AGE MYTH AND
ERIALITY

Iyth and Materiality: an Archaeology of Scandinavia AD *400–1000* considers
nship between myth and materiality in Scandinavia from the beginning
t-Roman era and the European Migrations to the coming of Christianity.
an interdisciplinary interpretation of text and material culture and exam-
the documentation of an oral past relates to its material embodiment.

the material evidence is from the Iron Age, most Old Norse texts were
wn in the thirteenth century or even later. With a time lag of 300 to 900
the archaeological evidence, the textual material has until recently been
as a usable source for any study of the pagan past. However, Hedeager
t this is true regarding any study of a society's short-term history, but it
be the crucial requirement for defining the sources relevant for studying
structures of the *longue durée*, or their potential contributions to a theo-
lerstanding of cultural changes and transformation. In Iron Age Scandina-
dealing with persistent and slow-changing structures of world views and
over a wavelength of nearly a millennium. Furthermore, iconography
date the arrival of new mythical themes, anchoring written narratives in
der archaeological context.

orse myths are explored with particular attention to one of the central
narratives of the Old Norse canon – the mythic cycle of Odin. In addi-
temporaneous historical sources from Late Antiquity and the early European Middle Ages are examined. No other study provides such a broad ranging and
authoritative study of the relationship of myth to the archaeology of Scandinavia.

Lotte Hedeager is Professor of Archaeology and Head of the Department of
Archaeology, Conservation and History at the University of Oslo, Norway.

IRON AGE MYTH AND MATERIALITY

An Archaeology of Scandinavia
AD 400–1000

Lotte Hedeager

Routledge
Taylor & Francis Group

LONDON AND NEW YORK

First published 2011
by Routledge
2 Park Square, Milton Park, Abingdon, Oxon, OX14 4RN

Simultaneously published in the USA and Canada
by Routledge
711 Third Avenue, New York, NY 10017

Routledge is an imprint of the Taylor & Francis Group, an informa business

British Library Cataloguing in Publication Data
A catalogue record for this book is available from the British Library

Library of Congress Cataloging in Publication Data
  Hedeager, Lotte.
  Iron Age myth and materiality: an archaeology of Scandinavia,
  AD 400–1000 / Lotte Hedeager.
      p. cm.
  "Simultaneously published in the USA and Canada"–T.p. verso.
  Includes bibliographical references.
  1. Iron Age–Scandinavia. 2. Scandinavia–Antiquities. 3. Material culture–
  Scandinavia–History–To 1500. 4. Oral tradition–Scandinavia–History–To 1500.
  5. Mythology, Norse. 6. Cosmology–Scandinavia–History–To 1500.
  7. Old Norse literature–History and criticism. 8. Scandinavia–History–To
  1397–Sources. 9. Scandinavia–Historiography. 10. Annales school. I. Title.
  GN780.22.S34H4 2011
  936.3–dc22
  2010038671

ISBN: 978–0–415–60602–8 (hbk)
ISBN: 978–0–415–60604–2 (pbk)
ISBN: 978–0–203–82971–4 (ebk)

Typeset in Bembo by Swales & Willis Ltd, Exeter, Devon

Printed and bound in Great Britain by
CPI Antony Rowe, Chippenham, Wiltshire

For friends, colleagues, and students from whom
I have learned so much

CONTENTS

LIST OF FIGURES

ACKNOWLEDGEMENTS

The following extracts have been reproduced with permission:

Prose Edda, 4–5. From *The Prose Edda* by Snorri Sturluson and translated by Jesse Bycock (Penguin Classics 2005). Translation copyright © Jesse Bucock, 2005.

Ynglinga Saga, 1–5, 7. From *Heimskringla or the Lives of the Norse Kings* by Snorre Sturlason, Dover Publications, 1990.

The following images have been reproduced with permission:

Fig. 3.11, 3.12, 3.13, 4.20A, B and C, 4.29, 4.30, 9.9B and C, 9.10, 9.12, 9.13, 9.14, 9.15, 9.16A. Drawing by Herbert Lange in K. Hauck, M. Axboe, C. Düwel, L. von Padberg, U. Smyra and C. Wypior (1985–89) *Die Goldbrakteaten der Völkerwanderungszeit*, vols 1–5, Münster Mittealterschriften 24, Munich: Wilhelm Fink Verlag. Reproduced by kind permission of Morten Axboe and Herbert Lange.

Fig. 4.6, 4.7. By kind permission of Erla Bergendahl Hohler.

Fig. 4.10. By kind permission of Per Persson.

Fig. 4.11A. From Gaimster, M. (1998) *Vendel Period Bracteates on Gotland. On the significance of Germanic art*, Acta Archaeologica Lundensia Series in 8, no. 27. Reproduced by kind permission of Lund University.

Fig. 4.11B. Arwidsson, G. (1977) *Valsgärde 7*, Die Grabfunde von Valsgärde III, Uppsala: Uppsala Universitets Museum. Reproduced by kind permission of the Museum Gustavianum, Uppsala Universitet.

Fig. 4.15B, 4.19, 4.22, 4.28, 4.31, 5.12, 6.8, 9.7, 9.8, 9.16B. Drawings by Olof Sörling, in Stolpe, H. and Arne, T.J. (1927) *La nécropole de Vendel,* Monografiserien 17, Stockholm: Kungl. Vitterhetsakademien. Reproduced by kind permission of Kungl. Vitterhetsakademien.

Fig. 4.16. From Ørsnes, M. (1966) *Form og Stil i Sydskandinaviens yngre Germanske Jernalder*, Copenhagen: The National Museum. Reproduced by kind permission of the Nationalmuseet, Denmark.

Fig. 4.21A, 4.25, 4.27. Drawings by Bengt Händel in Arbman, H. (1980) 'Båtgravarna i Vendel', i *Vendeltid*, Stockholm: Statens Historiska Museum. © Riksantikvarieämbetet, Sweden. Reproduced by kind permission of the Riksantikvarieämbetet, Sweden.

Fig. 4.23, 4.24, 5.1. Drawings by Sofie Kraft in Brøgger et al. (1917) *Osebergfundet*, Kristiania. Reproduced by kind permission of the Kulturhistorisk Museum, Universitetet I Oslo.

Fig. 5.5A–B, 5.15. Drawings from Lamm, J.P. (2004) 'Figural gold foils found in Sweden', in H. Clarke and K. Lamm (eds): *Excavations at Helgö*, vol. XVI, pp. 41–142, Stockholm: Kungl Vitterhets Historie och Antikvitets Akademien. Reproduced by kind permission of Antikverisk-toporafiska Arkivet, the National Heritage Board, Stockholm.

Fig. 5.7. Drawing here after Price, N. (2002), AUN31, Uppsala University. Originally from *The Viking World* by James Graham-Campbell. © Frances Lincoln 1980.

Fig. 5.13. Drawing by Eva Koch, in Axboe, M. (2005) 'Guld og guder', in T. Capelle and C. Fischer (eds) *Ragnarok. Odins verden*, Silkeborg: Silkeborg Museum. Used by kind permission of the Nationalmuseet, Denmark.

Fig. 6.2. The research area of Gudme. Data: Mogens Bo Henriksen. Drawing: Allan Larsen. Used with permission.

Fig. 6.3, 6.7, 7.2, 7.3, 7.4, 7.5, 7.6. © Nationalmuseet, Denmark.

Fig. 9.1, 9.3. Drawings from Bóna, I. (1991) *Das Hunnenreich*, Stuttgart: Konrad Theiss Verlag. Originally published by Corvina Press, Budapest. By kind permission of the artist, Mr János Balatoni, and Corvina Press.

Fig. 9.2. Drawing: Bjørn Skaarup. © Lotte Hedeager.

Fig. 9.9A. Drawing by Poul Wöhliche, in K. Hauck, M. Axboe, C. Düwel, L. von Padberg, U. Smyra and C. Wypior (1985–89) *Die Goldbrakteaten der Völkerwanderungszeit*, vols 1–5, Münster Mittelalterschriften 24, Munich: Wilhelm Fink Verlag. © Poul Wöhliche. By kind permission of Poul Wöhliche and Morten Axboe.

Fig. 9.11. Drawing from Lamm, J.P., Hydman, H., Axboe, M., Hauck, K., Beck, H., Behr, C. and Pesch, A. (2000) 'Der Brakteat des Jahrhunderts', *Frühmittelalterliche Studien*, 34: 1–93. Used by kind permission of Institut für Frühmittelalterforschung, Universität Münster.

Every effort has been made to obtain permission to reproduce copyright material. If any proper acknowledgement has not been made, copyright holders are invited to inform the publishers of the oversight.

Illustrations: full references

3.1   Map of Migration Age Europe, AD 406. Modified after McEvedy (1975: 17). McEvedy, C. (1975: 148). *The Penguin Atlas of Medieval History*, 8th edn, Harmondsworth: Penguin.

3.2   Map of Migration Age Europe, AD 420. Modified after McEvedy (1975: 19). McEvedy, C. (1975) *The Penguin Atlas of Medieval History*, 8th edn, Harmondsworth: Penguin.

3.3   Map of Migration Age Europe, AD 450. Modified after McEvedy (1975: 21). McEvedy, C. (1975) *The Penguin Atlas of Medieval History*, 8th edn, Harmondsworth: Penguin.

3.4   Map of Migration Age Europe, AD 476. Modified after McEvedy (1975: 23). McEvedy, C. (1975) *The Penguin Atlas of Medieval History*, 8th edn, Harmondsworth: Penguin.

3.5   Early Scandinavian animal style. Denmark. After Salin (1904: Abb. 134). Salin, B. (1904) *Die altgermanische Thierornamentik*, Stockholm and Berlin: Asher.

3.6   Early Scandinavian animal style. Lister, Norway. After Salin (1904: Abb. 490). Salin, B. (1904) *Die altgermanische Thierornamentik*, Stockholm and Berlin: Asher.

3.7   Style II. Udine, Italy. After Salin (1904: Abb. 655). Salin, B. (1904) *Die altgermanische Thierornamentik*, Stockholm and Berlin: Asher.

3.8   Style II. Uppland, Sweden. After Salin (1904: Abb. 554). Salin, B. (1904) *Die altgermanische Thierornamentik*, Stockholm and Berlin: Asher.

3.9   Style I. Kent, England. After Salin (1904: Abb. 700). Salin, B. (1904) *Die altgermanische Thierornamentik*, Stockholm and Berlin: Asher.

3.10 Style II. Wurzburg, Bayern. After Salin (1904: Abb. 641). Salin, B. (1904) *Die altgermanische Thierornamentik*, Stockholm and Berlin: Asher.

3.11 Gold bracteate, Funen, Denmark. Drawing by Herbert Lange after Hauck (1985–89: IK 75). Hauck, K. (1985–89) (ed.) *Die Goldbrakteaten der Völkerwanderungszeit,* vols 1–5, with contributions from M. Axboe, C. Düwel, L. von Padberg, U. Smyra and C. Wypior, Münster Mittealterschriften 24, Munich: Wilhelm Fink Verlag.

3.12 Gold bracteates. Nordic replica of a Roman gold medallion. Lilla Jored, Sweden. Drawing by Herbert Lange after Hauck (1985–89: IK 107). Hauck, K. (1985–89) (ed.) *Die Goldbrakteaten der Völkerwanderungszeit*, vols 1–5, with contributions from M. Axboe, C. Düwel, L. von Padberg, U. Smyra and C. Wypior, Münster Mittealterschriften 24, Munich: Wilhelm Fink Verlag.

3.13 Gold bracteates. Reverse side of Figure 3.12. Drawing by Herbert Lange after Hauck (1985–89: IK 107). Hauck, K. (1985–89) (ed.) *Die Goldbrakteaten der Völkerwanderungszeit*, vols 1–5, with contributions from M. Axboe, C. Düwel, L. von Padberg, U. Smyra and C. Wypior, Münster Mittealterschriften 24, Munich: Wilhelm Fink Verlag.

3.14 Style II. Uppland, Sweden. After Salin (1904: Abb. 570). Salin, B. (1904) *Die altgermanische Thierornamentik*, Stockholm and Berlin: Asher.

4.1 Style I. Tveitane, Norway. After Haseloff (1981: Abb. 21). Haseloff, G. (1981) *Die germanische Tierornamentik der Völkerwanderungszeit*, vols I–III, Berlin and New York: Walter de Gruyter.

4.2 Style I. Bifrons, Kent, England. After Haseloff (1981: Abb. 25). Haseloff, G. (1981) *Die germanische Tierornamentik der Völkerwanderungszeit*, vols I–III, Berlin and New York: Walter de Gruyter.

4.3 Style I. Nancy, Lothringen. After Haseloff (1981: Abb. 26). Haseloff, G. (1981) *Die germanische Tierornamentik der Völkerwanderungszeit*, vols I–III, Berlin and New York: Walter de Gruyter.

4.4 Style I. Kajdacz, Hungary. After Haseloff (1981: Abb. 487). Haseloff, G. (1981) *Die germanische Tierornamentik der Völkerwanderungszeit*, vols I–III, Berlin and New York: Walter de Gruyter.

4.5 Style I. Nocera Unbra, Italy. After Haseloff (1981: Abb. 388). Haseloff, G. (1981) *Die germanische Tierornamentik der Völkerwanderungszeit*, vols I–III, Berlin and New York: Walter de Gruyter.

4.6 Urnes style. Urnes Stave Church, Norway. After Hohler (1999, II: 235). Hohler, E.B. (1999) *Norwegian Stave Church Sculpture*, vols I–II, Oslo: Scandinavian University Press.

4.7 Ål Church, Norway. After Hohler (1999, II: 93). Hohler, E.B. (1999) *Norwegian Stave Church Sculpture*, vols I–II, Oslo: Scandinavian University Press.

4.8 Tunic band from Evebø Eide, Norway, with interwoven animal figures. From Dedekam (1925). Dedekam, H. (1925) 'To tekstilfragmenter fra folkevandringstiden. Evebø og Snartemo', in *Bergens Museums Aarbok 1924–25*, pp. 1–57, Hist.-Antik. Række 3, Bergen: Bergen Museum.

4.9 Late animal style. Gotland, Sweden. After Salin (1904: Abb. 607). Salin, B. (1904) *Die altgermanische Thierornamentik*, Stockholm and Berlin: Asher.

4.10 Belt buckle, Sutton Hoo, England. The eagle and the snake can be identified; however, two other species, one with its mouth closed, the other with an open mouth, cannot. Drawing by Per Persson. Used with permission.

4.11 Wolf, wild boar, and eagle. **A**: buckle from Zealand. Drawing by C. Borstam in Gaimster (1998: 77). Gaimster, M. (1998) *Vendel Period Bracteates on Gotland. On the significance of Germanic art*, Acta Archaeologica Lundensia Series in 8, no. 27, Stockholm: Almqvist & Wiksell International. **B**: Plate from a shield, Valsgärde, Sweden. After Arwidsson (1977: Abb. 146). Arwidsson, G. (1977) *Valsgärde 7*, Die Grabfunde von Valsgärde III, Uppsala: Uppsala Universitets Museum. **C**: Belt fitting from Esslingen-Sirnau grave 8, Germany. After Koch (1969). Koch, R. (1969) *Katalog Esslingen. Die vor- und frühgeschichtlichen Funde in Heimatmuseum*, vol. II, *Die merowingischen Funde*, Veröffentlichungen des Staatlichen Amtes für Denkmalpflege Stuttgart A14/II, Stuttgart: Müller & Graff. **D**: Detail from a Lombard gold-foil cross from Pieve del Cairo, Italy. From Haseloff (1956).

Haseloff, G. (1956) 'Die langobardischen Goldblattkreuze. Ein Beitrag zur Frage nach dem Ursprung von Stil II', *Jahrbuch des Römisch-germanischen Zentralmuseums Mainz*, 3: 143–63.

4.12 Belt buckle. Ejsbøl Moor, Denmark. Drawing: Eva Koch Nielsen, after Hedeager (1988, vol. 2: 317). Hedeager, L. (1988) *Danernes Land, Danmarkshistorie 2, 200 f.Kr.-700*, Copenhagen: Gyldendal og Politiken.

4.13 Humans cut into pieces. Detail from the Kirtscheim brooch, Germany. After Haseloff (1981: Abb. 1929). Haseloff, G. (1981) *Die germanische Tierornamentik der Vǫlkerwanderungszeit*, vols I–III, Berlin and New York: Walter de Gruyter.

4.14 Human cut into pieces. Mounting from a drinking horn. Söderby Karl, Sweden. Drawing by Harald Faith-Ell after Holmqvist (1951: fig. 5). Holmqvist, W. (1951) 'Dryckeshornen från Söderby Karl', *Fornvännen*, 1951: 33–65.

4.15 Human heads as part of the animals. **A**: Bridle-mount from Denmark. After Müller (1880: 185–403). Müller, S. (1880) 'Dyreornamentikken i Norden. Dens Oprindelse, Udvikling og Forhold til samtidige Stilarter. En arkæologisk Undersøgelse', *Aarbøger for nordisk Oldkyndighed og Historie*, 1880: 185–403. **B**: Bridle-mount from Vendel, Sweden. Drawing by O. Sörling (Stolpe and Arne 1927: pl. XXXVIII). Stolpe, H. and Arne, T.J. (1927) *La nécropole de Vendel*, Monografiserien 17, Stockholm: Kungl. Vitterhets Historie och Antikvitetsakademien.

4.16 Human head as part of the eagle. Bronze bird (shield-mount?), Gl. Skørping, Denmark. From M. Ørsnes (1966: fig. 160). Ørsnes, M. (1966) *Form og Stil i Sydskandinaviens yngre Germanske Jernalder*, Copenhagen: The National Museum.

4.17 Half man, half wild boar. Eagles are present on both sides of his head and two heads form the belt-buckle. Åker, Norway. After Gustafson (1906). Gustafsson, G. (1906) *Norges Oldtid. Mindesmærker og Oldsager*, Kristiania: Norsk Folkemuseum.

4.18 Men as part wild boar, part 'big animal/eagle'. Part of a Lombard gold-blade cross, Wurmlingen, Germany. After Haseloff (1956, vol. 3). Haseloff, G. (1956) 'Die langobardischen Goldblattkreuze. Ein Beitrag zur Frage nach dem Ursprung von Stil II', *Jahrbuch des Römisch-germanischen Zentralmuseums Mainz*, 3: 143–63.

4.19 Man 'composed' by animals. The 'beaks' of the lower animals are formed as animal heads. Vendel grave 1. Drawing by O. Sörling (Stolpe and Arne 1927: Pl. IX). Stolpe, H. and Arne, T.J. (1927) *La nécropole de Vendel*, Monografiserien 17, Stockholm: Kungl. Vitterhets Historie och Antikvitetsakademien.

4.20 Gold bracteates, from Denmark. **A**: Kølby. **B**: Kjøllegård, Bornholm. **C**: Skrydstrup. All figures drawings by Herbert Lange after Hauck (1985–89; A: IK 99, B: IK 95, C: IK 166). Hauck, K. (1985–89) (ed.) *Die Goldbrakteaten der Völkerwanderungszeit*, vols 1–5, with contributions from M. Axboe,

C. Düwel, L. von Padberg, U. Smyra and C. Wypior, Münster Mittealter-schriften 24, Munich: Wilhelm Fink Verlag.

4.21 Men in animal disguise. **A**: Torslunda stamp, Sweden. Drawing by Bengt Händel in Arbman (1980: 25). Arbman, H. (1980) 'Båtgravarna i Vendel', i *Vendeltid*, pp. 19–30, Stockholm: Statens Historiska Museum. **B**: Sword sheath from Gutenstein, Germany. Drawing by I. Müller, adapted from Böhner (1991: 38). Böhner, K. (1991) 'Die frühmittelalterlichen Silber-phaleren von Eschwege (Hessen) und die nordischen Pressblechbilder', *Jahrbuch des Römisch-Germanischen Zentralmuseums Mainz*, 38: 681–743. **C**: Two fighting men in animal disguise depicted on the 'long' gold horn from Gallehus, Denmark. Woodcut from 1641 by Ole Worm, here after Jensen (2004: 121; compare Figure 5.8). Jensen, J. (2004) *Danmarks Oldtid. Yngre Jernalder og Vikingetid 400–1050 e.Kr.*, Copenhagen: Gyldendal.

4.22 Warrior in disguise of a wild boar (left); both warriors are wearing eagle-helmets. Helmet-plate from Vendel, Sweden. Drawing by O. Sörling (Stolpe and Arne 1927: pl. XLI). Stolpe, H. and Arne, T.J. (1927) *La nécropole de Vendel*, Monografiserien 17, Stockholm: Kungl. Vitterhets His-torie och Antikvitetsakademien.

4.23 Wild boar warrior embroidered on the textile from the Oseberg ship grave, Norway. Drawing by Sofie Kraft in Brøgger et al. (1917). Brøgger, A.W., Falk, H. and Shetelig, H. (1917) *Osebergfundet*, Kristiania.

4.24 Woman in bird disguise embroidered on the textile from Oseberg, Nor-way. Drawing by Sofie Kraft in Brøgger et al. (1917). Brøgger, A.W., Falk, H. and Shetelig, H. (1917) *Osebergfundet*, Kristiania.

4.25 Warriors with wild boar helmets. Helmet plate stamp, Torslunda, Sweden. Drawing by Bengt Händel in Arbman (1980: 24). Arbman, H. (1980) 'Båt-gravarna i Vendel', i *Vendeltid*, pp. 19–30, Stockholm: Statens Historiska Museum.

4.26 Reconstruction of the Sutton Hoo helmet. After Speake (1980: pl. 5c). Speake, G. (1980) *Anglo-Saxon Animal Art and its Germanic Background*, Oxford: Clarendon Press.

4.27 Warrior fighting two bears. Helmet plate stamp, Torslunda, Sweden. Drawing by Bengt Händel in Arbman (1980: 24). Arbman, H. (1980) 'Båtgravarna i Vendel', i *Vendeltid*, pp. 19–30, Stockholm: Statens Histor-iska Museum.

4.28 Serpent-formed animals (with human heads as thighs). Shield-buckle mount from Vendel grave XII, Sweden. Drawing by O. Sörling (Stolpe and Arne 1927: Pl. XXXIII). Stolpe, H. and Arne, T.J. (1927) *La nécropole de Vendel*, Monografiserien 17, Stockholm: Kungl. Vitterhets Historie och Antikvitetsakademien.

4.29 Man in disguise of a bird – or with an eagle-helmet like the warriors on Figure 4.22. Gold bracteate from Kitnæs, Denmark. Drawing by Herbert Lange after Hauck (1985–89: IK 94). Hauck, K. (1985–89) (ed.) *Die Gold-brakteaten der Völkerwanderungszeit*, vols 1–5, with contributions from M.

Axboe, C. Düwel, L. von Padberg, U. Smyra and C. Wypior, Münster Mittealterschriften 24, Munich: Wilhelm Fink Verlag.

4.30 Man in disguise of a bird. Gold bracteate from Bolbro, Denmark. Drawing by Herbert Lange after Hauck (1985–89: 29). Hauck, K. (1985–89) (ed.) *Die Goldbrakteaten der Völkerwanderungszeit*, vols 1–5, with contributions from M. Axboe, C. Düwel, L. von Padberg, U. Smyra and C. Wypior, Münster Mittealterschriften 24, Munich: Wilhelm Fink Verlag.

4.31 Odin? in bird disguise. From a helmet plate. Vendel, grave 1, Sweden. Drawing by O. Sörling (Stolpe and Arne 1927: pl. VI). Stolpe, H. and Arne, T.J. (1927) *La nécropole de Vendel,* Monografiserien 17, Stockholm: Kungl. Vitterhets Historie och Antikvitetsakademien.

4.32 A shaman and his helping animals. Greenland. Drawing made by the shaman to Knud Rasmussen. After Rasmussen (1929). Rasmussen, K. (1929) *Intellectual Culture of the Iglulik Eskimos*, Copenhagen: The National Museum.

4.33 Lombard gold-blade cross with 'animal' ornamentation, however, humans have taken the place of animals. San Stefano grave 11–12. Petricia I Cividale, Italy. After Haseloff (1970: Tafel 4). Haseloff, G. (1970) 'Goldbrakteaten-Goldblattkreuze', *Neue Ausgrabungen und Forschungen in Niedersachsen*, 5: 24–39.

5.1 Humans sacrificed by hanging in a tree. Notice the horse heads in the top of the tree. Textile from Oseberg, Norway. Drawing by Sofie Kraft in Brøgger et al. (1917), here after Christensen et al. (1992: 242). © Gotlands Museum. Brøgger, A.W., Falk, H. and Shetelig, H. (1917) *Osebergfundet*, Kristiania. Christensen, A.E., Ingstad, A.S. and Myhre, B. (1992) *Osebergdronningens grav*, Oslo: Schibsted.

5.2 Seven humans lining up to be sacrificed by hanging. Picture stone (145 cm high) from Garda Bota, Gotland. From S. Lindqvist (1941–42: fig. 141), here after Imer (2004: 53). © Gotlands Museum. Lindqvist, S. (1941–42) *Gotlands Bildsteine*, vols I–II, Stockholm: Kgl. Vitterhets Historie och Antikvitets Akademien. Imer, L.M. (2004) 'Gotlandske billedsten – dateringen af Lindqvists gruppe C og D', in *Aarbøger for nordisk oldkyndighed og historie*, 2001: 47–111, Copenhagen: Det Kgl. Nordiske Oldskriftselskab.

5.3 Picture stone (309cm high). Lärbro St. Hammars. Notice the man hanged in a tree depicted on the third row. From S. Lindqvist (1941–42: fig. 81), here after Imer (2004: 60). © Gotlands Museum. Lindqvist, S. (1941–42) *Gotlands Bildsteine*, vols I–II, Stockholm: Kgl. Vitterhets Historie och Antikvitets Akademien. Imer, L.M. (2004) 'Gotlandske billedsten – dateringen af Lindqvists gruppe C og D', in *AArbøger for nordisk oldkyndighed og historie*, 2001: 47–111, Copenhagen: Det Kgl. Nordiske Oldskriftselskab.

5.4 Odin on his eight-legged steed Sleipnir depicted on the picture stone from Alskoga Tjängvide, Gotland. From S. Lindqvist (1941–42: fig. 137), here after Imer (2004: 50). Lindqvist, S. (1941–42) *Gotlands Bildsteine*, vols I–II, Stockholm: Kgl. Vitterhets Historie och Antikvitets Akademien. Imer,

L.M. (2004) 'Gotlandske billedsten – dateringen af Lindqvists gruppe C og D', in *AArbøger for nordisk oldkyndighed og historie*, 2001: 47–111, Copenhagen: Det Kgl. Nordiske Oldskriftselskab.

5.5 Gold foil figures (approx. 1cm) with embracing couples. **A**: Helgö, Sweden. After Lamm (2004: 89, Helgö 1101). Lamm, J.P. (2004) 'Figural gold foils found in Sweden', in H. Clarke and K. Lamm (eds): *Excavations at Helgö*, vol. XVI, pp. 41–142, Stockholm: Kungl Vitterhets Historie och Antikvitets Akademien (KVHAA). **B**: Helgö, Sweden. After Lamm (2004: 83, Helgö 2593). Lamm, J.P. (2004) 'Figural gold foils found in Sweden', in H. Clarke and K. Lamm (eds): *Excavations at Helgö*, vol. XVI, pp. 41–142, Stockholm: Kungl Vitterhets Historie och Antikvitets Akademien (KVHAA). **C**: Lundeborg, Denmark. Drawing by Eva Koch, after Thomsen et al. (1993: 88). Thomsen, P.O., Blæsild, B., Hardt, N. and Michaelsen, K.K. (1993) *Lundeborg – en handelsplads fra jernalderen*, Svendborg: Svendborg Museum.

5.6 Phallus-shaped stone from the Iron Age and a medieval stone cross on Sandeide churchyard, Norway. The photo was taken in 1912. The phallus-shaped stone was found during excavation in the church. Photo by H. Gjessing (1915), here after Myhre (2006: 216). Gjessing, H. (1915) 'Et gammelt kultsted i Sandeid. Frugtbarhetsgudeparets dyrkelse i Ryfylke og paa Jæderen', *Maal og Minne*, 65–79. Myhre, B. (2006) 'Fra fallos til kors fra horg og hov til kirke?', *Viking*, LXIX: 215–50.

5.7 A small phallic bronze figure, a naked, bearded man with a bracelet and a conical helmet, from Rällinge, Sweden. Here after Price (2002: 104, Fig. 3). Price, N. (2002) *The Viking Way. Religion and War in Late Iron Age Scandinavia*, AUN 31, Uppsala: Uppsala University. Original source: Graham-Campbell, J. (1980) *The Viking World*, London: Frances Lincoln.

5.8 One of the two gold horns (the 'long one') from Gallehus, Denmark. Woodcut from 1641 by Ole Worm. After Jensen (2004: 114). Jensen, J. (2004) *Danmarks Oldtid. Yngre Jernalder og Vikingetid 400–1050 e.Kr.*, Copenhagen: Gyldendal.

5.9 Detail of the long horn: a bearded man with long hair and long dress (in 'woman disguise'), carrying a drinking horn. Woodcut from 1641 by Ole Worm. After Jensen (2004: 114). Jensen, J. (2004) *Danmarks Oldtid. Yngre Jernalder og Vikingetid 400–1050 e.Kr.*, Copenhagen: Gyldendal.

5.10 Examples of gold-foil figures from Denmark. Drawing by Eva Koch, after Watt (1991: 96). Watt, M. (1991) 'Sorte Muld', in P. Mortensen and B. Rasmussen (eds) *Høvdingesamfund og Kongemagt*, pp. 89–108, Jysk Arkæologisk Selskabs Skrifter XXII:2, Aarhus: Aarhus Universitetsforlag.

5.11 Gold-foil animal figures from Sorte Muld, Bornholm. Drawing by Eva Koch, after Watt (1991: 98). Watt, M. (1991) 'Sorte Muld', in P. Mortensen and B. Rasmussen (eds) *Høvdingesamfund og Kongemagt*, pp. 89–108, Jysk Arkæologisk Selskabs Skrifter XXII:2, Aarhus: Aarhus Universitetsforlag.

5.12 Fighting warriors on a helmet plate from Vendel grave XIV, Sweden. One is dressed in a caftan, his counterpart in a chain-mail shirt. Drawing by O. Sörling (Stolpe and Arne 1927: Pl. VI). Stolpe, H. and Arne, T.J. (1927) *La nécropole de Vendel,* Monografiserien 17, Stockholm: Kungl. Vitterhets Historie och Antikvitetsakademien.

5.13 Women with her hair in an Irish ribbon-knot. Gold-foil from Gudme, Funen. Drawing by Eva Koch, here after Axboe (2005: 53). Axboe, M. (2005) 'Guld og guder', in T. Capelle and C. Fischer (eds) *Ragnarok. Odins verden,* pp. 41–56, Silkeborg: Silkeborg Museum.

5.14 Woman holding a cup. Drawing by Eva Koch, here after Mannering (1998: 263). Mannering, U. (1998) 'Guldgubber. Et billede af yngre jern-alders dragt', unpublished thesis, University of Copenhagen.

5.15 Gold foil figure dressed in 'fur'. Eketorp, Öland, Sweden. After Lamm (2004: 99). Lamm, J.P. (2004) 'Figural gold foils found in Sweden', in H. Clarke and K. Lamm (eds): *Excavations at Helgö,* vol. XVI, pp. 41–142, Stockholm: Kungl Vitterhets Historie och Antikvitets Akademien (KVHAA).

5.16 Gold foil figure; a naked bearded person with an impressive 'bead' neck-lace (of gold bracteates?). Sorte Muld, Bornholm. Drawing by Eva Koch, after Watt (2004: 212). Watt, M. (1991) 'Sorte Muld', in P. Mortensen and B. Rasmussen (eds) *Høvdingesamfund og Kongemagt,* pp. 89–108, Jysk Arkæologisk Selskabs Skrifter XXII:2, Aarhus: Aarhus Universitetsforlag.

6.1 Map showing the Gudme area and the production places for coins, glass, bronzes, and *terra sigillata* found in the Gudme/Lundeborg area. Modi-fied after drawing by Poul Erik Skovgaard in Thomsen et al. (1993: 96). Thomsen, P.O., Blæsild, B., Hardt, N. and Michaelsen, K.K. (1993) *Lundeborg – en handelsplads fra jernalderen,* Svendborg: Svendborg Museum.

6.2 The research area of Gudme. Data: Mogens Bo Henriksen. Drawing: Allan Larsen. Used with permission.

6.3 The big hall under excavation. The postholes are marked. Gudme, Funen. © Nationalmuseet, Copenhagen.

6.4 The gold-hoard from Broholm, Funen. After Jensen (2004: 57). Jensen, J. (2004) *Danmarks Oldtid. Yngre Jernalder og Vikingetid 400–1050 e.Kr.,* Copenhagen: Gyldendal.

6.5 Gold scabbard mouth from the Gudme area with two opposing animals forming a human mask. After Sehested (1878). Sehested, F. (1878) *Fortidsminder og Oldsager fra Egnen om Broholm,* Copenhagen.

6.6 Gold hoard from Lillesø. Gudme, Funen. © Nationalmuseet, Copenhagen.

6.7 Ring knobs of solid gold from sword hilts. Gudme, Funen. © National-museet, Copenhagen.

6.8 Group of warriors carrying swords with ring-knobs on the hilts (cf. Fig-ure 4.22, the warrior to the left). Drawing by O. Sörling (Stolpe and Arne 1927: Pl. XLII). Stolpe, H. and Arne, T.J. (1927) *La nécropole de Vendel,* Monografiserien 17, Stockholm: Kungl. Vitterhets Historie och Antikvitetsakademien.

7.1   Gold foil figures from Lundeborg, Funen. © Svendborg Museum.

7.2   Gold hoard from Fræer Nordmark, Denmark. © Nationalmuseet, Copenhagen.

7.3   One of the liturgical silver cups from the eighth century. Fejø, Denmark. © Nationalmuseet, Copenhagen.

7.4   Silver hoard from Sejrø, Denmark. © Nationalmuseet, Copenhagen.

7.5   Viking hoard from Vester Vedsted, Denmark. © Nationalmuseet, Copenhagen.

7.6   Reliquary gold cross. Orø, Denmark. © Nationalmuseet, Copenhagen.

9.1   Hunnish woman grave with an open-ended earring from Schipowo, Kurgan 2, Kazakhstan. Drawing by János Balatoni, after Bóna (1991: 59, fig. 19). Bóna, I. (1991) *Das Hunnenreich*, Stuttgart: Konrad Theiss Verlag.

9.2   Open-ended earrings of solid gold, pot-bellied and with pointed ends from Denmark. 14/82: Hammerslev, Randers county; C1419: Tjørnelunde Mølle, Holbæk county; 30/08: Glumsø, Præstø county; 11/38: Denmark, unknown; C3426: Vejlstrup, Ringkøbing county; C7403: Vils, Thisted county; 2/46: Svendsmark, Præstø county; 6/28: Vindblæs, Ålborg county; 10/27: Klipen, Åbenrå county. Registration numbers from the National Museum, Copenhagen. In addition, a gold ring similar to 6/28 is found in a weapon-grave from Vesterbø grave 16, Rogaland, Norway (S 1428). Drawing: Bjørn Skaarup. © Lotte Hedeager.

9.3   Levice – Léva (Slovakia): grave with open-ended earring and mirror. Drawing by János Balatoni, after Bóna (1991: 86, fig. 33). Bóna, I. (1991) *Das Hunnenreich*, Stuttgart: Konrad Theiss Verlag.

9.4   Distribution map of two of the most diagnostic artefacts related to the Huns: the pot-bellied, open-ended earrings of gold and silver and the bronze mirror. Redrawn by Per Persson after map from Werner (1956: map 10). Werner, J. (1956) *Beiträge zur Archäologie des Attila-Reiches*, Munich: Verlag der bayerischen Akademie der Wissenschaften.

9.5   Human masks on the earliest Style I fibulae from Scandinavia: **A**: Lunde, Norway. **B–C**: Galsted, Southern Jutland. **D**: Høstentorp, Zealand. **E**: Anda, Norway. **E–H**: Tveitane: Norway. After Haseloff (1981: Abb. 53). Haseloff, G. (1981) *Die germanische Tierornamentik der Völkerwanderungszeit*, vols I–III, Berlin and New York: Walter de Gruyter.

9.6   Human masks as part of the ornamentation on brooches. **A**: Galsted, Southern Jutland. After Haseloff (1981: Abb. 9). Haseloff, G. (1981) *Die germanische Tierornamentik der Völkerwanderungszeit*, vols I–III, Berlin and New York: Walter de Gruyter. **B**: Lunde, Lista, Norway. After Haseloff (1981: Abb. 3). Haseloff, G. (1981) *Die germanische Tierornamentik der Völkerwanderungszeit*, vols I–III, Berlin and New York: Walter de Gruyter.

9.7   Helmet from Vendel grave 1, Sweden with figural plates. Drawing by O. Sörling (Stolpe and Arne 1927: pl. V). Stolpe, H. and Arne, T.J. (1927) *La nécropole de Vendel*, Monografiserien 17, Stockholm: Kungl. Vitterhets Historie och Antikvitetsakademien.

9.8   Detail from the helmet from Vendel grave 1 (Figure 9.7). The small person wears a caftan. Drawing by O. Sörling (Stolpe and Arne 1927: pl. V). Stolpe, H. and Arne, T.J. (1927) *La nécropole de Vendel*, Monografiserien 17, Stockholm: Kungl. Vitterhets Historie och Antikvitetsakademien.

9.9   Gold bracteates. 'Balder's death'. **A**: Bornholm. **B**: Fakse, Denmark. **C**: Jutland, Denmark. **A**: Drawing by Poul Wöhliche after Hauck (1985–89; A: IK 595). **B–C**: Drawings by Herbert Lange after Hauck (1985–89; B: IK 51, C: IK 165). Hauck, K. (1985–89) (ed.) *Die Goldbrakteaten der Völkerwanderungszeit*, vols 1–5, with contributions from M. Axboe, C. Düwel, L. von Padberg, U. Smyra and C. Wypior, Münster Mittealterschriften 24, Munich: Wilhelm Fink Verlag.

9.10 Gold bracteate. Trollhättan, Sweden. 'Tyr who loses his hand'. Drawing by Herbert Lange after Hauck (1985–89: IK 190). Hauck, K. (1985–89) (ed.) *Die Goldbrakteaten der Völkerwanderungszeit*, vols 1–5, with contributions from M. Axboe, C. Düwel, L. von Padberg, U. Smyra and C. Wypior, Münster Mittealterschriften 24, Munich: Wilhelm Fink Verlag.

9.11 Gold bracteate. Sigurd the Dragon Slayer. Söderby, Sweden. After Lamm et al. (2000: Tafel V). Lamm, J.P., Hydman, H., Axboe, M., Hauck, K., Beck, H., Behr, C. and Pesch, A. (2000) 'Der Brakteat des Jahrhunderts', *Frühmittelalterliche Studien*, 34: 1–93.

9.12 Gold bracteate, Funen, Denmark. Drawing by Herbert Lange after Hauck (1985–89: IK 58). Hauck, K. (1985–89) (ed.) *Die Goldbrakteaten der Völkerwanderungszeit*, vols 1–5, with contributions from M. Axboe, C. Düwel, L. von Padberg, U. Smyra and C. Wypior, Münster Mittealterschriften 24, Munich: Wilhelm Fink Verlag.

9.13 Gold bracteates. Bjæverskov, Denmark. Drawing by Herbert Lange after Hauck (1985–89, IK 300). Hauck, K. (1985–89) (ed.) *Die Goldbrakteaten der Völkerwanderungszeit*, vols 1–5, with contributions from M. Axboe, C. Düwel, L. von Padberg, U. Smyra and C. Wypior, Münster Mittealterschriften 24, Munich: Wilhelm Fink Verlag.

9.14 Gold bracteates. Bjæverskov, Denmark. Drawing by Herbert Lange after Hauck (1985–89: IK 25). Hauck, K. (1985–89) (ed.) *Die Goldbrakteaten der Völkerwanderungszeit*, vols 1–5, with contributions from M. Axboe, C. Düwel, L. von Padberg, U. Smyra and C. Wypior, Münster Mittealterschriften 24, Munich: Wilhelm Fink Verlag.

9.15 Gold bracteates. Hjørlunde, Denmark. Drawing by Herbert Lange after Hauck (1985–89: IK 79). Hauck, K. (1985–89) (ed.) *Die Goldbrakteaten der Völkerwanderungszeit*, vols 1–5, with contributions from M. Axboe, C. Düwel, L. von Padberg, U. Smyra and C. Wypior, Münster Mittealterschriften 24, Munich: Wilhelm Fink Verlag.

10.1 'Wotan/Attila' image on a bracteate from Jutland from the fifth/sixth century (**A**) and 'Odin' image on a helmet plate from Vendel grave 1 from the seventh century (**B**). The images illustrate the gradual transmission from magician to warrior, however, the animal followers are still present.

A: Drawing by Herbert Lange after Hauck (1985–89: IK 25). Hauck, K. (1985–89) (ed.) *Die Goldbrakteaten der Völkerwanderungszeit*, vols 1–5, with contributions from M. Axboe, C. Düwel, L. von Padberg, U. Smyra and C. Wypior, Münster Mittealterschriften 24, Munich: Wilhelm Fink Verlag. **B**: Drawing by O. Sörling (Stolpe and Arne 1927: Pl. VI). Stolpe, H. and Arne, T.J. (1927) *La nécropole de Vendel,* Monografiserien 17, Stockholm: Kungl. Vitterhets Historie och Antikvitetsakademien.

PREFACE

> Every archaeological investigation, every historical study, is like a trial. Elementary justice requires that all relevant evidence be brought in, that all witnesses be found and called.
>
> *(Rausing 1985: 165)*

This book is written by an archaeologist; however, it draws on all available literary and archaeological evidence to explore the *mentalities* of the Old Norse world from the post-Roman era to the coming of Christianity around AD 1000. My intention has been to view the evidence contextually and ethnographically in order to demonstrate that an analysis of all sources available provide a hitherto missed opportunity for forming a new and more comprehensive perspective on the Scandinavian societies of the Late Iron Age.

In the decades after the Second World War, the dominant approach among European medievalists, whether historians, philologists, or archaeologists, was to deny myths and epic poetry from the Early Middle Ages any relevance as historical sources. The *Annales* tradition with its concept of *mentalité* was an exception, and Herwig Wolfram in 1994 explicitly stated that a modern historian, if responding to Ranke's demand to describe *wie es eigentlich gewesen ist*, 'must not only deal with what are superficially regarded as the "hard facts" but also take into account all the underlying meanings and connotations of the texts which express values alien to modern intellectual standards and experiences' (1994: 19). In the same vein, Ian Hodder claimed that archaeology should be redefined as cultural history and understood from the *inside* (Hodder 1986). It opened up a 'rehabilitation' of the written sources and this book is a result of this new direction of archaeological thinking. When using texts and material culture from different parts of Europe that cover half a millennium, some form of source criticism is needed in order to balance the different types of evidence. However, my overall social anthropological perspective added new perspectives to traditional historical 'source criticism'. In addition, I revitalise the texts by shifting them through the evidence provided by archaeology. That is indeed the basis for reinterpretation of Scandinavian societies AD 400–1000.

This book represents the final result of a research project that took its beginning in 1990 when I received a five-year research grant from the Danish Carlsberg Foundation. Needless to say, I am eternally grateful to the Carlsberg Foundation for giving me the opportunity to start on such a new and wide-ranging project (as a follow-up on my book *Iron Age Societies: From Tribe to State in Northern Europe 500 BC to AD 700*, 1992). Also I wish to thank the two departments at the University of Copenhagen, the Carsten Niebuhr Institute and the Institute of History, for housing the project.

At the same time, I was invited to take part in the large and ambitious project *The Transformation of the Roman World* – that was initiated by the European Science Foundation, and dealt with the transition from the Late Roman Empire to the Early Middle Ages (fourth to eighth century) in Western and Central Europe. It could hardly have come at a more suitable moment. The project had a thoroughly interdisciplinary approach that included archaeologists, historians, art historians, linguists, numismatists and other specialists from all over Europe. For more than five years I benefited from this fruitful interaction between disciplines and scholars. I am deeply grateful to Frans Theuws, Heinrich Härke, Janet L. Nelson, Mayke de Jong, Julia M.H. Smith, Walter Pohl and Peter Heather for opening the door to a new world of early medieval history and for guidance along the way.

The book was a long time in the making. Many articles and a couple of popular books have appeared in the meantime. It was not until spring 2004, spent at the Archaeology Centre at Stanford University as a visiting scholar, that the first draft of this book came into being. I am much indebted to Ian Hodder, Michael Shanks and Ian Morris for the invitation and for the ideal working conditions provided by the centre. Autumn 2003 was spent at the Department of Archaeology, Cambridge University, and autumn 2008, during the final phase of the editing, I was affiliated to the Department of Archaeology, University of Oxford. I take this opportunity to express my gratitude to those two institutions and to Catherine Hill, Helena Hamerow and Chris Gosden in particular.

Since 1996 I have held a position as Professor at the Department of Archaeology, University of Oslo. Here I have benefited from working with colleagues and graduate students to whom collaboration and intellectual generosity was always a first priority. I am proud to be a staff member of this department and grateful for the intellectual as well as the financial support I have received. Nick Thorpe, Winchester, did the language revision, and in the final editing I was assisted by Julie Lund and Sigrid Staurset. I am thankful to all of them.

Special thanks go to all friends and colleagues who generously commented on articles and papers at various stages, and provided me with books, and off-prints – published and unpublished, including master- and doctoral theses. They often covered areas and disciplines with which I am less familiar and thus helped me to navigate in this interdisciplinary field of early medieval Europe. It is impossible to name everyone, but many of you are represented in the bibliography. There are, however, two persons who cannot remain unnamed: Kristian, my lifelong partner, fellow archaeologist and best friend who has read and commented on the whole text, and Niels, our son, although he has never read an archaeological text.

Hindås, mid-summer 2010

INTRODUCTION

This book is about the relationship between myth and materiality in the Nordic Iron Age. It presents an interdisciplinary interpretation of text and material culture, two modes of expression that belongs together yet represent two different temporalities: the written historical documentation of an oral past long gone versus the contemporary material representation of those very same cosmological structures in action. They made their sudden appearance in the early fifth century and lived on for another half millennium or more before they were finally written down as a corpus of historical heritage. Therefore, to understand the relationship between myth and materiality it is necessary first to discuss their different historical temporalities.

Mentalités, as a society's contextual belief system expressed in collective representations (mythologies and symbols), are one of the well-known key concepts within the French *Annales school* of history, conceptualised at the time of Marc Bloch's and Lucien Febvre's founding of the journal *Annales d'histoire économique et sociale* in 1929. The *Annales'* paradigm was introduced to the discipline of archaeology in the 1980s, when archaeology was (re)defined as cultural history under the banner of post-processual archaeology (cf. Hodder 1986, 1987; Hodder and Hutson 2003; Bintliff 1991, 2004; Knapp 1992; Morris 2000; Andrén 1998c; Moreland 2001; Harding 2005; Thomas et al. 2006). Ideologies, world views, collective systems of belief, etc. became key concepts for understanding a society from the *inside*, as Ian Hodder argued for in the early days of the post-processual era (1986). In this approach, as in the *Annales* approach, *mentalités* at the same time reflect and are able to transform human life. In a process of mutual feedback between historical processes and what people and groups of people actually think and believe, premodern societies are structured and over time gradually transformed. In the *Annales* approach to history, historical time is analytically structured in three contemporaneous groups of processes, operating at different wavelengths of time, or durations:

the history of the short term, that is, the history of events, individuals etc.; the history of the medium term, that is, conjunctures such as social, economic history, demographic cycles, world view and ideologies (*mentalités*); and the history of the long term, that is, structures of long duration (*la longue durée*) such as the history of civilisations, of peoples, technology and – not least – persistent world views and ideologies (*mentalités*) (Bintliff 1991: 6 f.).

This classic *Annales* model of historical time, developed by Fernand Braudel in his pioneering work from 1949, *La Méditerranée et le monde méditerranéen à l'époque de Philippe II*, deals with different historical horizons, all of which are relevant to the discipline of archaeology. However, it is in particular the scale of long/slow-changing structures, *la longue durée*, that embraces the concept of *mentalités* and thereby serves as a powerful theoretical model for studying the development of past human societies *from the inside* in a long-time perspective. By definition then, any change in the collective representation of society has to happen gradually over time and therefore, ideally, should be visible in the material culture too. This, however, is not the case. On the contrary, the object world demonstrates radical changes in symbolic structures at certain historical moments, followed by long-term continuity and social resistance to change (cf. Kristiansen and Larsson 2005; Beck et al. 2007). It raises the question as to the relationship between formative historical events versus consolidating long-term structures (cf. Beck et al. 2007).

The aim of this book is to explore these temporal 'wavelengths' of the Scandinavian past, from the beginning of the post-Roman era and the European Migrations around AD 400 to the coming of Christianity around AD 1000. Adopting the *Annales* approach requires a truly interdisciplinary dialogue and therefore a huge body of evidence, material as well as textual, will be explored in the following chapters in an attempt to study the *mentalités* of the Scandinavian Iron Age. I define *mentalités* as the Old Norse cosmological universe displayed in text and material culture. However, while the material evidence is from the Iron Age, most Old Norse texts were written down in the thirteenth century or even later. With a time lag of 300 to 900 years from the archaeological evidence, the textual material has until recently been ruled out as a usable source for any study of the pagan past. True enough, from a traditional source critical point of view, the source material would have to be contemporary to be able to uphold its relevance – and thereby its value regarding Late Iron Age societies. This, however, is true regarding any study of a society's short-term history, but it should not be the crucial requirement for defining the sources relevant for studying long-term structures of the *longue durée*, or their potential contributions to a theoretical understanding of cultural changes and transformation. 'Pots and poetry' were used by the same people and therefore have to be analysed (albeit with different analytical tools) within the same cultural framework (Morris 2000: 27), although they represent different durations of time. Thus, artefacts and written texts are equally to be regarded as representations of the past (Hodder 1986; Hodder and Hutson 2003).

In approaching the *mentalités* of Iron Age Scandinavia, we are dealing with persistent and slow-changing structures of world views and ideologies over a wavelength of nearly a millennium. These were, however, in a process of mutual feedback with historical processes in Europe as well as in Scandinavia. In spite of the time gap between the material evidence from the Late Iron Age and the Old Norse sources, they will be highlighted as narratives of the pagan Scandinavian past. In addition, contemporaneous historical sources from Late Antiquity and the Early European Middle Age – the narratives of Jordanes, Gregory of Tours, and Paul the Deacon in particular – will be explored. As the first narratives of the Germanic peoples, they represent the history of those societies, peoples, or regions and thereby the conjuncture of the migrating Germanic peoples in the fifth, sixth and seventh centuries. Also, the short-term history of events will be paid some attention, particularly for the fifth and sixth centuries. This is the beginning of the post-Roman era during which the Germanic peoples were affected by, and literally involved in, the historical transformation of the Antique world into that of the Early Middle Ages. This should broaden the scope and consequently balance the long-term approach to how people construct and contest meaning through time.

As the structural basis for the book, one of the central mythical narratives of the Old Norse is explored as a representation of pre-Christian and early medieval *mentalités* in Scandinavia. That is, the mythic cycle of Odin, king of the Norse pantheon (Part I: A mythic narrative). The storylines are slightly different in the various narratives, but they may still be adopted as a point of departure. The aim is not to discuss the 'truest' or 'most ancient' history of Odin, but to approach the contextual belief systems expressed in these collective representations. The *meaning* of things is seen as essentially sub-conscious, as the 'neural equilibrium of individuals adjusted to their socio-economic and physical environment' (Bintliff 1991: 11). The key concepts from this mythological narrative will be used as the structuring basis to explore Old Norse society from the *inside*. The first question to be considered is the significance of memory and poetry (Part II: Words of identity); second, the meaning of art and objects will be explored (Part III: The constitution of 'otherness'). Third, the institutional framework of belief systems is considered (Part IV: Materiality matters). The final part of the book is devoted to the impact of the short-term history of Europe in the transitional phase from Antiquity to the Middle Ages in Scandinavia and its formative impact on the Scandinavia *longue durée* in the first millennium (Part V: The making of Norse mythology). Here the shortest wavelength of time, that of individuals and events, are taken as the point of departure and explored as leading to a thorough re-ordering of society. The history of individual time is thus explored as the foundation for changes in the structural history of Northern Europe and as such this book touches the current time-structure-agency debate within archaeology (i.e. Bintliff 2004; Harding 2005; Thomas et al. 2006; Beck et al. 2007).

PART I
A mythical narrative

1

THE MYTHIC CYCLE OF ODIN

The myth

Odin is best known in the context of Scandinavian mythology, although he is an old god who figures in the mythologies of other northern peoples as Woden, Wodan, Wotan or Woutan (North 1997). He has a priestly as well as a martial role, and he served as the patron of aristocrats, warriors and poets (Byock 2005: xviii). In Old Norse mythology, Odin appears as the head of the pantheon and as the king of the Asir gods (Nordberg 2003). His nature is particularly complicated and contradictory, and he is the most ambiguous in character and attributes of all the Nordic gods. His name derives from a word that would mean something like 'leader of the possessed'. In Old Norse the word *oðr* meant both 'poetry' and 'frenzy' (Lindow 2001: 250), and Odin is the furious ecstasy-god as well as the lord of inspiration and magic. He takes different names in virtually all the myths and more than 156 alternate names for him are known (listed in Orchard 2002: Appendix A), including All-Father, the High One and Val-Father, which means 'Father of the Slain' (Byock 2005: xviii). More than anything, however, he is the great sorcerer who uses his 'wisdom' to place himself atop the hierarchy of all living creatures (Lindow 2001: 250). In all, nine magical acts are ascribed to him. Among these are the following: he can appear in whatever shape he chooses – man, woman or animal; he commands the magic of the weather; with words he can extinguish fire, calm the seas and turn the winds; he can communicate with the dead; he possesses oral magic, *galdrar* (spells and chants) (Simek 1996: 97 f.) and the magic of writing – the runes (*Ynglinga Saga* chs 6–7). Through self-sacrifice and self-inflicted torture he attained the highest power, that is, made himself the master of runic magic. He sacrificed himself by spearing himself and by hanging in the World Tree (Yggdrasil), the holy tree, for nine stormy days and nights and through this suffering won magic, the art of runes, and powerful spells – that is, wisdom and knowledge.

With help from runic letters he could force hanged men's tongues to talk – that is, he could talk with the dead (*Hávamál* stanzas 138–40). Seen through the lens of myth runic, letters become something other than a primitive alphabet, as has been emphasised by many scholars (see Nielsen 1985 with refs). In addition, every rune had a particular name and could represent this particular concept on its own. The runes probably also had a specific numerical value which may have furnished the inscriptions with a further hidden layer (Simek 1996: 268). Runic letters could be used in black magic, and Odin is the god of runic knowledge as well as runic magic. The runic letters are the key to his feared power. The word 'rún/rúnar' thus means secret knowledge, or 'the knowledge of writing in verse' – and this means wisdom (Dumézil 1969: 52). Odin also plays a central role in the acquisition of the mead of poetry (wisdom, inspiration, skaldic poetry). Two stories are told: one in which Odin acquired the mead through shape changing, seduction, or rape of a daughter of the giant Suttungr, and subsequent theft, and the other where he achieved his particular wisdom by offering his one eye to the giant Mimir, from whose well he acquired the mead of knowledge as well as the runic letters.

Furthermore, two ravens belonged to Odin, named Hugin and Munin, which means 'Thought' and 'Mind/Memory', as a personification of Odin's intellectual and mental capacity. He had two wolves as well, and the eight-legged steed Sleipnir, who was used for trips to the realm of the dead. Gungnir ('swaying one') is mentioned as Odin's spear, probably the one by which Odin wounded himself while hanging in the World Tree, dedicating himself to himself. Odin is described as 'Gungnir's shaker' (Orchard 2002), and he uses the spear on the battlefield to throw it over an opposing army. The spear is also used for pointing out the heroes he wants for his *hird* in Valhal (i.e. a sign of death). At Ragnarok, the battle on the Last Day when the gods and the mythological present end, this particular spear will be crucial to the outcome. Odin is called by skalds the lord and god of the spear. Gungnir, together with Draupnir ('Dripper'), a fabulous golden ring from which eight equally heavy rings drip every ninth night, are decisive attributes for Odin's ability to uphold his power and position as king of the Asir. Like all other crucial attributes of the gods, these are manufactured by dwarfs who live underground.

This description of Odin may of course be conceived of as a purely literary fantasy, composed by Scandinavian narrators in early Christian times, that is, early in the thirteenth century AD. Alternatively, these stories may be seen as reflecting central myths of the pagan Nordic universe in the Viking Age and even centuries well before that, although transmitted with certain revisions and refashioning in a Christian context. Certainly, the versions of the myths vary widely and may not even reflect a coherent and uniform Nordic system of belief and religious practice held by social groups all over Scandinavia (Schier 1981; Schjødt 2004; Andrén et al. 2006: 13). If the myths have been changed in oral transmission through the centuries, such inconsistencies are, however, in the nature of mythology (in the sense of narratives). Whatever the original dates and origins of the Eddic poems, the pictures of the gods they give are fairly consistent (Lindow 2001: 14).

If the literary fantasy interpretation is accepted, we have to reject all written evidence from the North, which is the bulk of Old Norse literature. Consequently, we would be left to study the Scandinavian Late Iron Age entirely from the material evidence. True enough, this has been the case for almost all Scandinavian archaeology as a discipline since the Second World War. From the 1990s onwards, however, the post-processual and contextual approach has, to a certain degree, changed this *intra*-disciplinary attitude towards the field of history of Old Norse religion and literature. An integrated and *inter*disciplinary approach has appeared, and for that reason the archaeological evidence from the Late Iron Age has to some degree now become integrated into a historical perspective – or vice versa – the Old Norse sources are integrated into a material perspective (Andrén et al. 2006). Within this approach, archaeologists have at their disposal a wealth of textual, iconographic and archaeological material to explore. In the following, this interdisciplinary research strategy will be explored and challenged in an effort to capture shadows of what might have been central cognitive structures in Late Iron Age Scandinavia. As a point of departure, the description of Odin given above will serve as a case study. It will be explained by the supposition that it is a case of some general rule. Therefore, looking carefully into this may convey to us some basic information about the concept of sovereignty par excellence in the Old Norse world and at the same time revive notions of conceptual ideas that do not necessarily conform to our modern Western cosmology. In this particular case, it has no relevance whether Odin and the Old Norse pantheon of gods are transformed into human beings as they are in Snorri's writing ('euhemerism') or whether they are perceived as deities, as they certainly are in *The Poetic Edda*.

The constitution of primacy

The first thing to realise in the representation of Odin is what he is *not*. Although he is the king of the pre-Christian pantheon in Scandinavia during the martial Viking Age and preceding centuries, he is *not* the warrior king. As the one who decides the outcome, his connection to the battlefield is, however, clear. By throwing his spear over an army he claims it, and with the same spear he marks out the bravest warriors (i.e. he kills them) to gather them in for himself and include them in his own *hird* as *einherjar* (lone-fighters/warriors killed in battle) living in Valhal (the hall of the warriors killed in battle), Odin's magnificent guest hall (Nordberg 2003). Here they were served meat from *Sæhrímni* (literally 'sooty sea-beast', although Snorri makes it a boar), and it is cooked and consumed every night in Valhal but appears whole the next day to be eaten again. All in all, the *einherjar* have a splendid time with their fellow *hird*smen, fighting each other for fun every day, feasting and drinking in the evenings, and waiting for the last battle, Ragnarok, to come. Although Odin is not the warrior king (it is the Asir god Tyr who is specifically associated with battle and war) or himself a warrior, he is the lord of heroes – that is, the most famous warriors – who constitute his *hird*, he is the owner of a splendid hall and he is a generous host. The eight new gold rings produced by his own, Draupnir, every ninth night, continuously provide him with the ability to practise generosity by way of gift-giving, creating dependency and alliances.

To conclude, Odin behaves as an earthly and mortal king, of a kind familiar from the Old Norse literature where political alliances were forged by generosity, which meant gift-giving, including gold objects, feasts for the *hird*, and in the last instance, the fortunes of war. He is a hall-owner, which means he is the owner of a guest hall and public building of the sort familiar to Scandinavian archaeologists. So far the portrayal of Odin corresponds well with that of a king or *jarl* in pre-Christian Scandinavian society, except for the fact that his authority is not attached to a position as war-leader, as might have been expected.

However, the constitution of Odin's primacy encapsulates a variety of less tangible, although highly important, skills. Alone among the Asir gods, and in common with just a few in the whole Nordic pantheon, Odin masters the act of shape shifting, and can by the exercise of his will appear in the guise of a man, woman, or animal. In addition, his magical skills include the mastering of the runic letters as described earlier. Over and above its phonetic meaning, each rune had a symbolic value, being synonymous with a name or term connected to Nordic mythology. Thus, every rune had its own magical significance and possibly also a specific numerical value; thereby runic inscriptions may have contained a threefold message (i.e. Stoklund et al. 2006). Magic, that is, the art of runes, was potentially lethal to society and had to be monopolised and controlled. In many societies both the magic of the written word itself and the ability to read and write have been interpreted as a mystical craft that reveals divination, opens the secrets of sacred writing, guarantees the efficacy of amulets and holy talismans, and preserves ancestral knowledge. Literacy has been the main qualification of many holy men and learned scholars (Helms 1988: 12). Odin was the possessor and the true owner of the feared power that the secret knowledge created (Dumézil 1969: 52). By means of runic letters he could – as already mentioned – force dead men's tongues to talk and thereby achieved fateful knowledge about both past and present. Other kinds of sorcery were under his command, too. He mastered oral magic, *galdrer*, which means spells and chants (Halvorsen 1960), and through the use of words he could calm the seas and turn the wind, he could extinguish fire and he possessed the magic of the weather. To conclude, Odin was a great sorcerer whose magical skills made him the most feared among the gods in the Old Norse pantheon.

Apart from the runic letters, Odin also acquired or achieved the mead of poetry while offering himself, either by hanging in the World Tree or by giving his one eye (or by raping and stealing). In other words, the skaldic poetry, the inspiration to compose and the ability to remember the highly complicated metrical stanzas well known from the Eddic poetry belonged to Odin. In two cases these skills were acquired through devastating suffering. Odin was the principal skaldic poet and an expert on runic letters through a specific painful process of acquisition (or through shape shifting and rape), not because he was naturally gifted. Thereby this act must represent the concept of 'knowledge' and 'wisdom', that is, the ability to compose from inspiration and to remember from history.

The representation of Odin is not complete without mentioning his animal companions. Two ravens named Hugin and Munin, translated as already mentioned as 'Thought' and 'Mind/Memory', are closely connected with him. Every morning they set off to remote parts of the world and returned in the evening to advise Odin. In their roles as 'helping spirits' they encapsulated Odin's intellectual and mental capacity, and thereby were to be perceived as metaphors for an 'extended mind'. As specific representatives of Odin, the ravens make sense. They are impressive black birds with a good-sized beak and they are scavengers. In the Old Norse world they were well known from the battlefield, pecking the bodies of the fallen. And warriors who lost their lives in battle were, as already mentioned, supposed to be picked for an afterlife in Valhal as members of Odin's *hird*. While the two ravens may be seen as metaphors for cognition and cognisance, the two wolves, Freki and Geri ('the greedy one') represent ferocity, cruelty and the unpredictable aspects of Odin. Whether ravens or wolves, the animals are in a sense 'followers' representing Odin's extended mind and qualities. However, one more animal is closely connected to Odin, namely, the eight-legged steed Sleipnir. Riding the horse makes it possible to travel to the realm of the dead. In other words, this particular creature could cross the boundary between life and death, a boundary not even Odin himself was able to pass through on his own. Symbolically, Sleipnir may be seen as Odin's exclusive power to travel in all realms.

To sum up: the constitution of Odin's primacy is made up of some elements which are familiar from our own conceptual ideas of 'power', and others which definitely are not. On the one hand, Odin is depicted as an earthly king or nobleman in Scandinavian society, as the hall-owner with his *hird*, well known from the universe of the sagas and clearly recognisable in the archaeological record. On the other hand, his position and real power is interlinked with his knowledge (skaldic poetry, runic letters), his capacity as a sorcerer – not least his ability to change shape at will – and the skills of his zoomorphic helping spirits. Where Snorri's portrayal of the historical (euhemerised) god Odin has connections to the Sámi shaman, it is probably because Snorri recognised shamanic elements in the texts he knew relating to Odin (Lindow 2003). The crucial feature about Odin is, however, that his primacy and power constantly had to be negotiated and performed: it was embedded in social practice.

If this portrayal of Odin, as handed down through the literary sources, made sense in any respect to people of the Old Norse world, then we are faced with conceptual ideas and cognitive structures fundamentally opposed to our modern Western cosmology. It is the aim of the present book to explore these structures in a dialogue between written sources and material evidence.

Personification/Agency of objects

In the discussion above we have realised what might have made sense for people in the pagan past – a fundamental belief in a cognitive world of 'otherness' that has emerged from the Old Norse texts. Power and primacy were merged together with sorcery and knowledge, with shape changing and animal creatures in different guises as an 'extended mind', employing metaphors in a way we can hardly believe. The basic structural categories of the modern Western world obviously do not correspond to the fundamental categories of the ancient past when a body could exist beyond the boundary of the skin. Seemingly, words, humans and animals are not what we expect them to be. But what, then, of objects? Do they hold the same position as a neutral and unquestionable cultural category as they do in the world of today?

As already noted, two objects (a spear and a gold ring) are mentioned in connection with Odin. Gungnir and Draupnir, the spear and the ring, are both crucial to Odin's position as king of the Asir gods. It is obvious that they are not merely 'neutral' attributes of a specific god but inalienable to Odin in upholding his social position. Like Thor's hammer Mjollnir, Freyja's piece of gold jewellery Brísingamen, Frey's boar Gullinborsti and his ship Skídbladnir etc., all well known from the Old Norse sources, they are personified in the same way as animals such as Hugin, Munin and Sleipnir among others. As already mentioned too, Gungnir was thrown over the army fated to be slaughtered and it was used to point out the best warriors to fight the last battle, Ragnarok, against the giants, chaos and destruction. Thus Gungnir must be understood in metaphorical terms as the faith of earthly warriors and at the same time empowered Odin's ability to fight at Ragnarok. In other words, Gungnir was a 'gifted' spear of its own, not just an attribute of Odin, or a simple symbol of his power as a warrior. Obviously Odin was not a warrior, as already stated, and the spear was clearly not part of the prestigious – or kingly – war gear from the Late Iron Age. On the contrary, this was made up of highly decorated helmets and swords, of ships and riding equipment as familiar from the Old Norse and Old English literature as from the archaeological record. Although not a warrior, Odin was the primary god in the Nordic pantheon and an integral part of the martial elite culture not only in the North but also among barbarian peoples in Migration Period Europe, as will be argued below.

The other item attributed to Odin is the golden ring Draupnir. Every ninth night eight new rings dripped from it, permanently supporting Odin with gold and thereby providing him with supremacy in the rituals of gift-giving. For this reason it is obvious that Draupnir is a special artefact. However, the biography of the ring makes it unique, too. When Odin's most beloved son Balder died, Draupnir was placed on the funeral pyre and later followed him to the realm of the dead, named Hell's realm. Odin's other son went on Sleipnir to Hell to bring Balder back. However, Hell did not want to surrender Balder, and Balder handed Draupnir over as a gift for his father. A devastated Odin had Draupnir returned to him instead of his son. It may also have been Draupnir that played an important role in the Eddic poem *Skírnismál*, where it was used as a bribe to persuade the giantess Gerd to accept the Vanir god Frey as her husband and thereby unite the cosmic forces of chaos and fertility in a holy marriage (*hieros gamos*) (Steinsland 1991a).

In the earthly world of Old Norse societies, gold rings played a significant role as agents in the creation of political alliances and social relations and they are frequently found in the archaeological record, too. The written sources, whether Old Norse sources, early medieval law codes such as the Norwegian *Gulathings law*, or sources from early medieval Europe, give the impression that gift-giving was the decisive instrument in creating and upholding political alliances between lords and warrior-followers and among the warrior elite itself. Neither kings nor *jarls* held a political monopoly and powerful central rulers were lacking. In the continuous creation and negotiation of political primacy among the elite, gift-giving – often highly ritualised – played a significant role. Together with war gear such as swords and helmets, gold rings played an important ritual and ceremonial role when social and political identities were negotiated (e.g. Enright 1996; Bazelmans 2000). They were moveable wealth of specific symbolic value possessing a well-known biography; the most famous were named because they had a personality. Therefore they are not to be seen as ordinary gifts and symbols of wealth, although they certainly were that too, but as objects embodied with intangible qualities constitutive to them in the same way as Draupnir, Gungnir, Mjollnir, or Brísingamen. Persons and objects merged together (e.g. Appadurai 1986; Gosden and Marshall 1999; Kopytoff 1986; Meskell 2004; Gosden et al. 2004).

The 'lord of the ring' was just as solid a political reality in the Late Iron Age as a modern literary fiction in the realm of Tolkien. In the Old Norse sources, gold and gold treasures regularly play a central role in the construction of stories and the greed for gold reflects its potency as a vehicle of cultural values. For obvious reasons it should be expected that the gods had an unlimited access to gold, but this is definitely not the case. Gold, together with silver, bronze and iron, belonged to the dwarves. They lived underground and were especially talented craftsmen. As was the case for all the other vital possessions of the gods, the dwarves manufactured Draupnir and Gungnir.

To sum up: following these mythological schemes around Odin it becomes clear that objects embedded with specific qualities were crucial for upholding kingly power, as they may have been for earthly kings as well. Neither the metal nor the craftsmen were, however, under their control. The dwarves were outsiders, living on the outskirts of the civilised world. The objects they forged by means of magic were essential to upholding primacy among the gods.

The underlying nature of reality

The mythical narrative of Odin revealed that neither 'knowledge'/'wisdom' nor humans, animals and objects make up categories that fully conform to modern perceptions. Instead of emphasising categorisations and contradictions on the empirical level between words, humans, animals and objects, I propose that such categories were part of a broader cosmological system that empowered them with transformative meaning. To explore this further, I want to consider three main themes, all of which appear to be important in the construction of social identity and social dynamics in the mythical narrative concerning Odin as king of the Nordic pantheon.

First, the concepts of knowledge, wisdom and poetry occupy a prominent place in the constitution of Odin's supremacy, achieved through devastating suffering. Memory and remembrance, his external soul embodied in the raven Munin, stress the importance of the spoken word. Remembering and memory, however, do not exist by themselves. They have to be told – and retold – to people in order to persist, and must be given a material form, too (Meskell and Joyce 2003: 160). Although peoples all over the world now use literate means to represent the past, and written records have existed for millennia; the relating of past and present for social ends has for most of human history been done orally. Even in so-called traditional societies of today, it is well attested that there can still be skilled historians who neither read nor write (Tonkin 1995: 3). People remember what they need to remember, and forget, ignore, or invest with new meaning what no more makes sense. People remember or forget the past according to the needs of the present, and social memory is an active and ongoing process. Memory must be constructed (Lowenthal 1985: 210; Connerton 2006).

We can safely infer that memories are used and constructed by all societies, and as archaeologists we are familiar with the task ourselves when we interpret the human past and thereby contribute to the construction of memory for contemporary societies (Van Dyke and Alcock 2003: 1). In most traditional societies, genealogical knowledge is an important resource, used to support the legitimacy of a claim to political office or land as well as constituting the identity of the individual. Examples show that it is possible, for example, to 'remember' or 'know' thirty generations in all their references. Although it may be a social memory of no genuine authenticity at all, the existence of this, however, implies techniques of memorising, which are foreign to a Western tradition of textual memory (Tonkin 1995: 11). Writing allows people to stockpile data in masses, but when a society has to rely on human memory alone, it develops the necessary resources for the storage and transmission of data (Barber and Barber 2004). In societies without written archives, law books, religious books, etc., the spoken word, knowledge and memory in whatever form – practised or embodied – constitute the backbone of authority. Understandably, knowledge and memory are of formative importance to these societies, just as they are to the individual.

Fundamental to all societies, tribes, groups, families and individuals is knowledge about their origin and thereby about their identity. Ethnic identity, for example, has as much to do with myths of origin and a common knowledge about the past as it has to do with biological entities and genetic affiliations. When ethnic identities become a matter of structural importance, the matter of origins takes on a formative role in social and political reproduction – for society as a whole, or more exclusively among the ruling elite. Memory is constructed in a way that entails and transmits accounts of important persons, heroes, gods and events whereby the past is reinstated in the present. Social memory may be used to naturalise authority, to consolidate social identity and to establish or legitimise institutions, status, or relations of authority (Hobsbawm and Ranger 1983: 9). Control of a society's memory by and large constitutes a hierarchy of power, because shared images of the past commonly legitimate the present social order (Connerton 1989: 3).

The importance of a shared past for groups, tribes or nations is often articulated in periods of social and political stress (Connerton 2006). The post-Roman era of the fifth and sixth centuries is one such historical period of stress in the European past. It sees the formation of numerous new tribal histories in which origin myths and epic poetry go together to construct a 'shared knowledge' about the past. These myths identify a sacred origin and destiny of the peoples and their kings and they are of constitutive importance for the new barbaric – and Christian – kingdoms of the Early Middle Ages. Here Odin (Wotan) and Scandinavia play a formative role. This will be explored in Part II of this book, 'Words of identity'. Since memory and remembrance may be given a material form, this will be a matter for discussion, too.

Second, the importance of Odin's transformative capacities needs to be understood. The idea of somebody existing beyond his own skin, and the fact that one thing can become another, challenge a rational perception of the world. However, it must clearly have been comprehensible to, and taken for granted by, the people of the pre-Christian past. Odin's extended mind and out of the body capacities allowed him through the exercise of his will to change shape between man and animal as well as between male and female. Hybridity, metamorphosis and change are important intellectual concerns. Ordinary people may have been fascinated by change and transformation as an ontological problem because gender, ethnicity and kinship, principles that constituted identity in these societies, were vague structures (Meskell and Joyce 2003: 80). But by way of myth, the intangible was brought within the scope of what could be grasped.

Embodied animals, and their iconographic representations, may have been representations of stories and images recognisable for those with cultural knowledge in the same way as we can interpret Christian iconography. However, metaphors create new ways of conceiving the world. At the same time they both destabilise and reveal it (ibid.: 81). A rich body of archaeological, iconographic and textual material from Scandinavia reveals this hybridity, and supports the assumption that humans and animals were closely interwoven spiritually. This body of evidence will be explored in Part III of this book, 'The constitution of "otherness"', in both the relationship between human and animal and the social construction of gender. Special emphasis will be paid to the 'language' of clothing and sexuality.

Third, the mythical stories about Odin challenge our conceptual knowledge of objects and artefacts. Gungnir and Draupnir, as well as other items attached to the gods of the Old Norse pantheon, were not just artefacts on an empirical level. They were all personified, given names of their own, they had a well-known biography, and they carried a history of associations (Weiner 1992). They embodied special qualities and they were crucial for the gods in upholding their position. In that respect they were the key to ensuring the cosmological order of the universe. However, they were exclusive objects, manufactured and controlled by skilled craftsmen living on the edge of the civilised world. That is to say, the gods – and thereby humans too – were dependent on objects as embodiments of the cosmo-logical order. These objects were inalienable for the reproduction of social order and their manufacturing was out of reach.

Gungnir and Draupnir were merged with Odin in a way that made him what he was. We cannot describe Odin without referring to these two objects, just as we have to refer to Hugin, Munin, or Sleipnir – those objects and animals who in reality turned Odin from an earthly king into the king of the Asir gods. He was not just where his body was, but in many different places (and times) simultaneously. Those artefacts as well as the particular animals must be perceived as components of a particular type of divine identity and agency. They were embodied extensions of his power. Even the spear and the gold ring are emanations or manifestations of agency (Gell 1998: 21) where an agent is defined as one who 'causes events to hap-pen in their vicinity' (ibid.: 16).

In Old Norse societies, as in many other traditional societies, the process of gift-giving was highly ritualised and the display of wealth was incorporated in bodily practices. Movable wealth in the form of prestigious and artistic decorated warrior equipment, gold rings, jewellery and other personal belongings are well known from the archaeological sources, and the Migration Period is designated the 'Golden Age' of Scandinavia. Immense numbers of gold hoards were deposited during a few generations of the fifth and sixth centuries. In Marcel Mauss' exchange theory, they were to be considered as extensions of the person to whom they belonged (Mauss 1990), and following the terminology employed by Alfred Gell and Annette Weiner such objects (of art) were obviously seen as 'persons' in the same way (Gell 1998: 9; Weiner 1992; for a discussion see Godelier 1999). They had a life span and a personal biography (e.g. Kopytoff 1986), and they were embedded in social relations. They embodied specific historical relations and networks between people, but were also regarded as real animate persons who had the power to act in the world as humans do. They appear to have intentionality (e.g. Appadurai 1986; Gosden and Marshall 1999; Hodder and Hutson 2003: 102). They are, in the words of Alfred Gell, the equivalent of persons, or more precisely, are social agents (Gell 1998: 7). The manufacturing and circulation, as well as the embodiment of these artefacts, took place within an institutional framework of formalised acts and rites as part of the reproduction of social memory (Connerton 1989). In Part IV of this book, 'Materiality matters', these institutions will be explored. Special attention will be paid to the locality par excellence in the Nordic realm for the acquisition, production and transformation of precious objects and to the ritual deposition of such objects in the cultural landscape.

Fourth, the last part of the book, Part V, 'The making of Norse mythology', is an attempt to explain why there emerged a new symbol system of animal art in the Migration Period. During the fifth and sixth centuries, Barbarian Europe was fun-damentally changed and the early medieval Christian kingdoms came into being. In this specific historical context – the decades around AD 400 – the archaeological record reveals clear evidence that a new symbol-system had come into being in the Nordic realm. It is reflected in art-styles and iconography, in burial rituals, in cult practice and in settlement structure. We have to consider this a fundamental change of social practices – and social memory – in Scandinavia. It represented a new historical beginning for the non-Romanised, non-Christian societies of the North.

This change may therefore be just as significant as the one witnessed around AD 1000–1100 when Christianity was adopted and a new system of 'order in the world' fundamentally transformed the Nordic realm. In both historical periods the sense of what was reasonable, and what was unreasonable, in life may have changed within a few generations. The cultural historical context within which the transformation took place in the eleventh century is accepted and well attested as a powerful amalgamation between two institutions: the Church and the King. However, the social and cosmological transformation around AD 400 has never been fully recognised, or thoroughly debated; neither have the historical forces that triggered this transformation.

It is my hypothesis that the single most transformative component in post-Roman Europe was the Huns, an Asiatic steppe-people who appeared in the Black Sea region in the late fourth century and for more than half a century acted as a forceful, feared – and above all alien – military and political power that paralysed most of Europe. To contemplate these dramatic historical changes, I propose that the well-known king of the Asir gods in the North (Odin) emerged from the historical person Attila, the horrifying king of the Huns (who died in AD 453). Historical sources, epic poetry, iconography and animal art as well as the amount of Roman gold all point to the Huns – not as *the* single historical cause but as the catalyst in the transformation of Barbarian Europe into the Early Middle Ages. In Scandinavia it led to the formation of a new pagan cosmological world, which opposed the Christian world and lasted until the end of the Viking Period.

PART II
Words of identity

2

WRITTEN SOURCES ON THE PRE-CHRISTIAN PAST

Early Scandinavian literacy

In Scandinavia, the period known as the Middle Ages begins around the year 1000 – half a millennium later than the rest of western and central Europe. Only from this date onwards did Scandinavia consist of unified kingdoms and Christianity was established as a serious force in pagan Scandinavia. It is consequently only from this point onwards that Scandinavia has its own written history.

However, Scandinavia had not been totally illiterate in the preceding centuries. The runic script was used for magical purposes, as well as for messages, for protective charms, for memorials and so on, primarily written on wood but also on bone, metal and stone. There were, however, no extended literary texts in this form. The runic script was not especially Scandinavian: early runes are known from many Germanic peoples in fifth- and sixth-century Europe, in England, the Netherlands, Germany and central Europe (e.g. Düwel 1978; Fischer 2005; Stoklund et al. 2006). In those areas, however, the Roman script was adopted at an early date, and only in Scandinavia did the runic script develop further, during the Viking Period. This is the reason why the runic script is so well known from this area, although it also explains why we have to wait until as late as the twelfth century for Scandinavia to have a written history of its own. This does not, however, mean that the people of Scandinavia were without history, or without any knowledge of ancient events. Quite the opposite in fact, although their historical tradition was oral, transmitted from generation to generation within the constraints of rules and traditions of composition and performance.

From the 1990s, the post-processual research tradition in Scandinavian Iron Age archaeology began to employ the Old Norse sources from the twelfth to the fourteenth century in an attempt to better understand mentality, cosmology and systems of belief. However, the use of written sources from the thirteenth century as an explanatory framework for the Late Iron Age (from the sixth to the eleventh century) raises critical concerns. Historical documents of early Christian times cannot be treated as a reflection of 'genuine paganism'. On the other hand, we would go too far if we were to discard all written texts as useless for our endeavour. If used carefully and critically, the Old Norse texts yield valuable information, as demonstrated in many recent studies (Steinsland 1991a, b; Hedeager 1998, 1999a, c, 2000, 2001, 2004; Gansum 1999; Solli 2002; Price 2002; Herschend 1998, 2001; Andrén 1993; Andrén et al. 2004, 2006; Hines 2003; Melheim et al. 2004; Lund 2009).

In the modern world we tend to assume that statements in writing, especially in print, are more reliable than the spoken word. This is the result of our schooling in reading and writing and the constant use of documents for even the smallest transaction. In the medieval world, however, the living memory voiced by people of old age and experience persisted in a long tradition of remembered truth that contrasted with the artificial memory of written records (Clanchy 2001: 294 ff.). 'Objects, Voices, and Words' were in continuous dialogue in the Early Middle Ages, and were not yet dominated by the text (Moreland 2001: 53). Although there was a relative increase in written texts during this period, the literate elites continued to work orally. Medieval society remained 'fundamentally memorial' and the book itself was seen as a mnemonic device (Carruthers 1990; Moreland 2001: 35). It is obvious that the invention of written records could be a dubious gift to society because it transformed the flexible and up-to-date remembered truth into an artificial and static memory of the past. It altered, so to speak, the historical truth, because no ancient custom or narrative could be proved to be older than the memory of the oldest living wise person (Clanchy 2001: 296). In ancient Greece, Socrates was aware of the impact of writing when the Egyptian king Thamuzz, in Plato's *Phaedrus*, reproached the god who invented writing in the following way:

> If men learn this [the skill of writing], it will implant forgetfulness in their souls: they will cease to exercise memory because they rely on that which is written, calling things to remembrance no longer from within themselves, but by means of external marks; what you have discovered is a recipe not for memory, but for reminder.
>
> (*Plato:* Phaedrus, *274–5, cited from Clanchy 2001: 296*)

We might say that memory is humanity's remarkable ability to make the past present. Texts (written or spoken), monuments, artefacts, art, rituals, etc. serve as a memo technology, for the individual as for the culture. Therefore, pre-Christian Scandinavia can be compared to traditional communities, in which historical memory is integrated within a coherent whole of economic, political and religious institutions, represented as the world view of any given society. In the works of Claude Lévi-Strauss, Mircea Eliade and George Dumézil, however different, we have been taught that myth is ideology in narrative form (Lincoln 1999: 145 f.). Since much cosmological information is thought to be contained in myths (e.g. Weiner 1999; Barber and Barber 2004), special attention will be paid in the following to the myths of Old

Norse literature, primarily incorporated in *The Poetic Edda* and in *The Prose Edda* of Snorri Sturluson. In thirteenth-century Iceland, 'Edda' meant 'great-grandmother' (Byock 2005: xii), and in both cases we are dealing with 'remembered truth', that is, ancient wisdom that was transformed into literature in the Early Middle Ages.

The Poetic Edda and *The Prose Edda*

The Poetic Edda – or *The Elder Edda* – is primarily known from *Codex Regius*, dated to *c.* 1270 and another codex, called *AM 748*, written down a bit later (Lindow 2001: 14). There might have been a master copy dated to *c.* 1200 (Collinder 1972: 13). Both *Codex Regius* and *AM 748* are 'collected' works rather than composed by those who recorded them, and it seems also clear that they were compilations of other compilations (Lindblad 1954; Gunnell 2008: 299). However, the poems undoubtedly belong to a much older pre-Christian tradition; although there is no way to tell the original dates, some may go back to at least the sixth century AD (Collinder 1972: 15). The Eddic poems were essentially works that were presented 'live' by performers – they belonged to an oral tradition and were sung, spoken, or chanted with varying tones, rhythms and inflections. Thus, the *text* itself was only a limited part of the overall 'received' work (Gunnell 2008).

Found all over Scandinavia, some central motifs from the accumulated layers of belief are depicted in iconographic form from the sixth century onwards (Andrén 1993; Staecker 2004; Hauck 1970, 1983; Gaimster 1998; Axboe 2004; Hedeager 1997b; Wiker 2008). This also confirms that the Eddic poetry was well known all over the Nordic area, neither restricted to Iceland nor to the medieval period (Schjødt 2004: 121, 2008: ch. 4). It is a matter of fact that the mythological Eddic poems, despite their origin and date, present a fairly consistent picture of the Old Norse gods (Lindow 2001: 14; Steinsland and Meulengracht Sørensen 1994) and it is beyond debate that the Eddic poems of *The Poetic Edda* represent the oldest form of literature from Scandinavia, composed in a strict metric form as a contrast to the prose form of Snorri's *Edda* as well as the sagas.

The first text of *The Poetic Edda* is *Vǫluspá*, the Prophecy of the Seeress. In this lay the *volva* [seeress] tells of the creation of the World, the strife of the gods and the destruction of the earth. From his examination of both main manuscripts of *The Poetic Edda*, Terry Gunnell separates the layers into two very different types of poetic work. The layers of the first one, *fornyrðislag*, are for the main part composed in the third person and deal with ancient Germanic heroes. The audience is informed of earlier events by a narrator who acts as a middle man between the past and the present (the audience). The layers of the latter, *ljoðaháttr*, deal with the world of the gods and archetypical heroes such as Sigurðr Fáfnisbani who were dealing with the gods. They take the form of monologues and dialogues in the first person; there is no middle man, and the form forces the performer to take on the roles of the gods and their companion. Thus, the latter possessed strong dramatic qualities in performance, quite different form the former (Gunnell 2008).

The Prose Edda, or Snorri's *Edda*, was written as a handbook for aspiring Icelandic poets and skalds who needed to master the traditional forms of verse and the older stories since it was considered essential to 'know' the old myths. It is divided into four parts. The Prologue is a short introduction that differs significantly from the rest of the *Edda*. It is uncertain whether it was part of the original text, or whether some or all of it was a later addition. By harmonising Norse beliefs with Christian concepts, it tries to make the *Edda*'s stories more palatable to the medieval audience. The second section is known as *Gylfaginning* (the 'deluding of Gylfi'). This is the core of *The Prose Edda* and our best source of knowledge on the creation, the gods and their struggle, and the events leading to the destruction of the universe. It is organised as a dialogue between Gangleri and Odin's three manifestations, resembling the contests of wisdom found in *The Poetic Edda*. It is worth mentioning that this text is remarkably similar in all the important manuscripts of the *Edda*. The third section is called *Skaldskaparmal* (*Skáldskaparmál*), which means 'the language of poetry' or 'poetic diction'. The stories give the background for the references and allusions found in *The Poetic Edda*. Although *Gylfaginning* and *Skaldskaparmal* were written in somewhat different styles, and must have been gathered into one book after they were written separately, the two fit well together, containing almost no repetitions. The fourth and final section of Snorri's *Edda* is the poem *List of Metres*, called *Hattatal* (*Háttatal*), which was without doubt composed by Snorri himself in an attempt to flatter the Norwegian king. The text consists of 102 stanzas with a prose commentary offering technical explanations in between them (Byock 2005: xiv ff.).

Snorri Sturluson lived on Iceland from 1178/79–1241, and the sources for his *Edda* are the poems known from *The Poetic Edda* as well as other tales of the gods from unknown texts (Morris 1991: 4). Although he is named as the compiler of the work, it is not clear from the passage whether Snorri is the author of more than the last section, *Háttatal* (Byock 2005: xii). However, his *Edda* is a systematisation of the mythology, and the book itself must be regarded as a mnemonic. Both *Skáldskaparmál* and *The Poetic Edda* recount heroic legends that can be dated to the European Migration Period in the fifth and sixth centuries. Tales of legendary heroes (historical persons such as Attila the Hun and Ermaneric, ruler of the vast Gothic kingdom north of the Black Sea until suddenly attacked by the Huns in AD 376) originated during this era and became the basis for the epic cycles that were told during the Viking Age and must still have been told in the thirteenth century AD when they were written down (Lukman 1943, 1949; Byock 2005: xvi) (see Part V of this volume).

The texts give a reasonably coherent picture of the Northern cosmology, although pre-Christian Scandinavia had no single, organised religion (Andrén et al. 2006: 13). However, people shared a belief in the same pantheon of the Norse gods, just as they had a common world view (Schjødt 2004; Andrén et. al. 2006: 13 f.; Byock 2005: xvii). What we define as 'religion' is more appropriately termed a 'belief-system', a way of looking at the world. It was not an isolated orthodox structure but a way of living, simply another dimension of daily life and existence.

Thereby *The Poetic Edda* and *The Prose Edda* create a plausible setting for the material evidence from the Late Iron Age. Central myths representing the wisdom and knowledge of the pre-Christian world contain core elements that remain stable through time, although encrusted in new layers of meaning, and adapted to new contexts. As an example, extensive pagan wisdom still existed in pre-Reformation Icelandic society, in the guise of traditional esoteric knowledge, which then was transformed into Satan-worship and witchcraft in the seventeenth century (Hastrup 1990: 401). *Galdur* (galdring), *galdrastafir* (magic staves), *runes* (secret or occult), *skaldskapur* (poetry) and *hamrammr* (a person who could change shape at will) were so deeply rooted in everyday life and thought that they maintained their role as meaningful concepts long after the official introduction of Christianity (see also Gilchrist 2008 for late-medieval Britain; Mitchel 2009 for late-medieval Scandinavia; and Jóhanna Katrín Friðriksdóttir 2009 for Iceland). The runic staves from Bryggen in Bergen also indicate that the Eddic poems were still well known in Norway in the late Middle Ages. From another perspective it has convincingly been argued that mythological texts such as *The Poetic Edda*, some skaldic verses and Snorri's *Edda*, incorporate myths that explain fundamental ideas with regard to life and death in Nordic societies. These ideas retained their relevance even when the majority of the population on Iceland had become Christian (Clunies Ross 1994); however, the skaldic verses did not reveal Old Norse mythology itself (Clunies Ross 2008: 232). Evidence from Swedish court cases in the late fifteenth century indicates that the name of Odin was still important to people of late-medieval Stockholm; however, in other areas of Scandinavia it is likely that Odin continued to be regarded as a potential source of power late into the eighteenth century (Mitchell 2009).

Snorri's role in writing the *Edda* has long been a matter of debate. Some scholars have seen him as a creative literary artist; others as a far more reliable communicator of pre-Christian mythology[1] who had no obvious reason to disparage the faith of his ancestors, although he probably did not share it himself (Hultgård 1999). While Snorri's work was naturally influenced by Christianity – since he wrote in a Christian society – one may well wonder whether he could really have manipulated old and familiar myths to the extent of giving a false image of the pre-Christian cosmology still known to his audience. Within a Christianised society, pre-Christian traditions were still kept alive, although perceived through a Christian perspective, and therefore probably distorted. Also, we should not discount the possibility of some 'invention of tradition' (Hobsbawm and Ranger 1983), as authors such as Snorri were eager to incorporate traditional myths within a new framework, stressing the continuity between 'old times' and the new world they inhabited. But counting against this view are the observations that Snorri's narratives correspond in many details to other early medieval texts from elsewhere in Scandinavia, not least *The Poetic Edda*, and that his *Edda* was regarded in Iceland as the authoritative handbook for training poets in traditional verse forms (Byock 2005: xii). Therefore, we cannot afford to disregard Snorri's information and the information given in *The Poetic Edda*. Although there are some contradictions within each of the texts as well as between the texts, they nevertheless constitute a coherent cosmological unity (Raudvere 2004: 64).

If one pursues this argument, it follows that Christianity was a historical process rather than an absolute change of faith. 'Christianisation' in this definition meant that prior beliefs and concepts helped to shape new varieties of Christianity. Magic, be it of a Christian type or some sort defined by Christians as 'pagan', remained omnipresent in the daily lives of medieval people (Jong 2001: 131–68; Mitchell 2009). Yet I would go further. We are dealing not merely with folk magic, but with a *longue durée* of fundamental myths and systems of beliefs, whose roots were deeply anchored in the traditional pagan universe (Meulengracht Sørensen 1991a: 217–28). In the centuries following the introduction of Christianity, pagan myths were employed in the cultural memory as something that was still relevant and meaningful to people in Iceland; they were invoked to create a sense of continuity between past and present (Hermann 2009). This conclusion is supported by independent archaeological evidence, as I shall demonstrate in subsequent chapters.

Other Nordic texts

The great literature of early Scandinavia, written in the Old Norse language but in Roman script, includes other works of Snorri Sturluson, such as *Heimskringla*, composed *c.* 1230 with the encouragement of the king of Norway for the purpose of providing a coherent narrative of the Norwegian kings and their descent from the legendary Ynglinga kings of Sweden (*Ynglinga Saga*). According to Snorri, the *Ynglinga Saga* is, however, based on the *Ynglinga tal* (Enumeration of the Ynglingar), which is reproduced in his text. Unlike the anonymous mythological and heroic poems in *The Poetic Edda*, this one is composed by one of the earliest known *skálds* (poets), Thjódólf of Hvin, in the late ninth century AD. It is addressed to Rögnvald Heidumheiri (honoured highly) Óláfsson, king of the Vestfold district of Norway. Listed in the poem are twenty-two generations of Ynglinga kings, centred on Uppsala and predecessors to Rögnvald, together with the way in which they met their deaths and where they were buried. It has been a matter of debate whether *Ynglinga tal* is a much later composition (Krag 1991), although most scholars tend to agree with Snorri and accept *Ynglinga tal* as a genuine pre-Christian skaldic composition from the late ninth century which originally served a dynastic purpose (Skre 2007a). Thjódólf probably had access to traditions of east Scandinavian origin, flourishing among the Svea at the latest during the ninth century (e.g. Sundqvist 2002: 41 ff.). The Old Norse *skálds* honoured their kings by placing the ruler in a mythical context, as Thjódólf did for Rönvald, because the ancient myths might have been significant on several levels. For that reason they tend to reflect ritual aspects, popular belief and stylistic ideals (Lindow 2001: 16). To the contrary, Snorri and other early medieval writers moved in the opposite direction by transforming the myths into history and depriving the ancient gods of their divine status. In genealogical poems such as *Ynglinga tal*, as well as *Ynglinga Saga*, myth and history at the same time interact in a complementary way. By giving the royal families a divine origin, as for example Snorri did in *Ynglings Saga* and Thjódólf did in *Ynglinga tal*, their right to rule the land was legitimised (Sundqvist 1997, 2002).

Other sagas describe the history of the Icelanders, from the colonisation in the late ninth and early tenth centuries AD to the ceding of authority to the Norwegian king in the 1260s. *The Sagas of Icelanders (Íslendingasǫgur)* or 'family sagas' cover the earliest period of Icelandic history, which is roughly speaking the tenth century AD. The time of writing spans the period between the early thirteenth century and the middle of the fifteenth century (Nordal 2008: 315). The *Saga of the People of Laxardal (Laxdœla Saga)*, *Egil's Saga (Egils saga Skallagrímssonar)*, and *the Saga of Gunnlaug Serpent-tongue (Gunnlaug Ormstungas Saga)* are among those early family sagas that constitute the Icelandic foundation myth, describing the Norwegian families and their migration to Iceland. In a kinship society such as the Icelandic, with no central authority and no written record, and with relatively fluid social hierarchies, genealogies and geographical information about land, places and farms were crucial. Those two sets of information constituted the structures through which society framed its past and through which it revived its present, as the sagas confirm (Callow 2006: 300 f.). *The Sagas of the Icelanders* are decidedly the history and the historical legends of the founding families of Norwegian farmers settling on Iceland in a very specific time period of the recent past. Unlike other migrations myths of Europe, they have no mythological structure, no mythical origin in a timeless or very distant past, and the founding families were not descended from the gods (Byock 2001: 22 f.).

The scholarly approach towards the *Sagas of the Icelanders* is wary, and scepticism about their historical value is prevalent.[2] Were they literary fictions or historical facts, were they composed in the thirteenth century or did they represent a genuine oral tradition? To scholars who work in a historical–anthropological tradition, such as William Miller (i.e. 1990), Jesse Byock (1982, 1990, 2001), Carol Clover (1986, 1993) and Preben Meulengracht Sørensen (1992), it is obvious that the sagas were meaningful to the people who constructed them – they constituted the social memory of society, but they were not 'historical' texts in the positivist tradition (Callow 2006: 299). They represented Icelandic social memory and self-image, and this tradition in medieval Iceland was not 'a block of historical facts. Nor was it a fixed text. Tradition was a living and growing heritage of quasi-factual social recollection that served as the thematic core of each saga story, uniting saga-teller and audience with life in the Icelandic environment, past and present' (Byock 2001: 23).

The contemporary sagas *(Samtíðarsögur)* that covered Icelandic history in the twelfth and thirteenth centuries have traditionally been ascribed more historical 'truth' and 'historicity' than the 'family sagas' because they were written down shortly after the historical period they portray. *The Sturlunga Sagas*, for example, were part of the contemporary sagas; the historical period covered by this collection of sagas span from 1120 to 1264 and they were written down shortly after (*c.* 1300). From a comparison of the political relationships described in the *Sagas of the Icelanders* and in the 'contemporary sagas', it has convincingly been argued that those two collections of sagas were transformed into written form during distinct periods of time. The *Sagas of the Icelanders* reveals a much older and more original layer of Icelandic history than usually believed. It is unlikely, it is argued, that the authors of the *Sagas of the Icelanders* wrote fictional accounts of the past; it is more likely that they recorded something close to contemporary views of their own recent past (Callow 2006).

The latest sagas, the 'sagas of ancient times', are the *fornaldar sagas*, or the 'legendary sagas' (also 'Nordic sagas of antiquity'). This group consists of approximately thirty late-medieval Icelandic texts, generally subdivided into the overlapping sub-categories of adventure tales and heroic legends (Mitchell 2008). The *fornaldar sagas* were written down from the thirteenth century onwards and flourished in the late Middle Ages (Bandlien 2005: 29).

They tell of events that occurred, or that are supposed to have occurred, long before the settlement of Iceland, such as the *Saga of King Hrolf Kraki* (*Hrólf saga Kraka*). It goes back to events that might, or might not, have occurred in the Migration Period Danish kingdom of the Skjoldunga (Old English *Scyldinga*), showing close affinities to the Old English poem *Beowulf*, which was written down between the eighth and eleventh centuries AD (Byock 1998: vii). Another work is *Völsunga saga*, preserved only in a fifteenth-century manuscript. The fame of this tradition in northern Europe goes far back in time; scenes from the story are found in carved and sculptured presentations on, for example, Norwegian stave-churches and on a Swedish rock-carving from the Viking Age. In an encapsulated form it is known from Snorri's *Edda* and the heroic cycle constitutes more than a dozen of the lays in *The Poetic Edda*. In addition, the heroic and legendary sagas are well preserved in the ballade traditions of the Faroes, Norway, Sweden and Denmark, as well as in the Icelandic metrical romances (*rímur*). They are also well represented in the Danish *Gesta Danorum* from the late twelfth century (Mitchell 2008: 320).

Other sources from the Icelandic Middle Ages are *The Book of Settlements* (*Landnámabók*) and *The Book of the Icelanders* (*Íslendingabók*), which offer considerable information about the settlers, including genealogies and historical descriptions. The small *Book of the Icelanders* covers the history from the date of the first settlement in AD 870 up to 1120, and was probably written down between 1122 and 1132 by the Christian priest and *goði* Ari Thorgilsson, called Ari the Learned. *The Book of Settlements* accounts for approximately 400 *landnámsmenn* (farmers who took land) and their origin in Scandinavia, and like *the Book of the Icelanders* it reports specific information on people and places. It is agreed that Ari must have been one of the authors (Byock 1990: 15 ff.).

The last Icelandic source which has to be considered is *Grágás* (gray goose), the Icelandic Free State laws. The oldest manuscripts of *Grágás* are from the thirteenth century, but many of the laws long pre-date this period and show a legal system that operates without an executive central authority. The laws were not a set code, but instead a collection of rules that individuals could use to their advantage, or to the disadvantage of others (Byock 1990: 20f.). The individual's rights were upheld as a private responsibility, which implied extensive blood feuds, of the kind well known from the sagas (Byock 1982; Miller 1990). This is what makes *Grágás* reflect the social reality of early medieval Iceland in a unique way.

The most important Old English or Anglo-Saxon poem is *Beowulf*, preserved in a single manuscript, *Cotton Vitellius A. xv*, in the British Library. Its written form is usually dated to some time in the period from the eighth to the early eleventh century AD (Byock 1998: vii: Heaney 2008: vii); however, others have dated it to no earlier than around the turn of the eleventh century (Orchard 2002). The composition was certainly completed in England in the eighth century, but the poem is set among the societies of Scandinavia (the Danes, the Geats, and the Swedes) depicting events from the distant past, some of which appear to have occurred in the sixth century AD (Orchard 2002). The poem is a heroic narrative, more than 3000 lines long, concerning the deeds and faith of the Geatic hero Beowulf from the time when he leaves his land (that of the Geats in south-western Sweden) and crosses the sea to the land of the Danes (Zealand) in order to rid their country of a man-eating monster, his return in triumph and his rule as a king for fifty years, until he meets his own death in killing a dragon, his funeral, and lastly how he enters the legends of his people (Niles 2006). This is not a genealogical poem such as *Ynglingatal* and *Ynglings saga*, but a master narrative about one individual, Beowulf, and his path to commemoration.

Less attention is traditionally paid to *Widsith* ('Farway'), an Old English poem known only from the *Exeter Book* transcribed in the period AD 970–990. The 143-line poem might have been composed in a written form considerably earlier, while the three main parts of the poem clearly belong to an oral tradition stretching back to the sixth and seventh centuries (Chambers 1912; Malone 1962).[3] The text includes three mnemonic name lists in addition to the 'historical' references to the battle between the Goths of the Vistula and the Huns. The latter is also to be found in the Old Norse *Saga of Hervarar and Heidrik's crowning*, and in the Danish *Gesta Danorum*; however, by far the oldest source is *Widsith* (Malone 1962).

In Denmark, *c.* AD 1200, on the encouragement of the Danish king, Saxo Grammaticus (*c.* 1150 to *c.* 1220) wrote his Latin *Gesta Danorum* ('Deeds of the Danes'): the history of the Danish people from ancient times to the present (i.e. AD 1202), composed in sixteen books of unequal length. It was probably completed between 1210 and 1220; however, it was not published until 1514 (Clunies Ross 2008: 233). His intention is made clear in the very first sentence: 'To glorify the fatherland.' Accordingly he wrote in the same line of tradition as the early medieval (Germanic) historians such as Jordanes on the Goths, Gregory of Tours on the Franks, Paul the Deacon on the Lombards etc., on the brink of their conversion to Christianity. Books 1–9 are of particular interest: they retell old legends and myths, some of which are found in Snorri's *Edda* and other Old Norse sources. Because Saxo used Icelandic informants in addition to the written sources, *Gesta Danorum* contains a large number of Old Norse heroic and mythological tales otherwise unknown to us (Simek 1996: 276). Gods and giants, dragons and peculiar heroes are mixed together in a style far from the work of his contemporary, Snorri Sturluson (Fisher 1980). Although Saxo dealt with his sources fairly freely, *Gesta Danorum* does present tales found in a number of other Old Norse sources, not at least many of the *fornaldar sagas* (Mitchell 2008: 320).

Together with the sagas these works supply us with more detailed information on religious belief and practice, on world view and mentality than the Eddic poetry. Although they were compiled in a Christian milieu, they contain valuable information not found anywhere else about pre- and post-Christian myths and values (Morris 1991: 4). These historical accounts reach far back in time, incorporating ancient myths and stories, and tell of kings, heroes and events, some of which contain historical reality. Clearly, they are not historical sources in the modern sense of the term. The sagas, as well as *Gesta Danorum*, *Historia Norwegia* and other early medieval texts, should rather be interpreted as a mirror to attitudes (Morris 1991: 14). Like all other texts of the Old Norse they represent the social memory of particular social or geographical groups and they embody a heroic ethos linked to a religious cosmology. The only possibility of gaining an insight into the 'history' of Scandinavia in the fifth, sixth and seventh centuries lies in whatever information about Scandinavia these early medieval European texts contain. When linked to the archaeological record of the time, an independent chronological and interpretative context is provided that allows a fuller reconstruction of the Norse mythological universe (see Part III).

European sources

'From the mouth of the Rhine my fleet sailed over the sea in the direction of the rising sun to the land of the Cimbri [presumably Jutland], whither no Roman had ever gone before, either by land or by sea.' Thus wrote the Emperor Augustus around the time of the birth of Christ in *Monumentum Ancyranum*, an extract from his now lost autobiography reproduced on a temple wall in Ancyra (now Ankara) in Asia Minor. At that time, the region of Scandinavia was beginning to take its admittedly remote place in the Roman world view. Even though we find scattered 'information' in the early Greek sources and the Roman historian Pliny the Elder (*ob.* AD 79), it is first in the Roman historian Tacitus' work *Germania* at the end of the first century AD that we can talk about a 'real' description of the northern neighbours of the Roman Empire – the Germanic areas (i.e. Europe north of the Roman frontier along the Rhine and the Danube, and west of the Vistula). The composition of the *Germania* should probably be seen as a logical consequence of Augustus' interest in the Cimbric lands in the far distant parts of the world; in other words, in military terms. Tacitus was describing those areas which were beyond the border, but within the Roman sphere of interest, and his *Germania* distinguishes between various parts of Germanic territory and different Germanic peoples, many of whom, such as the Goths, the Svear, the Langobards, the Suebi, the Heruli and more, re-appear as tribal names in the Early Middle Ages. A number of the factual ethnographic details given by Tacitus are also found practically unchanged in Langobardic tradition five or six centuries later (Ausenda 1995: 32–3). Although the main purpose of Tacitus when writing *Germania* was to critique Roman society by extolling a 'noble savage' in the guise of the barbarian peoples outside the imperial realm (Halsall 2005a: 38 f.; Geary 2002: 22 f.), he nevertheless provides ethnographic information of unquestionable value.

A more substantial geographical description of Scandinavia comes from the middle of the second century AD in the work of the Greek geographer, astronomer and mathematician Ptolemy, who lived in Alexandria from *c.* AD 90 to *c.* 160. As a geographer, he sought to map and measure the then known world, which included north-west Europe. His world map is much closer to geographical actuality than that of the later Middle Ages, which is an ingenious composition with Jerusalem at the centre. In his 'Guide to Geography', *Geographiké Hyphégesis*, in eight books, Ptolemy states that there were four islands east of the Cimbric peninsula, 'Insulae Alociae' (Northern Jutland) and Insulae Saxonis (west and south of Jutland). These islands are together known as *Skandiai*, consisting of three small ones and one very large one, which was that furthest east and lay opposite the mouth of the Vistula. The large island was the true *Skandia*. He also gives the names of several different peoples (*Geographiké Hyphégesis* 2. 11).

Ptolemy's information was repeated *c.* AD 550 by the Ostrogothic historian Jordanes who wrote his *Getica* (*De origine actibusque Getarum*) (the history of the Gothic people) in Constantinople. The *Getica* is partly based on the now lost work on Gothic history by the Roman senator Cassiodorus, chancellor at the Ostrogothic court in Ravenna, Italy, in the first half of the sixth century.

Jordanes began his account with a geographical introduction in which *Scandza* (Scandinavia) was described quite thoroughly. This not only refers to Ptolemy, but also includes a surprisingly comprehensive account of a large number of named tribal areas, beginning with the northernmost, the *Adogitti*. Jordanes gives a careful account of the extraordinary circumstances in which they lived, in an area where there was unbroken sunlight for fourteen days in the summer, while there were forty days with no real daylight during the winter. This is because, he explains, the sun can be seen throughout its course during the summer while in the winter it does not rise above the horizon (*Getica* III: 19–20). However strange this must have seemed to someone residing in Constantinople or Ravenna, it is a reasonably correct account of the situation in the north of Scandinavia.

Amongst the many tribal groups Jordanes named are the Finns, the Lapps, the Svear, the East Goths, the Gaut-Goths, the Swedes, the Danes and the Heruli. They are all names well known in early medieval Europe in other contexts. This detailed description may be attributable to a certain King Rodulf to whom Jordanes refers: he had left his kingdom, that of the Ranii (possibly Romsdal in southern Norway), to seek sanctuary with the Ostrogothic king Theodoric (Callmer 1991; Skre 1998). He (or, indeed, some of his subjects) may have provided Cassiodorus with information about the Scandinavian peoples at the beginning of the sixth century. Even though several of the groups concerned can apparently be located, approximately at least, using either linguistic or archaeological evidence (Callmer 1991, after Svennung 1967), Jordanes' text is complicated, and its value as a source is much debated (see in particular Svennung 1967, 1972 with references; Søby Christensen 2002). What it does demonstrate, however, is the existence of tribal groupings as the basis of a geographical subdivision of Scandinavia, while the account of Rodulf indicates that the king was the political lynchpin of the tribe.

This perception is supported by, inter alia, Gregory of Tours' description of what seems to be a real historical event. In his history of the Franks, the *Historiae*, from the end of the sixth century, reference is made to a Danish king Chlochilaich (Hygelac) who, *c.* AD 515, brought a fleet to raid the Frisian coast but was slain by King Theuderic's son Theudebert, who had been despatched to the area with a large army (*Historiae* III: 3) (Wood 1994: 50).

The account of this episode contains several interesting points, as pointed out by Ian Wood (1983, 1994: 160 f.). First and foremost, the event itself must have been something quite special, simply because Gregory, who otherwise wrote very little about Scandinavia and the north-eastern regions, actually recorded it. Second, it is worthy of note that Gregory uses the term *rex* for the Danish king. Gregory was very careful in his use of royal terminology, and he always uses the term *dux* for kings of peripheral areas, or areas which were subject to Frankish overlordship such as the Bretons, the Frisians, the Continental Saxons, the Thüringians, the Alamanni and the Bavarians. When, therefore, he refers to Chlochilaich as *rex*, he concurrently recognises that the leader of the Danish fleet was effectively independent of the Frankish king. And it is finally noteworthy that the Danes are not mentioned at all after AD 515, either in the Frankish Annals or by Gregory. The explanation may be that the victory over Chlochilaich was such a serious defeat for the Danes that their raids and attempts to dominate the Frankish-controlled Frisian littoral ceased throughout the following centuries. The popularity of this story in the Germanic epic tradition, in, for instance, *Beowulf* (where Hygelac is his king) (e.g. Alexander 1973: 33) helps to underline the importance attached to the event. Southern Scandinavia never fell under Frankish hegemony as it was too far away, but after their defeat in AD 515 the Danes kept away from Frankish territory and consequently stayed out of European history for several centuries to follow.

3

ORIGIN MYTHS AND POLITICAL/
ETHNICAL AFFILIATIONS

Migration Period Europe: a historical survey

What are known as the European Middle Ages began around AD 400, succeeding Antiquity – the era of the Roman Empire. Around that time (more precisely on the last day of AD 406), Roman Gaul was invaded by a huge army of barbarians from many parts of Europe beyond the Roman frontier: Vandals, Sueves, Alans and Burgundians. In AD 410 Rome was sacked by another group of barbarians, the Goths. Not least symbolically, these two events marked an end of the West Roman Empire and the beginning of the Middle Ages, or the Dark Age, during which barbarian peoples in the following century settled all over the former Western Empire. From *c.* AD 400 to 560, Europe experienced formative political changes as armed barbarian groups were constantly on the move, searching for land and wealth – named fortune – on Roman territory. The Goths (East and West), the Vandals, the Lombards, the Burgundians, the Heruli, the Franks, the Anglo-Saxons and many more – together with Central Asian steppe nomads in the form of the Huns – are known from the written sources as players in shifting alliances and political confederations, both in mutual arrangements and with the Romans.

However, this was a long-lasting process, in reality starting two centuries earlier when the Roman emperor Marcus Aurelius spent more than twenty-five years on the northern frontier fighting the Marcomannii and Quadii, who were given assistance by other barbarian groups such as the Lombards (at that time settled at the mouth of the Elbe in northern Germany). For the first time in more than two hundred years the Romans had to negotiate a peace treaty with the barbarians to end a long-lasting conflict which they could not win. This in fact brought an end to the *Pax Romana* and 200 years of peace inside the Roman border. Shortly after, civil wars swept through the empire. Rival imperial armies elected their own emperors and Rome had definitely lost political control. This period of severe unrest lasted until the late third century and weakened the empire from the inside. Barbarian armed groups now penetrated far into the Roman provinces from the north. However, at the same time other barbarian groups enrolled in the imperial army, fighting their invading fellow tribesmen. No doubt, the third century gave rise to a changed relationship between the barbarians and the Romans, and it brought barbarians from all over Europe deep into the Roman Empire – both as allies and as enemies.

This political agony came to an end with the accession of Diocletian as emperor in the late third century. In the aftermath of Diocletian's long-lasting reign, in the first part of the fourth century Constantine the Great consolidated the division of the empire into an eastern (i.e. a Greek-speaking) and a western (Latin-speaking) part, himself maintaining supremacy. Constantine not only made Byzantium his new capital, as Constantinople, he also made Christianity the new official religion across the Roman world. Rome became the main centre of Christianity and the residence of the pope, while Ravenna in the north of Italy (in the Po Valley) became the new capital of the Western Empire.

However, peace was never restored. Armed tribal groups of barbarians, known from the written sources as the Goths, the Vandals, the Burgundians etc., swept down from the north through the weakened empire in astonishing numbers. At the same time the empire became fully dependent on barbarian groups, who gradually came to constitute the Roman army and were given land and allowed to settle in return for military service. This was especially the case in the densely populated western part (modern France and Spain), where the Visigoths were the first group to be settled after the sack of Rome in the early fifth century.

One more important political and military player in the late fourth and early fifth centuries has yet to be mentioned: the Huns. According to the written sources, they appeared in the Black Sea region *c.* AD 375, defeating the Goths, who at that time seem to have been in charge of a vast but loose federation, stretching from the Black Sea in the south to the Baltic in the north. This particular event precipitated the first large-scale movement by a barbarian group into Roman territory to be reported in the classical sources. This group, the Visigoths, formed only one branch of the previous Black Sea Gothic federation. The remaining group, now named the Ostrogoths, became allied to the Huns. This event became, as we shall later explore, one of the formative elements in the epic tradition of the European Middle Ages (see Part V).

For the next seventy-five years, until *c.* AD 450, the Huns became the dominant political force in barbarian Europe, settled as they were in the east Hungarian plain around the river Theiss (Figures 3.1–3.4). In a series of shifting alliances they destroyed their enemies and they sacked the Roman Empire. Attila, the most feared of their war-leaders, struck panic into most of the Continent over three decades, from around AD 420 to his death in AD 450. This is reported in the historical sources and it is reflected in the epic poetry from the Dark Age. The Huns no doubt became a catalysing force in the process of Western Roman decline and the large-scale barbarian migrations and invasions into Roman territory – thus in the formation of post-Roman Europe.

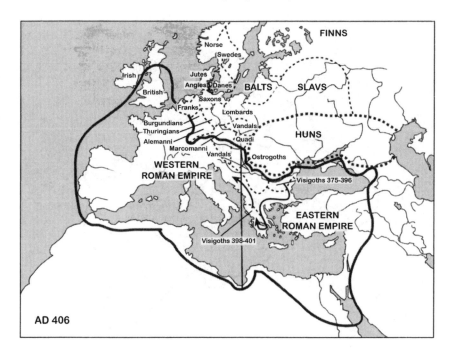

FIGURE 3.1   Map of Migration Age Europe, AD 406. Modified after McEvedy (1975: 17).

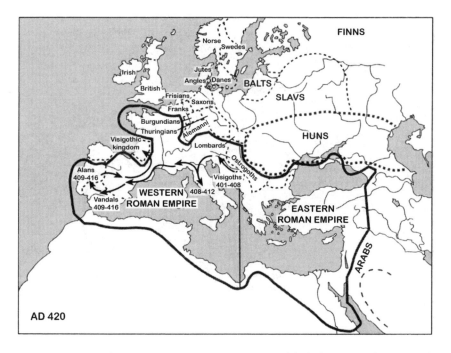

FIGURE 3.2   Map of Migration Age Europe, AD 420. Modified after McEvedy (1975: 19).

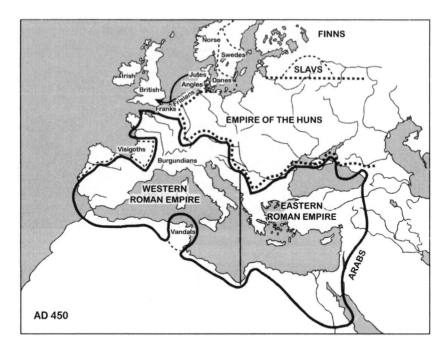

FIGURE 3.3 Map of Migration Age Europe, AD 450. Modified after McEvedy (1975: 21).

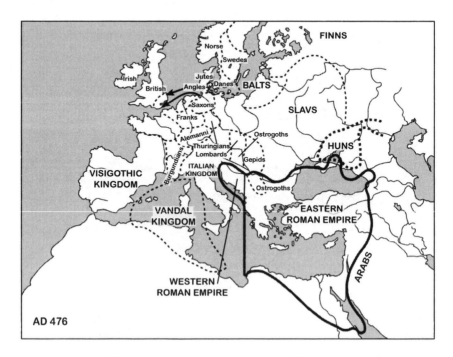

FIGURE 3.4 Map of Migration Age Europe, AD 476. Modified after McEvedy (1975: 23).

In short, this is the historical background to the Migration Period, the post-Roman era that transformed Europe from north to south. The Mediterranean (at least the former Western Roman Empire) became barbarised – with the Ostrogoths and later the Lombards ruling Italy, the Visigoths in Spain, the Burgundians in modern Burgundy in southern Gaul, the Vandals in North Africa, the Anglo-Saxons in Britain and the Franks in northern Gaul.

Until recently, these barbarian peoples considered to have swept away the classical world of the Romans and to be responsible for the decline of an ancient civilisation. Today, this is regarded as only partly true (e.g. Halsall 2005a, 2007; Heather 2006; Wells 2009). However, it has been viewed in significantly different ways. While German and English historians in particular have emphasised the barbarian migrations/invasions as the obliteration of a decadent and effete Roman civilisation, French and Italian historians have seen the barbarians as being responsible for the destruction of a strong Mediterranean civilisation, bringing about the Dark Age. While the first group refer to 'migrations' or 'Volkervanderung' as neutral terms for 'people on the move', the latter refer to 'barbarian invasions' (Halsall 2005a: 36; Härke 2000a).

European national history

However, the so-called 'Barbarian invasions' in many respects stand at the beginning of European history because almost all national histories in some way or another go back to a group of migrating barbarians: Anglo-Saxons in England, Goths and Lombards in Italy, Franks and Burgundians in France, Visigoths in Spain, etc. This is attested by the earliest versions of barbarian history, that is the history of the Gothic people (*De origine actibusque Getarum/Getica*) by the Ostrogoth Jordanes, written in Constantinople *c.* AD 550, the history of the Franks (*Historiae*) by Gregory of Tours, written in the late sixth century, the history of the Lombards (*Historia Langobardorum*) written in Italy by Paul the Deacon in the 780s and the elder *Origo Gentis Langobardorum* and *Codex Gothanum*, ecclesiastical history of the English people (*Historia Ecclesiastica*) by Bede in the 730s, and Isidore of Seville, who wrote the history of the Goths, Sueves and Vandals in Spain in the early seventh century (*Historia Gothorum, Vandalorum et Suevorum*). Most Western national histories of origin can thus be traced back to notions, however confused, of barbarian invasions or migrations (Veit 1989; Jones 1997; Geary 2002; Hills 2003; Halsall 2005a, b).

These migrating groups were mostly seen as unified and well-defined political entities with proto-national aspirations. They migrated along complex weaving routes, illustrated as 'spaghetti-like confusions of coloured arrows' from somewhere in the north to their final destination on Roman territory, almost as if these were predestined (Halsall 2005a: 36). Archaeology as a discipline has long served to establish and legitimise these national identities. As with the discipline of history, the dominant questions revolved around where these peoples came from, where they migrated to and what became of them. Thus, from an early stage, it was assumed that peoples of the Migration Period belonged to well-defined, ethnically homogeneous groups, and as biological entities had remained intact for centuries. They had, so to speak, been excluded from all kinds of historical change (Veit 1989; Geary 2002; Halsall 2005a).

The ethnic interpretation of archaeological culture areas on the continent remains inseparably linked with the name of Gustaf Kossinna, the German philologist (born 1858) who entered prehistory via his antiquarian study of the *Germani*, the Roman historian Tacitus' 'ethnographic' work from the late first century AD. He was by no means the first to attempt to ascribe archaeological finds to specific peoples. 'Clearly defined, sharply distinctive, bounded archaeological provinces correspond unquestionably to the territories of particular peoples and tribes' Kossinna wrote (in German) in 1926 (Veit 1989: 39). His main theme was to explore the origin of the *Germani* – the German people. The typological method enabled him to establish time horizons for the chronological ordering of the material past, and by means of the cartographic method he diagnosed culture provinces characterised by the greatest possible material homogeneity and bounded from neighbouring culture provinces (Veit 1989, 2000; Jones 1997: ch.1; Lucy 2005; Curta 2007).

This methodology of a one-to-one relationship between language, material culture and the peoples known from historical sources was widely adopted, not only among German archaeologists but also more generally among European archaeologists; for example, Gordon Childe in the 1920s and 1930s. Kossinna himself died in 1931, but the notion that specific 'peoples' must be hiding behind the various material groupings remained as a 'taken for granted' attitude. Archaeological cultures and ethnic units were equated. However, Kossinna's own approach had an underlying nationalistic, indeed racist, attitude that was adopted and further developed by the German National Socialists after 1933. Not only did Kossinna's *Kulturkreislehre* become the ideological justification for the Germans' claim for Polish territory as an act of return instead of conquest (Geary 2002: 35), but his concept of the Aryans as the Nordic race par excellence, superior to all other ethnic groups, supposedly justified the Holocaust and other ethnic outrages (Veit 1989, 2000; Trigger 1989; Jones 1997; Härke 2000a).

Since 1945, ethnic interpretations in the field of early European history have been strictly divided along the lines of the academic disciplines involved – medieval history, archaeology, philology and linguistics. Each had to evaluate their respective sources and generally avoided each other. This was perhaps a necessary outcome of the overstatements of the pre-war period. As a consequence, historians were left without dialogues with material culture studies, and vice versa: the archaeologist was left without any available interdisciplinary approach. Consequently, any attempt to establish late prehistory as a historical discipline was almost completely abandoned by the post-war generation of researchers.

With the post-processual contextual archaeology of the 1990s, ethnicity has in turn become a major theme of interest. The political reason is obvious, too. After the collapse of the Soviet empire and the political changes in Eastern Europe, ethnic questions and national identities have become fervently debated political questions, in Europe as everywhere today. Although German archaeologists have long avoided discussing and developing this field of research in their pursuit of being neutral and non-ideological, it was in fact a German historian, Reinhard Wenskus, who in a pioneering work of 1961, *Stammesbildung und Verfassung*, initially brought the idea of ethnic homogeneity into question. Wenskus' book on the formation of *gentes* (people) of the Early Middle Ages represents the first interdisciplinary approach to the question of ethnicity in the early historical period of central and northern Europe. Since then, it has not been possible to take the complexities of migration and the term 'ethnicity' for granted, and Wenskus' book remains today fundamental for ethnic interpretations of early European history (e.g. Wolfram 1970, 1990; Pohl 1980, 1994, 1997, 2000a, b; Pohl and Reimitz 1998; Geary 1983, 1988, 2002; Daim 1982; Liebeschutz 1992a; Heather 1994, 1998, 2006; Harrison 1991; Wood 1990, 1994; Jones 1997; Halsall 2005a, b; Veit 1989, 2000; Hills 2003; Lucy 2005; Hamerow 2005; Curta 2007).

Broadly speaking, the Germanic migrations represented the beginning of a new form of political community, which was based neither upon objective ethnic nor biological genetic connections. These early medieval peoples were groups that were brought together for political reasons and had thus conclusively broken with the old Germanic tribal groupings (Wenskus 1961). Multi-ethnic in character, these migrating peoples derived their ethnic identity from their connection with a particular war-king and warrior-group, whose traditions they adopted (see the description of Alaric and his Gothic federates in Liebeschuetz 1992a: 75, 1992b). Thus early medieval ethnicity was neither linguistic, nor geographical; it was ideological, military and political, a kind of 'peoples in arms' (Wenskus 1961; Wolfram 1990; Liebeschuetz 1992b; Harrison 1991). At least from the sixth century AD, ethnicity was defined by one's social role, even if it had originally derived from a notion of a cultural community (Amory 1993: 26; Heather 1998). Ethnicity, in other words, was not an objective category with a precise referent but a subjective process through which individuals or groups identified themselves against others, in particular situations and by certain criteria, usually in the context of conflict or war. Political divisions could be expressed through the symbolic manipulation of 'pre-existing similarities' and traditions for the purposes of unifying one community in opposition to another, people having to belong to one group rather than another (Barth 1969; Geary 1983: 16 ff.; Shennan 1989: 14). This definition implies the existence of specific ideological legitimation claims linked to core groups of people, normally that of the war-leader/king. Warriors would then gather under his ethnic umbrella, whatever their names.[1]

> Erzählung und Handlungsanweizung, Tradition und Gesetz, *origo et religio*, historische Legitimation und politische Strategie, Diskurs und Macht sind also eng verschränkt ... Die ethnischen Einheiten des Frühmittelalters sind also nicht nur durch subjektive Faktoren definiert, sie reproduzieren sich in der Praxis oder, besser gesagt, in Praktiken.
>
> (Narrative and blueprint for action, tradition, and law, *origo et religio*, historical legitimacy and political strategy, discourse and power are

consequently closely interwoven. Ethnic groups of the Early Middle Ages are thus not defined by subjective elements alone, they are reproduced in practice, or more precisely, practising.)

(*Pohl 1994: 22*)

This more complex and dynamic understanding of early medieval ethnicity is rather new (i.e. Jones 1997) and yet not fully integrated with an archaeological understanding of symbols in the material culture. Most research has been devoted to the identification of specific historical groups through material culture studies. Therefore we have overlooked or played down precisely those uniform cultural codes that come to the surface over much of Europe, in material culture as well as in rituals, myths and legends. In the fifth and sixth centuries, the 'Germanic peoples' were, essentially, a common Germanic warrior class on the move which, wherever it appeared, seized control of the native rural inhabitants or was paid a reward in corn or coin, or both, in return for Roman military service. As examples, the Lombards in Pannonia seem to have been a mounted warrior tribe, living on tribute and booty (Harrison 1991: 28) and the Goths under the leadership of Alaric spent twenty-three years of adventures within the empire, but were not in search of land (Liebeschuetz 1992b: 79). To these warrior elites, as to elites in general, communication of ethnicity and 'belonging' was an active process involved in the manipulation of economic and political resources alongside the creation of a common identity also in material culture.

It has been widely recognised that material culture is actively involved in the signification and structuring of ethnic affiliation (e.g. Hodder 1982; Jones 1997; Diaz-Andreu et al. 2005; Curta 2007). However, the collectivising of memory also plays a role in the creation, transmission and upholding of culture and ethnicity. It can be associated with different kinds of political strategies and with different forms of religious life (Rowlands 1993; van Dyke and Alcock 2003). Thus, although text and material culture are apparently unrelated, they are in fact ideologically interlinked when used to articulate a new system of power and values. The materialisation of new ideas and values occurs through the deployment of objects with symbolic meaning, the construction and shared use of public monuments, the formation of oral traditions, the telling of tales and the production of the written word (Marrais et al. 1996; Earle 2004; Marrais et al. 2004; Jones 2007). Sharing common cultural codes promotes a feeling of unity and shared world view, which could be especially accentuated – or mobilised – in periods of social stress. However, it also served to veil or to accentuate social differences and – in the case of the groups we shall be looking at here – common or different origin. In what follows I concentrate on the Germanic warrior elites, and evidence for their social and ritual life.

Migration Period cosmology and symbolism formed internal similarities and differences within the society of the Germanic warriors and, at the same time, also accentuated the differences between their world and the Roman world that many warriors would eventually join. It was in this turbulent political landscape of the fifth and sixth centuries that material culture became a symbolic materialisation of new social and political identities (as will be argued later). They created a new Romano-Germanic culture in which oral Germanic tradition including origin myths, tribal histories and royal genealogies was maintained and later written down as part of the Barbarians' (Germans') integration into the Classical Roman imperial tradition. Whether classified as 'social memory', 'collective remembrance', 'national memory', 'public memory', 'counter memory', 'popular history making', or 'lived history' (Connerton 2006: 315), these stories served to reconstitute the past in times of political turbulence. Despite their mythical character, these 'histories' are of prime relevance as myths of origin in the Migration era.

Origin myths from the Early Middle Ages

In early medieval ethnic histories, three origin myths recur, and in all of these, migration is a central theme. First, there is the Graeco-Roman story of the escape of the Trojans westwards after the fall of Troy; second, there is the biblical story of the emigré people of Israel; third, there is the story of the Goths migration from 'Scandza', that is, Scandinavia. The first and the second stories are understandable in the light of Graeco-Roman and Christian influences of the Late Antique Period, and the barbarians' interest in demonstrating connections with the civilised Mediterranean world. But the story that is less comprehensible from this perspective is the third one. It can be traced back to a certain Ablabius (*Getica* 28, 82) – whether he is a real or a fictive person – who in the mid-fifth century wrote a (now lost) history of the Goths (Hachmann 1970: 109 ff.; Heather 1993: 318, 1994: 328) or the Visigoths (Søby Christensen 2002: 345). This myth of migration from Scandza is also found in the majority of early ethnic-national origin myths; for example, those of the Lombards, the Burgundians, the Anglo-Saxons and the Heruli. Cassiodorus, drawing on Ablabius, wrote his *Historia Gothorum* in twelve volumes (*c.* AD 525) and dedicated it to Theodoric, king of the Goths.[2] Cassiodorus' objective was to make the Ostrogoths, and Theodoric's family the Amals, equal in birth to the Romans, whose ancestors had come (as every reader of the *Aeneid* well knew) from Troy. Cassiodorus' work is now lost; but he may well have included the story of the Goths' migration from the lands north of the Black Sea.

In creating a royal Gothic genealogy comprising seventeen generations between the first king, Gaut/Odin, and Theodoric's grandson Athalaric, Cassiodorus obviously used the Roman royal genealogy (with seventeen generations between Aeneas and Romulus) as a model. Yet, in the Old Norse *Grimnismal* in *The Prose Edda*, Odin says that 'Gautr' is his name among the gods (*Grimnismal* 54). The Old Norse form cognate with Gaut is Gautr (North 1997). Thus, although Cassiodorus' account incorporates a classical-literary motif, it perhaps represents his adaptation (and extension?) of a Gothic genealogy, which had been orally transmitted. Cassiodorus may at the same time have excluded a number of kings and lineages in order to present the Amals as the royal family of the Goths (Wolfram 1990: 29 ff., 1994: 31). While according to some researchers it remains a possibility that he constructed the genealogy of the Amals himself, without any basis in tradition, let alone historical reality (Heather 1989), it is more likely, as I will argue, that the Amals were central historical actors throughout Gothic history, and it is clear from Cassiodorus' own testimony that he wanted the credit for having 'drawn forth from the hiding-place of antiquity long-forgotten kings of the Goths' (*Variae* IX, 25.4). A closer look at the written sources implies, however, that the 'Amal dynasty' first developed into a family of some standing only as late as the middle of the fifth century AD during the reign of Valamer, Theodoric's uncle. Victory over a number of rival leaders may have been the reason. The Goths in Valamer's reign were only a conglomerate of several groups which had previously been under Hunnic domination (Heather 1998: 92–111).

Athalaric, in a letter to the Roman senate explaining why he had promoted Cassiodorus to the rank of praetorian prefect, praised, among his other merits, the writing of the *Historia Gothorum*. This letter in Athalaric's name was actually written by Cassiodorus himself.

> From Gothic origins he made a Roman history ... Think how much he loved you in praising me, when he showed the nation of your prince to be a wonder from ancient days. In consequence, as you have ever been thought noble because of your ancestors, so you shall be ruled by an ancient line of kings.
>
> (Variae *IX, 25.6*)

Jordanes, in his *Getica*, c. AD 550, adopted Cassiodorus' Amal genealogy, despite the fact that by the time he wrote this the Amals really had no further role to play in Italy. Thus Jordanes, like Cassiodorus, depicted the Amals as descended from the warrior king Gaut (Vries 1956: par. 372).[3] Moreover, Jordanes recounted the story that the Goths had originally come from Scandinavia. Cassiodorus and Jordanes were writing almost two hundred years after the Goths and their kings had adopted Christianity. Yet these learned historians credited the Goths with a pagan prehistory. The Ostrogoths were in this respect not so different from other Germanic groups, such as the Lombards (who from the 560s settled in Italy), or the Anglo-Saxons (who from the fifth century settled England). For Lombards and Anglo-Saxons alike, once they had become Christianised, ecclesiastical writers incorporated something of a pagan past into 'gentile' histories.

The production in Italy of the first documented Lombard royal genealogy seems to have been associated with the issuing by King Rothari in AD 643 of the Lombard law code known as the *Edictus Rothari*. Genealogy and law code are transmitted in the same manuscripts. The basic elements of this code are Germanic, and there are unmistakable similarities to, for instance, Scandinavian law (Boje Mortensen 1991: 68; Fischer Drew 1993: 26). Like the Gothic and the Roman royal genealogies, the Lombards consisted of seventeen generations back to Scandinavia and Gausus, Old Norse Gautr/Odin (cf. discussion by Vries 1956: par. 369).

The edict and the royal genealogy were later prefaced by a brief historical work, the *Origo Gentis Langobardorum,* probably written during the reign of King Grimoald (AD 662–671), in which the Lombards' origins and their name are traced back to Odin and Scandinavia. The *Origo* was taken over and greatly expanded by Paul the Deacon in his *Historia Langobardorum* (*c.* 790) to supply his own account of the Lombards' Scandinavian origins:

> If any one may think that this is a lie and not the truth of the matter, let him read over the prologue of the edict which King Rothari composed of the laws of the Lombards and he will find this written in almost all the manuscripts as we have inserted in this little history.
>
> (Historia Langobardorum *I, 21*)

In spite of the similarities between the royal genealogies and the origin myths found in the *Origo* and Jordanes' *Getica*, there are also many details that do not coincide. For this reason we must surely dismiss the notion that the Lombard origin myth is nothing more than a copy of the Gothic one. These dissimilarities also argue against the possibility that the authors of the texts were mere compilers. They had clear aims and intentions in producing their works, and were certainly aware of the meaning and importance of what they wrote (for further reading see Teillet 1984; Croke 1987; Goffart 1988).

The next question, then, is to ask whether these early histories should be taken as expressions of independent Gothic or Lombard oral traditions, still being maintained up to the time that they were documented in written form (Wolfram 1994: 32; on early histories generally see Dumville 1977), or alternatively as original literary compositions by the authors (Goffart 1988; Heather 1994; Søby Christensen 2002). The former hypothesis is supported by, for example, the Lombard royal genealogy described in the *Origo* and repeated by Paul the Deacon, to the effect that King Agilmund, the son of Agio and the final historical chief of the Lombards, belonged to the race or stock of the Gugingus (*Origo* c. 3, *Hist. Lang.* I, 14). The expression *ex genere Gugingus* has been related to the name of Odin's great spear Gungnir. From this, together with the Lombard royal inauguration ritual involving the transfer of the royal symbol (the spear or lance), as described by Paul the Deacon (*Hist.Lang.* I, 15), it has been argued that the Lombard kings were descended from Odin and thus whoever possessed the holy spear was entitled to be king (Gasparri 1983, 2000).

Another oral tradition may be expressed in Jordanes' *Getica* in written form:

> Of course if anyone in our city [i.e. Constantinople] says that the Goths had an origin different from that which I have related, let him object. For myself, I prefer to believe what I have read, rather than put my trust in old wives' tales (*fabulae aniles*).
>
> (Getica *V, 38*)[4]

In this particular case Jordanes refers to 'fabulae anilis' which is the same phrase well known from the vocabulary of Cicero as meaning an old woman telling a story to a circle of children. The Old Norse word 'edda' actually means 'great grandmother'

(Simek 1996: 69) and when ancient Greeks called stories 'geroia', they referred to the same tradition: the grandmother who took charge of the narrative activity of the group. In ancient societies the youngest living generation was generally educated by the oldest living generation, and this way of transmitting social memory must surely have contributed substantially to the traditions inherited in most ancient societies (Bloch 1992: 57 ff.; Connerton 1989: 39).

Other authors too commented on their own times and referred to their own particular sources. In Book I, c. 8 of the *Historia Langobardorum,* Paul the Deacon went so far as to apologise for what he had to write about the way in which the Lombards acquired their name from Odin: 'At this point, the men of old tell a silly story of the Vandals coming to Godan (Wotan)' and the chapter finishes: 'These things are worthy of laughter and are to be held of no account' (*Hist. Lang.* I, 8, *Origo* c. 1). Both Jordanes and Paul the Deacon claimed familiarity with oral traditions, which they despised yet felt obliged to mention.

Tribal legends or national histories are not attested for all the early medieval Germanic peoples, but only for those who perceived their ancestors as having come from Scandinavia. The royal families claimed divine origin and a relationship to the pagan (Nordic) pantheon. Another feature common to the Goths and the Lombards, and also the Angles, the Saxons, the Vandals, the Svear and the Herules, was that they were all mentioned, at an earlier date, by Tacitus, as being 'true and old names' (Wolfram 1990: 324, 1994: 34f.). These traditions seem to have played an important part in the formation of peoples (*gentes*) in early medieval Europe.

The Franks' origin myths, on the other hand, form a remarkable exception to the pattern. According to the *Chronicle of Fredegar,* written in the 660s, probably in Burgundy, the Franks came from Troy, where their first king was Priam. Thence they migrated to Macedonia, moving on to regions on the Danube and then, under the leadership of Francion, to the Lower Rhine, where they then settled and remained undefeated. The Trojan origin myth was also related in the *Liber Historiae Francorum,* written up in or soon after AD 727, but it seems not to have been known to Gregory of Tours (see Wood 1994: 33ff. for discussion). In his *Historiae,* completed AD 593–94, Gregory recorded a story that the Franks were 'commonly said' to have come from Pannonia, and had migrated via the Rhine (*Historiae* II, 9; Gerberding 1987; Wood 1994). The origin myth of the Franks may have been consciously constructed in opposition to the Gothic histories related by Cassiodorus and Jordanes (Wood 1994: 35), or it may be that the Franks adopted their myth from the Romans, and thus distanced themselves from the more generally accepted Nordic origin myth.[5] Such an explanation would also accord with the fact that the Franks, in contrast to other Germanic-Christian peoples, moved directly from paganism to Catholicism without going through an Arian phase. In this way the Franks distanced themselves from other 'barbarian' forms of Christian belief, perhaps because Clovis, who made himself sole King of the Franks in 486, saw himself as the successor to the Roman Emperor in the West.

Historical 'meaning' of the Scandinavian origin myth

If we accept that the early medieval historical writers referred to myths and legends, which, in one form or another, had a previous existence as oral traditions,[6] it does not automatically follow that we accept these stories as accurate accounts of genuine historical events (Meulengracht Sørensen 1992: 19).[7] These writers, nevertheless, depicted their own past in a way that had meaning for them, using their own criteria of accuracy and concrete representation. If some credibility was to be retained, there were limits, at any given time, to how far it was possible to alter a people's oral traditions or change its sacred tales and legends.[8] The legitimacy and the political dominance, which family histories and origin myths effect, would have disappeared if manipulated too obviously (Weiner 1992: 11). In other words, these stories cannot have been invented on the spur of the moment, but were most probably constructed, developed and altered over many generations, thus the stories' power derived from their being retold and performed as embodiments of social memory (Connerton 1989; Foley 1995; van Dyke and Alcock 2003).

This might help to explain why some of the Germanic peoples have a longer and more varied historical tradition than others. At the same time, it allows for the possibility that the royal genealogies of, for instance, the Amals, were constructed on the basis partly of fictive, and partly of actual, events. By adapting an oral tradition and circulating written explanations, Cassiodorus was able to construct a historical 'truth' that legitimised the power of Theodoric and his family. In any case, as Cassiodorus explained in the letter ghost-written by him to the senate of Rome on behalf of Athalaric, Theodoric's grandson and successor:

> He [Cassiodorus] extended his labours even to the ancient cradle of our house, learning from his reading what the hoary recollections of our elders scarcely preserved (*lictione discens, quod vix maiorum notitia cana retinebat*). From the lurking-place of antiquity he led out the king of the Goths, long hidden in oblivion. He restored the Amals, along with the honour of their family, clearly proving me [Athalaric] to be of royal stock to the seventeenth generation. From Gothic origins he made a Roman history, gathering, as it were, into one garland, flower-buds that had previously been scattered throughout the fields of literature.
>
> (*Variae IX, 25: 4–5*)[9]

The question of historicity is thus impossible to answer. Some kings may have been mythical; others perhaps were genuinely historical characters, but their connections with the Amals were merely a construction.[10] What is important in this context is that which unites the long lines of histories of the early medieval period, namely, the myth of pagan Nordic origin. In the specific case of the Amals, it was not only their founding father Gaut who had close links with the pagan past and maybe with Scandinavia, but also his son Humli/Hulmul, whom later written tradition depicted as the divine ancestor of the Danes (Wolfram 1990: 31, 37; 1994: 28).[11] If the Scandinavian origin myth of the Germanic peoples represented some ancient 'collective memory' of a tribal history, which was subsequently transformed into the language of myth and the sacred identity of the people, then what does this Scandinavian origin actually imply?

Jordanes himself put forward the classical authors' explanation, namely, that a population explosion in Scandinavia was the reason for emigration en masse. This, however, is something of a literary topos, and there is little reason to take it seriously. The same can be said for Jordanes' notion of the Nordic people's powerful and long-lasting fertility, thought to be due to climatic conditions, such as the long, dark winter nights. Nevertheless, that these explanations cannot be used to confirm the historicity of the origin myth does not imply that the Goths and many others did not, one way or another, originate in the north. Several independent and unrelated pieces of evidence, both philological and archaeological (e.g. Hachmann 1970; Christie 1995; Menghin 1985; Heather and Matthew 1991; Kazanski 1991; Näsman 1998; Svennung 1972; Hines 1984, 1992, 1993, 1994, 1995; Härke 1992a, b; Bierbauer 1994; Kaliff 2001), indicate that there may be more than a grain of historical truth in these stories. If Scandza is a literary motif, it might also reflect some long-gone historical reality (Wolfram 1994: 27 f.), at least for the warrior elites of the Goths, the Lombards and the Anglo-Saxons, and perhaps even for groups such as the Heruli, the Vandals and the Burgundians too. As a matter of fact, several of the tribal groups that settled inside the boundaries of the Roman Empire are said to have spoken a Germanic language and for that reason must have come from 'the north'.

What matters, however, is not whether these groups once set out in small and scattered formations from Scandinavia, but that their identity and self-perception was – or became – tied up with the Nordic regions.[12] Over generations, the origin myths would have been handed down and recreated in a multitude of ritual contexts, associated with the social reproduction of their elites.

When Theodoric became a Roman citizen, in AD 484 at the latest, he and his family, the Amals, also became *Flavii*. They became, in other words, relatives of the great Roman emperors of the first century, such as Vespasian, Titus and Domitian (Wolfram 1994: 33) in much the same way as eminent 'Goths' were allowed to become related to the Amals. As the Ostrogothic king of Italy, however, Theodoric created or continued to uphold a pagan Nordic ancestry. The question remains – what was it that made Theodoric, whose connections with Roman civilisation and with Christianity can hardly be denied, link the ancestry of the noble Amals and the Goths to a pagan Nordic origin? A similar question arises even if it was Cassiodorus who constructed the story.

One explanation might be that this origin myth was already so firmly rooted in the Ostrogoths' ideology that it could not be discarded, and therefore was transformed into the foundation of the king's authority and the 'nation's' legitimacy. Even if this was presented in a Roman literary style by Cassiodorus in order to explain the king's divine and ancient ancestry, it was hardly something that had been invented by Cassiodorus, or for that matter Theodoric. Had this been the case, it surely would have been completely worthless as an argument in legitimising the Ostrogoths' royal genealogy.

Genealogies and heroic legends have long been active agents and instruments of legitimation. However, Gregory of Tours could not do for the Franks what Cassiodorus or Paul the Deacon did for the Ostrogoths and the Lombards – that is, present a royal genealogy with sufficient time-depth, together with a detailed history of the migration. In his *Historiae* (II, 9) Gregory wrote:

> Many people do not even know the name of the first king of the Franks. The *Historia* of Sulpicius Alexander gives many details about them, while Valentinus does not name their first king but says that they were ruled by war-leaders.
>
> (Historiae *II, 9*)

Then followed an account of what Sulpicius Alexander had written about the early battles of the Franks. Here Gregory vented his irritation: 'A few pages further on, having given up all talk of "duces" and "regales", [Sulpicius Alexander] clearly states that the Franks had a king, but he forgets to tell us what his name was.' Having cited yet another authority, Renatus Profuturus Frigeridus, Gregory was finally forced to conclude: 'The historians whose works we still have give us all this information about the Franks, but they never record the names of the kings.'

He continues with the origin myth cited above: 'It is commonly said that the Franks came originally from Pannonia and first colonised the banks of the Rhine. Then they crossed the river, marched through Thuringia, and set up in each country distinct and city, long-haired kings chosen from the foremost and most noble family of their race.'

In all, Gregory was not able to give the Merovingian royal family an ancient genealogy,[13] nor could he provide the Salian Franks with an origin myth, because he neither had the sources to turn to, nor a common body of knowledge to manipulate. He could not create a story for the occasion, so he had to make do with naming Clovis as the fourth king of the Merovingian line, and all this in spite of the fact that, as Goffart once wrote: 'everyone agrees in recognizing Gregory's outstanding talent for anecdote' (1988: 113). It is obvious that Gregory knew little about the origin of the Franks, and that his ignorance reduced him to recording an origin-story that was inferior to the traditions which assigned other peoples a glorious and noble past (Geary 1988: 77).

This reticence was hardly due to the fact that Gregory's main objective was to document the history of the Church and the histories of the nobility at a local level, rather than explicitly to document the history of the Frankish people (Boje Mortensen 1991: 39; see Wood 1994 for a discussion). Even if he knew, but was reluctant to repeat, the story (known only from Fredegar, written *c.* AD 660) of Merovech's conception as the result of his mother's coupling with a sea-beast, what Gregory does tell of early Frankish and Merovingian history is hardly very impressive. It is also clear that the Franks had no place in Tacitus' reckoning of the old names of the *gentes* (Wolfram 1994: 34). Both archaeological and historical sources indicate that they started as a confederation in the regions immediately east of the Rhine (James 1991: 35 ff.) and, as such, they differ from other Germanic tribes in that they are a creation within the Roman Empire. In the written sources from the mid-third century onwards, a number of small groups – the Chamavi, Usipii, Bructeri, and Salii, amongst others – appear loosely associated under the name of Franks, 'the hardy', 'the brave', 'the fierce people', and only later acquired the meaning favoured by the Franks themselves, 'the free'. The name Frank designated a variety of tribes so loosely connected that some scholars have denied that they formed a confederation (Geary 1988: 78). However, the name conforms to that of other large confederations with classic confederation names: the Allemani in south-west Germany, 'all men', the Picts, 'the painted men' in the north of Britain, and the Goths, 'the men' in and around the eastern Carpathians and the Danube (Halsall 2005a: 45), and the Saxons in the north of Germany, their name being derived from 'seax', a short one-edged sword (Geary 2002: 141).

Some scholars have inferred from Gregory's personal notes in his *Historiae* that the absence of myths in some sense denied the Franks' historical legitimacy. For the warrior tribes of the Migration Period, the power of origin myths to create historical and ideological identity was so great that these could hardly have appeared out of thin air. Through the works of Cassiodorus, Jordanes, and (later) Paul the Deacon, it is evident that neither Christianity nor new political/geographical realities made the origin myths superfluous – perhaps they had quite the opposite effect. Social remembering – as well as social forgetting – is constitutive in the formation of a new identity, although anthropologists, archaeologists and historians have paid much more attention to the role of memory in transmitting knowledge and forming identity (Connerton 2006: 320 f.). However, Gregory seemingly did not use social forgetting in his creation of the Franks' early history.

The role of origin myths, early history and royal genealogies in the creation of the barbarian kingdoms of the fifth and sixth centuries has to do with the overarching concept of 'memory' and thus 'identity'. As expressed by Guy Halsall (2006b: 55):

> the creating of those kingdoms, and of their new identities, must be understood as the results of active, conscious decisions by many people as part of their struggle and conflicts within their own societies, because, in this, as in so many other periods of history, we have to put not just the social history back into the political, but the political back into the social, and above all we have to put the people back into their history.

Formation of a political mentalité

Political realities amongst the Germanic peoples seem to have been even more complex than those presented in the previous chapter. This complexity is perhaps best illustrated through the difficulties incurred by late Roman authors when they attempted to depict an extremely varied scene (Heather 1995a). As an illustration, Heather (1995a) describes how Claudian, on two separate occasions, gave an account of the different tribes that congregated round Alaric at the beginning of his career in the Danube regions. In one of these accounts he mentioned Sarmatians, Dacians, Massagetae, Alani, Geloni and Getae, and in the other, Visi, Bastarnae, Alani, Chuni, Sarmatians, Gloni and Getae. In much the same way, Sidonius Apollinaris named the tribes along the Danube as being the Bastarnae, Suebi, Pannonii, Neuri, Chuni, Getae, Daci, Halani, Bellonoti, Rugi, Burgundi, Vesi, Aliti, Bisalti, Ostrogothi, Procrusti, Sarmatae and Moschi. Even if some of those names can be credited to a literary tradition, it indicates that these and other authors' general understanding of the Germanic peoples, an understanding we have inherited from them, as large, ethnic, well-defined and homogenous *gentes* or nations, does not accord with fourth- and early fifth-century historical realities in central Europe. From this multitude, some tribes grew into historically well-attested kingdoms during the course of the fifth century, for instance, those of the Ostrogoths, the Visigoths, the Burgundians, the Vandals and, last but not least, the Franks.

All this was not, however, the result of successive concentrations of power or the expansion of some groups at the expense of others. It was a long and discontinuous process, in which various groups and kingdoms, torn by internal conflict and liable to fragment, frequently replaced one another. Some disappeared completely, others for a short time, only to reappear in the literary texts at a later date as having survived after all, or as resuming their old tribal names and political identities. Peter Heather (1995a) has shown how such groups, willingly or by force, could give up their political autonomy for a while, as happened with the Heruli, the Goths and the Rugi. In the case of the Rugi, a group that followed Theodoric from the Balkans to Italy in AD 489, Procopius wrote (*c.* AD 540):

> These Rogi ... in ancient times used to live as an independent people. But Theodoric had early persuaded them, along with certain other nations, to form an alliance with him, and they were absorbed into the Gothic nation [*ethnos*] and acted in common with them in all things against their enemies. But since they had absolutely no intercourse with women other than their own, each successive generation of children was of unmixed blood, and thus they had preserved the name of their nation among themselves.
>
> (Wars 7.2.1–3)[14]

For a period of approximately sixty years it seems that the Rugi succeeded through sheer willpower in holding on to an independent identity, separate from both the Ostrogoths and the Romans in Italy. Nor is this case unique. Certain other tribes managed to do the same, giving up their political autonomy yet retaining their identity, as, for example, the Goths and several other peoples did when they came under the control of the Huns. Priscus' account confirms that the Huns' political and economic dominance was established by force, yet most of the existing social hierarchy of the many Gothic groups remained unchanged, thus maintaining their internal structure, and, through that, their sense of identity (Heather 1995a).

Heather's research into the ethnic identity of those tribes and peoples who, according to their literary texts, disappeared, only to re-emerge many decades later, has led him to distance himself from the interpretation of ethnicity as something to be individually chosen (e.g. Barth 1969; Wenskus 1961; Geary 1983). It can sometimes be manipulated by individuals (or groups), but sometimes not. Furthermore, it is capable of operating at greatly differing strengths. It can be argued that there were two complementary models of being an individual or a group in the Roman world, whether Christian, Jewish, or pagan: an 'ethnicity' that was based on descent, custom, and territory, and a 'constitutional' identity based on law and adhesion. People realised and responded to this complexity and the heterogeneous nature of community, and the difference was largely one of perspective (Geary 2002: 55).

If this interpretation is accepted, origin myths suddenly become more intelligible. They represented a type of cultural memory, which answered current needs through periods of social and political stress. While identity may originally have been related to a specific 'ethnic' elite, new political groups would take shape during the Migration Period around a core of ethnic tradition, which would now bind together tribes with separate backgrounds in new political partnerships. Myths, by connecting the past with the present, provided the political–ideological glue needed to erect and maintain these kaleidoscopic groups of peoples as political units. This again implies that origin myths cannot have been conjured out of thin air, they were neither fiction nor literary compilations. Rather, they represented an ancient 'wisdom' for at least some of the new 'peoples', and must have contained a kernel of historical truth and familiarity if they were to serve as sources of legitimation.

Material manifestations: Germanic styles in a historical perspective

Historical–ethnic questions have traditionally dominated the study of the European Migration Period. However, archaeological research has focused excessively on what were often minor differences in the archaeological record and has therefore been unable to grasp the material significance of the new larger ethnic and political configurations that emerged in the Migration Period. Select aspects of material culture came to represent a materialisation of a new cosmological understanding of the world that supplemented the new historical narratives of the Migration Period.

Historical narratives are a basic human way of making sense of the world, as particular details are given meaning through their incorporation into story forms (Shanks and Hodder 1995: 225; for examples see Ricoeur 1989; Cohan and Shires 1988; Rimmon-Kenan 1983; Barber and Barber 2004). As cultural memory they bring the past into the present and transcend individual lives. Material culture has the same capacity to reproduce the past in the present by transmitting cultural knowledge from one human generation to the next. However, material culture also creates and shapes representations of the world that would otherwise not exist in the same forms (Gell 1998; Gosden 2006).

The Germanic animal styles represent this type of complementary identification in symbolic form. They also represented a conscious act of forgetting. Forgetting – as well as remembering – is constitutive in the formation of a new identity. While historians, anthropologists and archaeologists have in recent decades paid a great deal of attention to the role of memory in the transmission of cultural knowledge and the forming of identity, less attention has been paid to forgetting. Forgetting as a 'structural amnesia' is constitutive in the formation of new identity (Connerton 2006).

Following these premises, new elements of style, not least iconographic ones, are presumed to have been selected with a great deal of care, just as objects are very carefully selected for use in ceremonies because they are the bearers of important messages (Gell 1998). Style, then, participated in the creation and legitimation of power. Controlling and upholding style can therefore be regarded as a part of an elite strategy, in the same way as the control of rituals, myths, legends and symbolic objects – in short, everything that embodies the group's identity (e.g. Jones 1997). Seen in this light, the dominant art-style of Barbarian Europe in the fifth century, the so-called Scandinavian or Germanic animal styles, acquire a new, more significant, historical role (e.g. Salin 1904; Haseloff 1981; Høilund Nielsen 1997, 1998; Høilund Nielsen and Kristoffersen 2002).

With the ideological function of animal ornaments as my starting point, I shall now briefly summarise the ways in which the animal styles can be linked, not only to the Nordic peoples but also to the 'continental' warrior peoples: the Lombards, the Goths, the Alemanni, the Anglo-Saxons etc., whose myths assign them a Scandinavian origin. In short, I use the archaeology of animal styles to enhance and eventually support or disprove the historical narratives.

In his three volume work *Die germanische Tierornamentik der Völkerwanderungszeit*, Günther Haseloff has analysed the earliest developments of animal styles in Scandinavia, on the continent and in England, using typological, chronological and geographical criteria (Haseloff 1981). Haseloff confirms Helmuth Roth's earlier study (1979) and shows how the development of the earliest style of the late fourth and early fifth centuries (Nydam Style/Style I) was closely connected with southern Scandinavia, that is, Jutland, the Danish islands, southern Sweden and the southernmost parts of Norway. A remarkably rich variety of forms and figures (Figure 3.5), often with human features (masks) (Figure 3.6), developed in this area during the first half of the fifth century. It has not been possible to trace its immediate predecessors, either in Scandinavia or elsewhere. As Nydam Style/Style I contains a wide variety of elements, including some drawn from Late Roman carved bronzes, and some from Asiatic ornamental and polychrome work (Haseloff 1984), the only plausible conclusion is that the style, characterised by unique artistic skills and craftsmanship, originated in the Scandinavian region. Finds on the continent and in England are well represented from the latter half of the fifth century up to the end of the sixth, when a new style (Style II) emerges, homogenous across a

FIGURE 3.5 Early Scandinavian animal style. Denmark. After Salin (1904: Abb. 134).

FIGURE 3.6 Early Scandinavian animal style. Lister, Norway. After Salin (1904: Abb. 490).

FIGURE 3.7   Style II. Udine, Italy. After Salin (1904: Abb. 655).

FIGURE 3.8   Style II. Uppland, Sweden. After Salin (1904: Abb. 554).

wide area from Italy (Figure 3.7) to the Nordic countries (Figure 3.8) (Salin 1904; Lund Hansen 1992: 187 with references; Høilund-Nielsen 1998; Høilund Nielsen and Kristoffersen 2002).

Artefacts from the continental and Anglo-Saxon regions, usually relief brooches, can be divided into two categories. The first consists of Nordic brooches, either imported or copied; the second consists of Anglo-Saxon (Figure 3.9) and continental (Figure 3.10) brooches and other metal work with their own independent development. The Nordic brooches (whether 'originals' or 'replicas') were distributed along the Rhine, in Alemannia and Thüringia, and even in southern England once it had been settled by Anglo-Saxons (Hines 1984; Näsman 1984: map 10,

FIGURE 3.9   Style I. Kent, England. After Salin (1904: Abb. 700).

FIGURE 3.10   Style II. Wurzburg, Bayern. After Salin (1904: Abb. 641).

1991: figure 8). Continental Style I was prevalent in Pannonia, where it can be linked to the Lombards' presence, and also in the Alemannic regions of southwestern Germany, but it is also widespread over many other parts of the continent and southern England (Haseloff 1981: Abb. 359). It is worth mentioning the gilded silver brooch in Scandinavian or Anglo-Saxon style from grave 10, Saint-Brice, Tournai, that is, Childeric's grave (Brulet et al. 1990: Abb. 28; James 1991: 102). On the continent, Style I brooches were in circulation much longer than in Scandinavia, and developed into Style II,[15] a gently curving, interlaced animal design of ribbon-like form, executed in carved bronze (Lund Hansen 1992: 187).

Besides the brooches, Nordic gold bracteates are also dispersed over much of the continent, from England to Hungary and the Ukraine (Haseloff 1981: Abb. 92). The iconography of the bracteates, in contrast to that of the brooches, refers to scenes from Nordic mythology, revolving around the war-god and the king of the gods, Odin (Hauck e.g. 1978, 1986, 1987; Axboe 1994; Axboe and Kromann 1992; Hedeager 1997b) (Figure 3.11). It demonstrates that the Nordic pantheon and its mythology known through later texts of the early Scandinavian Middle Ages were already present in the Migration Period, as will be argued (Chapter 9). The bracteates have been interpreted as a political medium, used in situations where political relations were forged on the occasion of great feasts held in association with religious ceremonies and demonstrations of loyalty (Andrén 1991). Although the motifs and designs are unmistakably Nordic, the bracteates have obvious forbears

FIGURE 3.11   Gold bracteate, Funen, Denmark. Drawing by H. Lange after Hauck (1985–89: IK 75).

in Late Antique art and Byzantine emperor-medallions (Hauck 1985–86; Andrén 1991; Axboe 1991; Bursche 2000) (Figures 3.12 and 3.13).

Many of the Germanic peoples on the continent and in England possessed an understanding of the depictions on the bracteates and the brooches. From about the beginning of the fifth century up until the seventh, the Nordic figurative world was taken on board amongst the migrating Germanic peoples. It was imitated and elaborated, becoming an impressive elite style of a shared identity. Significantly, however, 'new' peoples, with no connection to the Scandinavian origin myth – for instance, the Franks – did not adopt animal ornament in their symbolic language, but instead used a bird: the Roman or Gothic eagle.

If we accept the recent trends within anthropology and archaeology that 'art' and styles are meaningful in what they do in shaping relationship between people (Gell 1998; Morphy 1999; Gosden and Hill 2008), the same must apply to changes in style. Such changes then become central to our understanding of social and political changes. The beginning of the Migration Period, during the first half of the fifth century, is marked by the introduction of animal ornament, in the form of a contorted multi-faceted single animal (Nydam Style/Style I). Towards the end of the Migration Period, however, the animal depiction is distorted almost beyond

FIGURE 3.12   Gold bracteate. Nordic replica of a Roman gold medallion. Lilla Jored, Sweden. Drawing by H. Lange after Hauck (1985–89: IK 107).

FIGURE 3.13   Gold bracteate. Reverse side of Figure 3.12. Drawing by H. Lange after Hauck (1985–89: IK 107).

recognition into a twisted pattern in which the four-legged animal, previously the dominant element in the composition, is less visible (Style II) (Figure 3.14). This phasing-out of animal depiction represents the conclusion of a long developmental sequence. The main difference between the two stylistic traditions is that the animal is the central motif in Style I, while in Style II the animals are eclipsed by complex ornamental patterns.

The origins of Style II (= Swedish Vendel Style A–C) have been much debated; some scholars have ascribed them to Scandinavia (Arwidsson 1942), some to Late Roman art (Lindqvist 1936), others to Italy (i.e. the Lombards) (Åberg 1947; Werner 1935; Haseloff 1956), and others to the south-west Alamannic regions (Haseloff 1981: 597 ff., 1984: 117; Lund Hansen 1992: 187). On the whole, this debate reveals that the new style was so homogenous that it is impossible to isolate a distinct 'region of innovation' in Europe, even if most scholars agree in dating its appearance to the latter half of the sixth century AD (560–570) (Lund Hansen 1992 for a discussion).[16]

When linked to their broad historical context, the rise and decline of Style I and II become meaningful. The arrival and the disappearance of early Germanic animal ornaments (Nydam Style/Style I) covers the crucial period between the Huns' first intervention in Europe and the period of the last great migrations, the Lombards'

FIGURE 3.14 Style II. Uppland, Sweden. After Salin (1904: Abb. 570).

conquest of Italy (AD 568). The development of the animal Style I is therefore closely linked to a historically documented period of great social change and the establishment of new 'Barbarian' kingdoms. Style I linked the migration warrior elites together, but also gave room for some ethnic differentiation. Once the new kingdoms were established, Style II came to symbolise this shared identity and close bonds between them. Finally, during the Viking Period the animal styles became solely the cosmological identification of the new expanding Viking kingdoms. The animal styles thus embodied a new, shared pagan identity among the large mobile tribal formations and later kingdoms of post-Roman Europe. In this they support the textual evidence of shared myths of origin in Scandinavia.[17]

PART III

The constitution of 'otherness'

4

EMBODIED IN ANIMALS

Scandinavian animal style AD 400–1200

The Scandinavian and Germanic animal style was, as we have seen, formed during the fifth century as a new abstract language of signs. It dominated until early Christianity, both among the Germanic tribes on the continent and among the Scandinavian peoples themselves. From the beginning to the end the animal styles were an inseparable part of the elite's material identity. In Part II, I demonstrated that the animal style is more than a decorative element, but conveys an intentional mythological message of a shared identity and destiny.

This has, however, been a matter of debate (Høilund Nielsen and Kristoffersen 2002). During the nineteenth century, typological sequences were linked to evolutionary or diffusionist hypotheses. In this tradition, art and style were associated with culture-areas, tribes or schools (Morphy 1999: 659). After the 1960s, art re-entered the anthropological and archaeological mainstream with an emphasis on meaning and symbolism (e.g. Hodder 1982). The interest was in how symbols were organised and how they encoded meaning, rather than in the meanings themselves. This approach closed the gap between the anthropology of art and the anthropology of religion (Layton 1991; Gell 1998). At the same time it stimulated interaction with other disciplines, in particular art history and archaeology. From then on it has generally been accepted that style encodes a form of cultural knowledge embedded in an institutional context (Morphy 1989: 3, 1999: 659). It is the nature of this cultural knowledge, the content of the form, which I shall decode in the following.

The development of the earliest Germanic animal style was – as already mentioned in Chapter 3 – closely connected with southern Scandinavia (Roth 1979; Haseloff 1981, 1984). An elaborate figurative and geometric style, the Nydam style/Style I, developed in this area during the first half of the fifth century AD (Salin 1904; Haseloff 1981) (Figure 4.1). From the latter half of the fifth century up to the end of the sixth, the styles were well represented in England (Figure 4.2), on the continent (Figures 4.3, 4.4) and Italy (Figure 4.5) (Roth 1979; Haseloff 1981; Hines 1984; Näsman 1984: map 10, 1991: fig. 8). From the end of the sixth century, Style II emerged and this art-style was homogenous from Italy to the Nordic countries (Salin 1904; see also Lund Hansen 1992: 187 with references; Høilund Nielsen and Kristoffersen 2002) (cf. Figures 3.7, 3.8, 3.10, 3.13).

Style II is, like Style I, remarkably uniform, and both styles are found on elite jewellery and weapons from most parts of Europe (Speake 1980; Høilund Nielsen 1997, 1998). Style II continued into the late seventh century AD, and from then on it is no longer possible to define a common Germanic animal style. Once Catholic Christianity had put down firm roots, a new iconographic style developed: one that blended insular with Frankish elements, and was closely connected to the Irish/ Anglo-Saxon mission which began in Friesland in 678/79 and reached central and south Germany during the first half of the eighth century (Roth 1979: 86).

While this style was indisputably linked with missionary activity, and it can be found on a great variety of different ecclesiastical objects, it is not restricted to

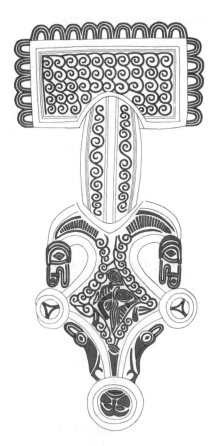

FIGURE 4.1   Style I. Tveitane, Norway. After Haseloff (1981: Abb. 21).

FIGURE 4.2   Style I. Bifrons, Kent, England. After Haseloff (1981: Abb. 25).

FIGURE 4.3   Style I. Nancy, Lothringen. After Haseloff (1981: Abb. 26).

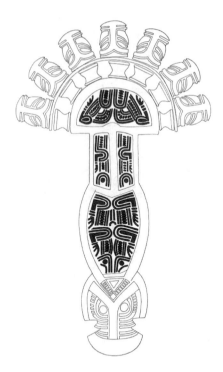

FIGURE 4.4   Style I. Kajdacz, Hungary. After Haseloff (1981: Abb. 487).

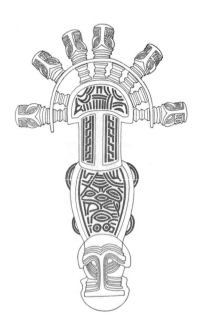

FIGURE 4.5   Style I. Nocera Unbra, Italy. After Haseloff (1981: Abb. 388).

'church art' alone. A wide variety of secular objects of precisely the same kind as earlier were now decorated with this new Christian style – dress accessories, riding equipment, stirrups, spurs, bracelets and so on – thus signalling a new form of ideological legitimisation for their owners (Wamers 1993). The elites of southern Scandinavia, however, reinvented the Nordic animal style as a response to this expansion of Christianity. The once disintegrated animal figures recovered their zoomorphic character, the new style from the eighth century onwards absorbed some insular elements, such as decorative plant motifs, but this was only briefly. First and foremost they maintained the cosmological universe of the Old Norse animal style.

It was not until AD 1100 that the Nordic animal style ceased to develop (the Urnes Style) (Figure 4.6). Gradually the animals were extended and woven together with plant motifs to look like plants (Anker 1997: 237; Hohler 1999) (Figure 4.7). Finally they disappeared, and new animals were introduced in the form of Christian iconography *c.* AD 1200 when both Christianity and the medieval kingdoms in Scandinavia were consolidated. This consolidation is reflected in the new 'official' history, first and foremost illustrated by *Gesta Danorum* (Saxo Grammaticus) and *Ynglinga Saga* (Snorri Sturluson), and the adoption of the new major international style – the Romanesque – with its unambiguous Christian symbols (Karlsson 1983: 81; Wilson 2008: 337).

Christian iconography and Christian myths are inseparable: they are signs and symbols, visual and textual, of the same. Therefore, it becomes evident that Christian iconography and art could not take pre-Christian symbols on board, except during a short period of transition.[1] If we assume that the pre-Christian visual art functioned in the same way as the Christian, then it becomes explicable that the Germanic – or Scandinavian – art style could not incorporate Christian symbols: they represented a cosmology in fundamental opposition to the Northern

FIGURE 4.6   Urnes style. Urnes Stave Church, Norway. After Hohler (1999, II: 235).

FIGURE 4.7   Ål Church, Norway. After Hohler (1999, II: 93).

belief system. Although the animal styles are not easily comprehensible to a modern mind, and although they vary through time, they extemporise on the same theme – the *animal*. The animal's organising power in pre-Christian society – from the Migration Period to late Viking Age – is beyond dispute. Pagan iconography and pagan myths are connected in the same way as Christian myths and Christian iconography, serving as 'mediators, facilitating communication with the other world. They were meant to reflect and provide an approach to this other world' (Duby 2000: 2; Tinn 2009). Therefore, in order to understand the Old Norse belief system, we must also understand the role of the animals.

Animals in the styles

In AD 747, St Boniface, on a Christian mission to the pagan Saxons in Germany, wrote a letter to Cuthberg, Archbishop of Canterbury, in which he condemned the Saxons' foolish superstitions in dress, in particular the use of broad edgings with figures woven into them, well known from archaeological dress textiles (Figure 4.8): 'those ornaments shaped like worms, teeming on the borders of ecclesiastical vestments; they announce the Antichrist and are introduced by his guile and through his ministers in the monasteries to induce lechery, depravation, shameful deeds, and disgust for study and prayer'.[2] Also, in 742 St Boniface addressed a letter to Pope Zacharias to make him aware of what he knew from his informants: that even in Rome women wore phylacteries and knotted ribbons (i.e. Style II) in the guise of charms around their wrists and calves.[3]

That the same motifs and compositions were maintained for centuries indicates that the ornamentation was heavily loaded with meaning and not just upheld through habit and taste. The constant transformation, the inevitable testing of new elements, the changing compositions etc. support the idea that animal

FIGURE 4.8 Tunic band from Evebø Eide, Norway, with interwoven animal figures. From Dedekam (1925).

ornamentation also had an indisputable significant religious function in pre-Christian societies. The role of the animal styles as an inseparable part of pre-Christian material culture, not least in connection with the elite classes, implies that the animals also had a corresponding central position in the perception of the world (Kristoffersen 1995, 2000a, b; Glosecki 2000; Gaimster 1998; Magnus 2001, 2002; Lindstrøm and Kristoffersen 2001; Jakobsson 1999, 2003; Hedeager 1999a, 2004, 2005a; Lundborg 2006).

That this perception of the world underwent changes over a period of 800 years is hardly a surprise. What is surprising, however, is the consistency, in spite of stylistic variations, of one fundamental element that connects all the styles, namely, *the animal*. From animals being primarily a simple classificatory element, suitable for chronological and style divisions in the cultural historical tradition,[4] archaeological enquiry has now shifted to understanding the cognitive and symbolic meaning of animals. Symbolic representation operates within a particular set of cultural codes, and the animal representations therefore become part of cognitive and cosmological structures. As such the styles are not just 'art for art's sake', but embody symbolic forms of complex cultural knowledge. Animal representations must therefore be understood within the cosmological world of which they were part (Morphy 1989: 2, 1999: 659 ff.). Here the texts of Norse belief system may help us to decode their meaning.

Nordic animal ornamentation does not only incorporate animals, it *is* animals – that is, it is entirely a paraphrasing of a many-faceted repertoire of animal motifs: whole and half animals, small animals and large animals, animal fragments and anatomically complete animals, along with animal heads without bodies and animal bodies without heads. In complicated patterns they blend and blur, in and around each other, creating dense, smooth-surfaced ornamentation (Figure 4.9). This complex representation, far removed from naturalistic animal depiction, reveals that the styles do not attempt to mirror the animals themselves. Instead, these representations ought to be understood as representations of the animals' mentality, that is, their significance is embedded in the form of artistic expression.

Complexly composed animals may express a reality that is more revealing and more ambiguous than a naturalistic representation ever could. Species are created

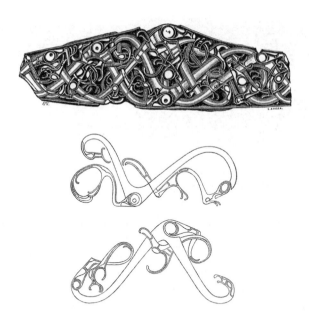

FIGURE 4.9 Late animal style. Gotland, Sweden. After Salin (1904: Abb. 607).

that cut across all categories by transgressing the boundaries of what is considered 'natural' (Morphy 1989: 5; Ingold 2000: 130); for example, hybrid forms such as a bird with a serpent-like body, a four-legged animal with a bird's head, etc. Such ambiguity is an important structuring element of the animal style. The ambiguous representation, in which a figure is shown on closer inspection to represent something entirely different, reflects a hidden meaning, so that one level conceals another. This ambiguity makes the styles more powerful than it otherwise would be possible to achieve through the written or spoken word (Kristoffersen 2000a: 265; Lindstrøm and Kristoffersen 2001). As a special mode of expression, the styles may be seen as a visualisation of the metrical forms of skaldic poetry (Salin 1922; Lie 1952; Herschend 1997a: 48; Andrén 2000: 26; Lundborg 2006), which is far more complex than the Eddic poems in terms of structure, metre, length and diction. This complexity makes them extremely difficult to understand (Lindow 2001:15).

The artistic complexity and the artistic continuity that characterise the Nordic animal styles (i.e. Salin 1904; Roth 1979, 1986a; Haseloff 1981, 1984), and their affiliation to an elite milieu throughout the entire Iron Age and Viking Age, show us how culturally significant they were. Their multi-layered complexity suggests that they incorporated an abstract order and also the physical order of the universe (Roe 1995: 58).

In spite of the abstract and extremely stylistic language, it is possible to discern certain naturalistic animal species/categories in the stylistic representation. A recurring motif in the early styles is the bird with the hooked beak, that is, the bird of prey. Another is the serpent or other serpent-like animals (Figure 4.10). Furthermore, the wolf and the wild boar appear, although not as frequently. Attached to

FIGURE 4.10 Belt buckle, Sutton Hoo, England. The eagle and the snake can be identified; however, two other species, one with its mouth closed, the other with an open mouth, cannot. Drawing by Per Persson. Used with permission.

the war-gear (in Style II) are the following trio: wolf, wild boar and eagle (Høilund Nielsen 1999) (Figure 4.11a–d). The Viking styles are on the whole less naturalistic. The snake ('the serpent formed animal') and the 'big animal' together with the 'gribedyr' are dominant in the later iconography (e.g. Klindt-Jensen and Wilson 1965; Fuglesang 1982; Wilson 2008). The animals, whether they are recognised as specific animal species or as imaginary ones, appear threatening and prepared for action, that is, they are wild and powerful animals. Among the domesticated animals the naturalistic horse (stallion) is the only one to be found sporadically, primarily from the eighth century (south Scandinavian style E) (Ørsnes 1966). However, some scholars have argued that the main creature in the Vendel styles (and Style II) is the horse (Olsén 1945; Roth 1986b).

Another characteristic feature of the early styles (Nydam, Style I–II) as well as the Anglo-Saxon so-called 'helmet'-style/Style I and the 'ribbon' style/Style II (Kendrick 1938) is the representation of animal heads inside each other, as part of

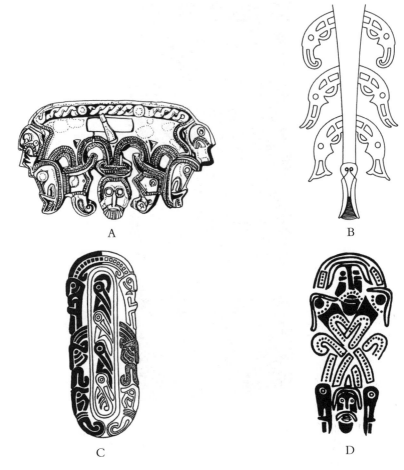

A   B

C   D

FIGURE 4.11 Wolf, wild boar, and eagle. A: buckle from Zealand. Drawing by C. Borstam in Gaimster (1998: 77). B: plate from a shield, Valsgärde, Sweden. After Arwidsson (1977: Abb. 146). C: belt fitting from Esslingen-Sirnau grave 8, Germany. After Koch (1969). D: detail from a Lombard gold-foil cross from Pieve del Cairo, Italy. From Haseloff (1956).

each other, or as separate animal heads but part of other animals (Figure 4.12). To this complexity human representations are added (Hedeager 2010). Human bodies are also reproduced cut into pieces (Figures 4.13 and 4.14) (Haseloff 1970), and human faces are included in animal representations: bodies with human heads, human faces as part, normally the thigh, of a beast or bird of prey (Figures 4.15 and 4.16). On the unique buckle from Åker, Norway, a man is represented as half human, half wild boar (his arms and legs are two animals) (Figure 4.17), and this motif is repeated on the German/Lombard gold blade crosses (Figure 4.18). A similar composition is seen on a mount from Vendel, Sweden (Figure 4.19). On the so-called C-bracteates – the ones with a 'rider' as the central motif – man and

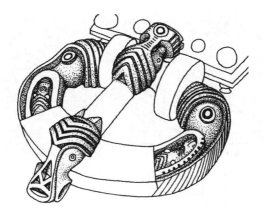

FIGURE 4.12 Belt buckle. Ejsbøl Moor, Denmark. Drawing: Eva Koch Nielsen, after Hedeager (1988, vol. 2: 317).

animal (the so-called horse) is only one individual (Figure 4.20a, b), and a man in bird disguise is surrounded by animals: a bird, a wolf, a stag, and two snakes (Figure 4.20c). Especially on the gold scabbard mounts from the Migration Period, two symmetrical animals can at the same time create a human head. This is what Hayo Vierck, and later Siv Kristoffersen, adopting the words of Claude Lévi-Strauss, has termed 'split representation' (Vierck 1967; Kristoffersen 1995). They are adopted to express the symbolic transformation – or shape shift – which is also to be seen when an animal head is transformed into a human mask when turned upside down (Magnus 2002: 112).

FIGURE 4.13 Humans cut into pieces. Detail from the Kirtscheim brooch, Germany. After Haseloff (1981: Abb. 1929).

FIGURE 4.14   Human cut into pieces. Mounting from a drinking horn. Söderby Karl, Sweden. Drawing by Harald Faith-Ell after Holmqvist (1951: fig. 5).956).

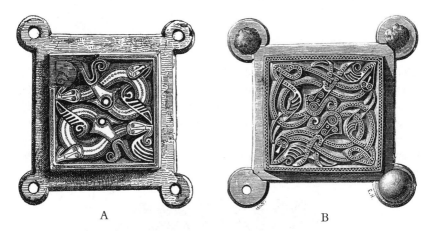

A   B

FIGURE 4.15   Human heads as part of the animals. A: bridle-mount from Denmark. After Müller (1880: 185–403). B: bridle-mount from Vendel, Sweden. Drawing by O. Sörling (Stolpe and Arne 1927: pl. XXXVIII).

FIGURE 4.16   Human head as part of an eagle. Bronze bird (shield-mount?), Gl. Skørping, Denmark. From M. Ørsnes (1966: fig. 160).

FIGURE 4.17 Half man, half wild boar. Eagles are present on both sides of his head and two heads form the belt-buckle. Åker, Norway. After Gustafson (1906).

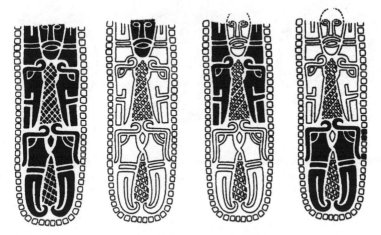

FIGURE 4.18 Men as part wild boar, part 'big animal/eagle'. Part of a Lombard gold-blade cross, Wurmlingen, Germany. After Haseloff (1956, vol. 3).

The semantic potential of animal ornamentation is complex, multi-dimensional and ambiguous, and it is quite impossible for a present-day observer to understand it in full. I suggest, however, that it is possible to draw some general conclusions.

FIGURE 4.19   Man 'composed' by animals. The 'beaks' of the lower animals are formed as animal heads. Vendel grave 1. Drawing by O. Sörling (Stolpe and Arne 1927: pl. IX).

A   B   C

FIGURE 4.20   Gold bracteates, from Denmark. A: Kølby. B: Kjøllegård, Bornholm. C: Skrydstrup. All figures drawings by H. Lange after Hauck (1985–89; A: IK 99, B: IK 95, C: IK 166).

First, the animal renderings are representations, not naturalistic depictions. The depictions not only cross the boundaries between various animal species but also the boundary between animals and humans. Second, the animals represented are not domestic, but wild, powerful and aggressive. Third, species in the iconography were depicted as amalgams of human and animal parts. Human bodies may be fragmented, cut into pieces.

The figurative art

In the previous section it was argued that the animal styles – consciously or un/ sub-consciously – reflect cognitive cosmological structures in pre-Christian Nordic societies, both on the continent and in England. Even when the structural levels in the styles include highly abstract and often unconscious principles that reflect social and universal order, they are hardly a conscious representation of the myth (Roe 1995: 58). The mythic level, on the other hand, is represented through the obvious visual message, with the iconography and oral rendering referring to the same 'story'. The recognised mythic level can, however, be found in the naturalistic and therefore immediately more accessible iconographic art from the Iron Age, especially the gold bracteates.

Special attention has been paid to those bracteates where several of the scenes depicted appear to be an illustration of central myths in Nordic mythology; for example, Balder's death (e.g. Ellmers 1970: 210; Hauck 1978: 210, 1994), or the sacrifice of Tyr, who, in order to save the world, placed his right hand in the mouth of the Fenris wolf (e.g. Oxenstierna 1956: 36; Ellmers 1970: 202, 220; Hauck 1978: 210). The majority of bracteates ('C-bracteates') reflect he who has been interpreted as the 'king' of the Asir, Odin, in his most powerful position, that is, as magician and boundary crosser in the guise of a bird (e.g. Hauck 1972, 1978, 1983; Hedeager 1997a, b, 1999a)[5] 'riding' a large animal – a hybrid between a horse and a moose (it has antlers and a beard, it is a pacesetter as it is always shown in movement). It is not uncommon to see traces of breath coming from its mouth, that is, the animal is animate. Birds and snakes often follow on the journey – and sometimes a fish is recognisable too (Hedeager 1999a: 229f., 2004). Shape shifting, that is, a person in the disguise of a bird, together with animal followers, is a recurrent component in the iconographic universe of the bracteates (see Figure 4.20). At the same time it constitutes a central element in the religious complex that modern anthropologists and historians of religion classify as 'shamanism'. In Old Norse sources the word shamanism is, of course, never found because it is a modern analytical concept. However, several words – or terms – are used to characterise this concept (Strömbäck 1935). Examples are *seið, galdr, seiðgaldr, seidlæti, volva, seiðstaf, hamr* and many more (du Bois 1999: 53, ch. 6; Mundal 2006: 287). In the following section, the concept is used entirely as an analytical category and an academic construction to serve as a tool for describing patterns of ritual behaviour and belief (Price 2001: 6, 2002).[6]

From the Migration Period to the Viking Age depictions of humans in animal form can be found, primarily attached to the helmets from the rich warrior graves in Vendel, Valsgärde in Uppland and the Sutton Hoo grave from East Anglia, as well as the iconography on the helmet plate dies from Torslunda, Öland. Most commonly portrayed is the so-called wolf warrior (Høilund Nielsen 1999: 332) (Figure 4.21), but warriors in wild boar skin (or wild boars in human skin?) can also be found, on closer inspection; for example, on one of the helmet plates from Vendel, where one of the depicted warriors quite clearly has a wild boar's head

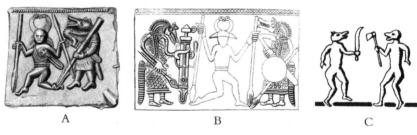

A   B   C

FIGURE 4.21 Men in animal disguise. A: Torslunda stamp, Sweden. Drawing by Bengt Händel in Arbman (1980: 25). B: sword sheath from Gutenstein, Germany. Drawing by I. Müller, adapted from Böhner (1991: 38). C: two fighting men in animal disguise depicted on the 'long' gold horn from Gallehus, Denmark. Woodcut from 1641 by Ole Worm, here after Jensen (2004: 121; compare Fig. 5.8).

(Figure 4.22). On the belt buckle from Åker a man, crowned as a king, has human head and hair, whereas his legs and arms are in the form of two wild boars (Figure 4.17). A boar-warrior (Figure 4.23) and another person in bird disguise, probably a woman, are depicted on the tapestry from the Norwegian Oseberg ship-grave (Figure 4.24).

The helmets themselves display a complete animal symbolism; on the crest sit the wild boar (Figure 4.25) and bird of prey (Figure 4.22), and the helmet from Benty Grange (Glosecki 1989: fig. 6) with a gilded boar on the crest materialises this image. The animal figures are, however, to a greater extent part of the helmet's composition. On the Sutton Hoo helmet, for example, the snakes lie like a crest from the neck to the bridge of the nose, whilst the bird protects the face in front, its beak reinforcing the protection of the bridge of the nose. Its wings make up the helmet's eyebrow arches, and the wing tips rest on the temples, where the most

FIGURE 4.22 Warrior in disguise of a wild boar (left); both warriors are wearing eagle-helmets. Helmet-plate from Vendel, Sweden. Drawing by O. Sörling (Stolpe and Arne 1927: Pl. XLI).

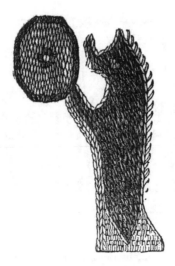

FIGURE 4.23 Wild boar warrior embroidered on the textile from the Oseberg ship grave, Norway. Drawing by Sofie Kraft in Brøgger et al. (1917).

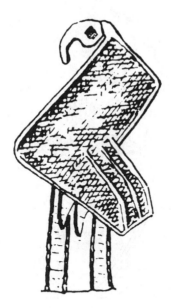

FIGURE 4.24 Woman in bird disguise embroidered on the textile from Oseberg, Norway. Drawing by Sofie Kraft in Brøgger et al. (1917).

vulnerable part of the face is located. And here we find two wild boar heads (Bruce-Mitford 1979: 35; Glosecki 2000; Hedeager 1999c) (Figure 4.26). The splendid helmets from these centuries often incorporate those three animals, and all are significant 'spiritual guides' in the shamanistic world view: the snake who collects

FIGURE 4.25 Warriors with wild boar helmets. Helmet plate stamp, Torslunda, Sweden. Drawing by Bengt Händel in Arbman (1980: 24).

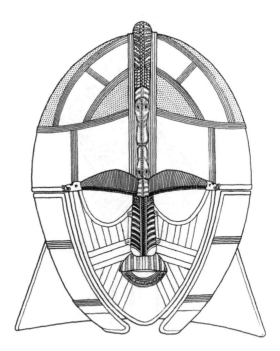

FIGURE 4.26 Reconstruction of the Sutton Hoo helmet. After Speake (1980: pl. 5c).

knowledge from the underworld, the bird who flies to all corners of the world to obtain information, and the large animals, in this case the wild boar, who protects the journey to the other side. The figural plates depict mythical scenes that may have been well known among the elite warrior milieu in pre-Christian times.

Sutton Hoo, with its unique equipment, illustrates the animals' inseparable connection with the Nordic and Anglo-Saxon pagan elite of the seventh century.[7] Animals are to be found everywhere: on belt buckles of gold, the snake and bird of prey are discernible (see Figure 4.10), the impressive drinking horns have end plates formed as bird's heads, on the shoulder clasps in gold and cloisonné the wild boar, wolf and snake are found, and on the purse in gold and cloisonné a bird of prey is catching a duck and the man is flanked by two carnivores (Bruce-Mitford 1979: fig. 73, fig. 80). This composition is repeated on the helmet plate dies from Torslunda (Figure 4.27) and the helmet plate from Valdgärde, Sweden (Arwidsson 1977: Abb. 142). On the front of the shield sits a bird of prey with its claws out, ready to attack. On the top of its neck there is a beast of prey baring its teeth, its thigh is a human head and its tail is a serpent in artistic arabesque (Bruce-Mitford 1979: fig. 20). On the back of the shield there are fittings with birds of prey, beasts of prey and a face: a peculiar mixture of animals and humans (Bruce-Mitford 1979: fig. 23). The principals in the animal ornamentation are, in other words, found on independent figurative decorations, in which the animal characters – the bird of prey, the snake and the aggressive animal – are fundamental components, with animals and humans part of the ambiguous composition.

It is possible to conclude, first, that humans are rendered in animal form – as a wolf, wild boar or bird – from the Migration Period to the Viking Age and that human faces are incorporated in animal figures. Second, hybrid bodies are one of the clearest indications that we have to change our ontological assumptions in regard to the 'natural' classification of human versus animals (Meskell and Joyce 2003: 88; Hedeager 2010). A third observation is that the bird (birds of prey), the snake, and the four-footed aggressive and powerful animal are the recurring animal

FIGURE 4.27 Warrior fighting two bears. Helmet plate stamp, Torslunda, Sweden. Drawing by Bengt Händel in Arbman (1980: 24).

characters, sometimes united in one and the same animal, eventually also in combination with a human. This principle is upheld through the Viking Age. Fourth, the animals are inseparable from the warrior elite and from the religious scenes depicted in the Oseberg textiles. And, fifth, domesticated animals (except for the stallion) cannot be identified.

Animals in names

Certain personal names in Old Norse literature as well as in the Germanic literature of the Early Middle Ages consist of animal names. When a list of names from Old Norse literature contains animal names, it shows the influence these kinds of identification marker must have had at the time. Animal names appear either alone as a symbolic name (as a prefix to a name) or as a hyphenated, two- or three-part, name in combination. Bear, wolf, eagle and serpent were predominant in the names, while species such as fox, wild boar, beaver, raven, hawk, falcon and sparrow were less common. Among the domesticated species, horse, cock and goose occurred in names (Janzén 1947). It is significant that men are given animal names much more frequently than women (Jennbert 2006: 137).

The Germanic and Scandinavian hyphenated names typically contain the following species: wolf, bear, boar, dog, bull, deer/stag, buck, ram, worm (snake, dragon), marten, horse, wild animal, eagle, falcon, crow and swan. Most of these species are powerful and combative animals, although not all, and there are no obvious connections between women and, for example, swans or deer, or between men and bears (Müller 1968: 216 f.). The oldest hyphenated names contain bear-wolf, eagle-wolf, or boar-wolf combinations (ibid.: 209). Other common combinations are eagle-boar, eagle-boar-wolf and eagle-worm/snake (Speake 1980: 78). Like Joakim Werner (1963), George Speake calls attention to these names and the combinations of animals found in Style II (see Figure 4.11), although we should be aware of course of the danger in reading too much into these similarities (Speake 1980: 78).

In Old English literature most of the clans take on animal names; for example, Beowulf, Bjørn (bear), Bera, Bjarki, Eofor (wild boar), Wulf (wolf), Hjort (deer), Svann (swan), Ottr (otter). The name 'bear' in particular appears be associated with great heroes (Glosecki 1989: 204). There are also warrior–names that include animals, such as 'Battle-Bear', 'Battle-Wolf', 'Sword-Wolf' and 'Hird-Wolf' (Müller 1968: 211). On the rune stones from Istaby, Blekinge (Sweden), three generations of men from the same family are mentioned: 'Battle-Wolf', 'Sword-Wolf' and 'Warrior-Horse-Wolf'. The memorial stones were erected in the seventh century AD (Jansson 1987: 119; Price 2002: 373).

It is notable that certain animal names appear regularly in the compounded names, especially the wolf and permutations of wolf, bear, wild boar and eagle. Other seemingly obvious combinations are, however, unusual, such as boar-bear, bear-raven, eagle-raven, boar-raven, eagle-bear and eagle-snake (Müller 1968: 209).

From this summary outline we can conclude that the animal species used in names, whether as single names or as compounded names, are more often than not wild animal species. It is a reflection of the specific male warrior milieu in the written evidence. In addition, the combination of animal names largely refers to the combination of animal species found in the iconography of the Late Iron Age (especially Style II). Second, the preferred species are powerful and aggressive, which fits well with the contemporary warrior culture, too. The combination of animal species in the compounded personal names was certainly not a matter of chance, but the essence of the person and the bearer of personality. 'You do not have a name, you *are* a name, just as you *are* a body' (Milde 1988 cited in Meskell 1999: 111) may be just as relevant to the people of the Old Norse world as it was to the people of Ancient Egypt. From the above we may conclude that the species in the animal iconography and warrior names with the very same species point to an intricate connection between warfare, humans and animals, which I shall explore further.

Humans as animals – animals as humans: *hugr – hamingja – fylgjur*

The iconography, stylistic as well as figurative, along with the name traditions all point towards the idea that animals and humans represent coordinating principles in pre-Christian cosmology. This is fundamentally different from Christianity. The core doctrine of the Christian belief was based on the understanding that humans were created in God's image and as such fundamentally different from all other living things. Man was the master of all living things. In medieval and Renaissance theology and philosophy, nature was created to serve the interests of mankind, and even if this did not always happen in practice, animals were at any rate morally and aesthetically given this role. The animals served as moral allegories to create meaning in the cultural universe of the Middle Ages, whether religious or profane (Ingold 1994; Ferguson 1961: 8 f.; Flores 1996: x f.).

In spite of the scientific revolution, in which human biology has been included in the realm of the animal, the Western world has nevertheless upheld the Enlightenment's concept of nature: animals continued to be treated as fundamentally different from humans. Animals are seen as 'over-exploited', 'endangered', 'protecting' or 'protected', that is, unconditionally subordinate to human domination; and humans themselves are seen as unique animals, whose dominance is a natural consequence of intellectual and cultural superiority. And from this anthropocentric perspective it is hard to comprehend an animistic culture such as the pre-Christian Norse system of belief, where the boundaries between humans and animals are fluid (Tapper 1994: 48; Ingold 1994). It is, however, notable that belief in shape changing has had a long afterlife in some (remote) parts of Europe (Davidson 1978; Ginzburg 1983; Raudvere 2001: 107; Price 2002: 376 ff.).

Nordic iconography from the Migration Period onwards created a new world of hybridity that portrayed animals and humans as overlapping taxonomies. The images of the iconography depict humans in animal shape – such as the wolf, wild boar or bird of prey. All three are wild animals: truly powerful and aggressive animals. The wolf and the wild boar are unequivocally connected to the Iron Age warrior milieu, while the eagle/bird of prey is linked to the earliest bracteates that portray Odin crossing over to the other world. Odin is the central figure in the Nordic pantheon and 'king' of the Asir, not because he is the greatest hero but because he is in control of the specific magical power called *seið* that enabled him to change shape. This was first pointed out by the historian of religion, Dag Strömbäch in 1935, but has only recently been taken on board in Iron Age studies (e.g. Hedeager 1999a, c; Price 2002; Solli 2002; Nordberg 2003). Snorri Sturluson described Odin in the following way:

> Odin could change shape. The body lay just like when asleep or dead, whilst he was a bird or four-footed animal, fish or snake, journeying in a blink of the eye to distant parts, to carry out his own or other men's errands.
>
> (Ynglinga Saga 7)

Everywhere in Old Norse texts Odin appears in the guise of others; he crossed the boundaries between human and animal, and between male and female. As already mentioned (see Part I), Snorri's description of Odin corresponds to the archetypal shaman (Strömbäck 1935; Glosecki 1989; Lindow 2003), and the iconography supports the significance of zoomorphic guiding spirits – the bird, the snake and the large animal (Hedeager 1999a, 2004).

As a recurring theme in the Old Norse texts, we find the idea of the 'spirit' which can leave the body either in human or in animal form: *hugr, fylgjur,* or *hamingja.*[8] *Hugr,* 'spirit' or 'soul', is able to leave the body, either in the disguise of a human being or an animal (Davidson 1978). However, the *hugr* is beyond human control and is best described as 'thought', wish, desire, or direct personality. Clearly this indicates an Old Norse 'soul faith' (*sjæletro*), in which every person can own/possess several 'souls'. *Hugr* only becomes visible when a person is in a certain state of mind, and this is beyond human control (Mundal 1974: 42). In the guise of an animal, the *hugr* reveals the moral quality of its 'owner', exposing his or her intentions, just like the *fylgja*: a powerful bear or an aggressive wolf (Raudvere 2003: 71).

The dual nature of the human mind is most clearly articulated in words such as *fylgjur* and *hamingja. Fylgja (*the plural *fylgjur*) refers to a sort of 'doppelgänger' or *alter ego*, which attaches itself to a person, often at birth, and remains with them throughout their entire life. After death, the *fylgja* may transfer to another person within the family. Etymologically the word is translated as *fylgja,* 'followers', or related to *fulga*, that is, 'skin', 'cloak' or 'animal clothing', or third as *fylgja* – afterbirth (Simek 1996: 96; Glosecki 1989: 186; Orchard 2002: 122). The *fylgja* appears in the shape of an animal or a woman, and usually it is only visible at times of crisis when it can act on its own instead of the person. It can be seen in dreams or when you are awake (Morris 1991: 120 ff.). One of many examples is to be found in Njal's Saga (ch. 23) where the main character, Gunnar Hamundarson of Hlidarend, appears to Hoskuld in a dream as a big bear with two small bears as his followers. In the morning Hoskuld knows for sure that he has seen the *fylgja* of Gunnar in his dream.

The *fylgja* can best be understood as an externalised soul, although the Christian concept of a 'soul' had no relevance to people in the Old Norse world. Rather it was the embodiment of personal luck, and bound by a belief in destiny. It shared many similarities to *hamingja* (Orchard 2002: 122; Simek 1996: 96).

Hamingja is the embodiment of the good fortune of the family and it passes from one family member to another. In contrast to the *fylgja*, the *hamingja* can also be transferred to someone outside the family when a person dies (Simek 1996: 129; Orchard 2002: 129). But there seems to be a second meaning to *hamingja* as well. *Hamr*, which also means 'skin' or 'animal clothing', can be perceived as the interim shape of a person's *hugr*, obtained through *hamhleypa*, that is, shape changing, which often takes the disguise of an animal or a woman (Simek 1996: 129). Usually this 'free soul' will appear in the shape of a bird, but also as a bear, wolf or whale (Glosecki 1989: 184). On other occasions it can be as a stately woman. The more powerful the animal/woman, the more it is able to triumph over other free and/or hostile spirits. When, during shape shifting, the human *hugr* transforms into an animal (or a woman), then it means that the person *becomes* this animal (or woman), and crosses over to the Other World while the physical body lies still, as when asleep or dead. In the process the human becomes animal and the animal human.

There is no clear distinction between *fylgja* and *hamr* (Raudvere 2003: 71), both could take on a physical shape outside the body. The main difference seems to be that a person's *hugr*, that is, 'spirit', can by shape changing materialise in different animal guises, while the *fylgja* is an immutable symbolic expression of the person's moral qualities. It materialises as a particular 'helping spirit' in animal form and has more mythological character (Raudvere 2001: 102 f., 2003: 71). The animal *fylgja* is an extra somatic soul, supplementary to the 'body soul', that is, an *alter ego* in animal disguise belonging solely to the immaterial world (Mundal 1974: 42–3).

The idea of *fylgja*, and *hamr*, as presented in Old Norse literature, places it centrally in the general complex of traditional shamanistic perception and cultural traits (Strömbäck 1935). From our perspective both *fylgja* and *hamingja* are immediately understood as symbols of power. But this barely relates to the understanding of the term in the pre-Christian world, in which both *fylgja* and *hamr* were perceived as literal descriptions. Although spiritual, they were definitely real – the animals (or the women) were at the same time both spiritual and embodied. *Fylgja* and *hamr* were alternative ways of being that endowed their 'owner' with transcendental reality (Glosecki 1989: 186). However, it is only in connection with shape changing that it is relevant to regard it as fully materialised in a living creature, representing a specific person. While the animal is acting, the man himself is put out of the running (Mundal 1974: 42–3).

The wolf, the bear, the wild boar and the bird of prey are, as pointed out above, particularly powerful animals in Nordic nature. Although most mammals, as well as birds, can be *fylgja* and *hamr*,[9] with the horse as an exception (Davidson 1978: 141), it is these particular four that are prominent because they are connected to the elite classes and as such also appear in the surviving material culture, as well as in texts including the runic stones (personal names). It is, in other words, these animals which in specific situations gave their skin or shape to humans. Shape shifting was dangerous and it was real; it was not just a symbolic action. Throughout the saga literature and in the mythological texts, shape changing is presented as a concrete reality (Raudvere 2001: 103 ff.). Even in *Hrólf saga Kraka* from the fourteenth century AD, a detailed description can be found of a battle between rival animal spirits: in the hall at Uppsala, King Adils' wild boar suddenly materialised, presenting a dangerous opponent for Hrolf and his men. Its presence was the result of the evil king's *seiðr*-like supernatural powers. At the same time as the wild boar disappears after the battle with Hrolf's dog Gram, Adils appears back in the hall.[10]

Both *fylgja* and *hamingja* give a person a certain degree of transcendental power without necessarily turning the individual into a shaman. The person becomes her/his *fylgja* – in other words, King Adils, during the battle in the hall, *was* his *fylgja*, the wild boar, and his *hugr* had taken this particular shape while the body lay somewhere else. This was not a symbolic action, but perceived as reality by Hrolf and his men, and Adils' power and wickedness could only be expressed through the strength of his magical powers, *trolldómr*.

One final example is located in *Annales Lundenses* from *c.* 1250/1265. In this part of the Lund annals (describing events up to AD 856), a Danish prince actually becomes a white bear before battle (lines 36–50):[11]

> The Emperor Arnulf from Rome marched with God's help against the Danes, who were making war under the leadership of three brothers: Godefrid, Sigefrid and Ivar. In accordance with God's will, Arnulf marched against them with an army. Two of the brothers doubted whether their side would be victorious, but were comforted by the third [Ivar], which incited them to fight in a manly way without fear, and then went into his tent. However, Godefrid wanted another word before the battle, and opened the tent in order to ask his brother some questions. When he did so, he saw him in the form of a white bear, walking around the floor and scratching at the ground with his claws; in appearance and behaviour he was like a wild animal. When Ivar, who had been changed both in form and nature, saw his brother standing in the door, he said: 'you can fight a battle, dear brother, but you will not get victory'. These princes and the other enemies of the Christians were all but annihilated by the Emperor Arnulf in a series of terrible battles.

As kingly power was described through the ability to transform into a wild animal, so too was it for Odin as king of the Asir: not because he was the best warrior but because he was the greatest magician. And the highest-ranking Nordic *trolldóm* was to master the art of shape shifting; in other words, the ability to transform into animal guise (Raudvere 2001: 86). Each of the animals was associated with a particular set of characteristics. In the following I will therefore take a closer look at those animals whose physical characteristics are recurrent and recognised in artistic expression: the bird, the wild boar, the wolf and the bear. The serpent or snake holds also a special position in the animal-art; in particular Style II is organised around serpent-ornament (Figure 4.28).

My point of departure will be the animals from sixth- and seventh-century iconography. They express a certain naturalism, which partly fades away with the more abstract styles of the Viking Age. My examples will demonstrate that the artistic expressions of the fifth to seventh centuries AD conform to the written evidence of the thirteenth and fourteenth centuries AD. This testifies to a common historical origin.

The snake

Old Norse cosmology was permeated with a fundamental belief in shape changing, that is, a person's capacity to act outside their body/skin in another shape, and hybridism, that is, having a double being (Bynum 2001).[12] The animal par excellence at mastering shape shifting is the snake. Once a year it casts off the slough. Also, it swallows other animals for food, that is, incorporates other – sometimes living – species to become a double being, an entity of parts. It lives underground, it can swim and climb. It is a reptile, dependent on the sun and the temperature to live and, like the bear, it hibernates during the winter to return to life in spring. The viper is a poisonous snake, and it gives birth to offspring even more poisonous than the adults. It moves silently and quickly and attacks with great speed.

In mythology, folklore and belief the symbolic significance of the snake is almost universal. Certainly in Old Norse literature the snake is a recurrent motif. Under the sea, the World Serpent, also known as the Midgard Serpent, encircled the earth, biting its own tail. When the serpent emerges at Ragnarok it means the end of men

FIGURE 4.28 Serpent-formed animals (with human heads as thighs). Shield-buckle mount from Vendel grave XII, Sweden. Drawing by O. Sörling (Stolpe and Arne 1927: pl. XXXIII).

and gods. Its central position in Nordic mythology is obvious: it was an offspring of the god Loki, and Odin threw it into the sea. The snake held an important role in the central myth about Odin and the way he obtained the mead of poetry as Snorri Sturluson relates in *Skáldskaparmál* (The language of poetry). Here Odin made himself into a snake to be able to pass through a crack in the cliff where the mead cauldron was kept. Also, as already referred, Odin's ability to change shape is described in *Ynglinga Saga* (ch. 7).

There are several reasons why there existed an intrinsic link between the cult of Odin and the snake (Speake 1980: 88). It is telling that the personal name Orm (serpent), as in Gunnlaug Serpent-*tongue* and Orm Barreyiar*skjald*, is attached to the spoken word. Gunnlaug has a serpent-tongue, indicating that he is able to poison by way of words, and Orm is a skald, which means that he is dependent on Odin and the mead of poetry to perform successfully. As a name or a kenning it is, however, not found in the extended lists of Odin's names. Nor is it present in the dwarf names, giant names, names of troll-wives, giantesses or valkyries listed by Andy Orchard (2002), Rudolf Simek (1996) and Neil Price (2002). The serpent no doubt held a special and ambiguous position in the Old Norse world.

The serpent as a symbol continued into Christian times as a pagan identifier, associated with the Devil. This is obvious from the origin myth of the Old Testament, but it is also attested in the previously discussed letter from St Boniface to the Archbishop of Canterbury in AD 745, in which he condemned ecclesiastical vestments with 'those ornaments shaped like worms' on the borders (Speake 1980: 91).

As illustrated in the above, the snake is the most common of the species in the animal-iconography. It exists in personal names too, as the names of Gunlaug Ormstungu (Gunnlaug Serpent-tongue) or Orm Barreyiarskjald,[13] but not in the compound animal names and in alternate names (kennings) for the gods, the giants or the supernatural beings in general, or for persons in the Icelandic sagas.

The eagle[14] and the raven

Within the shamanistic world view, the bird is a traditional *fylgja* animal, and the archetypal way to depict the shaman is in the guise of a bird. The central figure on the bracteates is recurrently depicted in this way (Figures 4.29 and 4.30), interpreted as Odin presented at the height of his powers – during a journey to the other world. He is depicted with an eagle's head, or an eagle escorts him. The eagle is the lord of the skies: it sees everything and it can, more than any other animal, travel over great distances. It is powerful and dangerous and with its beak and claws is capable of attacking an enemy shaman bird *fylgja*, and will do so. The eagle is a constant element in stylistic and iconographic art from the Late Iron Age, often in combination with the wolf/wild boar and humans, and it is included in the names of people in conjunction with the wild boar, wolf and snake. The warriors, whose helmets are decorated with two horn-shaped, snake-like bird of prey heads, can be seen on the Vendel Period helmet depictions and on one of the helmet-plate dies

FIGURE 4.29 Man in disguise of a bird – or with an eagle-helmet like the warriors in Figure 4.22. Gold bracteate from Kitnæs, Denmark. Drawing by H. Lange after Hauck (1985–89: IK 94).

FIGURE 4.30 Man in disguise of a bird. Gold bracteate from Bolbro, Denmark. Drawing by H. Lange after Hauck (1985–89: 29).

from Torslunda. The bird was incorporated in the Vendel Period helmet composition, placed over the face, with the wings spread out over the eyes, and with either a bird or wild boar on the wing tips, just by the temple – a very vulnerable spot (see Figure 4.26). Women could presumably also take the form of a bird, according to the representation on the Oseberg textile (see Figure 4.24).

In Eddic poetry, as in skaldic poetry, Odin is the Raven-god. Two ravens sit on his shoulders and tell him everything they see and hear. At daybreak they fly all over the world and return in the morning. From what they tell Odin he becomes the wise. Their names are Hugin (Thought) and Munin (Mind/Memory), and although Odin is worried they might not come back in the morning, he is most concerned about Munin. Odin is repeatedly identified by his bird companions in the iconography of the bracteates from the Migration Period and on the helmet plates from the Merovingian Period (Figure 4.31). The motif is traditionally related to the trance-state journey of shamans, and the concern about their safe return might describe the danger the shaman faces on the soul journey (Simek 1996: 164; Lindow 2001:188).

However, a closer look on the iconography of the gold bracteates and the helmet-plates reveals that the depicted birds are different species; from the form of the beak some are undoubtedly depicted as eagles, others have a long and strong beak similar to ravens. Ravens are normally undisguised in animal iconography, whereas the 'bird-disguise' is that of an eagle.

Why, then, did ravens from the fifth century AD onwards hold that special position in Norse mythology as the mind and memory of the prime Asir god? The raven is the biggest and most impressive bird in the North in addition to the birds of prey. It is coal-black with a long and powerful beak and big staring eyes, it has a strong and differential voice, in average it measures 65cm long, has a wing span of 1.25m, and it weighs more than 1 kilogramme. A closer look at the nature of the raven reveals that it has a liminal position, eating all kind of small mammals in addition to fruits, plants, snakes, etc. It is a scavenger, and for that reason is known as the bird of battlefields where it first goes for the eyes of those killed in the fight. It is an old saying in Scandinavia that 'one raven does not peck the eyes of the other'

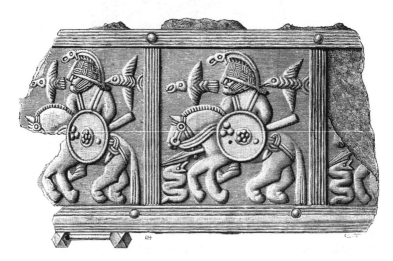

FIGURE 4.31   Odin? in bird disguise. From a helmet plate. Vendel, grave 1, Sweden. Drawing by O. Sörling (Stolpe and Arne 1927: pl. VI).

(like the English saying that dog does not eat dog). Also the saying 'to steal like a raven' (or steal like a magpie) refers to their habit of taking things with a shining surface in particular. Among farmers it is well known that ravens take newborn lambs at the moment they are born when the mother sheep is unable to protect her offspring. However, a pole with a dead raven tied to it and placed on the field keeps other ravens away. Ravens live in lifelong relationships and the couple remains together the year around. They are superior flyers, they fly high in the sky, and *two* black dots up in the sky are occasionally ravens. Like the eagle, they travel great distances, but unlike the eagle, the ravens act two by two. In addition they are shy and watchful.

The wild boar

The wild boar, the toughest, most aggressive and most stubborn animal in Iron Age Europe, was unparalleled as a symbol for the fatalistic warrior philosophy, where one fought to the death and against all odds. The wild boar was a recurring name (*eofor*), and it decorated helmets from the Vendel Period. In the first century AD, Tacitus wrote of the Aestii (on the Baltic) who spoke a language more like British than Suebic, and who worshipped the Mother of the gods, that their warriors wear, 'as an emblem of this cult, the device of a wild boar, which stands them in stead of armour or human protection and gives the worshipper a sense of security even among his enemies' (Tacitus *Germania* 45). From a shamanistic point of view the warrior takes on the symbolic power of the animal when transformed. Beowulf also wears a wild boar helmet and this might imply that the wild boar on the crest expressed the helmet's supernatural powers, that is, the wild boar is *fylgja* for the person wearing it during battle (Glosecki 1989: 190 f., 2000: 9 f.). From this it follows that the wild boar is not just a symbol or a label for a warrior's attachment to a specific tribe or king, as has been proposed (e.g. Høilund Nielsen 1997, 1998, 1999: 332); it is something more. However, the wild boar does seem to have a certain affiliation to the Uppsala kings. According to Snorri, the famous gold ring Svíagrís (Svía-boar) belonged to King Adils and it was an heirloom or item of regalia for the royal dynasty of the Ynglings. The helmet-plates from Vendel near Uppsala depict wild-boar-helmets and warriors in the guise of a wild boar (cf. Figure 4.22). The Ynglinga dynasty in Uppsala claimed descent from Yngvi-Freyr (Davidson 1988: 49; Simek 1996: 122, 147, 306) and the Vanir-god Freyr had a boar called Gullinborsti (golden bristle). The golden wild boar is also found on the helmet from Benty Grange in England on which the boar's bristles have been gilded (Davidson 1988: 50). Beowulf's wild boar helmet named Hildisvin (battle-boar) suggests that the warrior with the wild boar on the helmet was his *fylgja*; in other words, he was a wild boar when he fought, and he acquired the character of a wild boar, just as Beowulf fought to the death against all odds. On one of the helmet plates from Vendel, the warrior not only wears a wild boar helmet but takes the form of a boar with huge tusks (see Figure 4.22). The same figure can be found on the Oseberg tapestry (see Figure 4.23), as well as on the belt-buckle from Åker (see Figure 4.17).

On this particular representation the man, half-human, half-wild boar, wears a crown indicating his elevated position. Finally, the connection between battle and the wild boar is preserved in the word *svínfylking*, which means boar-formation and denotes the wedge-shaped battle formation (Davidson 1988: 50).

The wolf

The wolf travels great distances and is, like the bird, a valued animal-guide for shamans, who in their state of ecstasy also journey great distances. The wolf has stamina, great powers of resistance and is resilient. It is also bloodthirsty – that is, it can attack solely with the aim of killing (Glosecki 1989: 191).[15] Wolf is also the most common animal in the compounded personal names, often in combination with bear, eagle, or wild boar, or it is attached to battle, *hird*, sword, etc. In Old Norse literature one particular type of warrior is mentioned as *Ulfheðnar*, which etymologically means 'wolf coat' or 'wolf fur' (Müller 1967, 1968). The earliest example can be found in *Haraldskvæði*, a laudatory poem to the Norwegian king Harald Hårfager (860–940), composed by Tórbjorn Hornklofi around AD 900 (see Part I). In the translation of Neil Price (2002: 367):

> They [the ships of Harald's fleet] were loaded with farmer-chiefs and broad shields, with Vestland spears and Frankish swords; *berserkir* screamed, the battle was on, *ulfheðnar* howled and shook their spears.
> Of the *berserkr*-fury I would ask, about the drinkers of the corpse-sea [blood]: what are they like, these men who go happy into battle?
> Ulfheðnar they are called, who bear bloody shields in the slaughter; they redden spears when they join the fighting; There they arrange for their task; there I know that the honourable prince places his trust only in brave men, who hack at shields.
>
> (*Haraldskvæði 8, 20, 21*)

Here, as in later Old Norse literature, the wolf is presented as being on a par with the *berserkr*; in other words, within the elite troops of the king. The warrior in wolf guise is, on many occasions, reproduced iconographically: on the helmet plate die from Torslunda on Öland and on two contemporary metal plates from Germany, at Gutenstein and Obrigheim (Böhner 1991: 717 f.) (see Figure 4.21). The text as well as the iconography illustrates warriors with wolf *fylgja*, that is, when in battle the warrior *was* the wolf and had the characteristics of a wolf – in Haraldskvæði described as blood on the shields, the red spears – the symbol of wild slaughter and the wolf howl. A similar transformation is described in the Volsungesaga, written down in the thirteenth century although it goes back to a much older epic tradition, referred to in *The Poetic Edda*. During a revenge raid, King Sigmund and his son Sinfjotle dressed in wolf coats, yelled as wolves and attacked the enemy by biting their throats. That day, it is told, they could not take off the wolf coats. Only after a longer stay underground, which means by sorcery, did they succeed at last (ch. 8). Again we recognise the wolf warrior, not dressed up as a wolf, but in the figure of the animal itself.

In the stylistic expressions from the sixth and seventh centuries, the wolf-like carnivore with the exposed canine teeth appears in connection with wild boar, the bird of prey and the human. This motif is also found on the shield plates from Sutton Hoo (Bruce-Mitford 1979: fig. 23) and Valsgärde 7 (see Figure 4.11). As already mentioned, 'wolf' was the most common animal in the compounded personal names.

The eagle, the wild boar and the wolf all have specific characteristics that make them powerful *fylgja*; together they represent rapidity, ferocity, stamina and aggression. As *fylgja* animals they protected and defended the warriors, whose combat equipment and impressive personal accessories were covered in art indicating their actual presence, and where the name signals to the rest of the world that they bear the same characteristics and powers as the animal. This perception of the world expressed in Iron Age figurative art is unthinkable without a shamanistic belief system in which *fylgja* and shape changing are the central concepts. Neither *fylgja* nor shape changing are, however, perceived as magical acts in Old Norse literature, where they often appear. This is fundamental to the understanding of the relationship between animals and humans when it appears as late as the Early Middle Ages (Price 2002: 364). Folk belief changed only gradually (e.g. Ginzburg 1983; Pluskowski 2002) and the Old Norse concept of the 'soul' ceased to exist in a Christian context during the thirteenth and fourteenth centuries (Mundal 1974: 15).

As is known from the many Eurasian shamanistic groups, the bird and wolf are traditional shamanistic guiding spirits and the Old Norse cosmology does not deviate from this. It is in accordance with this tradition that Odin's animal creatures are the two ravens, Hugin ('thought') and Munin ('mind/memory'), and the two wolves, Freki and Geri, which mean 'the greedy ones'. It should be noted that among the animal bones from the impressive 'royal' burial mounds from the sixth/seventh century in Old Uppsala, traditionally ascribed to the Ynglinga kings, there were remains of bear and goshawk in addition to bones from domestic animals (Sten and Vretemark 1999) and in the nearby settlement bones from red deer, elk and reindeer in addition to considerable quantities of wolf bones are found (Ljungkvist 2006). Among a total number of 156 alternate names (kennings) for Odin known from Old Norse literature, eleven refer to shape changing: two eagles, four bears (one stallion-wolf-bear), and five ravens (for surveys see Price 2002: 101ff.; Orchard 2002 Appendix A). Eagle/bird, wolf, and bear are recurring animal species attached to Odin. The bird as well as the wolf is a reiterated motif in the artistic expression from the Late Iron Age; however, the most archetypical of all the shamanistic guides, the bear, is missing.

The bear

Of all animals it is the bear that has the most anthropomorphic characteristics. It is a plantigrade and creates footprints from heel to toe, and it swings its arms like a human when it walks. Its head is round like a human head, it can sit with its back resting against a tree, it loves honey, it weans its offspring and when it cries it sounds like a baby. Its language is complex and it has a well-developed emotional repertoire. In other words, the bear would seem half human. It is also as strong 'as a bear' and potentially the most dangerous of all animals in the northern hemisphere. If mankind is the master of domesticated land, the bear is master of the wilderness. Both hunt in each other's territories. This apparent competition between equals usually breeds both fear and respect (Glosecki 1989: 198 ff.; Byock 1998: xxv ff.).

More than any other animal, the bear is associated with shamanism through the bear-cult. Like the shaman, the bear journeys between this world and the other, when it hibernates in the winter and returns to life in the spring. The bear also has a dazed and dramatic awakening after its ecstatic sleep. The huge male is a shaman of superior power (Glosecki 1989: 198 ff.).

In traditional cultures from Lapland to Labrador the body of the bear is sacred (Davidson 1978: 130; Price 2002: 247 with references). When a bear is killed or captured, this only occurs because the bear itself allowed it to happen. It gives itself, in other words, to the hunter (Ingold 2000: 121). Among all the north Eurasian groups, the majority of rituals and the greatest number of taboos are associated with the bear and bear hunting, and these are regulated and administered by the shaman. He is the only one who can change shape between human and animal by force of will (Ingold 2000: 123). During the hunt the bear was treated like a *person*, and after the killing, its nose was cut off and tied to the face of the hunter, as an expression of the respect the hunter wished to show the bear. Later on the hunt was re-enacted as a full-scale drama and the hunter apologised for having slaughtered the bear – their own relative – to provide food for the tribe (Glosecki 1989: 203). In addition it was a common practice to drink the blood to obtain power and courage from the bear (Davidson 1978: 130). By giving itself to the hunter, the bear not only handed over its physical mass but also part of its skills and potential to the humans. If the hunt was performed in the right way and the dead bear and its bones were treated correctly, vitality and rebirth were ensured. In this way, man and bear are dependent on each other in a symmetrical relationship. In order to survive, the humans had to kill the animal. In an animist ontology, as for example among the Sami, the bear hunt thus has a fundamentally different meaning than that of simply providing food. The bear hunt is essential to the renewal of the World (Ingold 2000: 114).

Among the Sami, this connection between the bear and humans was traditionally expressed by addressing the bear as 'grandfather', and here ritualised bear hunts were held until recently. Each ceremony ended with the burial of the bear's bones (Näsström 1996 with references). In Scandinavia this well-known circumpolar bear cult is primarily attached to the Sami (Zachrisson and Iregren 1974). However, it is also noted in Finland, where the national epic the *Kalevala* (46) describes a bear ceremony in detail (Näsström 1996: 76). Correspondingly close ties between bears and humans are reflected in Old Norse literature and can be found as late as the fourteenth century AD, in *Hrólf saga Kraka*, where a man and a bear – in the guise of the hero Bodvar Bjarki – are tied so tightly together in mystic union that it can only be understood as a genetic affinity (Glosecki 1989: 198 ff.; Byock 1998: xxv ff.). This idea of a special connection between bear and man is reflected in folk belief. In 1555 Olaus Magnus, Father of the Church and historian, published his great work on the Norwegian peoples, *Historia de gentibus septentrionalibus*, in which he in deadly earnest mentions the existence of mixed marriages between bears and humans (Näsström 1996: 75).

The most obvious and revealing version of the human bear can be found in the word 'berserker', which etymologically consists of ber (bear) and serker (skin or cloth). However, Snorri, and his successors well into the nineteenth century, confused 'ber' with 'berr', that is, naked. From this they concluded wrongly that the warriors went to battle naked, without weapons (Davidson 1978; Simek 1996: 35). Instead, they are to be perceived as warriors, whose *fylgja* were bears, fighting in its guise, but not necessarily wearing bear fur/coats. In Old Norse literature the *berserker* is described as the most feared of all warriors, and they are mentioned along with *ulfheðnar* as Odin's warriors. In his *Ynglinga Saga*, Snorri describes Odin's warriors as furious dogs or wolves who bit into their shields and were strong as bears or bulls. They killed people and neither fire nor iron could harm them. According to Snorri this state is named *berserkergang* (to go berserk/mad/furious) (ch. 6). The *berserker* is best seen as a picked warrior who fights in a state of ecstasy, without knowledge of either pain or fear. The berserker controlled the most powerful and dangerous magic – shape shifting (Glosecki 1989: 205 f.; Byock 1998: xxix; Näsström 2006). However, this power to 'go berserk' ceased with the coming of Christianity, as is related in *Eyrbygga Saga* 61 (Raudvere 2003: 109).

The greatest heroes in Old Norse and Old English literature have names connected to the bear, reflecting its magical power. There is Bodvar Bjarki from *Hrólf saga Kraka* – his name means 'little bear of battle'. He is the son of Bera – 'she-bear' – and of Bjørn – 'he-bear'. In a noteworthy episode, a huge bear is seen fighting alongside Hrólf and his men, biting and slaying the enemy with its paws and itself invulnerable to weapons. Meanwhile, the *berserk* Bodvar Bjarki is asleep. When he is woken, the bear disappears (and Hrólf is slain). Certainly the bear was Bjarki's *fylgja*, which disappeared when he himself turned up on the battlefield (Orchard 2002: 123).

Bjarki is the most obvious Germanic bear-son and a direct analogy to Beowulf, whose name means Bee-wolf, that it, wolf and bee, a synonym for the bear that seeks the same honey from which kings used to make their mead (Byock 1998: xxix f.). The bear was *fylgja* for the most powerful of shamans in the Eurasian regions, and for the greatest mythological heroes in Old Norse and Old English literature, as it was a frequent *kenning* for Odin (Glosecki 1989: 206).

The central and special ritual position that the bear had in Scandinavia during pre-Christian times is reflected in many ways; the bear burials, bear furs in graves, just as drilled bear claws and bear teeth are found often in very rich graves such as the Norwegian weapon grave from Snartemo of the Migration Period (Hougen 1935; Mansrud 2004, 2006). Bear claws in Norwegian graves from the Migration Period are interpreted as symbolic expressions of *hamskifte* related to shamanistic characteristics of an Odin cult (Krüger 1988; Fredriksen 2006). Furthermore, the elite warrior costumes from the Migration Period burials at Evebø-Eide in Norway and Högom in Sweden are interpreted as representing 'bear-warriors' (Bender Jørgensen 2003).[16]

In artistic expression the bear is pretty much non-existent: it is not an element in the animal art, it is not present on helmets, and there are no known warriors in bear guise from the Vendel Period's rich iconography. A warrior-bear may be depicted on the Oseberg textiles (Christensen et al. 1992: 244), and on a so-called *volva-stick* from a female grave in Klinta on Öland, dated to the Viking Age (Price 2002: fig. 3.67). The only iconographic reproductions of the bear come from the Torslunda helmet-plate die (see Figure 4.27), on a helmet plate from Valsgärde 7, and on a lance in Vendel grave 12 (Böhner 1991: 698). Quite coincidentally, Torslunda is situated very close to Björnhövda, that is, bear-head. Bearing in mind the significance of a slaughtered bear in shamanistic cult, then perhaps it could be argued that the name is an expression of a bear cult connected to a particular place.

The die does not show the warrior in the guise of a bear, but rather in battle with two bears. On one side it looks as if he will be eaten by one of the two bears, and on the other side it looks like he has wounded one of them fatally with his sword. The bear is the largest, strongest and most taboo of all animals; it was *fylgja* for the most powerful shamans/sei∂-men and the wildest of warriors and it gave its name to the greatest of mythical heroes in the Nordic countries and East Anglia. It could appear in the guise of a man in the same way as the shaman could appear in the guise of a bear (Ingold 2000: 114). The ritualised enmity between shamans/warriors and the animal *fylgja* is a recurring theme in Eurasia, often associated with initiation rites. Among the Gothic Heruli, as well the Scythians, the slaying of a bear, a wild boar or a 'four-legged animal' took place as part of the *rite de passage* into manhood (Wolfram 1990: 107 f.).

The die could therefore be explained as reproducing the initiation rite of a great warrior, rites that transformed them into 'berserkers'. By killing a bear, drinking its blood and eating its meat (the Christian term), the man became a part of the animal, the animal part of the man and the warrior became one with his *flygja*. This is the concrete physical uniting of animal and human. On the Torslunda mould the bears try to eat the man, while the man attempts to kill the bears – an identical relationship is portrayed in gold and cloisonné on the purse-lid from Sutton Hoo, but this time the composition relates to a wolf (Bruce-Mitford 1979: 110).

The *Hrólf saga Kraka* tells how the most archetypal bear-warrior/*berserk*, Bodvar Bjarki, initiated a young man, Hott, to become a *berserk* himself (ch. 23) (Byock 1998: 51):

> He [Bodvar Bjarki] picked up Hott and carried him to where the beast lay dead. Hott was trembling violently. Bodvar said, 'Now you will drink the beast's blood.' For a while Hott was unwilling, although certainly he dared do nothing else. Bodvar made him drink two large mouthfuls as well as eat some of the beast's heart. After that Bodvar seized Hott, and they fought

each other for a long time. Bodvar said, 'You have now become remarkably strong, and I expect that from this day forward you will have no fear of King Hrolf's retainers.'

(Hrólf saga Kraka *ch. 23*)

Shortly after Hott became a *berserk* in Hrolf Kraki's *hird*, from then on taking the name of Hjalti.

Although the motif of two antithetical creatures placed symmetrically around a human being is rooted in classical art (Böhner 1991: 702 f.), it has no doubt been adapted and transformed into a meaningful expression in the iconography of the Nordic Iron Age on a par with the bracteates. Do these two portrayals express what originally had been the initiation of the bear warrior, *berserker*, and wolf warrior, *ulfheðinn*, respectively? Was this equivalent to a warrior, paying careful consideration to particular ritual actions, killing and eating his *fylgja*, the bear, wolf or wild boar, in order to be united with the animal and attain its particular traits and powers? In battle these bear, wolf and wild boar warriors were terrifying because everyone knew what violent magical powers they commanded.

The bear was a highly significant animal in the Old Norse world. It is connected to the greatest of heroes and to Odin's own warriors. Its lack of representation in the iconography throughout the entire Iron Age and the Viking Age is therefore quite remarkable. Perhaps the only explanation is that the bear, whether in animal or human guise, was so feared and considered so taboo that it could not be depicted.

Embodied and transformative existences

The wolf warrior, bear warrior and wild boar warrior represent three different forms of combat, symbolised by the three animal species. The bear represents the solitary, independent and majestic figure with huge power and noble conduct that nevertheless can in a fury destroy everything and everybody in its surroundings. The wolf, however, always fights as part of a pack with strong solidarity. It is sly and bloodthirsty. Thus *berserk* and *ulfheðnar* represent two different ways of fighting in the Viking Age and Late Iron Age. The *berserk* is the individualistic warrior whose reputation was created through his impressive courage and ability to fight. At the same time he should never attack an un-armed or powerless enemy. Thus the *berserk* is seen in contrast to the *ulfheðnar*, the Viking warrior group par excellence who attacked in force to plunder and destroy. Whereas the bear was a noble enemy, the wolf was cruel and sly. In addition there was the wild boar, associated with devastating power and savagery. *Svínfylking* is the name for warriors in a wedge formation with one person in front, after that two, then three, etc. – which means in a formation corresponding to the shape of a boar's snout. In Old Norse literature the wild boar *hamr* seems mostly attached to the act of protection, just as the wild boar helmet may have protected the head during battle (Davidson 1978: 138 ff.).

The wolf warrior, the bear warrior, and the wild boar warrior are not exclusively Nordic phenomena. As battle groups they appear in the contemporaneous Germanic culture where the names are also in use (Müller 1967, 1968). Male groups who fought in fury and made up an exclusive class whose members were allowed to transcend normal rules and laws are known among the Germanic peoples long before the Viking Age (Davidson 1990: 66). Together with other forms of shape shifting and sorcery, the belief in a military brotherhood whose members were transformed into wolf warriors to fight evil spirits and other transcendental armies have remained part of folk belief in many parts of Christian Europe well into the eighteenth and nineteenth centuries (Russell and Russell 1978; Ginzburg 1983; Raudvere 2001: 107f.; Price 2002: 376 ff.; Pluskowski 2002).

These warrior groups were elite troops, but it is unlikely that their unique equipment and uniforms merely signified adherence to some specific king or military rank alone. The intimate connection between the Uppsala kings and the wild boar, with Freyr as the symbolic link, is real, but it does not automatically imply that all wild boar *fylgjer* can be attached to this royal family. They were generally feared and fearless warriors whether they fought solitary as *berserk*, in groups or brotherhoods as *ulfheðnar*, or in wedge formations as *svínfylking*. But their real strength lay in the fact that they were in command of a dangerous spiritual dimension – shape shifting. They could appear in the guise of their *fylgja*, their doppelganger, and were therefore perceived, both physically and actually, not as man but bear, wolf or wild boar. The spiritual dimension was perceived as a transcendental reality.

The metamorphosis between animal and human in the iconography displays the same transcendental perception. Hybridity and metamorphosis between people and animals (and things) underscore this deeply rooted conceptualisation of humanity in Old Norse society. Shape changing created new types of beings that demonstrated overlapping taxonomies, and new ways of conceiving the world. The wolf, the wild boar and the eagle could do what human beings were not capable of doing, namely, cross the threshold to the spiritual world. In their guise, man could therefore transcend the boundary between life and death. Once we understand that contact with the other world had to pass through animals in the Old Norse system of belief (Figure 4.32), we also understand why the Scandinavian – and Germanic – animal styles were maintained up until the introduction of Christianity. It also explains why animal iconography and Christian iconography were incapable of blending into a new, official, artistic style. During a transitional period, the Urnes style continued to exist within Christian contexts, on altars, church portals, liturgical artefacts. etc. (see Figures 4.6 and 7.3). In AD 1200 it was perhaps necessary to retain the well-known animal style because the animal iconography communicated the same fundamental principles as Christian iconography, that is, the door to immortality. But in Christianity this path had definitely nothing to do with animals. This is exemplified on the gold-foil crosses from seventh-century AD Lombardy (Italy), where human beings replace the animals (Figure 4.33).

Textual evidence, whether the sagas or the Edda, confirms that certain people – and gods – manifested themselves in animal form, literally becoming embodied

FIGURE 4.32 A shaman and his helping animals. Greenland. Drawing made by the shaman to Knud Rasmussen. After Rasmussen (1929).

in animals. The words *hugri*, *hamr* and *fylgja* testify to the specific Nordic belief in
a spiritual world of animal helpers and followers. When a person was gifted with
supernatural powers, he or she was called *hamrammr* (shape strong), or might be
described as *eigi einhamr* ('not of one shape'), suggesting that he or she had the possibility to change shape. The term *hamfarir*, which means 'shape-journey', is used to
express a sort of shamanistic practice in which the spirit travels in animal form while
the body rests in a sleep or trance (Morris 1991: 98). No doubt shape changing and
metamorphosis were regarded as natural phenomena. In the thirteenth century AD
this was still regarded as a fact of nature. Intellectuals, religious leaders, and ordinary people were fascinated by change as an ontological problem: the fundamental
fact that one entity could be replaced by something completely different (Bynum
2001).

However, the Church demonised animal metamorphosis and transformed it
into an evil practice indulged in by witches. In the later Middle Ages animal metamorphosis became associated with the demonic aspect of the female gender and by
that time it had become synonymous with sexual promiscuity, bestiality and heresy
(Morris 1991: 123–5). Tales of vampires, fairies, angels and werewolves reveal a

FIGURE 4.33 Lombard gold-blade cross with 'animal' ornamentation; however, humans have taken the place of animals. San Stefano grave 11–12. Petricia I
Cividale, Italy. After Haseloff (1970: Tafel 4).

fascination with, and horror at, the possibility that a person – actually or symbolically – might become a beast possessed by demons, or an angel inspired to prophecy
(Bynum 2001: 25 f.).

According to Old Norse cosmology, men and women imbued with supernatural powers could transform themselves into animals like the pagan gods Odin,
Freyja and Loki, and animals were an integral part of the cosmic world. The ravens,
the wolves and the horse of Odin, the boar and the cat of Freyja etc., as well as the
many animals in Yggdrasil, all bear witness to the importance of animals in Norse
mythology (Morris 1991: 98). Many animals were thought to have supernatural
powers (such as the snake, the bear, the wolf and the boar) and many were con-
sulted for information about the future by obtaining auspices through observing the
movements of, for example, specific birds or a specific horse (e.g. Tacitus *Germania*
10). In the cosmic world of the Old Norse system of belief, animals were an integral part because they possessed knowledge of nature and conveyed it to humans
and gods. Humans transgressing their bodily boundaries by becoming animals were
therefore nothing unnatural, just slightly unusual. Fluidity, hybridity and metamorphosis were considered as simple facts of nature. In this process, body parts were
integrated in animal wholes to indicate ambiguity and shape shifting, illustrating the
Old Norse saying *eigi einhamr*, that is a person 'not of one shape'.

However, metamorphosis and hybridity are different in 'nature'. Metamorphosis is a process, while hybridity is not (Bynum 2001: 28 ff.). A hybrid is an entity
of two or more parts and it is visible; we actually *see* what a hybrid is. Like the
creatures in the animal styles, a hybrid is a double/triple, etc., being. Here, eagle,
wild boar, snake, beast, etc. and humans constitute hybrid forms that encapsulate the power and ability of all species. The same might be seen in the hyphenated personal names with two or three names in combination: animals as well as
battle/war/fight-synonyms. On the contrary, metamorphosis goes from one entity
to another and is essentially narrative. The metamorphosis is a process going on
from beginning to end, and is comparable to the little death of the shaman/bear/
seið-man/women in the stage of soul journey/winter hibernation. It is a constant series of changes and replacements. Metamorphosis breaks down categories
by breaching them: man becoming wolf or bear, male becoming female, youth
becoming a tree, etc. In opposition to this, hybridity is about contradictions. In a
hybrid form, contradictory categories are forced to co-exist (Bynum 2001: 28 ff.),
such as when man, wolf, snake, eagle and wild boar co-exist in the animal iconography. I shall explore this transformative capacity and its implications in the next
chapter.

5

OTHER WAYS OF 'BEING IN THE WORLD'

Analytical categories and perceptual realities

By now it should be apparent that our conceptual categories of humans and animals as binary oppositions were inappropriate to people of the Old Norse world. Although the scientific revolution has revealed only minor differences in the gene pools between Homo sapiens and all other living species, we still perceive animals as fundamentally different from the human race and therefore subordinated. Nature, and the animals within it, has become dependent on the human race for survival, exploitation, or protection, and we, the modern peoples of the Western world, are only dependent on animals for obvious practical reasons – or reasons of leisure (pets, etc.) (Ingold 1994, 2000; Franklin 1999), Although ethical questions regarding domestic animals and the protection of wildlife have come more into focus, the relevance of this bifurcated structure of living species for earlier periods is rarely questioned (Jennbert 2003, 2004; Hedeager 2003, 2004; Oma 2004, 2007; Mansrud 2004, 2006).

In the study of prehistory, animals are traditionally regarded in purely economic terms. This is of course valid if they are found in settlement contexts, but in sacrificial contexts such as burials and bogs the concept of the 'animal' is rarely questioned. However, some animals such as dogs, horses, and bears were sometimes buried separately in inhumation graves like their human counterparts (Mansrud 2006). Bears were always consumed before the burial, while dogs and horses are buried whole although they are also part of social practice linked to 'food consumption' (Jennbert 2003: 147).[1] In addition to these rare burials, scattered bones from horse and other domestic animals, such as cattle, pig, goat and sheep, are frequent in Norwegian graves from the Iron Age, whereas wild animals are never present (except for a hare and a bird) (Mansrud 2006, 2008). The fragmentation has been regarded as a logical consequence of the process surrounding the ritual meal, which very likely took place in relation to the ritual event. However, human skeletal remains from Iron Age inhumation graves are also often fragmented. Funerary rites generally involved a deliberate fragmentation of the human body, not only through the process of burning but also in the subsequent treatment of the burnt remains. The bones are smashed and only a fraction of the cremated bones were kept for the burial deposition, while, one way or another, the remaining part appears to have been redistributed (Gansum 2004; Kaliff 1997; Kaliff and Oestigaard 2004; Oestigaard 2007). In some cases, bone remains were removed from cemeteries shortly after the burial. Archaeologically, those graves have been described as 'robbed', although it is equally possible that the remains were deliberately removed.

In recent years a number of scholars have challenged the assumption of bodily integrity after death (Kaliff 1997; Brück 2004, 2006; Oestigaard 1999, 2000) and the ideology of individual personhood (Brück 2004, 2006; Chapman and Gaydarska 2007; Fowler 2004; Mansrud 2008; Strathern 1988). This criticism of bodily integrity is the result of mounting evidence that animal and human bodies were often deliberately fragmented in later prehistory. I would rather distinguish between different cosmological domains with different perceptions of 'self'. Thus, the 'heroic' self is highly integrated, whereas the ritual trance (soul journey) disintegrates body and person. Finally, the dead body enters yet another domain where the 'self' and its materiality are disintegrated (Brück 2004, 2006; Chapman and Gaydarska 2007; Jones 1998). Thus, in the Scandinavian Iron Age, the end of a human lifecycle did not necessarily involve the maintenance of bodily integrity. Through a process of deconstruction, skeletal remains achieved an afterlife and thus outlived the living person in a variety of contexts. Bodily remains were imbued with agency and a biography of their own; a well-known example of this from a later period is the use of skeletal remains as relics in a medieval Christian context (Brown 1988; Geary 1978).

There are examples of burials in which a part of the human skeleton (the head) was carefully replaced by the corresponding animal part (Arbman 1943: 384; Jennbert 2004: 200), literally forming a hybrid being. The same may be true of a Vendel-period warrior-grave from Birka, Sweden, where a moose antler was placed in contact with the head of the deceased. On top of him lay a younger man in an unnatural position, with his head separated from the body (Olausson 1990).

Human sacrifice was common during the Iron Age, and yet in discussions of Norse religion its role remains enigmatic (but see Näsström 2001).

The bog people from the Early Iron Age are obvious examples[2] and in graves from the Viking Age it is well attested too (Price 2008: 266 f.). The textual evidence, from the Roman historian Tacitus writing in the first century AD (*Germania* 9, 39, 40), or the Arabian diplomat Ibn Fadlan in the early tenth (AD 922) century, confirms this ritual practice among Germanic and Nordic peoples. The Oseberg tapestry has a scene in which humans have been sacrificed by hanging in the World Tree as part of a major ritual drama (Christensen et al. 1992: 242) (Figure 5.1) and the same scene appears on some of the picture stones from Gotland[3] (Figure 5.2). In the provincial lawcode *Gutasaga* from the early thirteenth century AD, it is

FIGURE 5.1   Humans sacrificed by hanging in a tree. Notice the horse heads in the top of the tree. Textile from Oseberg, Norway. Drawing by Sofie Kraft in Brøgger et al. (1917), here after Christensen et al. (1992: 242).

recorded that people from the whole of Gotland celebrated a *bloð* at which their own sons and daughters were sacrificed (*Gutasaga* 1994: 101) and the Icelandic sagas – for example, *Eyrbyggja saga* (ch. 10) as well as *Landnámabók* (e.g. ch. 73) – describe human sacrifice (children, adults and the elderly) as a recurring part of the Norse religious worship (Näsström 2001).[4] In addition, a striking number of early Ynglinga kings were ritually killed according to the *Ynglinga Saga*.[5] In particular, the legendary story of King Aun of Uppsala describes how his sons were sacrificed to Odin when his own life was threatened.[6] This may reflect an ancient tradition of rulers carrying out son sacrifices at times of crisis (Sundqvist 2002: 253 ff.). The best-known example is found in the *Flateyjarbók*, written in Iceland in the late fourteenth century. The account of Earl Håkon in the fight against the Jomsvikingar (*c.* AD 980–990) suggests that Håkon was accustomed to ordering human sacrifices:

> The earl had a son called Erling, who was seven years old and most promising. And it happened like this, that Thorgerd [a divinity] wanted this sacrifice from him and chose his son Erling. And when the earl thought his prayer and his invocation were heard, it seemed to be better for him, if he let the boy be taken by his slave Skofta. And he allowed him to kill him [Erling] in that manner which Håkon was accustomed to use and he gave him [Skofta] advice on it.[7]

Some scholars have questioned king sacrifices and considered it to be historical fiction (i.e. Lönnroth 1986), while others have seen it as reliable and indeed a clear

FIGURE 5.2   Seven humans lining up to be sacrificed by hanging. Picture stone (145 cm high) from Garda Bota, Gotland. From S. Lindqvist (1941–42: fig. 141), here after Imer (2004: 53). © Gotlands Museum.

trace of sacred kingship and *bloð* in Old Norse (i.e. Steinsland 1991a; Näsström 2001: 59 ff.; Sundqvist 2002: 253 ff.). However, archaeology testifies that human sacrifices belonged to the ritual tradition of Old Norse, where it could take many forms. Written and archaeological sources often confirm each other. The Arab traveller, Ibn Rustah, met a group of Scandinavian Vikings in Russia and wrote about them some time after AD 922 (Sørensen 1973: 76 ff.). He describes a chamber grave of a type well known from Scandinavia (Price 2002: 46). When a leading man dies, Ibn Rustah relates, they dig a grave in the ground formed like a big house. Together with clothes, gold bracelets, coins, food, drinking vessels, etc. the dead body is placed in the chamber. Also, the woman that he loved goes into the grave while still alive. Then they close the entrance and she dies there. The sagas contain a great many references to live burial and sacrifice (summarised in Ellis 1943), and the archaeological record confirms sacrificial descriptions (Price 2002: ch. 3).

Both humans and animals were sacrificed by hanging, in addition to other ways of ritual killing. The Christian clerk Adam of Bremen describes a *bloð* in Uppsala (chs 26–27) in the second half of the eleventh century AD.[8] This ritual drama took place every ninth year in the sacred grove surrounding the temple and it lasted nine days. During this period one human and seven animals (all male) were sacrificed and their bodies suspended in the trees.[9] Although Adam himself never witnessed this ritual practice, he refers to an eyewitness who saw seventy-two hanged bodies, humans, dogs and horses, which were left to putrefy as part of the sacrificial process. Another source describes a similar bloð from Lejre on Zealand. In the chronicle by Thietmar of Merseburg, written down in AD 1012, it is recorded that no less than ninety-nine human beings, together with horses, dogs and cocks (in the absence of birds of prey) were sacrificed every ninth year (Sundqvist 2002: 134, 2004; Näsström 1996: 77, 2001; Solli 2004: 270–1). Thietmar had not himself witnessed the ritual, but relates what he has been told. In spite of the methodological problems in using Adam's and Thietmar's narratives, other independent sources also testify to hanging offerings in sacred trees – for example, Frösjö (Iregren 1989) – as well as human sacrifices (Sundqvist 2002: 135). The accounts are – as already mentioned – confirmed visually on the Oseberg tapestry and on one of the Gotlandic picture stones. At the end of the branches on the holy tree at the Oseberg tapestry – the one with the hanged bodies – there are heads of horses, as if the tree itself is a horse[10] (see Figure 5.1). Yggdrasil in Old Norse means 'Odin's horse' (Simek 1996: 375).

Animals sacrificed like humans are documented in the archaeological remains from below the altar in Frösjö church in Jämtland (Iregren 1989). Here five bears were sacrificed together with a variety of other animal species (moose, red deer, squirrel and domestic animals). From the spatial distribution of the bones on the ground it has been argued that bears were hanged in the tree and left to putrefy. Occasional human remains were found as well.[11] Bones and charcoal were carbon dated to the period between AD 745 (+/- 85) and AD 1060 (+/- 75). A related example comes from the settlement centre of Uppåkra in Southern Sweden, dated between AD 550 and 1050. Here bones from humans and animals were found commingled in distinct concentrations together with weapons (particularly spears), which suggest sacrificial activities within the settlement area.[12] In the account of Ibn Rustah from AD 922, he tells of the 'medicine man' among a group of Vikings in Russia (probably a seið-man) who assigned men, women and cattle for sacrifice. When he had made a decision concerning who among them was to be sacrificed, they had no possibility of evading his order and they were all hanged on a pole (Sørensen 1973: 77).

Also, the small gold images from the sixth to the ninth century AD, the gold-foil figures, make no distinction between humans and animals (e.g. Watt 1991, 1999, 2004; Jansson 2003; Lamm 2004). Although the majority are human representations, whether couples or single figures, some show animals (primarily boars or pigs). The gold-foil figures are ascribed to purely ritual practice since they are found in postholes in halls and other special buildings, such as the 'temple' in Uppåkra (Larsson 2007). Thus, in this ritual context gold-foil figures depicting humans or animals are treated likewise.

To conclude: human sacrifice of various forms is well attested during the Iron Age. Humans and some animal species apparently played similar roles in ritual communication with the other world through sacrifice and in burial rituals. Iconography, material sources, and written evidence thus provide us with a holistic view of

Old Norse religion, in which sacrifice of humans and animals played an important role. According to this broad view of Old Norse cosmology, the self could, under certain conditions, enter into a process of transformation. Body and 'self' were both separated and fragmented in various constellations. With this as a point of departure, I shall now discuss sex and gender representations and the way these are embedded in the overlapping human–animal taxonomies.

Phallus, fertility, and death

In the present day, sex and sexuality have implications of morality and privacy. Nakedness, urinating, defecating and copulation are acts performed in secrecy. Although natural, they are definitely not considered 'natural' acts such as eating and drinking. However, it was not until sixteenth-century Europe that it became bad manners to urinate and defecate openly in front of others, to eat from a communal plate with the fingers, to blow one's nose in the hand, etc. (Elias 2004: 135; Hodder and Hudson 2003: 108). Likewise, open nakedness was the rule rather than the exception. Thus it was common practice, at least in the towns, to undress at home before going to the bathhouse. 'How often', says an observer, 'the father, wearing nothing but his breeches, with his naked wife and children, runs through the streets from his house to the baths' (Elias 1994: 138). No clothing was worn in the steam baths, and every evening everyone undressed completely before going to bed (and the bed could be shared with a guest as a gesture of hospitality). Also, the attitude towards the relations between man and women has changed during the civilising process. Only very gradually did a stronger association of sexuality with shame and embarrassment, and correspondingly more restrained behaviour, spread to the whole of society, as Norbert Elias has shown (1994: ch. IX). Extramarital relationships were entirely public and not surrounded with secrecy. Like a banquet, free access to brothels could be offered to high-ranking guests as part of official hospitality. The example of Emperor Sigismund, who in 1434 publicly thanked the city magistrate of Berne for putting the brothel freely at the disposal of himself and his men for three days, illustrates this (Elias 1994: 149).

Although traditionally overlooked – or at least not considered important – nakedness and sexual symbolism are recurring motifs on early medieval church carvings, while a great number of sculptures in the Romanesque period are devoted to sexual themes of one kind or another (Weir and Jerman 1986: 9). Copulation and sodomy, mega-phallic males, female exhibitionists with exposed vagina and anus, exhibitionist animals such as apes and beasts, etc., all of which to a modern observer look oddly bizarre and vulgar, are, however, numerous on churches all over France, northern Spain, England and Ireland, inside as well as outside. These motifs are definitely not what one expects to represent religious and public life in the Christian Middle Ages. They have been explained as sacrilegious figures, as magical fertility symbols, or as 'Christianised' pagan idols of some ancient fertility religion (ibid.: 10). However, they may just as well be iconographic images whose purpose was to give visual support to the Church's moral teaching in the Early

Middle Ages by dealing with matters of great public concern – the sexual *mores* and salvation of medieval folk whose approach to sex was very different from ours. For example, the grotesque female exhibitionist might illustrate a nearly unbelievable misogyny among the monks who regarded Woman as unclean, and the copulating couple might be seen as a message of warning to the common people revolving around an honest fear of sin and retribution (Weir and Jerman 1986). Regardless of the true meaning, however, the motifs themselves, their location on churches, and their numbers are in itself telling.

Thus, if sex was not a discursive category *per se*, neither nakedness nor copulation had to be 'removed behind the scenes', and human sexual relations were not surrounded by the fear and shame of our 'civilised' world (e.g. Elias 1994 [1936]; Taylor 1996; Laqueur 1990; Meskell 1996, 1999; Schmidt and Voss 2000; Meskell and Joyce 2003). This same open perception of sexuality is also attested among the ancient Greeks where hundreds of vase-paintings depict naked men and women (young men and women being shown as strikingly similar), phallic males, sexual intercourse among the same sex and among men and women, men engaged with women in anal intercourse and even frontal views of women urinating (Dover 1989: 135). Among the ancient Greeks, however, the ugly, drunken satyrs were amoral creatures who obeyed their impulses and masturbated constantly. By contrast, a youth masturbating or penetrating an animal is a rare subject (ibid.: 97). Roman culture deliberately built its sexual taxonomy on practices. A man performing a 'normal' sexual act of penetration was a *futuere* (inserting his penis into the vagina), an *irrumare* (into the mouth), or a *pedicare* (into the anus). All other acts were regarded as abnormal. Persons were categorised according to their preferred sexual activity; for example, as *pathicus* (anal intercourse), *fellator* (performing oral sex on a man), or *cunnilingus* (pleasure women). However, the term *cinaedus* was so broad that it could be applied to men who performed oral sex on men or women, or even womanisers. When Roman authors used the phrase *cinaedus*, they implied a Roman citizen inclined to be penetrated in a same-sex relation. In the late Republic, even prominent statesmen, including Julius Caesar, were openly slandered as being *cinaedi* (Williams 1999: 259 ff.; Skinner 2005: 18f.). In the highly stratified ancient Roman society, there existed firm rules of behaviour and appearance for upper-class men who were expected to avoid whatever might seem 'feminine' (in movement, gesture, or dress). Apart from clothing and other visible markers, rank was associated with moral repute and sexual conduct. In Roman as well as in ancient Greek society, gender roles were pre-arranged upon an axis of dominance and submission. Sexuality was a symbolic code for social difference and sexual beliefs and values were components of more extensive gender systems (Skinner 2005: 20).

In ancient Greece, as in Rome and medieval Europe, morality and privacy were perceived very differently from our modern notions. It is only from the sixteenth century that there emerged a growing consciousness of the body itself, followed by constructions of barriers and boundaries between one body and the next. It is indicated in numerous ways of changed daily routines of eating, sleeping, spitting and toilet behaviour, as argued by Norbert Elias (1994). These changes emerged centuries before the 'one-sex-model' (to use the terminology of Thomas Laqueur (1990)) developed into the 'two-sex-model' of our own time.[13] This discursive separation of spheres of sexuality from other spheres of life clearly constrained a fuller understanding of past sexuality as an embedded sphere of social life, cross-cutting other cultural categories. Perhaps sexuality included so many aspects of daily life that it made no sense to isolate it as an explicit category (Meskell 2000a).

One of the primary lessons to be learned from recent historical studies of sexuality is an understanding that sexual diversity in the past was more variable than conventional historical and archaeological narratives have allowed (Dowson 2000c; Voss and Schmidt 2000). Regarding Old Norse society, we might as well be open to the possibility that the sexual and the religious/ritual were unified in ways we may find inappropriate (i.e. Steinsland 1994a, 1994b, 1997; Price 2002; Solli 2002, 2004). To get around the obviously indecent elements in both texts and the material culture, most scholars since the nineteenth century have referred to 'fertility cult' as a 'neutral' reproductive element in Old Norse religion that need not be explained (Solli 2002: 200).[14] It contains the same aura of neutrality and 'distance' expressed in the term 'sexual intercourse' (Cadden 1995: 2).

The most well-known metaphorical connection between the phallus and fertility is a horse penis named Volsi that was worshipped as a cult object. It came from a farm in the northern part of Norway, which was visited by King Olav the Saint, according to the *Flateyjarbók* (*Ólafs saga helga*, 265–6). The story runs as follows: in autumn when the draught horse was slaughtered, the family (according to the heathen tradition) ate the meat and preserved the horse's phallus (*vingull*). The farmer's son brandished it in front of his mother, sister and a female thrall, and passed it to his mother while intoning this verse:

> Here you can see,
> a good stout *vingull*
> chopped off from
> the horse's father.
> For you, serving-maid,
> this *Volsi* [phallus] will be
> lively enough
> between the thighs.[15]

The housewife carefully dried it, wrapped it in linen and preserved it with leeks and various herbs preventing it from putrefying. Every evening she unwrapped the phallus and muttered a formula to it, and it is told that she placed all her faith in it and held it to be her god. The text describes how it was growing in size and could stand up beside her whenever she wished. When the ritual started – after the king and his men had arrived and had been seated – it was started with the words: 'empowered are you Volsi'. Then the phallus was passed from person to person among all members of the household, and everyone said a stanza that ended: 'Accept, Maurnir (Mornir), this sacrifice'.[16]

Mornir is the recipient of Volsi, and the narrative has been interpreted in different ways. Mornir might be synonymous with a plurality of fertility goddesses or it may have been recorded as a sword name, that is, a symbol of the phallus (Simek 1996: 365), and therefore related to the cult of Frey. However, the cult has also been interpreted as an ancient fertility cult, actuated by women, and related to the farm as a *hieros gamos*, an erotic meeting between gods and giants, between chaos and cosmos (Steinsland and Vogt 1979).[17] Whatever the explanation may be, it is obvious from the *Volsa tháttr* that the phallus and fertility were closely associated in a cult, which was clearly related to the farm and presided over by women (Price 2002: 217 f.). Furthermore, the worship might in a literal sense incorporate masturbation, as Price convincingly proposes. When the phallus during the ritual was passed to the daughter, the text says that 'they shall make wet/the *vingull* tonight'[18] and the masturbation element is underlined in the stanza spoken by the female thrall after receiving the *Volsi*:

> I certainly could not
> refrain from
> thrusting him inside me
> if we were lying alone
> in mutual pleasure.[19]

Neil Price (2002: 219) has summarised the most important sexual elements in the *Volsa tháttr* in the following way:

*   The horse penis is personified (even deified) as *Volsi*, probably a derivative of *volr*, 'staff' (Turville-Petre 1964: 317).
*   It is carefully conserved with herbs that may themselves have functions connected with sexual potency.
*   The horse phallus is in the care of a woman, possible a *volva*, who also presides over the ritual; it is to women that the ritual is primarily directed.
*   It is the main item of 'equipment' used in the rite.
*   It is believed to increase in size during the rite, and to acquire a degree of independence.
*   In two or three instances (strophes 1, 9, and possibly 6) there are explicit references to its use for masturbation.

To Price, as to most other scholars, there seems little doubt that the *Volsa tháttr* does contain early elements of ancient cult, and this has been rendered probable by the study of the Eddic poem *Fjǫlsvinnsmál*. Here the same motif occurs and it is argued that the entire Old Norse cosmology is represented in a symbolic language of sexuality (Heide 1997). Also, the horse phallus might be an equivalent to the *volva* staff (or *vice versa*) (Steinsland and Vogt 1979: 103; Price 2002: 219). This association of the sorcerer's staff with a horse phallus might reflect the obvious sexual association between women and animals in a sorcery context (*volve, valkyri*). The relationship might also be reflected in the Christian Middle Ages, where the witch as a diabolic and sexually dangerous figure is illustrated through her particular relationship (including shape shifting) with animals (Morris 1991: 93 ff.).

The name 'Volsi' also emerges in the doom-laden line of kings and heroes descended from the eponymous ancestor Volsunge, Odin's grandchild.[20] He was married to a giantess, so the line of Volsunge carried the blood of both the Asir and the race of giants (Orchard 2002: 386 f.). 'Volsi' is the family name of Odin's offspring, but it is also the Old Norse word for penis, whether that of horse or man (Vries 1956 I: 409), and human males and stallions do indeed have proportionally large penises outside their bodies (Laqueur 1990: 32). These similarities touch once again on the delicate question of the relationship between humans and animals (horses) and a phallus cult as an integral part of rituals and rulership in Early Scandinavia.[21]

The most persuasive example of the involvement of sexual intercourse in elite rituals is to be found in the Arabian diplomat Ibn Fadlan's often quoted testimony, *Risala* [22] from a 'Swedish' Rus burial on the Middle Volga in AD 922.[23] From this he reported comprehensive sexual activity during the entire period of the funeral ritual. During nine days of preparatory rituals, a (thrall)-woman who volunteered to follow the chief in death had intensive sexual intercourse with the men in the camp. On the ninth day, when the dead body was brought into a tent on the funeral ship and animals had been sacrificed, she went from one tent to the other in the camp and performed sex acts with the men in each tent. One after the other, they said, 'Tell your master that I have done this out of love for him' (Foote and Wilson 1980: 409). Apparently, after having drunk some kind of intoxicant, six men brought her into the tent on the ship, and besides the dead body she had intercourse with each of them. Immediately thereafter the four of them held her arms and legs while the remaining two strangled her. An old woman, who presided over the ceremony, simultaneously stabbed her with a knife.

Ibn Fadlan's account is the most explicit report (if it is to be believed) of sexuality forming an integral part of rituals in Old Norse religion. However different, the *bloð* in Gamla Uppsala may convey a similar impression. Adam of Bremen reports that songs were performed during nine days (like the Rus-burial) of ritual sacrifices, and he adds that they were so indecent that they ought to be kept secret (Adam of Bremen, ch. 27). Concerning the human sacrifices, Brit Solli has opened a provocative and stimulating discussion of the sexual connotation of the process of hanging (Solli 2002: 156 ff., 2004: 271). No doubt sacrifices by hanging were devoted to the gods (or more exactly to Odin, God of the Hanged).[24] The human hanging offering was a well-attested practice among the Nordic peoples from the sixth century AD, according to Procopius (*De bello Goth.* Book II, ch. 15, part 23) replacing other sacrificial killings, including the sacrifice of the 'bog-people' (some were hanged as part of a three-fold killing). Solli's hypothesis revolves around an initiation in which the hanged may – or may not – survive. However debatable, it is pregnant with meaning that the physical action of hanging left the male genitals exposed – erect and achieving ejaculation. It is well known in modern sexology (and practised in some sadomasochistic milieus where it may lead to the death of the practitioner) that suffocating in connection with hanging/stranglehold provokes a heightened state of sexual excitement (Gormsen 1967: 173; Solli 2002: 155). The same phenomenon has been put forward by Robert Graves (1961: ch. 8) as the reality behind the myth of the five-fold bond (and the beating) of Hercules. He was bound with willow thongs (wrist, ankles and neck) to bend him backwards over a T-shaped trunk of oak. He was beaten until he fainted, then flayed, blinded, castrated, impaled with a mistletoe stake, and finally hacked into joints on the altar stone. Graves suggests that Hercules was the type-fossil for a sacrificial king and explains that he had a fertility role. The effect of the five-fold bonds may well have been to cause erection and ejaculation.[25]

The process of hanging/strangling affects all males in the same significant physical way (Gormsen 1967: 171 ff.), whether human, horse, or dog, and unifies in one ritual act sexual power, death and fertility.[26] This might explain why the procedure for ritual killing by hanging or strangling was so important; the usual slaughtering was carried out by stabbing the animal or cutting the throat to let the blood flow. This did not lead to any sexual reaction. The same specific importance of stabbing has been ascribed to the central sacrifice ritual in the Indo-European Vedic tradition in which a stallion sacrifice, Ashvameda, and the sacrifice of a young male, Purpusamnedha, is ritually attested. For a full year neither stallion nor youth were allowed to have sexual intercourse, which implied that they had accumulated semen. During the ritual process, both stallion and youth were tied to the holy tree, Asvattah, and they were both strangled. In the Vedic mythology this ritual act symbolised the re-birth of the fertility god, and through ejaculation the semen symbolised the coming year. No doubt erection and ejaculation were highly important in this most central of the Vedic rituals (Puhvel 1970).

The compound of fertility, death and sexual power is recognisable on the picture stones from Gotland, themselves of obvious phallic form (Figures 5.2 and 5.3). Odin (or a mounted hero) arrives on Sleipnir at the hall of Hell or at Valhal, where a woman (a valkyrie or Hell herself) greets him with a mead cup (or mead horn). The horseman has transgressed the boundary between life and dead in a phallic condition (however, the sword and the phallus are metaphorically depicted as one). This may be understood as a metaphorical unification of life and death through an erotic meeting (Steinsland 1997) (Figure 5.4). Correspondingly, this unification is conveyed on several occasions in *Ynglingatal* where the dead king is described as being 'on his way to an erotic meeting with Hell' (i.e. ejaculating), and in the sagas where young warriors who have lost their lives at sea are 'embraced by Ran's nine daughters' (Steinsland 1997: 106 f.).[27] In the magnificent commemorative poem for his drowned son Bodvar, Egill Skallargrímsson (in *Sonatorrek* 10: 'grievous loss of my sons') describes him *á munvega,* 'on the god's joyful road', that is, he is on his way to Ran (Steinsland 1997: 106 f.). *Ynglingatal* indicates that at the moment of death the ruler was welcomed to an erotic meeting with a mythical woman, although this

FIGURE 5.3   Picture stone (309cm high). Lärbro St Hammars. Notice the man hanged in a tree depicted on the third row. From S. Lindqvist (1941–42: fig. 81), here after Imer (2004: 60). © Gotlands Museum.

does not necessarily refer to any *hieros gamos* celebration (Sundqvist 2002: 168, 288). Generally speaking, however, the texts picture death as a delightful erotic journey. This motif occurs so frequently that it must reflect a general religious idea and not a random poetic expression (ibid.: 289; Fredriksen 2006: 278).

Sexual intercourse is never depicted in the iconography of Scandinavia, although the embracing erotic couple, however dressed, is a recurring motif on the gold-foil plates (Figure 5.5). When found in context, they come from central postholes in ceremonial buildings from the Late Iron Age, and from cult houses or central places such as Helgö in the Mälar area, Gudme on Funen, Uppåkra in Scania, Hov in Hedmark/Opland, etc. (Watt 1991, 1999; Jansson 2003: map; Lamm 2004: 52). The motif has been interpreted as Frey and Gerd, the Vanir god and the giant woman, symbolising the intercourse between fertility and chaos as part of sacred kingship (*hieros gamos*). It has been argued that this particular myth gave cosmological legitimacy to the kingly marriage by reinstating the mythical past in the

FIGURE 5.4 Odin on his eight-legged steed Sleipnir depicted on the picture stone from Alskoga Tjängvide, Gotland. From S. Lindqvist (1941–42: fig. 137), here after Imer (2004: 50). © Gotlands Museum.

      A   B   C

FIGURE 5.5 Gold-foil figures (approx. 1cm) with embracing couples. A: Helgö, Sweden. After Lamm (2004: 89, Helgö 1101). B: Helgö, Sweden. After Lamm (2004: 83, Helgö 2593). C: Lundeborg, Denmark. Drawing by Eva Koch, after Thomsen et al. (1993: 88).

present (Steinsland 1991a). Whatever the explanation,[28] this erotic motif is related to certain place names such as *god-*, *hov/hof* (hall/sanctuary),[29] *holy*, *borg*, *lund* (grove) etc., which were linked to central rituals.[30]

From these examples it can be argued that sexuality might have been deeply interweaved not only in the religious practice of the Nordic past but in political negotiations as well. Commemoration and remembrance were fundamental to these peoples, and the construction of memory, whether through burials, ceremonies, runic stones, heroic tales, or picture stones, was part of an active strategy of remembering. Anders Andrén has previously explained the Gotlandic picture stones as 'doors to the other worlds'. He suggested that the motifs illustrated the same heroic poetry that was ritually performed (Gunnell 1995, 2006, 2008) in the impressive warrior graves in the Mälar area from the sixth century onwards, such as Vendel, Valsgärde and Old Uppsala. On Gotland the stones served as commemorative monuments, like the burials at Vendel and Valsgärde (Andrén 1993). This explanation carries conviction, although the memorial stones might have been metaphorical in another sense as well as doors. The picture stones all have an impressive phallic form, which makes them 'doors to the Other Worlds' in another way. If sexual intercourse was an integral part of chiefly burial practice, it clearly makes sense to frame the commemoration of a dead hero in this form (door/phallus) and to place the most important motif – the (phallic) hero arrives in Valhal and is welcomed by a *valkyri* with the mead cup or horn – on its head.

Although picture stones are only found on Gotland, undecorated three-dimensional white phallic stones are widely attested from Norway, placed on – or close to – barrows and cemeteries, and thus underlining the relationship between the phallus and death. Traditionally they have been dated to the late Roman and Migration Periods (Solberg 1999); however, they clearly belong to the Late Iron Age as well (Myhre 2006).[31] Carved into the surface of some of the stones, on both the head and the 'shaft', are cup-shaped pits, well known from Bronze Age rock-carvings where they are interpreted as a sign of the uterus, that is, a symbol of femininity. This obviously ambiguous sexual connotation has been interpreted by some scholars as symbols of an ancient fertility cult connected to Njord (Solberg 1999), while others have considered them as metaphors for a holy marriage (*hieros gamos*) between life and death (Steinsland 1991b, 1994a, 1994b, 1997).[32] Lately they have also been explained as metaphors for sexual ecstasy in the worship of Odin (Solli 2002: 126, 200).

In an important contribution to the discussion of the phallic stones, Bjørn Myhre observed that thirty-two (i.e. more than half) of the known stones are found close to farms with medieval churches. Several of the stones were located on churchyards, and most of them have been found close to farms with sacred names, among others *Hov/Hove* (heathen cult buildings). According to Myhre, the phallic stones might therefore have belonged to the cult sites known as *hov*. This was either a separate building on the farms of the elite or the main room of the hall building. The *hov* represented an official cult, like the cult in Old Uppsala. Here Adam of Bremen describes an impressive phallic Frey statue. In the private cult, however, *horg* is mentioned as a heap of stones. Scholars agree that special stones or wooden statues might have been placed on the *horg*, representing the god. Myhre suggests that some of the monuments, where phallic stones have been located, were *horgs* rather than burial mounds. In *Landnámabók, Flateyjarbók*, in some sagas (e.g. the saga of Hardar), and in medieval laws special stones are mentioned. In the Middle Ages it was prohibited by law to worship these stones, and some of them belonged to the group of phallic stones (Myhre 2006). The connection between Old Norse cult sites, Christian churches, and the worship of the phallus was archaeologically confirmed through the excavation of a white phallus-shaped stone beneath the choir of the medieval Sandeide church, Rogaland in 1912 (Figure 5.6). A similar stone, found in the medieval churchyard of Volda, Sunnmøre, indicates that this was no coincidence (Gjessing 1915: 70; Myhre 2006: 216).

Apart from the picture stones and the Norwegian white stones, phallic images from the later part of the Iron Age are unusual. However, a carved wooden phallus from the early ninth century AD was uncovered in the rampart of the Danevirke at Thyraborg – that is, the southern system of the fortification defending the Danish kingdom in Jutland during the Viking Age (Hellmuth Andersen et al. 1976: 58). It is 23cm long, broken at the base and might have been longer. The phallus seems to have been erected and might have belonged to a wooden idol (Graham-Campbell

FIGURE 5.6   Phallus-shaped stone from the Iron Age and a medieval stone cross on Sandeide churchyard, Norway. The photo was taken in 1912. The phallus-shaped stone was found during excavation in the church. Photo by H. Gjessing (1915), here after Myhre (2006: 216).

1980a: 153) – or it may have been complete in itself, eventually intended for practical use (Price 2002: 221).

A small phallic bronze figure – a naked, bearded man with a bracelet and a conical helmet – from Rällinge, Södermanland in Sweden, is the most significant and unambiguous sexual image from the Late Iron Age (Figure 5.7). It is dated to the Viking Period and is traditionally associated with Frey due to its obvious potency (Ström 1999: 175 ff., fig. 28: 166), but other gods have been suggested (Price 2002: 220, 2006). According to Adam of Bremen, three statues were placed in the temple in Old Uppsala, and the one named Fricco (Frey) was equipped with an impressive phallus. Frey is the fertility god of the Old Norse. He is the Vanir god who was given to the Asir as a hostage (together with his father Njord and his sister Freyja). The two men were the most distinguished among the Vanir, and the Asir made them cult leaders. Two boars are attached to Frey, one is *Slidrugtanne* (dreadful teeth) and the other *Gullinborsti* (gold-bristle). He married the giant woman Gerd (*hieros gamos*). Additionally, he was one of the important early kings among the Swedes. He succeeded his father Njord, who himself succeeded Odin. He erected a large temple in Uppsala and established his principal residence there. As peace and prosperity made people wealthy, the more he was worshipped among the Swedes. According to Snorri Sturluson he was buried in one of the large burial mounds there (*Ynglinga Saga* 10). Frey's other name was Yngvi, and for that reason his descendants are called the Ynglinga, later to become the founders of the Norwegian royal lineage as well (Ström 1999: 175 ff.; Simek 1996: 378–9; Lindow

FIGURE 5.7 A small phallic bronze figure, a naked, bearded man with a bracelet and a conical helmet, from Rällinge, Sweden. Here after Price (2002: 104, fig. 3). © Frances Lincoln 1980.

2001: 12). Here again we meet a royal line descended from an eponymous ancestor who was married to a giant woman (i.e. the sexual intercourse between chaos and cosmos) and who himself personified the power of fertility and virility.

From all these examples we may conclude that in Old Norse societies sexuality and religion co-existed. This interpretation also has implications for our understanding of social and political dynamics. Sexuality did not exist as a separate sphere, or as a conceptual category of its own, but is rather to be perceived as an organising principle involved in many aspects of daily life and ritual practice. This will be further illustrated in a discussion of the concept of penetration. The phallus, whether belonging to the stallion or to the human male, was not merely a metaphor for a fertility cult. It was also a symbol of the power of penetration.

The power of penetration

In the Norwegian *Gulathings law*, outlawry was the penalty if a man accused another of being *sannsorðenn* (provably sodomised). Also, full personal compensation must be paid

> if a person says to another man that he has given birth to a child. The third is if he compares him to a mare, or calls him a bitch or a harlot, or compares him with the female of any kind of animal. ... Then he can also kill the man as an outlaw as a payback for those words that I have now spoken, if he takes a witness to them.
>
> (Gulathings law *196*)[33]

The Icelandic code *Grágás* provides for a sentence of full outlawry (exile for life) for the utterance of any of the words *ragr*, *stroðinn*, or *sorðinn*. Indeed, to avenge these three insulting terms one had the right to kill[34] (*Grágás II*: 392) (Clover 1993: 373–4 with refs; Bandlien 2005: 99). The same accusation is listed in Norwegian laws, that is, the *Gulathing law*.[35] Both *stroðinn* and *sorðinn* refer explicitly to the sex act in which a man played the passive role, while the other performed the action of *streða* or *serða*, indicating the male role in intercourse. The sexual meaning of *ragr* instead implied the general condition of being effeminate (Jochens 1998: 74). When used about a woman, *org* (the feminine form of *ragr*) has been 'translated' as an individual who was inclined to engage in perverse sexual acts. However, Bjørn Bandlien has convincingly argued against this interpretation, and puts forward the definition of a woman who desired a man far below her own social standing (Bandlien 2005: 77f.).

Thus, concerning an accusation against somebody (implicitly a man) taking the form of sexual defamation (*níð*), the law not only prohibited it, but the maximum penalty for this crime equated with the penalty for murder. The outrage always demanded revenge and the insult might simply have been meant as a challenge to fight (Meulengracht Sørensen 1992: 199). However, the strongest and most ritualised form of *níð* was that expressed in skaldic poetry. Because of the complicated and ambiguous character of skaldic poetry, the accusation could be hidden in metaphors with a double meaning. The purpose was primarily to bring about the disgrace of certain persons, as exemplified in the poem about the first Christian missionaries on Iceland. Here it is told that the bishop had 'borit' nine children and Torvaldr (the other missionary) was the father to all of them. Thus, the poet makes use of the dual meaning of 'borit' as 'carried' (during the christening ceremony) and 'given birth' respectively, as he does with the dual meaning of the word 'faðir', father. It thus carries a double meaning. According to one, the bishop had been used as a woman and given birth (and thereby was *ergi*). According to another, it is a harmless poem about the two missionaries who fulfilled their duties and baptised nine children. This example may well illustrate why *Grágás* prohibited poems about any named person (Meulengracht Sørensen 1983: 53–5, 1992: 200 f.; Clover 1993).

However, *nið* also had a particular meaning in Norse mythology linked to death. *Níðhögg* (nið-blow) is the name of the dragon associated with Yggdrasil, the World Tree (*Yggr* is one of Odin's names, 'Terrible One', *drasilis* is 'horse'. Yggdrasil might thus perhaps best be translated as 'Powerful-breathing horse of the Terrible One' (Price 2002: 109)). The *Níðhögg* was an important symbol of chaos and the looming end of the world, and it appears in the very last stanza of the Eddic poem *Völuspá* (Prophecy of the Seeress (*völva*)) where at Ragnarok the dark dragon comes flying from *Nidafjöll* (-mountain) and the *Níðhögg* is mentioned at the very end, just when the cosmic world is gone (Lindow 2001: 239).

It is commonly accepted among scholars that *nið* was not a question of biological reality (after all, pregnant and childbearing men are metaphorical constructions); it was instead a sophisticated form of gendered insult, to be equated with the 'murder' of someone's honour. That is why *nið* has the secondary meaning of death. The conceptualisation of *nið* is aimed at the person who was suspected of being the object of sexual penetration, whether man, woman, or animal. The masculinity of the practitioner is not the moral problem. In Old Norse society the physical act of penetration had no moral connotations, neither if one man penetrates another, turning his anus into a vagina (and metaphorically making him pregnant), nor if he practised sodomy, called *tidelag*. What was deeply defamatory, however, was to accuse a man of having being subject to penetration by another man – or a male animal – or of being transformed into a female or a female animal. The *nið* was subjected to a transformation into 'female', not specifically into an animal (Solli 2002: 143). In short, *nið* is an accusation of unmanliness and softness, that is, the person is *argr* (*ergi, ergjask, ragr*, etc.) (Clover 1993: 385; Meulengracht Sørensen 1983: 13, 1992: 199; Bandlien 2005: 98 ff.).

Ergi has attracted much attention in the study of Old Norse mythology, not least because it is so inextricably linked to Odin's *seiðr*, which is a form of magic and divination. It is widely agreed that this form of sorcery was closely related to the concept of 'shamanism' as an analytical term (i.e. Strömbäck 1935; Eliade 1964; Clunies Ross 1994; du Bois 1999; Hedeager 1997a, b; Price 2002; Solli 2002; Bandlien 2005).[36] 'But in promoting this sorcery (*seiðr*), lack of manliness followed so much that men seemed not without shame in dealing in it; the priestesses were therefore taught this craft', as Snorri writes (*Ynglinga Saga* ch. 7). *Seiðr* was attributed to female practitioners (the *volva*, the *seiðr*-woman) because seiðr was an act that damaged a man's virility and hence his reputation. As *ergi* is traditionally explained as 'sexual perversion' (i.e. Lindow 2001), it has troubled researchers for decades, explicitly because of the obvious connotation of passive homosexuality (i.e. Clunies Ross 1998: 33–4) manifested as 'a third sex' named *queer* (Solli 1998, 2002, 2004).

Heterosexuality defines itself as the negotiation of homosexuality and is the precondition for the conceptualisation of homosexuality (Halperin 1995: 44). However, the Old Norse language had no explicit term for heterosexuality and the translation of *ergi* presents a hermeneutic problem in itself. Unconsciously we bring *ergi* into our own normative sexual terminology as a mark of identity, although the word may relate to a practice within a fluid sexual system. 'Homosexuality' as a term may therefore be inadequate when referring to an experience as *ergi*. 'Homosexuality' was an invention of the late nineteenth century, as Michel Foucault has demonstrated (1985), and it was closely related to a new understanding of sexuality and the sanctity of the nuclear family. By comparison, there was nothing in Greek culture – whether in art, law, or cult – which suggested that heterosexuality was natural and homosexuality unnatural. The Greeks regarded male homosexual desire as a natural part of life, and it was solely the differentiation between the active and the passive role in same-sex relations which was of profound importance (Dover 1989). The Gothic people, the Heruli, and the Scythians are all said to have practised pederasty between warriors and boys. However, by slaying a bear or a wild boar as part of an initiation ritual, boys achieved manhood and were no longer the target of male desire (Wolfram 1990: 107f.). The moral distinction that mattered was that between male prostitution and a homosexual ethos – the first prohibited by law (to Athenian citizens), the second regarded as part of nature (Dover 1989). This takes us back to Norse 'ergi'.

The multi-faceted meaning of *ergi*, and the state of *argr* and *ragr* when attributed to men, has been summarised as follows (Price 2002: 211):

- 'morally useless' in a general sense,
- 'unmanly', with strong connotations of perversity and taking the female role in sexual acts,
- 'one who employs sorcery, and specifically *seiðr*',
- 'cowardly'.

However, Carol Clover has convincingly pointed to the matter of age in relation to the concept of *argr* and *ergi*. Thus, in *Hrafnkels Saga* it is related that 'everyone becomes argr who (or: as he/she) gets older' (ch. 8). It should be obvious therefore that *argr* was not perceived as an act, but as a *condition*. The intimate relationship between *argr* and old age supports the idea that *argr* only metaphorically expressed sexuality (Clover 1993). This change of sex- or gender-affiliation owing to age is also exemplified in the *Egils saga Skallagrímssonar*. As an old man living 'innan stokks' (the women's domain), Egill was no longer part of the public world of his youth and manhood, and even the thrall women treated him with no respect, laughed at him, teased him, etc. Egill ends his life not only surrounded by women, but in a sense as one of them. In *Sonatorrek* (1) Egill himself complains about his weakness and the softness of his 'bore (drill bit) of the foot/leg of taste/pleasure'. In Clover's explanation the bore becomes a metaphor for the tongue, sword and penis – all three have softened and for that reason Egill ends far down the gender scale as a powerless, effeminate geriatric. 'Sooner or later, all of us end up alike in our softness – regardless of our past and regardless of our sex' (Clover 1993: 385). Thus, sex changed progressively through life and was not a generalised category related to gender. To become *argr* was to become soft, impotent and powerless – including a man on whom a sexual act was performed.

In the extremely competitive and aggressive Scandinavian society in which blood feuds were taking place everywhere, often lasting for many years and several generations (e.g. Byock 1982; Miller 1990), the concept of honour evolved around reputation, respect and prestige. Social life and reputation was hierarchically organised and arranged according to dominance and submission, powerful and powerless. At the bottom of the social scale, female thralls were routinely subjected to rape and traded as sexual subjects. In the account of a Viking market at Volga in 922, the Arab diplomat Ibn Fadlan describes how the Vikings (the Scandinavian Rus) regularly had sex with their slaves, often in public, and in groups of both sexes. This activity took place both in front of potential buyers and their own formal partners, whether wives or girlfriends, who seemed unaffected (Sørensen 1973: 70; Price 2005). Rape of a free woman, however, was a serious matter. The Icelandic law code *Grágás* compares it with murder (of a free woman's honour), and it was enough to ruin her reputation for the rest of her life. A male relative of the woman had the right to kill the perpetrator of even an attempted rape (Price 2005).[37]

Within this social hierarchy, power was explicitly connected with metaphors for penetration – by the sword, penis, or tongue. Those who penetrated – with words, with weapons, or with the phallus – were the powerful ('males'); those who became penetrated were the powerless ('females'). In a social setting, sexuality provided a symbolic code for dominance and submission, throwing light on power and thus status differences, and the penis therefore became a symbol of power rather than a sign of *real* sex (Laqueur 2003: 134). The most severe accusations in the Old Norse society evolved around 'effeminacy' and penetration, implying that sexuality and hostility were two sides of the same coin. At the same time it also reveals the underlying threats and fears in a social hierarchy based on gender roles.[38]

Women in men's image

According to the early medieval Icelandic law code *Grágás*, all freeborn women on Iceland had responsibilities comparable to those of men, and they could participate at the *thing*, although they were not permitted formally to negotiate in the law court or allowed a role as peace negotiators. *Grágás* also confirms the power and position of women inside the household (Bandlien 2005: 13). Throughout their life they maintained the right to own property independently and when they acted as heads of households, they were required to tithe 'in the same manner as men'. Like men they were also subjected to outlawry for a wounding or a killing (Byock 2001: 196).

According to *Landnámabók* (The book of the settlements), which is a catalogue of the first settlers who came to Iceland from *c.* AD 870, thirteen of the more than 400 'founding fathers' (the original land claimants) of Iceland were in fact women (Jesch 1991: 79 f.; Clover 1993: 367). The catalogue was written in the twelfth century AD, although the oldest surviving edition is from the thirteenth century. Despite some of the names of peoples and places probably being invented, or creatively deduced, the overall picture of the early settlement on Iceland must be correct. *Íslendingabók* (The book of the Icelanders), written in the late 1120s by Ari Thorgilsson, only lists the four most prominent settlers of Iceland, one for each of the four quarters of the country. One of these four 'noble settlers' is, however, a woman, Auðr, daughter of a Norwegian chieftain. According to *Landnámabók*, where she is mentioned as one of the thirteen founding fathers, she married a Norse king of Dublin who was killed in battle, as was her son. In secrecy she prepared a ship and set off to Iceland (where two of her brothers were living) with her family of unmarried granddaughters and a retinue of twenty free men. After marrying off the granddaughters she settled in Breiðafjörður in the west of Iceland as head of the household, and distributed land to her shipmates and freed slaves. Although Auðr probably is unique and represented the maximum a woman could achieve, she is nonetheless representative of women who took the initiative to emigrate and undertook a male role as head of a household (Jesch 1991: 79 ff.; Herschend 1998: 137–48).

There are several examples of female skalds, and women might even have taken part in organised piracy (i.e. Viking activity) (Clunies Ross 2000). One such example is found in *Stjǫrnu-Oddadraumr*, part of the *Fornaldersögur* written down in the thirteenth and early fourteenth centuries. A certain Earl Hjorvard on Gotland equipped his daughter Helgunn with three longships simply to get rid of her. Later on in the story it tells how she sent shield-maidens to King Geirvid on Gotland, challenged the king to a battle where both sides met on longships, how Helgunn fought in the guise of a she-wolf and the king's troop was reduced, and lastly how Helgunn's warriors surrendered when the king killed the she-wolf with his sword (Andrén 2008). In addition, Andrén points to the similarities between the Icelandic *Stjǫrnu-Oddadraumr* and the Danish *Skjoldunga saga*. The latter mentioned that a shield-maiden from Gotland, Vebjørg, joined the army of the Danish King Harald Hildetand at the battle of Brávalla with a large force.

In other sagas, such as *Laxdæla saga* and *Gísla saga Súrssonar*, women take up arms to avenge close relatives. Although only Guðrún in the latter succeeded in taking blood vengeance, the attempts are generally viewed with respect and admiration. According to the *Laxdæla saga*, some women dressed in men's clothes and carried weapons (Jesch 1991: 207), and in the *Saga of King Heidrek the Wise* a certain Hervör calls herself 'Hervarðr' to become the captain of a band of Vikings (Norrman 2000). The text presents her in the following way:

> Bjarmar's daughter was with child; and it was a girl of great beauty. She was sprinkled with water, and given a name, and called Hervör. She was brought up in the house of the jarl, and she was as strong as a man: as soon as she could do anything for herself she trained herself more with a bow and shield and sword than with needlework and embroidery.
>
> (*The* Saga of King Heidrek the Wise *ch. 10*)

Brynhild, in the *Saga of the Volsungs*, is the 'shield-maiden' or woman warrior par excellence:

> Sigurd (the hero) said: 'The best day for us would be when we can enjoy each other.' Brynhild said: 'It is not fated that we should live together. I am a shield-maiden. I wear a helmet and ride with the warrior kings. I must support them, and I am not averse to fighting.' Sigurd answered: 'Our lives will be most fruitful if spent together. If we do not live together, the grief will be harder to endure than a sharp weapon.' Brynhild replied: 'I must review the troops of warriors, and you will marry Gudrun, the daughter of Gjuki.' Sigurd answered: 'No king's daughter shall entice me. I am not of two minds in this and I swear by the gods that I will marry you and no other woman.' She spoke likewise. Sigurd thanked her for her words and gave her a gold ring. They swore their oaths anew. He went away to his men and was with them for a time, prospering greatly.
>
> (*The* Saga of the Volsungs *ch. 25*)

Brynhild as a warrior-woman is no exception in the world of the Middle Ages. Saxo Grammaticus, in his *Gesta Danorum*, writes about these women:

> In case anyone is marvelling that this sex (female) should have sweated in warfare, let me digress briefly to explain the character and behaviour of such females. There were once women in Denmark who dressed themselves to look like men and spent almost every minute cultivating soldiers' skills; they did not want the sinews of their valour to loose tautness and be infected by self-indulgence. Loathing a dainty style of living, they would harden body and mind with toil and endurance, rejecting the fickle pliancy of girls and compelling their womanish spirits to act with a virile ruthlessness. They courted military celebrity so earnestly that you would have guessed they had unsexed themselves. Those especially who had forceful personalities or were tall and elegant embarked on this way of life. As if they were forgetful of their true selves they put toughness before allure, aimed at conflicts instead of kisses, tasted blood, not lips, sought the clash of arms rather than the arm's

embrace, fitted to weapons hands which should have been weaving, desired not the couch but the kill, and those they could have appeased with looks they attacked with lances. Now I shall return from this by-way to my main narrative.

(Gesta Danorum, *Book 7: 192*)

To Saxo, who as a Christian cleric did not approve of warrior women because they refused their role as sexual beings, this was only a further example of the chaos in Denmark before the Church had brought order and stability (Jesch 1991: 178). According to Saxo, those fighting women lived in the old heathen Denmark, which they in fact may have done (Pohl 2004: 32). Roman, Late Antique, and early medieval authors who deal with wars commonly report on barbarian/Germanic women on the battlefield. Fighting women 'in male attire' were not imaginary at all; their dead bodies were reported from battlefields as, for instance, on Balkan examples during the Gothic raids in the third century and after battles with the Huns in the fourth and fifth centuries. Before AD 238 a majority of all available sources about Germanic women mention women at war, and warrior women are described by Procopius, Jordanes, Paul the Deacon, Adam of Bremen – among many other sources (Pohl 2004). Also, Homer describes Amazons as men's equals as long as they fight. When they lay dead on the battlefield however, they were classi-fied as women. Recurrent in the description of all fighting women, from Homer to the Icelandic law code, is their cross-dressing. Fighting women always wore male dress. Dress constituted and embodied the social signs of gender to such a degree that only when the mail coat – 'the wrong sign' – was removed, and the body lay dead, did the 'wrong' gender also die (Pohl 2004). Regardless of their status as liter-ary fictions or historical realities, all these women assumed a cultural role as men. They had, so to speak, female sex but male gender.

Furthermore, the written sources tell generally of women who organised not only their lives but also their sex lives in a self-assured and almost aggressive way unparalleled in other parts of Europe. Clover (1993: 367) as well as Price (2005) point to the fact that married women took lovers but this went unpunished. Women who divorce, take political decisions on their own, and act independently are socially superior to their husbands (Magnúsdottir 2008: 46). Female promiscuity and erotic aggression in the sagas confirms that women with enough social power were not particularly hindered by the usual sexual constraints of Icelandic society. In general, adultery was no crime and no reason for divorce. *Eyrbyggja Saga* (ch. 47), *Grettirs Saga* (ch. 91), and *Íslendinga Saga* (ch. 21) all describe married women taking lovers. This is also reflected in mythology. Among the gods themselves there are several examples. One of these concerns Odin's wife Frigg, who is accused of having slept with his two brothers, Vé and Vili (Price 2005).

Thus, the principle of ranking was more important than gender, and the law codes confirm this convincingly, as a woman (a daughter) could be considered a man (a son) in the absence of a biological son: 'better a son who is your daughter than no son at all' (Clover 1993: 370). The name *drengr*, which is conventionally regarded as the essence of masculine excellence, is used for exceptionally powerful women as well. Clover argues that the distinction between sex and gender seems oddly inappropriate in a culture that permits biological females to serve as juridical men, and she argues that 'woman' is a normative category, something to be negotiated. Might it be that a warrior society such as that of Scandinavia more or less allowed the transgression of conventional gender roles when biological women became gendered males, and thus accepted – if not required – female violence (Pohl 2004: 32). In this world masculinity had a positive value, even when it was bestowed on women. High rank was masculine.

A cognitive world in which biological women could legally become men, where gendered women could be described in positive terms as *drengr*, where biological males might turn into females and become pregnant (by means of sorcery), and where both men and women by virtue of age end alike, both gender and sex are certainly fluid categories. Thus the principle of sex was not so final that it could not be overridden by other social discourses. While a woman who acted like a man was admirable, a man who acted like a woman was despicable. The normative was masculinity, regardless of biological sex. The fear of losing masculinity, which cross-cut all the way through the world of the Old Norse, had nothing to do with the female sex *per se*, but with the condition of powerlessness and the lack of will (Clover 1993: 379).

Not all men were masculine, potent, brave, honourable and held power. Some women exceeded some men in each of these categories as has been demonstrated, mostly by virtue of their rank. The most striking positive characteristics related to the ideal Icelandic woman are resolution, harshness and courage, all of which were indeed manly qualities in Icelandic society. For the sake of honour she was allowed to transgress the gendered boundary and while doing so she was regarded as admirable and honourable. This transgression was only acceptable when her husband or other male members of the family were unable to satisfy the requirements of maintaining honour (Meulengracht Sørensen 1992: 237), including when a daughter was considered a son in the absence of a brother (Clover 1993: 370).

In Viking society, males were often seasonally absent – trading, raiding and warring. Some lost their lives. Women had to serve as family heads in such situations. The independent role granted to women in Icelandic society no doubt reflects an economic and social necessity. Or put another way, economic power and rank go before gender, but are framed in male ideology. However, gender identities were strictly upheld, as we shall see in the next part.

Gender images/identities

In Norse society normative gender roles had to be upheld, as illustrated through gender-specific dress codes and behaviour. Snorri specifically attests the essence of womanhood and manhood while presenting the correct way to describe a woman and a man respectively in skaldic poetry:

A woman shall be referred to by all female adornment, gold and jewels, ale
or wine or other drink that she serves or gives, also by ale-vessels and by all
those things that it is proper for her to do or provide. It is proper to refer to
her by calling her dealer (*selia*) or consumer (*lóg*) of what she hands out, but
selia (willow) and logs are trees. Hence woman is called in kennings by all
feminine tree-names. And the reason a woman is referred to by gemstones or
beads is that there was in antiquity a female adornment that was called 'stone-
chain' that they wore round their necks. Now it is made into a kenning,
so that woman is now referred to in terms of stone and all words for stone.
Woman is also referred to in terms of all Asyniur or valkyries or norns or *disir*
((divine) ladies). It is also normal to refer to a woman by any of her activities
or by her possession or descent.

(Skáldskaparmál *30–2*)[39]

Thus it is clearly stated what womanhood is about. It revolves around specific manners and behaviours, primarily focused on offering beer or mead (and food) (e.g.
Enright 1996), on the wearing of jewellery (gold and beads), as well as the ability
to carry out sorcery and/or foretell the faith (*norns*, *disir*). To these are, of course,
added her property and her lineage.

The complexity and variability of femininity, covering a vast range of positions related to age, marriage status and 'profession' are, however, demonstrated
in the Old Norse texts (Göransson 1999: 163). Frequent mentions are made of
the young woman ready for marriage, the married, the divorced, or widowed, as
well as woman as housewife, mother, queen, frille (mistress), thrall, or skald. To
these should be added female sorcerers, seeresses and wise women. They are *volva*
(staff-bearers), *seiðkonur* (seið-women), *spákonur* (prophesy woman/wife), *spámeyjar*
(prophesy-maiden), *spákerling* (old prophesy woman), *vísendakonur* (wise woman/
woman who knows), *galdr-women* (like *seið*-woman), *vitka* (a kind of sorceress),
heiðr (both a category of sorceresses and a personal name, especially for volvas),
fordæða, flagð (kona), fála, hála, g'ygr, skass (all with a rough meaning of 'witch',
with a range of negative connotations), *fjolkyngiskonur* (sorceress) (Price 2002: 112
ff.). In addition a special category of female sorcerers are related to the act of 'riding', which is illustrated in the *mara*, synonymous with the 'nightmare' (Raudvere
1993; Price 2002: 119 ff.). Finally there are all kinds of mythological women; for
example, in the guise of birds, as valkyrie, norns, dísir, fylgja, or as giant women.
Lastly there are men dressed like women or in the guise of a woman. Some women
are powerful by virtue of age and social position, some by profession, some are 'real'
living women, and some are mythological or cosmological perceptions of women.
However, they ought to be treated as different, but necessarily linked aspects of the
world view because – as Price has argued – both 'image' and 'reality' were different
products of the same social mind (Price 2002: 112).

The elaborate terminology for sorceress associates women with prophecy, magic
and wisdom, that is 'words'. The sagas show how these wise women were esteemed
in medieval Iceland; they wandered, visited farms and were welcome guests. They

practised low magic, although some were involved with higher forms of magic and divination. Such women, whose sorcery affected the entire community, were feared, venerated and held a high status in society (Morris 1991). The *volva* (a seið-woman) is another gendered identity attested from textual evidence confirmed in the archaeological material. From the description in *Eiríks saga Rauða* (the saga of Erik the Red) it appears that the costume (including fur and skin from different animals), jewellery (coloured beads) and the staff all embodied her profession.[40] Women with a staff (a metaphorical phallus) are illustrated in the iconography (on the picture stones, gold foils, amulets and the Oseberg tapestry), and they are also well attested in the burial evidence (Price 2002: ch. 3). The particulars of the *volva*'s clothing confirm the complexity and symbolic value of her dress, serving to transform the wearer into a *volva* and at the same time emit a complex message of secret knowledge and magic power to the viewer.

Thus, female gender identities are a complex network of signifying practices, varying for individuals over time and intersecting with class, age and marital status. Elaborate hairstyle and costume, together with attributes such as the drinking cup/horn and jewellery (necklace, bracelets and fibulas) are significant markers of female identity on the picture stones and on the Oseberg tapestry, as well as on the small female amulets from the Viking Age,[41] and on the gold-foil plates.

From the instructions given by Snorri, manhood, on the other hand, is described as being in distinct opposition to womanhood:

> [A man] shall be referred to by his actions, what he gives or receives or does. He can also be referred to by his property, what he owns and also if he gives it away; also by the family line he is descended from, also those that have descended from him. How shall he be referred to by these things? By calling him achiever or performer of his expeditions or activities, of killings or voyages or hunting, or with weapons or ships. And because he is someone who tries out (*reynir*) the weapons and is a doer (*viðr*) of killings, which is the same thing as an achiever – *viðr* is also a word for tree, there is a tree called *reynir* [rowan] – on the basis of these terms poets have called men ash or maple, *lund* [grove, tree] or other masculine tree-names, and made reference to killings or ships or wealth. It is also normal to refer to a man using all the names of the Asir. Names of giants are also used, and this is mostly as satire or criticism. Using names of elves is thought complimentary.
>
> (Skáldskaparmál *30–32*)[42]

Thus, according to Snorri, manhood revolves around 'action': what he gives, what he takes and what he is going to do, including 'killing'. Weapons and ships are significant masculine metaphors. Also, he can be named after his property – what he owns or what he has given away; and he can be named after his stock or after his offspring's. Iconographically, masculinity is depicted as 'bearded martiality'. The mounted bearded warrior with his weapons and occasionally with his ship, too, is attested on the picture stones from Gotland, on some of the runic stones, on the

Oseberg tapestry, on the early medieval Swedish tapestries from the churches in Överhogdal (Härjedalen) and Skog (Hälsingland) (Göransson 1999: figs 57, 59, 61, 63, 65), and can be identified in the rich burials, too. The mounted warrior is a motif on some of the helmet plates from the sixth and seventh centuries (cf. Figure 4.31). The wardrobe is carefully depicted, leaving no doubt about the importance paid to correct dress. All in all, masculinity is generally performed through action, and the sex-specific attributes are the beard, martial equipment and the costume.

Men practised magic and sorcery too. Like their female counterparts they belong to a number of different categories. Most common are seiðr-terms, such as *seið-maðr* (seið-man) and *seiðskratti* (evil-seiðr-sorcerer?). Another category consists of galdr-terms, such as *galdramaðr* (galdr-man), *galdrkarl* (galdr-man), *galdrsmiðr* (galdr-smith), *galdrmeisstari* (galdr-master), etc. To these can be added *spámaðr* (prophesy-man), *falsspámaðr* (false prophesy-man, or man who prophecies falsely), *vitki* (sorcerer), *fjolkyningsmaðr* (sorcerer), *vísendamaðr* (man who knows), etc. Although male sorcerers and wise men are well attested in the universe of the sagas, they are clearly not regarded with same social respect as the *volvas* and the other female magicians. On the contrary, they appear as excluded and socially problematic (Price 2002: 126)[43] and Snorri does not even mention this skill.

Thus we may conclude that the categories of masculinity and femininity were strict social constructions, negotiated on an individual level through lavishly elaborated garments, jewellery, hairstyle and weapon adornments. Those are significant for gendered sex, age and class (see Treherne 1995; Sørensen 1997, 2000; Göransson 1999). Among these, dress has the function as a primary means of non-verbal communication or 'signalling'. The components of dress, including clothing, jewellery, weapons, hairstyle and beard (Gansum 2003), emit constant, complex messages, intended by the wearer and understood by the viewers. Objects represent and affect gender as well, and like dress they are discursively involved in the creation and interpretation of social differences (Sørensen 2000). In addition, the phallus, breasts and beard are biologically significant attributes in verbal as in non-verbal communication.

The rich body of textual, iconographic, and burial evidence from early Scandinavia confirms that gender was embodied in dress, jewellery, weapons, hairstyle, etc. (Bazelmans 1999, 2002; Wiker 2001), consequently a high degree of social control was exercised over Old Norse dress, as laws prohibited biological women to dress in male garments, and vice versa (Göransson 1999: 262). Both the Norwegian *Gulathing law* and the Icelandic law code *Grágas* clearly express this view: 'If a woman dresses in men's clothing or cuts her hair like a man or uses weapons in a dangerous way, that should be punished by the lesser outlawry (*fjörbaugr* = life money). It is the same punishment if a man dresses like a woman.'[44] However, the sagas often describe these women as being headstrong or bold, and the question therefore arises of whether the authors of the sagas accepted women warriors, maiden kings, and 'daughters who act like sons' as belonging to a different gender and therefore not guilty of breaking the strict dress code. At least the sagas never mention any prosecution or punishment, although 'cross-dressing' was generally considered to be something of a problem because the cultural gender model was thereby seriously challenged. Therefore, 'transgender' might be a better term for those who acted socially in the intermediate space between the poles of male and female gender, as these women clearly did (Norrman 2000: 378).

Betwixt and between: gold-foil figures on display

Beyond those fields related to the domestic household sphere, Snorri mentions one specific type of female 'action', and that is the ability to foretell the future. Also, the *Eddas* associate women with prophecy, magic and wisdom, and these women were feared and respected in Old Norse society (Morris 1991). Some of these women were dressed in a way that transformed the wearer into a *volva* (i.e. a seið-woman), and they were equipped with a staff. It is clearly attested that various kinds of staffs played a major role as a metaphor or symbol of the phallus (Price 2002: 217, 2005; Heide 2006).[45] Therefore, in addition to the weapon of magic, the *volva*s were 'armed' with a phallus symbol (or a real phallus such as Volsi) too, and the seið ceremony might have imitated an intercourse in which the *volva* received not the male, but the phallic deity symbolised by the staff (or horse phallus). Just as 'Volsi' is the Old Norse word for penis, 'Volva' is the corresponding name for the female genitals (vulva) although the usual Old Norse term was 'wand-bearer' (Simek 1996: 367; Price 2005).

'Armed' with male weapons these women ended up at the powerful 'male' end of the scale (together with their mythological counterpart – the armed *valkyrie*). On the same scale, *seið*r-men, *galð*r-men, prophesy-men, etc. might have ended far down it because they were 'armed' with 'female' weapons. Both male and female magicians were, however, ambiguous figures, transgressing the cultural and sexual boundaries between gendered men and gendered women. *Seiðr* has to be understood as 'a sexual defined metaphor for the practice of sorcery itself' (Clunies Ross 1998: 33):

> conceptualized as feminine in a society that equates the act of sexual penetration with masculinity and the function of receptivity with femininity. Because the shaman and the sorcerer are considered to be possessed and so penetrated by the spirits, their role is thought to be like that of a woman in a sexual encounter.
>
> (*Clunies Ross 1994: 209*)

Seiðr might therefore have included masturbatory orgasm by the performer (Jochens 1996: 74; Price 2002: 219, 2005). The *seiðr*-men might have been dressed in a way that embodied their role and encapsulated their ambiguity, that is, they might be cross-dressing men.[46] Such men are represented on the picture stones from Gotland[47] in typical flowing female dress, some holding drinking horns, but they have beards and perhaps also helmets (Göransson 1999; Price 2005). Also, there is a bearded 'woman' with a drinking horn on the golden horn from Gallehus, Jutland

(Figures 5.8 and 5.9). Among the burials there are also biological men buried in female dress and with female jewellery.[48] They too might have received the power of the phallus in a sexual performance – real or symbolic – turning them into females, and thus making them *ergi*. However, it was not the sexual act *per se* that caused the accusation of being *ergi*, but the effeminacy and humiliation that this sexual act implied. It is well attested that strangers, newcomers and trespassers in many societies and at many times have been subjected to homosexual anal violation as a way of reminding them of their subordinate status (Dover 1989: 105). The phallus was the most powerful weapon because it killed a man's honour, that is, he became socially killed, and it was the medium through which the practitioner (man or woman) was penetrated during the *seiðr* performance. Sexuality/orgasm might have been of fundamental importance in ritual practice as the medium through which life and death was most commonly united (Meskell 1999: 124).

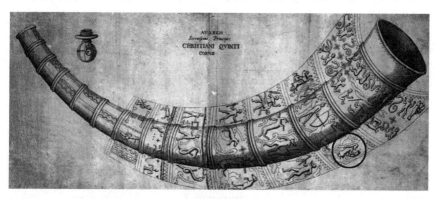

FIGURE 5.8   One of the two gold horns (the 'long one') from Gallehus, Denmark. Woodcut from 1641 by Ole Worm. After Jensen (2004: 114).

FIGURE 5.9   Detail of the long horn: a bearded man with long hair and long dress (in 'woman disguise'), carrying a drinking horn. Woodcut from 1641 by Ole Worm. After Jensen (2004: 114).

If we accept the still rather scanty evidence of biological men in the guise of women, they were socially 'honour-less' outsiders using 'female' skills as sorcerers and magicians and thus constituted a liminal group in the Scandinavian society. On the contrary, women 'dressed' with a weapon or phallus (staff) as men constituted a group of socially 'accepted' outsiders, some with a majestic position in society. The *volva* (staff-bearer) was the real power, and the most feared, in society and their power far exceeded even the most powerful kings and warriors (Price 2002). Thus, the boundary between gendered males and females was ritually exceeded when biological men dressed as women and women 'dressed' with weapons or a staff (phallus) as men. When both dress and objects are media through which gender operates, cross-dressing has a profound impact on the viewer. The ambiguity of the physical body when it lacks the social signs normally attached to it – dress, ornaments, hairstyle, etc. – was threatening because it encapsulated a powerful representation of the entire gender-scale, whether socially respected such as the *volva*, or socially despised such as the *seið*-men.

The gold-foil figures are the single most common group of figurative representations from the Later Iron Age. Much effort has been devoted to them on hair, dress and articles of clothing, and the presentations are very naturalistic. In contrast to this, the anonymity of the faces is all the more remarkable compared to the individuality given not only to dress and associated artefacts but also to the hands (Mannering 1998, 1999, 2006, 2008; Back Danielsson 1999, 2002, 2007).[49]Only the head, hair, hands and feet are left as discursively relevant parts of the body and gender is thus constructed through exclusion of the body from visibility. In addition, some of the figures seem to be masked (Figure 5.10). Masking is not just about

FIGURE 5.10   Examples of gold-foil figures from Denmark. Drawing by Eva Koch, after Watt (1991: 96).

someone 'dressing up' or playfully concealing their identity, as we are familiar with the practice from present-day carnivals or fancy-dress balls (Back Danielsson 1999, 2002; Napier 1986; Gunnell 1995: 146 ff.; Mitchell 2006). Masks that combine features of both sexes, or masks that have both animal and human attributes, are known from a wide group of pre-industrial societies where they communicate esoteric knowledge and *sacra*, the symbolic template of the whole system of belief and values in any given culture. In these cultures masking is associated with 'rites de passage', or other rituals marking change and transformation, and the masks themselves are regarded as objective embodiments of power or the capacity to will their use (Turner 1967: ch. IV).

The gold-foil figures consist of three major categories of images: embracing couples, single figures and a small group of animals, primarily boars (Figure 5.11). All human figures are clothed. The female dress is a long skirt and shawl/cloak, while the male dress is trousers, cloak or a caftan. There are a great variety of styles, from very rich to simple. The caftan, carefully depicted with broad, richly decorated, bands, is well known from the warrior costume on the Vendel Period helmet plates (Figure 5.12). While the women wear their long hair in a characteristic Irish ribbon-knot hairstyle (Figure 5.13) similar to the ribbon-knots on the procession-horses from the Oseberg tapestry, most men have shoulder-length hair. All men on the double-figured gold foils are beardless and so are most men on the single-figured foils. The visible artefact associations for the figures are arm-rings, fibulae, cups and staffs, traditionally regarded as typical gender-specific items attached to women. Generally, the figures fit into the description of womanhood given by Snorri. Even more remarkable is the complete absence of manly signs, except for

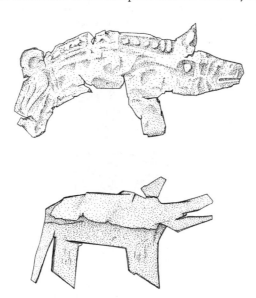

FIGURE 5.11 Gold-foil animal figures from Sorte Muld, Bornholm. Drawing by Eva Koch, after Watt (1991: 98).

FIGURE 5.12   Fighting warriors on a helmet plate from Vendel grave XIV, Sweden. One is dressed in a caftan, his counterpart in a chain-mail shirt. Drawing by O. Sörling (Stolpe and Arne 1927: pl. VI).

FIGURE 5.13   Woman with her hair in an Irish ribbon-knot. Gold-foil from Gudme, Funen. Drawing by Eva Koch, here after Axboe (2005: 53).

FIGURE 5.14   Woman holding a cup. Drawing by Eva Koch, here after Mannering (1998: 263).

the warrior-dress (the caftan). No weapons or any other martial equipment are depicted, and the men are not bearded. Also, the single figure men carry a staff and cup (see Figure 5.10), as do the single figure women (Figure 5.14). It indicates that none of the male figures are gendered males. The beardless figures, dressed as men/warriors and with their hair cut as men, are, however, 'armed' with female attributes such as the staff and cup like the *volva/valkyri* and thereby attain a special category of socio-sexual identity or a 'third gender'.

Most of the figures, both the embracing couple and the single figures, are framed by a portal. They appear, so to speak, on the doorstep – metaphorically in a stage of transformation. The single figures clearly meet and welcome someone, while the double figures meet each other on the doorstep. The doorway has a significant symbolic connotation related to death and transformation. The Gotland picture stones have the form of a door, and Ibn Fadlan describes the specific function of door and doorstep relating to the funerary ceremony among the Vikings on the Volga. The woman who is going to marry the dead chief ceremonially was lifted over an artificially constructed doorstep three times, from which vantage point she looked into the Other World. Doors and doorsteps represented the liminal, transformative passage between this world and the Other World, between life and death.

There are other anthropomorphic figures. Some are described as *wraiths* (Ratke and Simek 2006). Those figures apparently do not wear clothes, or they are dressed only extremely schematically and have no indication of gender-specific attributes; they are neither male nor female (ibid.: 259). One group is dressed in what looks like fur, that is, they are in 'animal cloth' (Figure 5.15). Another example shows a naked bearded person with an impressive 'bead' necklace that might be interpreted as a bracteate's 'collier' (Watt 2004: 212) (Figure 5.16). Most figures in these groups

FIGURE 5.15   Gold-foil figure dressed in 'fur'. Eketorp, Öland, Sweden. After Lamm (2004: 99).

FIGURE 5.16   Gold-foil figure; a naked bearded person with an impressive 'bead' necklace (of gold bracteates?). Sorte Muld, Bornholm. Drawing by Eva Koch, after Watt (2004: 212).

are not stamped but rather cut out individually, and their iconographic representations present a stage of liminality: between life and dead, or man and animal, or man and woman.

Much effort has been devoted to understanding the different motifs and the function of the gold foils (e.g. Steinsland 1990; Watt 2004; Ratke and Simek 2006), although no single explanation fits all the different motifs and none of the explanations have been found to be particularly convincing. However, the foils clearly have some traits in common: they are made of gold, they are tiny, they are related to specific sites and buildings with ritual connotations, and the figures all seem to indicate a stage of transformation – *rites de passage* (van Gennep 1960).[50]

Similar hybrid persons are depicted in the ritual scenes on the Oseberg tapestry, on the Gotland picture stones, and on the golden horn from Gallehus (e.g. Figure 5.9). Some of the figures on the gold bracteates from the Migration Period are seemingly transgressing normative sex as well (Motz 1994; Wiker 2001; Martel 2007); for example, a naked bearded man with breasts;[51] a longhaired person – traditionally explained as the god Tyr with his hand in the mouth of the Fenris wolf (cf. Figure 9.10) – who has, however, breasts, long hair and mini-skirt;[52] and the persons on the 'three-gods bracteates' are men who are clearly represented as naked except for mini-skirts.[53] From the first century AD Tacitus' *Germania* (43: 4) reports that 'the Naharvali [a Germanic tribe in the north] proudly point out a grove associated with an ancient worship. The presiding priest dresses like a woman.' To understand the meaning, it may be suggested that their sexual ambiguity represented a specific conceptual category related to ritual power.[54] Their supernatural skills made them responsible for undertaking of ritual performances such as *seið* and divination in the Late Iron Age.

In the *Eddic* lay *Lokasenna*, Odin himself, who was the master of *seiðr*, is taunted by Loki for wearing female dress when he made prophecies:

> But thou, say they, /on Sáms Isle (the Danish island Samsø) once
> wovest spells like a witch:
> in warlock's shape/through the world didst fare:
> were these womanish ways, I ween.

> (Lokasenna *24*)[55]

Odin on his part taunts Loki with bearing children and for eight winters being a woman and milking cows:

> thou winters eight/wast the earth beneath,
> milking the cows as a maid,
> and there gavest birth to a brood:
> were these womanish ways, I ween.

> (Lokasenna *23*)

Similar accusations are found in the lay of *Helgakviða Hundingsbana I* in which Sin- fjotle accuses Guthmund of being a *volvi* and practising sorcery:

> A witch wast thou/on Varins Isle,
> didst fashion falsehoods/and fawn on me, hag:
> to no wight would'st thou/be wed but to me,
> to no sword-Wielding swain/but to Sinfjotli.

> (*Helgakviða Hundingsbana* I, 38)[56]

Hybrid persons are ritually powerful and socially dangerous at the same time. Ambiguity need not be synonymous with androgyny, homosexuality, or *queer*. Men in the guise of a bear, a wolf, or a boar are not accused of sodomy; they are regarded as powerful magicians, sorcerers and 'shamans' transforming themselves into animals. Like Odin temporarily and Loki on a more permanent basis, their gender position can best be understood as 'liminal'; as transgressing all the world's boundaries – between male and female, centre and periphery, and male and animal (Bandlien 2005: 350, 2006).

When rituals erased the boundary between the sexes, the strict laws on body, dress and adornments attempted to stabilise social gender – woman as (free) woman and man as (free) man. Gender was the order of things, closely linked to a social identity. In Old Norse society sex was a cultural and economic issue too – lavish clothing and costumes, animal-ornamented jewellery, weapons, etc. created the 'self' in a gendered setting.[57] To be a man or a woman was to hold a social rank, a place in society, to assume a cultural role.

Thus apparently contradictory forces held Norse society together. At the core of society strictly bounded and gendered roles defined rank and status, honour and dishonour. Power was framed in a male ideology, and female behaviour was used as a degrading sexual metaphor for weak men. In liminal situations, however, whether at the moment of death or in battle, a powerful cosmological world of transformative gods and helping spirits/animals transgressed the boundaries between animals and humans, and between gendered sex. Warriors and animals were unified in battle; sexes were converted in important rituals. In the process, powers were released and wisdom achieved. Thus, the cosmological and social order of things balanced each other in a constant exchange of earthly and divine forces/powers that were mediated through animals and ritual specialists and supported by sacrifice and excessive rituals.

PART IV
Materiality matters

6
COMMEMORATIVE PLACES

Objects as agents

The task of archaeology is to reconstruct past societies on the basis of material remains – to archaeologists artefacts matter. Contextual analyses of individual burials have long provided a profile of social relations. However, far from passively 'symbolising' social forms, material culture is now more often regarded as being created by the same media that express them. Material objects are not only functional items vital to the social process, they are integral to it. In social anthropology, Marcel Mauss first established this image of material culture in an essay from 1925 on *The Gift* (1990). Central to his argument is the concept of the gift as a material embodiment of the relationship which exists between two persons in their mutual obligation to give and return gifts (Miller 1999: 416).[1]

According to this understanding of material culture, objects become invested with meaning through the social interactions in which they are engaged; they accumulate 'biographies'. Specific objects – 'prestige objects'– whether stone axes or finely decorated swords, may be specially produced for such social transactions. In this way they 'materialise' specific values and social institutions.

Since artefacts change so gradually over time, particularly in pre-industrial societies, they also represent a sense of stability and permanence. This illusion of change-lessness reinstates, so to speak, the past in the present (Connerton 1989; Meskell 2004; Tinn 2007: 20), and specific material objects may be actively involved in the creation of cross-generational continuity by being passed on to the next generation; for example, a famous sword. Heirlooms were one of the key media in the performance of memory (e.g. Connerton 1989; Rowlands 1993; Van Dyke and Alcock 2003; Meskell 2004). So, it may be argued that the continual process by which meaning was given to things is the same process by which meaning was given to persons.

A metaphor for describing these processes is that of 'biography' – 'the cultural biography of objects' (Kopytoff 1986; Appadurai 1986; Gell 1998; Gosden and Marshall 1999; Meskell 2004). The famous sword Skrep may illustrate this capacity. Saxo Grammaticus relates that it was so powerful that it was kept underground (hoarded) only to be retrieved in times of great danger, as happened when the Saxons threatened the Danish kingdom. It was decided that the battle between the two territories should be settled through single combat between the sons of the two kings. The old Danish king dug up Skrep and gave it to his son Uffe ('the Weak'). The story goes that the power of the sword, which 'sang' when it was slashed, gave victory to the Danish prince, despite his nickname.

Other objects imbued with histories and power could be ceremonial dress and adornments, or deified objects such as the phallus Volsi. Animal iconography added a visual code for communicating meaning and quality (see Part III). In this way cosmological meaning was materialised in specific objects, which I shall discuss in Chapter 9.

This capacity of material culture to attain power through its long history (biography) or through specific symbolic decorations (materialisation) is what Alfred Gell in his book *Art and Agency* (1998) called secondary agency.[2] Such objects and art 'caused events to happen in their vicinity'. Social agency can thus be exercised relative *to* 'things' and *by* 'things' (as well as animals) (Gell 1998: 17). By contextualising the concept of agency in ethno-historical contexts, animation, power and divinity can be ascribed to specific objects under the assumption that they have undergone certain rituals or are subjected to certain artistic expressions; for example, animal ornamentation. When social anthropology states that material culture is more than symbolically loaded objects, it must be assumed that this was also the case in the archaeological past. If so, then objects were embedded in similar interchangeable relations of meaning, power and agency between humans, animals and material culture. In the following I shall describe the process through which this took place in Norse society.

Like persons who had to go through a process of socialisation/initiation to come into being with a particular cultural identity, objects only come into being through a particular process of manufacturing and initiation into a particular system of categorisation (Miller 1999: 416). They are brought into existence (they acquire an 'origin') through a process of transformation – what Gell (1992) calls the technology of enchantment and what Mary Helms (1993) classifies as skilled crafting. Both regard this as a value-laden activity, serving to produce items associated with the mastering of social–political–religious leadership.[3] To Gell (1992) such art products serve two main purposes. At first, they are produced to serve the purpose of being displayed on specific occasions when political power is being legitimised by association with supernatural forces (ancestors, deities, etc.). Second, they are produced to serve the purpose of ceremonial or commercial exchange. If they enter into a system of exchange, they will circulate in the most prestigious sphere of exchange. The value of such objects stems from the technical process they objectively embody and the fact that it is difficult to obtain the finished product.

Artisan production presupposes a certain technical level of excellence, and magic is an ideal means of technical production (e.g. Gell 1992; Helms 1993; Eliade 1978; Herbert 1984, 1993). Therefore the role of metalworkers – especially blacksmiths and jewellers – deserves special attention. Besides the technicalities of metallurgy and metalwork, their craft also included an obvious symbolic and ritual element (Rowlands 1999; Haaland 2004, 2006; Haaland and Haaland 2007, 2008; Barndon 2004), which gave them a special status. Mastering metallurgy meant controlling a transformation: from iron ingots to the tools for agricultural production and the weapons on which protection or aggression depended; from ingots, bars and items of gold and silver into ritual objects central to the symbolic universe of society.[4] Blacksmiths and jewellers are usually associated with power in traditional societies because they forge the implements by which the natural and social world may be dominated (i.e. Eliade 1978; Maret 1985; Herbert 1984, 1993; Gell 1992; Helms 1993; Rowlands 1999; Barndon 2004; Gansum 2004; Haaland 2004, 2006; Haaland and Haaland 2007, 2008; Meskell 2004).[5] Furthermore, they create objects that mediate between mankind and the supernatural.

The smith's work requires esoteric knowledge that enables him to manipulate the dangerous forces unleashed in the process of transforming shapeless metal into a finished product; this especially holds true when sacred objects are cast, or specific types of jewellery associated with status and/or ceremonial use are produced. Because of the secret knowledge inherent in such activities, smiths were both powerful and feared (Eliade 1978: 99). As Eugenia Herbert explains (1993), in traditional societies the nature of their work set smiths apart from other people. Often they are ethnically different, or at least regarded as 'others', precisely because they mediate between the natural and the supernatural. The smith has magical powers, often holding a high position in society (Herbert 1984, 1993; Helms 1993; Rowlands 1971; Haaland 2004, 2006; Barndon 2004; Haaland and Haaland 2007, 2008). However, his ambiguous position, half-technician and half-magician, could also place him at a disadvantage in society. He then had to live a separate and secluded life, regarded with disdain by the elite in order to hide the fact that he possessed the technical mastery which was necessary for any ruler in the mediation between himself and those he ruled (Gell 1992).

From anthropological and ethno-archaeological case studies there is a substantial body of evidence to support the idea of iron production being restricted by taboos, just as the process of smelting and transformation is associated with sexual intercourse. This association is played out as the (phallic-like) tuyere ('pipe') is inserted into the body of the furnace by the male blacksmith, and as the bellows are blown. The slag coming out of the tap hole is associated with women giving birth to the iron bloom. Thus, in a comparative perspective, the blacksmith is associated with secrecy, with transformations from nature to culture, and with sexual connotations (Haaland 2004; Barndon 2004).

In order to obtain the necessary metal, the artisan often has to take part in trading activities (Maret 1985: 76). Together with poets, troubadours, carvers and musicians, smiths constitute a group of specialists whose frequent long-distance travel associates them with spatial distance and foreign places. As such, they might achieve a great reputation; as Mary Helms argues, artisans coming from outside were often believed to be superior. Such specialists, as well as travelling religious experts, came to embody the supernatural qualities of the world beyond the settlement. They roamed between cultivated and settled space and the wild and dangerous territories beyond its pale (Helms 1993: 35–9).

Cosmology, magic and materiality are united in the work of blacksmiths and artisan smiths, and that goes for Old Norse society as well. They further endowed the quality that ensured the efficacy of rituals and the legitimacy of the elite (Helms 1993: 13–26; Saunders 1999). Therefore, the study of symbolism, magic and technology belong together. Until recently archaeo-metallurgists have focused on the technological aspects of artefacts. However, in European cultural traditions there are a wide range of myths, legends and folktales on the magic and rituals of the smith, iron and iron-working (Budd and Taylor 1995; Haaland 2004).

More recently, research on blacksmiths has focused on the use of bone – from animals and also humans – in the process of carbonisation of iron bloom, that is, making steel (Gansum 2004). From excavated Iron Age smithies in Scandinavia, forges and bone-coal are found together, and experiments have demonstrated that bone-coal mixed with charcoal transforms carbon into iron bloom and into steel. Terje Gansum concludes that this smithing process of mixing species – animals and humans – has a deeper symbolic meaning. Thus it was possible to transfer an ancestor into a sword blade. If we consider the possibility that a famous warrior after his death had his cremated bones transferred into the symbol of power par excellence, the sword, his strength, spirit and luck was passed on into that weapon and it became personified. The meaning of named swords suddenly takes on a new significance (Kristoffersen 1995: 11; Gansum 2004: 51; Jakobsson 2003).

This technology of mixing bones from animals and humans in the smithing process also has conceptual similarities to the animal style. Thus the taxonomies between persons, animals and things are once again deconstructed and objects were embodied with intangible qualities in quite the same way as the gods' attributes; Gungnir, Draupnir, Mjollnir, and Brísingame. In the sagas, in the Edda and in Saxo Grammaticus there occurs a particular group of named swords to whom be ascribed agency, as they clearly 'caused events to happen in their vicinity' (Gell 1998: 17): Tyrving, Gråsida, Kvernbitt, Gram, Fetbreid, Bastard, and Skrep can be mentioned.

Common characteristics of all these pieces of material culture are that they have famous biographies, dwarves made most of them, and betrayal and murder followed them (see Gansum 2004: 49 ff.). This grants smithing a special place in Old Norse mythology.

The smith in Old Norse sources

The magician-craftsmen and artisans par excellence in Old Norse mythology are the dwarves, who produced the objects through which the cosmic order is sustained; for example, Odin's spear Gungnir and his golden ring Draupnir, Thor's hammer Mjollnir, Freyja's golden necklace Brísingamen (flaming necklace), and Frey's boar Gullinborsti (Golden bristles) and his magical ship Skíðblaðnir. They brewed the mead – the drink of wisdom, poetry and inspiration that constituted Odin's supremacy. Also, they exercised the functions of chanters, teachers, wise men, magicians and ritual officials, and in the mythical–heroic sagas they provided the hero with his mighty weapon. They are also remembered through folklore (Motz 1983, 1993). Their dwelling place was among the rocks and in boulders, that is, underground and away from the daylight.

The names of dwarves given in the lists in *The Poetic Edda*'s lays *Voluspá* and *Thulur* are an important source of further information. In all, 148 different dwarf names are known, including Alvíss (all-wise), Dagfinnr (day-Finn/magician), Draupnir (dripper), Raðspakr (counsel-wise), Skirvir (craftsman), Úri (smith), Viðr (wood) and Yngvi (lord – Freyr?) (listed in Orchard 2002: app. B). However, they also created the world out of the body of the slaughtered giant. They took his skull and made thereof the sky above the Earth, and under each corner they set a dwarf; their names are Vestri (west), Austri (east), Suðri (south) and Norði (north).[6] These represent the four cardinal points, a geographical division that belongs to a world view in which the horizon is crucial. Therefore, the linking of the dwarves to heaven might indicate that they also held a position as astronomers (Motz 1993). Two other dwarves, Nyr (growing/new) and Niði (fading moon) are designations of the waxing and waning moon.[7] The dwarf Alvíss is destroyed by the rising sun[8] and another is described as 'day-shy' (dagskjarre),[9] while Dvalinn (dawdler) is termed the 'friend' or 'playmate' of the sun. In *Voluspá* (stanza 48) dwarves are denoted as 'the wise ones of the mountain' and they might additionally have a relation to funerary rituals, as they have the powers of healing and crafting. As a group (a body of professionals), they are also presented as 'the host of Dvalinn' (stanza 14), who had wandered forth from the 'stone of the hall' to Joruvellir (sandy plain), an undefined mythological place. In some way it appears to be linked with Aurvangar (the gravelly wetlands), which appears to be the place where the dwarves live (Simek 1996: 25, 180). Here we may find a reference to a ritual procession (Motz 1993: 92).

In the world's first age, the happy 'Golden Age', the gods had special talents for skilled metalworking. But when this talent was destroyed by the arrival of giant women from *Utgard*, the gods had to 'create' (although they had always been around) the dwarves and place them in the underground world, among stones and cliffs, where they controlled precious metals and produced much-coveted objects. Like the *Asir* in the Golden Age, the dwarves constituted a male society and were – for social and not biological reasons - unable to reproduce themselves.

They possess no family, the race of dwarves does not encompass women, and they do not create offspring. Subsequently the dwarves became the gods' craftsmen, creating technical wonders for their masters, sometimes willingly and sometimes under duress. However, the gods remained dependent on the dwarves, who crafted the objects that ensured success in the gods' struggles against the giants, which upheld the cosmic order. Although Snorri designates Odin and his priests as 'forgers of songs' (Eliade 1978: 98), neither Odin nor any of the other *Asir* gods were in command of forging.

One of the 'personified' dwarf-smiths is known from the mythological circle of *The Poetic Edda*, namely, Reginn (i.e. the mighty) from the lay *Reginsmál*. The storyline is depicted on a Swedish rock carving from the Viking Age at Ramsundsberget (Andrén 2000) as well as on the Anglo-Saxon *Frank's Casket*, dating from the first half of the eighth century (Davidson 1982: 134). This is part of the great epic cycle of the Volsunga, which tells the story of the fall of the Burgundians after the attack by the Huns in AD 437. Known from a number of Old Norse sources, the *Volsunga Saga* became the core of the *Nibelungenlied* in a Christianised German version from *c.* AD 1200 (see Chapters 2 and 8 this volume).[10] In this epic cycle about Odin's grandchild Volsunga and his descendants, Reginn the Smith is an important, although subordinate, character. His family was composed of a father (no mother is mentioned) and two brothers (no sisters); the father, Hreidmar, was an odd person who knows magic; one brother, Utter, had the shape of an otter (and was killed by the god Loki), and the second, Fáfnir, changed himself into a dragon to guard the golden treasure. In the story, Reginn acts like a human being and travels, like human smiths were supposed to do, to a foreign king to become his master smith. Later he went on to another ruler, Volsung's son Sigurd, whom he fostered in his youth. He revealed to him the nature of Fafnir's treasure and encouraged him to kill the dragon. Reginn is the only one who knows how to forge a sword with the necessary (magical) power to kill Fáfnir, and he knows the right magical acts to perform to ensure that Sigurd wins the fight. Only with this particular sword, named Gram, was Sigurd able to kill the dragon Fáfnir (Reginn's brother), lay his hands on the gold, gain wisdom (from the blood of the beast) and gain a new name: *Fáfnirsbani* (Killer of Fafnir) as the proof of his decisive deed. This episode may exemplify the initiation of a young hero in Old Norse society: instruction in the wilderness, a deed of strength and courage, the gaining of wisdom and of a new name. In this the dwarf Reginn holds the role of the master of initiation (Motz 1993: 83).

Although Reginn at first sight behaves like a human being, he is not an integrated member of human society. He is a long-distance traveller and a skilled artisan smith, he travels between realms of kings, he masters magic, and his brothers master shape changing. Even the strongest king is dependent on him. Furthermore, there were no women present in his family, neither mother, nor sister, or wife, and he had no children. He is a dwarf, a stranger among humans, a liminal figure belonging to the world outside, and he is the master of initiation.

One of the most famous smiths in the Old Norse texts is, however, Volund the Smith, known from a lay in *The Poetic Edda, Vǫlundarkviða*. This is an Old Norse version of the widely known story of the master smith, adapted to Nordic maxims. His name occurs in a variety of forms; for example, Wayland, Weland and Welund (Orchard 2002: 389). The oldest example of the Volund myth is from the first half of the eighth century AD, carved in relief on the Anglo-Saxon 'Franks Casket'.

In Scandinavia the myth is illustrated on a picture-stone from Gotland, from approximately the same time or slightly later (Jakobsson 2003: 149). Volund is the tragic figure of the semi-divine hero-smith, captured and mauled by the king, robbed of his gold and sword, held prisoner and forced to create high-quality weapons and jewellery for his captor. With revenge as its central theme, the poem must have provided a logical and intelligible story line for its audience.

The ability to grow wings and fly like the wind to escape the greedy king, as Volund did, is typical of the master smith who could change shape like the shaman to mediate between human society and the supernatural world.[11] Volund's pedigree and family relations are a good illustration of the smith's position in the cosmological world of the Old Norse texts. As the son of a Finnish king, his origin was clearly defined as that of an outsider; in Old Norse sources a Finnish (or Saami/magician) background always indicated someone who represented dangerous magical forces from outside. Volund, who is called 'king of the elves', was married to a valkyrie, a giant woman from the outside world, and they settled in Wolf-dale. She was a skilled weaver, herself the daughter of a king and in control of shape changing. After nine (seven plus two) years she flew away in a swan cloak.

Although Volund is not a dwarf, he is not a human being either; he is most at home in the outside and dangerous world where he was captured by a human king and brought into society. His forge is situated on an isolated islet, and he himself is a feared person in control of the gold (Bæksted 2001: 278–81). Although married, he has no children, so he does not belong to any family group; he is set apart from society. As the master smith in control of gold as well as skilled crafting, he fabricates prestigious objects essential for the kingly ideal. In revenge he kills the king's two sons and from their skulls makes two silver drinking cups and from their teeth and eyes jewels for the royal couple: 'He hewed off the heads – of the hapless lads, their bodies buried – "neath the bellows pit"'.[12] In other words, he forged the sons into the doom-laden objects (the scene pictured on the Franks Casket) by means of their own bones in the bellows pit. This carefully explained practice might reveal a deliberate use of human bone in the smithing process, making it what Gell (1992) describes as a 'technology of enchantment', or Helms (1993) as 'skilled crafting'; this is where the master smith transformed metal into 'embodied existence' (Gansum 2004; Oestigaard 2007).

Like the Asir gods, the worldly king is dependent on the smith to produce these emblems of royal power. In other words, the king depends on Volund the Smith, his captive, to retain his royal power. Here, the artisan smith clearly had to live a separate and secluded life (as the king's captive on an isolated islet) in order to hide the fact that he was the only person with the necessary technical and magical knowledge to mediate the relations between the ruler and the ruled (Gell 1992).

Summing up, such skilled smiths, whether dwarves or men, have certain specific traits in common. They all belonged to the realm outside human society. By way of magic, the objects they forged were embodied with a certain quality/agency making them essential to the powerful position and ideological legitimisation of the elite, whether gods or human kings. They were – in one way or another – skilled long-distance travellers; they mediated between the settled heartland of human society and the dangerous outside world. Only Volund has a wife (although a giant woman who left him after nine years and flew away), and they constituted a male society unable to reproduce themselves. They are never seen feasting, making love, waging war, or taking part in any of the other activities which make up social life. They are seen in the light of their craft and wisdom, as mythical representatives of a profession that has parallels among the astronomers–healers–skalds of Old Norse society (Motz 1983, 1993; Gansum 2004; Oestigaard 2007). In all, they were the practitioners of Wisdom.

Gold in the Old Norse sources

In *Volsunga Saga*, treasures of gold generate the greed that constitutes the main story line. In Old Norse sources, gold and gold treasures regularly play a central role in the construction of stories. Time and again we meet the devastating greed for gold as an archetypal theme in myths and stories; here and in other heroic tales, such as *Beowulf,* Saxo's *Gesta Danorum* and Snorri's *Ynglinga Saga,* the highly ritualised competitive gift-giving system endows the gold with authority and power (Mauss 1990: 1–7, 60–3; Enright 1996; Herschend 1998; Bazelmans 1999, 2000; Härke 2000b). Gold itself is personified in the name Gullveig, which means 'golden-drink, golden-intoxication' or 'golden-power'; altogether, it implies a 'personified greed for gold'.[13] Gold was a potent vehicle of cultural values and it could function as a medium of power, of art, and of exchange (Herbert 1984: 301–2). The amount of gold treasures from the fifth century AD confirms this general idea.

The 'Golden Age' of Scandinavia is the Migration Period. Immense quantities of gold were deposited in the fifth and sixth centuries, in the course of only a few generations.[14] The written sources, whether the Old Norse ones or texts from continental early medieval Europe, convey the impression that gift-giving was the crucial instrument in creating and upholding political alliances. Movable wealth items with strong symbolic connotations were the most prestigious gifts in this highly ritualised process (Bazelmans 1999, 2000; Le Jan 2000; Enright 1996; Herschend 1998). Much gold and silver, and many swords and other prestige goods, must have circulated as gifts without leaving any traces in the archaeological record (cf. Theuws and Alkemade 2000). However, if the strategy of gift-giving included an element of competitive display, it was more likely to play a central role in political strategies. In such cases we should expect to find evidence of the ritualised use of prestige goods in hoards and in graves (Barrett et al. 1991: 240).

According to the early written sources, gold treasures and their powerful enchantments were associated with members of the upper social stratum. However, treasure legends preserved in folklore from later periods feature people of a lower social standing. These later tales contain an element of ludicrousness never encountered in the Scandinavian legends from the Early Middle Ages and the Late Iron Age, where the value of the treasures is bound up with the notion of faith. Gold represented its owner's honour and riches, and as such it was equivalent to happiness. Stealing a treasure not only meant robbing someone of his riches, but also to steal his good fortune, and thus condemned him to a dismal fate. For this reason, those who managed to steal a treasure were struck by dire punishments (Zachrisson 1998).

To sum up, objects of gold were central to political strategies primarily because such treasures had been acquired by honourable and daring acts performed in far-away places. In the Late Iron Age and Early Middle Ages, items of gold represented the honour and respectability of their owner. To secure or maintain dominance in the social hierarchy of early medieval societies, gold had to be appropriated and controlled by the elite. By the added value of highly qualified artisans, however, gold was transformed into something that embodied additional values crucial to elite identities in the Nordic realm.

Places for acquisition and transformation

No matter the type of skilled craftsmanship – forging, jewellery, carving, weaving, pot-making, etc. – it represents a radical transformation of the materials of which the objects are composed. The value of the artisan's work is conditioned by this technical sophistication represented in the 'art of transformation'. This also included the added value of distance (Helms 1993). Crafting and long-distance trade must not be understood as purely economic transactions: they embodied qualities and values linked to distant origins within a larger cosmos (Helms 1993; Marrais et al. 1996; Gell 1998; Saunders 1999; Heide 2006).

Long-distance trade and exchange in the Roman and Migration Periods in Scandinavia has long been discussed from different perspectives, such as 'trade', 'economy', 'prestige-goods', 'gifts', 'war booty', 'payment' and so on. Initially, Roman tableware was manufactured in the empire and brought to the Nordic area either by long-distance traders or as ceremonial gifts in the context of inter-elite alliances. In the Migration Period, however, gold came into the barbarian world primarily as a military payment by the Romans. Here it was transformed into Germanic/Norse prestige objects essential for gift-giving. This reversal from Roman to Germanic prestige goods represents an essential shift in the relations Germanic societies entertained with the outside world.

It is highly unlikely that any prehistoric society ever saw activities and objects associated with distant origins in a neutral light. Elite graves from all over prehistoric Europe contain foreign objects as a significant part of their display; be they from the Hallstatt or La Téne periods (with Greek and Etruscan imports), from the Roman Period (imports from Greek and Italy), or from the Migration and Merovingian Period (with Byzantine and Frankish objects). Elite graves in Scandinavia followed these changing patterns. In late prehistoric Europe it meant that foreign objects were closely connected with social prestige. How are we to understand this?

Objects obtained from distant places have two things in common. First, whether crafted or uncrafted, they all had to pass the boundary between the unfamiliar world outside and the familiar 'inner' world of a given society. Furthermore, they represented unequal access to symbols of status and authority. Mary Helms, who has investigated how various traditional cultures interpret space and distance in cosmological terms, has argued that social and political power are associated with information about strange places, peoples and things (Helms 1988, 1993, 1998). In all non-Western native cosmologies, people and things coming from 'afar' are invested with a range of symbolic meanings, and with qualifications such as superiority, inferiority, or danger.[15]

In well-functioning societies, bad things are banished and good things are acquired from 'outside'. Helms (1993) argues that places 'out there' are represented by two axes: one situated horizontally (geographical distance), and the other vertically (cosmological distance). A morally informed and 'cultured' social group representing the centre is surrounded on all sides by a cosmological realm 'out there', which, as Helms expresses it, 'is believed to contain all manner of visible, invisible and exceptional qualities, "energies", beings, and resources, some harmful, some helpful to those at the centre' (ibid.: 7). When geographical and supernatural distance correspond to one another, horizontal movement, away from the social centre, is also a departure into an area that is seen as increasingly 'different', and therefore increasingly supernatural, mythical and powerful. Often objects acquired from geographically distant places carry associations with ancestors and cultural heroes (Helms 1988).

The point of Helms' argument is that objects acquired from the world beyond the confines of a traditional society are considered to be powerful, and potentially beneficial either to society at large or to its leaders. In order to comprehend how a Roman vessel – or a cowry shell – may become a more powerful object than a locally manufactured iron buckle, we have to regard power not merely as a function exercised by people but also as an entity or quality that may be acquired or accumulated, and as an existential reality that may be connected to wealth or weapons and also to other objects. In this sense, power is a spiritual energy enabling an individual to interact with the forces of the natural and supernatural world. Objects obtained from 'outside' tend to channel and concentrate such energy, and the individual in possession of such goods will become associated with the power with which these objects are infused (Carmichael 1994; Herbert 1993: 1–5).

The fundamental quality attributed to such 'prestige goods' or 'luxury goods' is that they encapsulate the forces of a dangerous universe. Helms sees similarities between travellers, who communicate with the dangerous but potentially powerful outside world, and religious practitioners – shamans, priests and diviners – because the latter also explore and control a realm outside human society. She includes artisans in this category, for high-level crafting is an act of creation that involves some kind of communication with the outside world; craftsmen, as already argued, tend to be liminal figures credited with supernatural powers. This must have been particularly true if they crafted sacred objects. Both the skilled metalworker and the skilled trader act as intermediaries between society and a domain characterised by 'intangible energies that must be tapped and transformed via the artisan's various skills into cultural formats that encode qualities identified with whatever is thought to constitute true humanness' (Helms 1993: 15). Likewise, the organisation of expeditions and expertise in shipbuilding and navigation also represent the ability to mediate successfully between one's own society and the outside world. For obvious practical reasons, the final stages of shipbuilding often take place on the beach; but the beach is also a liminal zone, separating land and sea, the gateway to a dangerous world full of desirable objects (ibid.: 21).

The argument developed by Helms is of course a matter for further debate; however, it offers a new paradigm for understanding the cosmology of acquisition and transformation in traditional societies, and therefore it might be helpful for understanding Old Norse society. For the Nordic realm before AD 800 there is no textual evidence of any specific locations of religious or political power, such as monasteries or other sacred sites, cities, or royal palaces, where production, exchange and ritual display might have been located. Archaeological sources and toponymic (place name) evidence provide the only basis for analysing the concept of super-ordinate centres. Still, Old Norse literature does throw some light on the essential components of places of superior quality in the Scandinavian world view.

For example, the hall assumed great importance in the ideological universe of the texts (Herschend 1997a, b, 1998, 1999; Enright 1996). It is therefore remarkable that the word 'hall' hardly ever occurs in Scandinavian place names. The reason may be that the Scandinavian language of the time used another word, that of *sal*, as in Old Upp*sala*, On*sala*, Oden*sala* or just *Sal*: the god whose name is compounded with *sal* is always Odin, king of the gods (Brink 1996). The word *sal* is often linked with *zulr'* (*thyle*), that is, the term for a particular type of leader or priest. The *thyle* is regarded as a poet, that is, a skald or storyteller; in other words, the person who preserves the treasure hoards of mystical and magical knowledge that was essential to understand the Eddic poems. He was the cult leader who understood the cult activities and uttered the proper magical words. His main function was to speak, whether this was to recite verses and sacred stories, to declare the laws, or to function as the spokesman for a king or earl during a feast, a cult festival or a legal moot (ibid.: 256–7). The *thyle* was one of the specialists who controlled society's esoteric knowledge on the king's behalf.

Apparently *sal* means the king's and earls' assembly hall, cult hall, or moot hall: the place in which the functions of 'theatre, court, and church' were united (Herschend 1998). The *sal* or the hall was the centre of the human micro-cosmos, the symbol of stability and good leadership. The hall was also the location where communal drinking took place, which had the purpose of creating bonds of loyalty and fictive kinship; alcohol was the medium through which one achieved ecstasy, and thus communion with the supernatural (Enright 1996: 17). The high seat, that is the seat with the high-seat posts, served as the channel of communication with the supernatural world. Since the hall with the high seat served as the geographical and ideological centre of leadership, it is understandable that, as the literature tells us, earls and kings could oppress and ruin each other by simply destroying their opponent's hall (Herschend 1995, 1997a, b).

The multifunctional role of the hall thus extended beyond the site itself. The hall was at the centre of a group of principal farmsteads; it was the heart of the central places from the later part of the Iron Age,[16] which existed all over Scandinavia, as is now increasingly recognised. Among these are: Gudme/Lundeborg on Funen; Sorte Muld on Bornholm; Lejre, Boeslunde, Jørlunde, Kalmargård, Tissø on Zealand; Nørre Snede, Stentinget, Drengsted and Ribe in Jutland; Trondheim, Borre, Kaupang and Hamar in Norway; Slöinge, Helgö, Birka, Uppåkra, Vä, Old Uppsala, Högum, Vendel and Valsgärde in Sweden (e.g. Jørgensen 1995b; Andrén 1999; Larsson and Hårdh 1998; Larsson 2004, 2007; Myhre 2003a, b; Zachrisson 2004a, 2004b; Sundqvist 2004; Skre 2007b, c, 2008a, b). Characteristically, many of these sites are located a few kilometres inland, relying on one or more landing places or ports situated on the coast (Fabech 1999). Although this is still a matter of debate, such central places undoubtedly served as a basis for some form of political or religious control exercised over a larger area; the radius of their influence went well beyond the site itself.

In his innovative analysis of the toponymic evidence, Stefan Brink (1996)[17] argued that, rather than being a precisely defined site, such central places should be understood as a somewhat larger area encompassing a number of different but equally important functions and activities. Both toponymic evidence and archaeological finds suggest that this was a recurring pattern. It means that it is inadequate to refer to these sites as 'trading sites', 'cult sites', or 'meeting or thing places', emphasising only one of their many functions. Instead, such locations should be perceived as multifunctional and composite sites. In addition to their 'official' function as trading and market sites, and as centres where laws were executed and cults were established, these central places were probably also associated with special functions such as the skilled crafting of jewellery, weapons and clothing. They were also the residence of particularly privileged warriors or 'house-carls'. While archaeological research has revealed a range of such activities, the picture becomes clearer when the place names are brought into play. Names around Gudme and other such places demonstrate the presence of a pagan priesthood, of military units and warriors, of the most prominent smiths, and so on. Some of these central places, such as Gudme/Lundeborg, originated in the Late Roman Period (AD 200–400), but the majority only emerged after AD 400. In fact, it looks as if most of these multifunctional sites did not post-date the seventh century, although some remained centres of power and of economic activity well into the Middle Ages.

Central places as 'centres of the universe'

A central place with sacred functions represents the whole universe in symbolic form; it is deliberately constructed as the 'centre of the universe', be it a Christian cathedral or a pagan cult site organised around a sacred pool, a world tree or the like, as Mircea Eliade has made clear in several publications (1961, 1997).[18] Byzantine churches, it has been argued, embodied all the features of the Christian universe. According to Eliade, citing historians of church architecture, the four parts of the interior of the church symbolise the four cardinal directions. The interior of the church is the universe. The altar is Paradise, which lay in the east. The imperial door to the altar was also called the Door of Paradise. During Easter week, the great door to the altar remains open during the entire service; the meaning of this custom is clearly expressed in the Easter Canon: 'Christ rose from the grave and opened the doors of Paradise unto us.' The west, to the contrary, is the realm of darkness, of grief, of death, the realm of the eternal mansions of the dead, who await resurrection of the flesh at the last judgement. The middle of the building is the earth. As Eliade argues, the earth is rectangular and is bounded by four walls, which are surmounted by a dome. The wider topography around the church was similarly organised to reflect Christian cosmology (Rosenwein 1989: 203; Jong 2001).

In Lund, the seat of the Danish archbishop in Scania from the twelfth century onwards, the whole Christian world was deliberately replicated in the city. The topography of the churches built after Lund became an archbishopric in AD 1104 mirrored the supposed location of important saints' graves in the Christian world. The cathedral was situated in the centre of the city (like Jerusalem in the Christian world). To the east, churches were built that were dedicated to patron saints from Asia; in the western part of the city the patron saints were European ones; in the northern part of the city the main patron saint was St Olav, buried in Trondheim, in the far north of the Christian world. Thus, Lund was constructed as a sacred city, a microcosm of the Christian world (Andrén 1998a, 1998b, 1999).

A Christian topography apparently emerged all over the Christian world. Pilgrimage in Late Antiquity and the Early Middle Ages integrated the Holy Land and its sacred sites into a new Christian landscape. In this landscape the 'places of the saints' (*loci sanctorum*) were the real landmarks, because they established a connection with the heroic history of the Church (Jong 2001).

Christianity established itself in a Roman world full of sacred places and sacred spaces, and had to 'compete' by creating its own sacred topography (cf. Markus 1990; Jong 2001). In early medieval Scandinavia, Christianity was gradually incorporated into the cosmology of a Norse religious world, after centuries of contact and mutual influence prior to the beginnings of a formal conversion around the year AD 1000. Anders Andrén has argued that, as part of this process, the whole landscape, including the parishes with their churches and manor houses, became organised according to Christian principles of topography (Andrén 1998b, 1999). These principles serve as a useful guide to our question: how could a sacred place be organised to repeat the paradigmatic work of the Norse god(s)?

The creation of sacred places in pre-Christian Scandinavia must have been embedded in Norse cosmology, of which, however, very little is known. In a society without any form of central public power, a precarious peace had to be constantly negotiated. Here the most important institutions were the home, the hall and the *thing*, where social and legal negotiations took place. According to the sagas, these institutions were the sacred foundations of society, the focal points in the topographical structure of the Icelandic universe in the Early Middle Ages. The most common locations for combat and open attack were outside the precinct of the farms (*utangards*): in woods, near rivers and in areas bordering on the wild interior, that is, the 'outside' dangerous world. An attack on the hall or the home, or to take up arms at the *thing*, counted as the worst possible outrages in Icelandic society. The world depicted in the sagas practised a distinction between the sacred and the profane (Olason 2000: 131–5). Land and settlement were organised in accordance with a clear perception of 'centres of the universe', in the form of the hall. This is supported by Frands Herschend's study of archaeological and textual evidence for the hall in Late Iron Age Scandinavia, including *Beowulf* and *The Fight at Finnsburg* (1997a, b, 1998). Here kingly power could not be exercised without a hall, however temporary such a structure may have been. Therefore, the struggle for power among the leading families revolved around destroying each other's halls – the backbone of their power. It was political rather than economic warfare, with destruction as its main purpose (Herschend 1998: 37).

To sum up, landscapes and settlements of the Early Middle Ages and the Late Iron Age, be they archbishoprics, churches or manor houses/halls, were organised according to a specific cosmological structure. This fits the general explanation of 'sacred places' and 'sacred spaces' offered by Eliade. A sacred space was constructed as the 'centre of the universe', sharply differentiated from the profane world surrounding it (Eliade 1997: 379–80). For that reason it is relevant to explore the Old Norse centre par excellence: the home of the gods.

Asgard: home of the gods

It is far from clear what the pre-Christian universe in Scandinavia looked like, but there are some common features attested in *The Poetic Edda* as well as in Snorri's *Edda* that are worth exploring. At the heart of the Norse literature and its view of the world is the World Tree, Yggdrasil; it is an evergreen ash whose roots reach out to the ends of the inhabited universe (Andrén 2004). Mankind lived under one root, the giants under another, and Hel, the realm of the dead, is located under the third. Beneath Yggdrasil, according to *Vǫluspá* (19) lies Urd's well, where the gods would meet and hold council before Ragnarok (*Grimnismal* 29, 30); according to Snorri (*Gylfaginning* 14), this is the location for Mimir's well, which holds all wisdom and understanding in the world.[19]

Nine worlds are mentioned more than once, but never clearly specified. The Asir gods lived in Asgard, the Vanir in Vanheim, and mankind inhabited Midgard. Beyond the human world lies Utgard, home of the giants and demons; in the east, separated by rivers, lies Jotunheim, the world of the giants. In the north, and beneath Midgard, is Hel, the residence of those who died on land of illness or of old age. While Alfheim is the world of the elves, earth is that of the dwarves. There are two further worlds, one possibly inhabited by the dead heroes in Valhall and the other by the most powerful gods, called 'the Holy and Mighty Ones' in *Alvíssmál* in *The Poetic Edda*. It is not clear, however, whether all these various worlds were oriented towards the World Tree, and it has proven impossible to come up with a convincing blue-print of Scandinavian views of the 'other world' (Davidson 1993:

69). Furthermore, the two 'axes' of the cosmic world – one horizontal, and one vertical – are a matter of debate (Schjødt 1990).

In Old Norse texts the representation of Asgard, home of the gods, produces many problems of interpretation. Snorri is the one who frequently mentions Asgard and gives the most detailed description in *Gylfaginning* in his *Edda*, and in *Ynglinga Saga*.[20] In addition to being part of a didactic work about the art of skaldic poetry, the *Gylfaginning* is also a systematic presentation of pre-Christian mythology, as argued above. In the following I shall briefly describe this cosmic world of the north.

Although Yggdrasil is the undisputed centre of the universe, Asgard figures as the home of the gods and the residence of the Asir. A giant built Asgard on Idavoll. The gods had a temple, Gladsheim, and a separate hall for the female Asir, called Vingolf. Gladsheim, the 'bright home' was Odin's residence,[21] and maybe also the location of Hlidskjalf (his high seat – a throne or a chair – from whence he overlooked the whole world[22]); furthermore it contained Valhall, where Odin gathered the warriors slain in battle. In *Gylfaginning* (13) Snorri says Gladsheim was the temple of Odin and twelve other gods; inside and outside, it was made of gold, and it was the best and greatest building in the world. Another crucial element of Idavoll was the forge. In the beginning, hammers, anvils and tongs were created. From then onwards, the gods themselves were able to produce all the implements they needed. They forged iron ore, made woodcarvings and had sufficient gold to make their houses, and even their furniture, out of precious metal. As mentioned above, this age is called the Golden Age, the happy first age of the world, before the arrival of women from the dangerous outside world of Utgard, which meant that the gods lost their skills as artisans, and their control over precious metals.

When they first settled on Idavoll, where a giant constructed Asgard, the gods founded the world of the Asir. The skilled and powerful carpenter who created Asgard belonged to the world outside. Judging by its impressive hall, Asgard was also the centre of ideals of kingship. From his high seat, the link between Earth and Heaven, Odin, that is, the hall-owner, was in contact with the Other World through his helping spirits, the two ravens Hugin (Thought) and Munin (Mind/Memory). Asgard was also a place where skilled crafting took place, particularly metal work; at first the gods had unlimited time for it, and also boundless access to gold. In addition to this, Valhall is the place for Odin's *hird* (armed followers) of human heroes. A roof of spears and shields covers the hall, and armour is piled on its benches.[23]

According to Old Norse tradition, Asgard lost its paradise-like status after the war that ended its Golden Age. From then on, the Asir lost control of the highly skilled crafting that had been their monopoly; they also lost direct access to all precious metals, including iron, copper, silver and gold. As a remedy, the myths explain, the gods created the dwarves, who were now to become the skilled artisans in charge of iron and precious metals. The Golden Age became what it is throughout human history: a paradise lost, and the object of intense nostalgia. Asgard's original splendour was eclipsed forever; the Asir themselves had become dependent on dwarves for gold, skilled crafting and magical treasures. Although its status declined, Asgard still remained the central part of the universe according to northern mythology.

The phenomenology of religion clearly attests that no sacred site has ever been organised as a 'neutral' construction, according to random or shifting criteria. It is embedded in the cosmological world of society. It may therefore be suggested that Asgard constituted the conceptual framework for Scandinavian central places – places for production, exchange and ritual performance.[24] This hypothesis can be tested archaeologically.

A 'central place' par excellence: Gudme on Funen

Gudme on the Danish island of Funen fits the general model of a 'central place' as defined above, but in some ways it even superseded it (Figure 6.1). First, Gudme is among the earliest of these places, and may even be *the* earliest, for it had already gained its central position during the Late Roman Period. Second, Gudme is bigger and the settlement area more extensive than that of any of the other central places hitherto found in south Scandinavia (Jørgensen 1994); its great hall, situated in the centre, is unique because of its size and its construction. Third, the sheer amount of archaeological finds from the area is overwhelming; this applies especially to the number of gold finds and superb jewellery produced by skilled craftsmen. Fourth, the evidence of place names connected with the sacred is more persuasive in the vicinity of Gudme than anywhere else. We have to consider the possibility that Gudme may have occupied a unique place in the cosmology of the Nordic realm

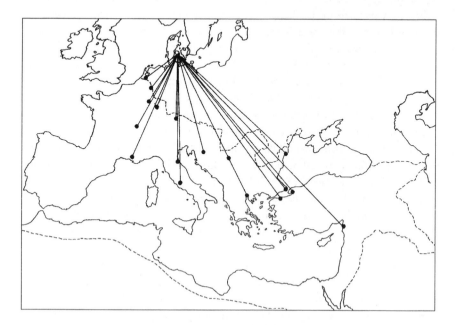

FIGURE 6.1   Map showing the Gudme area and the production places for coins, glass, bronzes and *terra sigillata* found in the Gudme/Lundeborg area. Modified after drawing by Poul Erik Skovgaard in Thomsen et al. (1993: 96).

in the middle of the Iron Age.[25] Because of its size and the nature of its finds, studying Gudme/Lundeborg can give us more insight in the characteristics of a 'central place', and also provide a model of comparison that is helpful to the interpretation of other sites in Scandinavia.

Gudme is made up of a complex of sites in an area on the east coast of the Danish island Funen (Thrane 1987). Apart from the locality of Gudme itself, which is the inland settlement area, to the west there is also Lundeborg, a trading port situated on the coast of the Great Belt (between Funen and Zealand), and to the north the extensive cemetery of Møllegårdsmarken (Figure 6.2).[26]

The settlement of Gudme (Nielsen et al. 1994) is located approximately 4km inland. While the surrounding area was inhabited from *c.* 100 BC until the Early Middle Ages, this particular settlement, of which about 500,000m^2 has been documented, existed from *c.* AD 200 to *c.* 600 (Jørgensen 1995a: 215 and figure 14). A

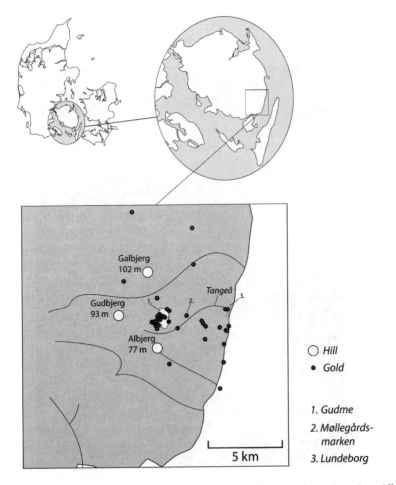

FIGURE 6.2   The research area of Gudme. Data: Mogens Bo Henriksen. Drawing: Allan Larsen. Used with permission.

range of small excavations in the central area revealed a settlement organised in fenced farmsteads. These are similar to other farmsteads in Denmark from the Late Roman and Migration Periods. The number of contemporary farms is unknown, but judging by the estimated size of the settled area there must have been at least 50 farms *c.* AD 400, the peak of activity of the settlement. Besides common farmsteads, three exceptional houses have been excavated (Sørensen 1994b). The largest building – a hall[27] – was nearly 50m long and 10m wide, with eight sets of posts, each with a diameter of more than 80cm, to support the huge roof construction. The size of these posts may indeed indicate a second floor or a construction similar to the Norwegian stave-churches (Gansum 2008), as recently proposed for the cult-building in Uppåkra (Larsson 2007) (Figure 6.3).[28] Two wide doorways in the centre of the building led into a particularly large room. According to the excavator, the house was a log-construction (cogging). Two smaller houses nearby were constructed in the same manner. They had a length of approximately 25m, and a width of nearly 10m. Compared to the normal farmsteads with a maximum length of 35m and a standard width of 6–7m, the size of the hall (and the width of the smaller houses too) is unparalleled in

FIGURE 6.3   The big hall under excavation. The postholes are marked. Gudme, Funen.
© Nationalmuseet, Copenhagen.

Denmark before the Viking Age. In fact, nothing like it is known in Denmark before the Viking Age. Surprisingly, the hall-houses represent a building tradition and a technical knowledge with no background in local traditions.

At Gudme itself, and scattered across the whole area, numerous hoards, treasures and single finds of precious metals, especially gold, have been found. Roman coins (gold, silver and copper) (Kromann 1994) were present in amazing numbers, either as hoards or as stray finds. Hoards containing scrap silver (amongst others Byzantine tablewares cut into pieces), scrap bronze such as part of a Byzantine statue, and even scrap gold, all point to extensive forging and casting activity. This impression is supported by finds of drops of melted gold, silver, bronze and glass as well as hammer scales of iron slag and small strips of gold foil. Among the finds from the plough soil were a Frankish silver bird fibula and some gilded fragments of a Roman bronze helmet. Other hoards or treasures contained golden jewellery, necklaces, bracteates, etc., mostly of local Scandinavian origin, but also some of Byzantine provenance. In their studies of the gold bracteates, Morten Axboe and Karl Hauck have drawn attention to the fact that the Gudme area played an important part in the development of gold bracteates and their iconography, although it cannot have been the only place in Scandinavia with such a role (Axboe 1994; Hauck 1987, 1994). In addition, the largest[29] Danish gold hoard from the Migration Period was recovered in the same area: the hoard from the nearby manor of Broholm with more than 4kg of golden arm-rings, necklaces, bracteates and the like (Figure 6.4). Besides the

FIGURE 6.4   The gold-hoard from Broholm, Funen. After Jensen (2004: 57).

jewellery, neck-rings, arm-rings, finger-rings, bracteates, fibulae with inlayed gar-
nets, etc., the local hoards contain scabbard mouths, some with marvellous filigree
work (Figure 6.5), some shaped as a gold spiral (Figure 6.6), as well as intertwined
pairs of rings for pommels of the so-called ring swords (Figures 6.7 and 6.8) which
have been interpreted as the customary *insignia* for members of the royal Frankish *hird* (retinue of warriors) (Steuer 1987, 1989; Jørgensen 1995a). Although the
settlement has not yet been fully excavated,[30] the results are already impressive: a
huge settled area with a monumental building at its heart – a hall measuring around
500m², like the royal palace in Copenhagen today – and with an overwhelming
amount of metal finds, scrap metal as well as masterpieces, in and around the central
settlement area.

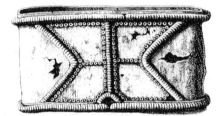

FIGURE 6.5 Gold scabbard mouth from the Gudme area with two opposing animals
forming a human mask. After Sehested (1878).

FIGURE 6.6 Gold hoard from Lillesø. Gudme, Funen. © Nationalmuseet, Copenhagen.

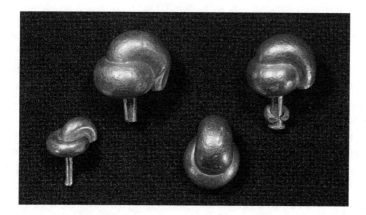

FIGURE 6.7   Ring knobs of solid gold from sword hilts. Gudme, Funen. © Nationalmuseet, Copenhagen.

FIGURE 6.8   Group of warriors carrying swords with ring knobs on the hilts (cf. Figure 4.22, the warrior to the left). Drawing by O. Sörling (Stolpe and Arne 1927: pl. XLII).

The coastal site of Lundeborg

Lundeborg is situated on the west coast of Funen, on both sides of the mouth of Tange Å, a small stream connecting Lundeborg and the Great Belt with its hinterland around Gudme (Thomsen et al. 1993; Thomsen 1994) (see Figure 6.2). The Iron Age finds recovered here were distributed over an area of some 900m along the coast and 30–75m inland. From the third century AD (Late Roman Period) until AD 700/800 (early Viking Age), different kinds of activities were going on at this coastal site. However, only one-tenth of the estimated settlement area has been excavated; the objects found are mostly from the third and fourth centuries and thus it is unclear what the place looked like in the Migration Period. The objects found at Lundeborg stem from both trading activities and crafts. The commodities are mainly Roman glass beads, glass vessels and *terra sigillata*. Germanic brooches, arrowheads and metal fittings for swords and scabbards have been found as well.

A remarkable feature of Lundeborg is the evidence of extensive craft activities. Tools from all the Iron Age crafts are represented: those of carpenters, bronze-, silver- and gold-smiths, blacksmiths as well as craftsmen working with amber, bone and antler. Small weights, silver *denarii* and gold pieces have also been found. Iron ingots seem to have been imported from Poland. More than 8000 unused and broken iron rivets from ships have been found. No doubt a wharf with extensive facilities for shipbuilding and repairs must have been located on the coast for the whole period.

So far no traces of proper houses have been recovered. There are traces of small structures (approximately 4m x 5m), interpreted as huts for seasonal use, and dating to the early phase, that is, the third and fourth centuries. According to the excavator, the many activities at Lundeborg were probably limited to specific periods during the year (Thomsen 1994).

The cemetery of Møllegårdsmarken

Møllegårdsmarken (Albrectsen 1971; Christoffersen 1987) is the huge cemetery situated between Lundeborg and Gudme close to the stream Tange Å (see Figure 6.2). About 2300 graves have been excavated and ploughing has destroyed many more. The graves are primarily cremation graves, with many urn graves among them; these have been dated from the first century BC up to the early fifth century AD. There are no traces of later burials; the same holds true for all the other known cemeteries in the Gudme region. Thus far, this picture corresponds with burial practices from all over Denmark: there is a hiatus from the fifth to the eighth century (early Viking Age) (Hedeager 1992a). Still, cremations at the cemetery may have continued during the fifth and sixth centuries. Møllegårdsmarken is unique in many respects, mostly because of the number of graves and the amount of Roman objects, but also in view of the cremation graves that predominate. These are often richly furnished; however, they never contain weapons.

Recent excavations at Møllegårdsmarken have produced new evidence concerning the organisation of the cemetery. They revealed what are possibly small houses for ritual purposes and tracks running through the area (Madsen and Thrane 1995). Although Møllegårdsmarken ceased to be used, the extensive cemetery located at the brink of Tange Å, halfway between Gudme and Lundeborg, must have been well known and visible in the Migration Period landscape. The prevailing impression of Gudme–Lundegård–Møllegårdsmarken is that of an important area in which the specialised production of luxury goods took place, aimed at the rituals of life and death typical of Germanic gift-giving societies (Enright 1996; Hardt 1998; Bazelmans 2000).

Gudme's sacred features

Apart from being an important archaeological site, the Gudme area also contains a significant number of place names with allusions to pre-Christian religion. Many of these place names are 'holy', and on the basis of such toponymic evidence, the conclusion can be drawn that the area also had religious significance. Gudme itself means 'the home of the gods', that is, the place where the ancient god/gods were thought to live (Kousgård Sørensen 1985). At a distance of 1.5 to 2.5km to the north, west and south of Gudme, there are three hills with sacral names: Gudbjerg to the west means 'the hill of the god/gods', Albjerg to the south means 'the hill of the shrine' and Galbjerg to the north has a less clear meaning, but may be interpreted as 'the hill of sacrifice' (Kousgård Sørensen 1985), although an explanation of the word *gal* as *galdr* may be more plausible (Figure 6.2). *Galdur* should rather be translated as 'magic'; the word *galdr* in Old Icelandic refers to sorcerers' songs in the sense of a 'charm' or 'spell'. *Galdur* was an important element in Icelandic witchcraft, which was practised as late as the seventeenth century; it indicates that in Iceland, the spoken word was the most important instrument of supernatural power (Hastrup 1990: 387). In Nordic mythology Odin himself was, as we know, the great sorcerer in control of *seið*, the technique of the soul journey, and the one who also mastered oral magic, *galdra* (i.e. Strömbäk 1935; Eliade 1984: 160; Hedeager 1997a, b; Price 2002; Solli 2002). This is yet another reference to chants and spells being central to witchcraft; *galdr* also testifies to the power embedded in metric forms (Hastrup 1990: 388–9). All this indicates that Galbjerg means 'the hill of *galdring*', that is, the hill of magic. It is of course impossible to date these place names with any precision, but according to philologists, the Gudhem names stem from the Migration and Merovingian Periods. This is consistent with the archaeological record (Thrane 1987: 40).

Gudme's great wealth in combination with sacred place names suggests that the site was not just a central place for 'commercial' trade and production but one with sacred connotations: a place where master artisans transformed bars, ingots, and coins of gold into symbolic objects such as bracteates and ornamented scabbard mounts. It is also a place that housed important rituals and sacrifices. Against this background, Karl Hauck has argued that the iconography of the gold bracteates points to the establishment of an Odin cult in Gudme, connected with sacred kingship (Hauck 1987, 1994). A recurring motif of a probable shape shift/soul journey should illustrate Odin's journey to the Other World (see Part III, Figure 4.20). This motif is the most common on bracteates, but other central motifs from Old Norse mythology are found as well (Ellmers 1970: 202, 210, 220; Hauck 1978: 210, 1994; Oxenstierna 1956: 36)[31] (see Figures 9.9–9.11). Initially the Scandinavian gold bracteates imitated the Byzantine emperor's medallions, symbolically connecting Roman Emperors and Asir kings.

If Gudme was indeed the main home of the Odin cult as suggested, the central area framed by the sacred hills would have been a place of ritual display and communication. I shall therefore pursue the parallels between Gudme and Asgard in order to see how well myth and reality correspond.

Gudme: the paradigmatic model of Asgard?

It is suggested that Gudme was the main centre of the Odin cult during the fifth and sixth centuries AD. Three sacred hills – the hill of the god/gods, the hill of the shrine, and what has been interpreted as the hill of magic (*galdring*) – framed the central locality, a place that – like Christian churches – served as an entry to the sacred. Following Eliade, the construction of Gudme as a sacred place reiterated the creation of the world.

In the Christian world of the Middle Ages, Palestine, Jerusalem and the Temple represented the centre of the world: the rock on which the temple of Jerusalem was built was the navel of the earth.[32] If Asgard was perceived as the religious centre of the Norse world/of the Odin cult, a possible context for Gudme begins to emerge. Something resembling the centre of Asgard-Gladsheim, according to Snorri 'the best and greatest building in the world' and the hall of Odin may have been in the minds of those who built the central hall of Gudme. With its 500m² it is the largest building known from Denmark before the Viking Age, constructed with a measure of technical knowledge without any precedent in local tradition. Together with two smaller houses, the hall represents a complex and extremely accomplished building that was most likely created by skilled craftsmen who were outsiders – as was the mythological Gladsheim. Gladsheim's centre was Odin's high seat, from which he surveyed the entire world. In Gudme, the high seat in the hall must have been a similar centre, which connected divine and kingly power – eventually supported by the power base represented by the two stores. From this elevated place, the king had a privileged view of the supernatural world, and access – like Odin – to the secret knowledge essential to his authority.[33] Especially in its dual role as *hof*, Terry Gunnell has argued that the hall potentially might be seen as a microcosm in which the performance of 'a first-person work' such as *Grímnismál* or part of *Hávamál* by someone such as a *goði* might have underlined the close connection between the king in the high seat and the gods (Gunnell 1995, 2006: 239). Other poems seem to be intended for outdoor performance and they might have involved an element of role play (Gunnell 1995, 2006). The *ljóðaháttr*, those of the layers who are dealing with the world of the gods and archetypical heroes, have a strong dramatic quality in performance that demanded some form of acted character presentation in voice and/or action. In short, the form forced the performer to take on the role(s) of the characters, the gods and their followers, who were 'brought to life' in front of the audience (Gunnell 2008). It seems therefore likely that the skalds, which performed in those mythological dramas as gods and heroes, had to wear ritual dresses and specific objects, and that they might have been masked, too; the gold foils are the apparent candidates as images of those figures. They are found in number at most 'central places' and Gudme is no exception. In total 102 gold-foil figures – all of embracing couples[34] (some obviously of the same sex) have been excavated within a limited area exactly where Tange Å meets the Great Belt (Figure 7.1). The archaeological evidence from the construction of the hall to its rituals conforms to the mythological Gladsheim.

The hall in Gudme is situated in a location held by archaeologists to be the 'workshop area' because of the many finds of workshop material, especially from metalwork (Jørgensen 1995a). In a traditional archaeological view such 'workshop areas' and 'workshop production' are treated as marginal to social and political life, but this interpretation is too narrow. Skilled crafting, especially forging and the work of jewellers – and probably woodcarving as well – were the hallmark of political and ideological authority in traditional societies. In the process, ideals of cosmic order were re-created and re-expressed in a tangible form (Eliade 1978; Helms 1993: 180). For this very reason, Old Norse mythology situated the workshop area close to the hall. Highly skilled metalwork was not merely a craft, it was an integral part of political and religious power, and something closely linked to ideals of kingly authority. Again, the archaeological evidence corresponds to the mythology.

The excavations in Gudme have shown that the big hall and the workshop area were located in the central and southern part of the settlement; the dwellings of the high-ranking warriors, however, were situated to the north of this area (Jørgensen 1995a: 212). In Old Norse mythology Odin's *hird* of (dead) human heroes lived in a separate hall, Valhall, situated in that part of Asgard which is close to Gladsheim. Although this is highly speculative, Valhall may be located to the north, for this was where Norse mythology situated the realm of the dead.[35] The high-ranking warriors living in Gudme may have been dedicated to Odin, as high-ranking warriors from the Viking Age are known to have been.

Continuing our exercise of testing the correspondences between Asgard and Gudme, the next element to be accounted for is the lake in the western part of the central settlement, and some springs connecting Gudme Lake with Gudbjerg to the west and Galbjerg to the north. Careful investigation has yielded no indication that the lake was used for sacrificial purposes. In Old Norse mythology, the springs reflected the significance of the mythical springs tapped by Urd's well (the 'well of fate') and Mimir's well (the 'spring of wisdom'), rising from below the roots of Yggdrasil, and may as such belong to the centre of the cosmic world. This is the place where the gods hold council, and Mimir's well is known as the source of Odin achieving his wisdom.

There are other streams in the Gudme area. Tange Å rises near the sacred hill of Albjerg, to the south of the central settlement area. It passes Møllegårdsmarken cemetery on its way to the coast at Lundeborg. This great cemetery was associated with the cosmological realm of the dead, the world of Hel, where those who died on land, of natural causes, were buried. Snorri situated it somewhere in the north, separated from Midgard by rivers, so one needed to cross a bridge in order to get there.[36] In his *Edda*, Snorri identifies Niflheim with Hel,[37] a mythical place in the icy north. Møllegårdsmarken is located between the centre of the world (Gudme) on the one hand, and the outside realm, where Utgard is to be found, on the other. In that it corresponds to the location of Hel.

Lundeborg on the coast, the transitional zone between civilisation and a threatening 'world out there' of giants, demons and chaos, was the place where long-distance travellers entered inner space, the domain of the familiar. It was the transformative, liminal zone between land and sea where prestige goods from 'beyond' entered society as well as a place where specific kinds of skilled crafting took place, such as extensive repairs to ships (Thomsen et al. 1993: 73).

Organising expeditions and mastering shipbuilding and navigation are all prerequi-
sites for skilled long-distance travelling, and therefore part of the process of bringing
resources of ultimate cosmological qualities into society (Helms 1993: 21).

To enter Gudme from the coast, from Utgard, may therefore have entailed a
process of initiation. Gudme, as a sacred place of the gods, must have been anx-
iously guarded against unwanted incursions. A sacred place such as Gudme was
both accessible and inaccessible, a place of great repute, that was also forbidden to
the uninitiated, and for this very reason a powerful model to emulate; this is a characteristic that Gudme shares with many other sacred places, both past and present.
The entrance to this secluded zone may have been the stream Tange Å, passing
through the realm of the dead on the northern bank and with its source close to the
sacred 'mountain' Albjerg, 'the hill of the shrine', south of Gudme's central area.

Entering Gudme was a passage through the entire cosmic landscape that ranged
between Utgard and Asgard, the outside and the inside. Put differently, those who
arrived in Lundeborg, after a long and arduous voyage across the sea, were then
taken, by gradual stages, to the impressive hall at Gudme, the home of gods and
kings.

The archaeological, topographic and toponymic evidence at Gudme conform
to the description of Asgard. We may therefore conclude that it was modelled
on the sacred topography of Asgard. In addition, the enormous amount of gold
found in Gudme's centre as well as in its surroundings suggests that those who
built this complex central place perceived it as a sacred place. According to Old
Norse mythology, gold and silver deposited in the 'Underworld' were not meant
to remain out of sight forever; these were divine treasures, furnishing jewellers
with the necessary gold for their artisan work. In Gudme, something similar may
have applied: treasures were deposited, that is, put underground in the realm of the
dwarves; however, they may still have been 'visible', at least to the initiated. They
could equally well be meant for the use of jewellers, themselves symbolic representations of the skilled dwarves, transforming gold into sacred objects.

Cosmological emulation

By focusing on Gudme as a symbolically constructed place that represented cosmological order, I have expanded its interpretation beyond traditional references
to 'trade', 'power', 'richness' and so on. In this it also corresponds nicely to Mary
Helms' model of skilled crafting (Helms 1993). If we follow Helms, Gudme can
be understood as a central place where Roman tablewares and Byzantine gold
were acquired, transformed and brought into the realm of the Norse sacred world.
Lundeborg, a site of shipbuilding and other kinds of skilled crafting, served as the
liminal zone between inland Gudme and the other world across the sea.

In addition, the archaeological evidence of Gudme as a cosmological replica of
Asgard confirms that Norse mythology relating to Asgard as the home of the gods
originated in the Iron Age. In some respects Gudme is an extraordinary place; in
others it shares many features with other places in Scandinavia that have also been

called 'central places' or 'places of extraordinary power'. Gudme may in fact be the key to a better understanding of comparable sites, for this archetypal sacred place, embodying the 'nostalgia for *Asgard*', is likely to have served as a model for emulation throughout Scandinavia, albeit with more humble results. All these different versions of sites inspired by Gudme fall into the category of what archaeologists today call 'central places' (e.g. Larsson and Hårdh 1998). These sites can be regarded as paradigmatic models of the cosmic world, deriving their structure and organisation from archetypal sacred places (Eliade 1997: 382–5) such as Gudme on Funen, and probably also from contemporary important sites such as Helgö in the Mälar area (Lundström 1968: 278–90; Zachrisson 2004a, b), and Uppåkra in Scania (Larsson and Hårdh 1998; Larsson 2004, 2007). These are archaeologically well-defined settlement areas, which I have classified as 'multifunctional and composite central places' because they combine the function of 'trading sites', 'cult-sites' and 'production places', and possess a hall (or *sal*), gold finds, etc. within a constricted area (Jørgensen 1995b). The puzzle of such complex central places in the Late Iron Age of south Scandinavia can be solved by comparison with the cathedrals and monasteries of the Middle Ages. All were places of power, created to be paradigmatic models of the universe, be it pagan or Christian ones.

7

THE COSMIC ORDER OF LANDSCAPES

Hoards as ritual and economic agents[1]

The 'Golden Age' of Scandinavia is − strictly speaking − the Migration Period. Immense numbers of gold objects were deposited over a few generations in the fifth and early sixth centuries AD. They comprise highly artistic rings (neck- and arm-rings), adornments for weapons, dress accessories, bracteates, so-called payment rings, etc. These gold hoards fascinate and challenge archaeologists and historians of religion because they signal 'wealth' and 'power'. From the point of view of profit and economic strength, it is easy to understand our 'rational' approach towards the gold depositions, although no consensus exists as to the meaning of these hoards.

They have, broadly speaking, been explained as treasures, that is, 'economic' depositions meant to go back into circulation, or as tactical gifts, that is, ritual sacrifices meant for the supernatural world and a way of creating alliances with the Other World. Therefore the discussion revolved around the question of whether the hoards were, or were not, meant to be capable of retrieval. For that reason the landscape situation became crucial; deposition in bogs or lakes makes it unlikely that the hoards were meant to be retrieved, but if they were deposited on agricultural land or in settlement areas, it spoke in favour of temporary deposition. All over Scandinavia, Migration Period hoards have been found both in central settlement areas, in − or very close to − houses, and in marginal areas, in bogs, rivers, streams, on or just off the coast, etc. (e.g. Geisslinger 1967; Fonnesbech-Sandberg 1985; Hines 1989; Hedeager 1992a, 1999b). Neither the hoards, nor the specific types of artefacts display a dominant association with either bogs or dry land even if certain tendencies among the types are discernable (Hedeager 1992a).

For the last decade the ritual explanation has been dominant (e.g. Fabech 1991a, b, 1994a, b, 1998, 1999), and the gold objects were considered to be actors in a symbolic communication with the gods (see Hedeager 1999b). However, we find the same kinds of objects in Viking Period hoards (Kilger 2008), which have traditionally been considered as 'treasures'. The only difference is that the Migration Period hoards consist of gold objects; a majority of the hoards from the Viking Period consist of silver items. Consequently, either the traditional explanation of the Viking hoards as 'rational' treasures must be questioned, or the 'ritual' explanation of the gold hoards reconsidered. In both periods, portable items of precious metal are placed in the ground, and only occasionally are the same kinds of artefacts found in burials, where weapons, helmets, and belt buckles dominate.[2]

Hoards are among the most difficult prehistoric source material to understand. I propose to consider the deposition of Migration and Viking Period hoards as part of a cognitive mapping of the landscape. It emerges from a study of their location that they were deposited in marginal or liminal areas in the landscape such as bogs, seashores, streams, lakes, etc. (i.e. Hedeager 1999b; Wiker 2000, 2001; Spangen 2005; Lund 2009). Finds from these kinds of localities are among the most impressive and spectacular. I now wish to illustrate some of these finds.

A prime example is the area around Gudme/Lundeborg on Funen (see Figures 6.5, 6.6 and 6.7) where the Broholm gold treasure including several solid neck-rings, bracteates, ingots, etc. (with a total weight of approximately 4kg) was found on the border of a wetland area between Lundeborg and Gudme (see Figures 6.2 and 6.4) (Thrane 1987: fig. 20; Geisslinger 1967: 164). The Elsehoved treasure with seven *solidi* mounted like bracteates, a brooch with gold, filigree, precious stones, etc. was found on the coast south of Lundeborg (Thrane 1987: fig. 20; Geisslinger 1967: 64). Hesselager Fredskov with a golden chain, a solid gold neck-ring, bracteates, etc. was found about 100m from the coast north of Lundeborg (Thrane 1987: fig. 20; Geisslinger 1967: 63, 126–7). However, not all gold hoards from Gudme/Lundeborg were found in marginal areas; a great many were located in the central settlement area, too (Thrane 1987: fig. 21). However, some of the most outstanding treasures were located in the coastal zone or in the wetland areas peripheral to the main settlements (e.g. Figure 7.1).[3]

Among other finds from the Migration Period, the hoard from Fræer Nordmark should be mentioned. It was found in a small bog in northern Jutland and consists of five solid gold neck-rings with a weight of more than 2kg (Geisslinger 1967: 77 and tafel.1) (Figure 7.2). At Kitnæs on the seashore of northern Zealand there was an impressive find of twenty-one gold bracteates, a brooch with gold, filigree and precious stones and several other objects (Hauck 1985–89: cat. nos. 92–4).

Many spectacular Viking hoards continue the tradition from the Migration Period depositions. From the small island of Fejø a treasure with six liturgical silver cups was found on a slope on the coast (Figure 7.3) (Skovmand 1942, II: 35). This hoard belongs to the tenth century. Another deposition from approximately the same time is at Mandemarke on the island of Møn, consisting of three arm-rings of gold, six silver arm-rings, a silver chain with animal heads, two Thor hammers, etc., deposited very close to the beach, and three gold rings from approximately the same locality.[4] Furthermore, a very similar find from the island of Sejrø was also found at the beach (Figure 7.4).[5] Two arm-rings of gold from Store Gråsand

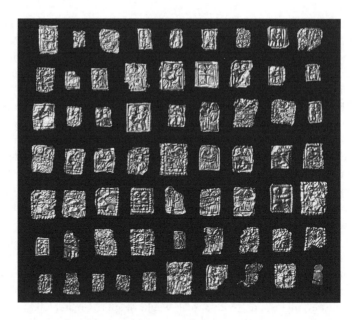

FIGURE 7.1   Gold foil figures from Lundeborg, Funen. © Svendborg Museum.

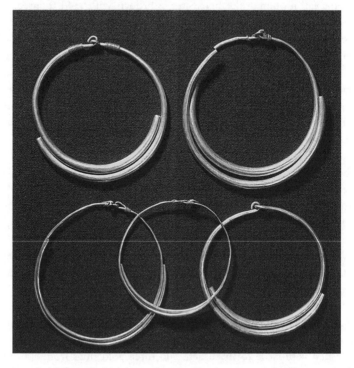

FIGURE 7.2   Gold hoard from Fræer Nordmark, Denmark. © Nationalmuseet, Copenhagen.

FIGURE 7.3   One of the liturgical silver cups from the eighth century. Fejø, Denmark. © Nationalmuseet, Copenhagen.

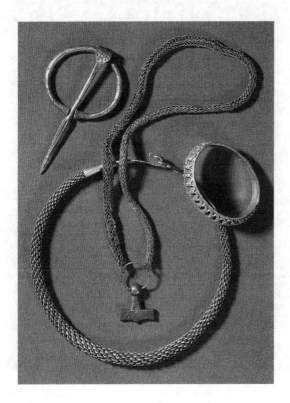

FIGURE 7.4   Silver hoard from Sejrø, Denmark. © Nationalmuseet, Copenhagen.

in Jutland were found in a bog[6] and three golden arm-rings, possibly from the same deposit, were found in a boggy area close to a stream near Tved in southern Jutland.[7] Among the hoards from the ninth century AD is the one from Erridsø in Jutland with four Permic silver rings, several bars and ingots. With a weight of more than 1kg, this is the biggest silver find from this century listed in Roar Skovmand's catalogue.[8] Among the rather few finds from the period AD 1016–1150 coming from wetland areas are the hoards from Tessebølle and Store Tårnby, both on Zealand.[9] The hoard from Tessebølle consists of 590 silver coins, and the hoard from Store Tårnby, one of the biggest coin hoards from this period, of 2253 silver coins together with a silver cross and several small pieces of silver pendants. A hoard with unusual large amount of gold objects is found at Vester Vedsted in Jutland, dated to late tenth century (Figure 7.5).

After AD 1000 finds from wetland areas, coasts, etc. come to an end and from around AD 1150 the hoards consist mainly of coins. Among the very few finds located on 'marginal land' from the period AD 1150–1240, the most impressive is a large and very beautiful relic cross with a plaited chain ending in animal heads, all

FIGURE 7.5 Viking hoard from Vester Vedsted, Denmark. © Nationalmuseet, Copenhagen.

made of gold. It was found on the small island of Orø near the coast of Zealand, and the cross had been deposited very close to the seashore (Figure 7.6) (Jensen et al. 1992: no. 34) in exactly the same way as spectacular hoards from the earlier periods were placed in the landscape. In the same period plenty of coin hoards have been deposited in a quite different context, namely in churchyards. We must therefore ask whether both kinds of depositions should be regarded as buried treasure or as ritual depositions.

Torun Zachrisson (1998) discusses a special group of finds from the Early Middle Ages containing relic crosses, silver bowls and chains with animal head ends. These came from the Swedish provinces of Uppland and Gästrikland, but hoards of the same character are known from south Scandinavia as well. In both areas they were deposited in marginal areas and coastal regions. Zachrisson argues that the objects possibly have a liturgical and Christian character, belonging to the owners of the first private churches, and she stresses the parallels in metaphoric language between these silver hoards and the late runic stones (ibid.: 216).

To sum up: during the long period from the fifth to the sixteenth century AD, the hoarding of wealth changes character both regarding the content and the mode

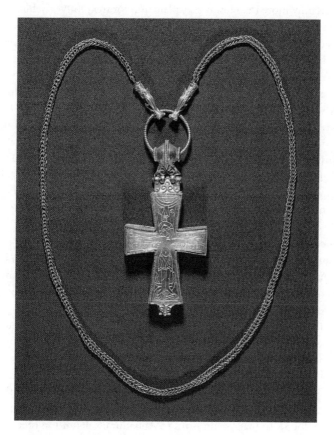

FIGURE 7.6 Reliquary gold cross. Orø, Denmark. © Nationalmuseet, Copenhagen.

of deposition at the transition to the Early Middle Ages. Hoards are now clearly related to settlement areas, to towns and castles[10] and to churches.[11] Some were buried on agricultural land, often connected to burial mounds, boulders, etc.,[12] and only a few were deposited in wetland areas and bogs, or at the coast.[13] The hoards have a different character, too. While hoards from the Migration Period and the Viking Age often contain what we, following Weiner (1992) and Parry and Bloch (1993), describe as *inalienable* objects, hoards from the Middle Ages mostly consist of *alienable* silver coins. As a consequence, the deposition of hoards as well as the hoards themselves seems – not surprisingly – to reflect a different cosmic order in the Late Iron Age to that in the Christian Middle Ages.

By contrasting the Christian hoards from the Middle Ages with the pagan hoards from the Iron Age, I have established two different depositional patterns. I suggest they correspond to a sacred versus a profane depositional tradition. In the following I take a closer look at the ritual tradition.

'Tournaments of value'

There is certainly more than just one explanation for the motives behind the deposition of hoards, whether from the Migration Period or later. Each hoard, and each of the objects within it, has of course its own unique cultural biography, which we will never be able to unravel. However, a majority of the hoards conform to a patterned distribution that is not random.

The first parameter is the frequency of deposition. Most hoards belong to the fifth/early sixth century or the tenth century AD. They reflect two very short 'horizons of investment'. The second parameter is the location of deposition: half of them are deposited in so-called marginal or liminal areas; the other half are not. Why is this so?

Each period in question, the Migration Period and the Viking Age, is characterised by an unusual flow of precious metal from abroad combined with significant warlike activities in Europe. If metal objects (such as gold or silver rings, swords, etc.) were kept in circulation as gifts and personal belongings, there would be no evidence at all in the archaeological record. But if the strategy of gift-giving included an element of competitive display, or 'tournaments of value' in the words of Arjun Appadurai (1986: 21), thus gift-giving would spiral into forms of conspicuous consumption. We should therefore expect to find evidence of ritualised consumption in hoards and in graves (Barrett et al. 1991: 240).

The written sources, whether Old Norse from the Viking Age or sources from early medieval Europe, agree that gift-giving was a decisive instrument in creating and upholding socio-political alliances. Whether characterised as *inalienable* or *alienable* objects (see Parry and Bloch 1993: 8; Weiner 1992; Godelier 1999), moveable wealth of specific symbolic value circulated as rewards from the Migration Period onwards (e.g. Bazelmans 1992, 1999, 2002; Theuws and Nelson 2000; Smith 2005). In that, it conforms to Appadurai's definition of 'tournaments of value' as:

complex periodic events that are removed in some culturally well-defined way from the routines of economic life. Participation in them is likely to be both a privilege of those in power and an instrument of status contests between them. The currency of such tournaments is also likely to be set apart through well understood cultural diacritics. Finally, what is at issue in such tournaments is not just status, rank, fame, or reputation of actors, but the disposition of the central tokens of value in the society in question. Finally, though such tournaments of value occur in special times and places, their forms and outcomes are always consequential for the more mundane realities of power and value in ordinary life.

(*Appadurai 1986: 21*)

No doubt the 'tournament of value' was an important political instrument throughout the last half of the first millennium AD (e.g. Enright 1996; Theuws and Nelson 2000; Bazelmans 1999, 2000; Smith 2005), but these two particular periods not only created special opportunities for access to gold and silver but they also claimed extraordinary investments of these values in social and political reproduction. Gold and silver held an exceptional position in political strategies because they were accessible only from outside the local system – that is, from the 'world out there'.

The idea of bestowing honorific gifts was embedded in a system of cultural values and as such was highly ritualised. Even if gift-giving was highly ritualised throughout the Late Iron Age, the intense competitive display in the Migration Period and the Viking Period must be considered historically exceptional. Both periods were characterised by warfare and social stress, resulting in a reorganisation of landscape and settlements, including larger landholdings and farms (e.g. Hedeager 1992a; Høilund Nielsen 2005).

Although half the gold hoards from the Migration Period are found in areas which in a local context are marginal or liminal, generally they cluster in fertile agricultural areas such as Gudme/Lundeborg. This pattern is seen even more clearly in Sweden, where a majority of the gold finds come from the most fertile provinces of Scania and Västergötland (approximately 22 kg, i.e. more than half the gold from mainland Sweden in the Migration Period). However, the hoards from the Viking Period are to a greater extent found in areas which can be characterised as areas of expansion in the Viking Age, at least as far as the Middle Swedish province of Gästrikland is concerned (Zachrisson 1998: 87).[14] These areas are defined as marginal to the previous Late Iron Age settlement structure.

There is thus a strong tie to economic power in the hoard depositions in addition to their ritual impact. They forged a strong local synthesis. Local environmental boundaries must have constituted one of the main features in people's perception of the cultural landscape because they enclosed the specific region by which people defined themselves (Fokkens 1996: 209). Within these borders people shared a common past, they shared the history of their land and they were connected by ties of kinship, alliances, etc. to each other. Therefore depositions of sacred objects of gold and silver added new cosmological power to the landscape – a new sacred topography was created.

Sacred topography

The fact that physical boundaries or liminal areas such as rivers, streams, coastlines, bogs, etc. were used for the deposition of hoards during the Migration Period and the Viking Age indicates that these areas played an important role in people's perception of the landscape. Both periods are characterised by extensive changes in settlement structure and land use (e.g. Hedeager 1992a). Old boundaries were changed and new land was taken into agricultural use; the cultural landscape was dramatically reorganised (see Høilund Nielsen 2005). It had to be followed up by a cultural and cosmological underpinning.

Torun Zachrisson has paid special attention to the establishment of borders in relation to the Icelandic *landnám* as outlined by Dag Strömbäck (1970) (Zachrisson 1998: 197). With reference to the *Svarfdoela Saga*, Zachrisson describes the practice of initiating new land through a ritual deposition of something highly symbolic and highly personal on the boundary of newly taken land. However, to legitimise this ritual deposition – and thereby the claim on the land – witnesses had to be present (Zachrisson 1998: 199).

The most personal objects to give were objects of gold and silver, because these metals embodied the honour and respectability of the owner. However, although ritually deposited, such treasures were neither hidden nor forgotten. On the contrary, they must have been 'official' knowledge. Even long after being buried they were as conspicuous as the burial mounds or the burial places in people's perception of the landscape. What traces were left of this sacred knowledge of buried wealth in later sources?

In folklore there is a rich vein of legends in which treasures are a common theme, as pointed out by Zachrisson (1998). Such treasure legends must have existed in the Early Middle Ages and the Late Iron Age, but not many are preserved. From a structural point of view, however, they are uniform over time. The main theme is that the treasures are visible in the landscape in one way or another, particularly by means of the light from a fire at the spot where they were placed. But, as Zachrisson states, the treasure was impossible to retrieve because it was protected. Some kind of animal, whether a dragon, hen or dog, guarded the treasure, or the treasure could be bound by means of magical incantations uttered at the time of deposition. Odin himself, according to the *Ynglinga Saga* (ch. 7), was able to see all gold and silver buried in the ground and he knew the right poetry to break the magical incantations and the right words to bind the guards. Only by means of *galdra* (sorcery) was it possible for Odin to remove the gold and silver (Zachrisson 1998: ch. III).

In the older treasure legends, gold treasures and their powerful enchantments are linked to people from the upper social stratum, whereas treasure stories from later periods involve people of much lower social standing. Likewise, the later legends have an element of absurdity in them, which is never seen in the earlier tales, where the value behind the treasures is connected with the conception of happiness. Gold and silver represented honour, riches and as such the happiness of the owner. Stealing a treasure in those days not only meant stealing someone else's riches in gold and silver but also taking another person's happiness and thereby influencing the faith of this person. It is a commonplace that persons who manage to steal a treasure suffer a dreadful fate (ibid.).

The historical sources support an interpretation of historical change in the perception of depositions from 'sacred' to 'profane'. The legends further add to our understanding of the ritual powers embodied in their deposition and their 'illegal' retrieval. In the 'archaic' pre-Christian cosmology, gold was an integral part of a person's 'happiness', which supports the idea of certain objects being incorporated into the person (Fowler 2004). During the Christian period this connection seems to have faded away and the coin hoards from the medieval period (up to AD 1550) have a status as hidden 'economic' treasures, buried in houses or in churchyards at places deliberately chosen as the best places for safekeeping. Losing one's money in the Middle Ages meant 'bad luck' in a purely economic sense. Precious metals in the Late Iron Age, however, possessed a mythical dimension, and as such they held a different place in the cosmological order than they did in the more modern world of the Middle Ages, although 'wealth' was still the focus.

The hoards from the Migration Period and from the Viking Age were intentionally deposited in the liminal area between cultivated/domesticated land and nature (see also Johansen 1996: 97; Wiker 2000, 2001; Spangen 2005; Lund 2009), often in the transitional zone between land and sea, between land and water. A majority of sacred place names, that is, names containing Odin, Tyr, Frey and God, are also located here (Andersen 1998: 26; see also Jakobsson 1997: 91 for part of Sweden). The transitional zones between land and water appear to hold a special position as places for negotiating with the Other World, as recalled in *Reginsmál*, *Vǫlundarkviða* and the saga of *Egils saga Skallagrímssonar* (Lund 2006, 2008, 2009). Once deposited, the hoards shaped the landscape for generations by creating a sacred topography in people's minds. Their biographies represented the link between past and present, between this world and the Other World, and as such they gave legitimacy to the land by becoming part of the discursive knowledge of the people who lived in this particular area.

By focusing on a cognitive landscape interwoven, as it must have been, with myths and stories about heroes and ancestors, spirits and gods, I incorporate the treasures in the construction of such 'biographies of power'. Protected in the realm of the dwarves, the hoards became ritual agents in a sacred landscape (Gansum 2004; Oestigaard 2007).

I further propose that hoards were deposited in periods of great social stress and radical changes in the organisation of the settled land. They constitute a cosmological instrument that balanced the conflicting forces of economic and religious rationality. As runic stones made visible social claims to power and land, so the hoards provided ritual compensation to the gods and guaranteed their support in a period of social and political changes. Although hidden, the hoards remained ritually 'visible' for generations, continuing to play an active role in people's negotiation with the past. As gifts to the gods, they embodied the art of 'keeping while giving' (Weiner 1992), adding sacred power and prestige to their owners.

PART V

The making of Norse mythology

8
KNOWLEDGE PRODUCTION RECONSIDERED

Epic poetry and historical reality

During the fifth, sixth and seventh centuries AD of northern Europe, myths, legends and poetry existed as 'remembered history': 'Whether memory changes or not, culture is reproduced by remembrance put into words and deeds' (Vansina 1985: xi). Myths and histories persist as long as they are able to account for, and adapt to, unforeseeable events and new developments. Prominent myths therefore take on different forms at different moments in time. Despite these variations, the myths or legends retain a core of substance, of 'hard facts' – perhaps a name, a time, a place – probably transformed into an archetypical situation. Without this accepted echo of historical 'truth', the myth or legend loses its capacity to unite the past with the present (Howe 1989: 4). The corpus of historical accounts is based on a few topics such as origins, migrations, descent, wars (over land, women, or wealth) and natural catastrophes, and they deal mainly with leaders and the elite. In this they reflect central issues of authority, power and legitimacy (Vansina 1985: 120).

Tradition encompasses memories of memories, and they change over time. In a society without writing, oral tradition must bear the brunt of historical reconstruction (Vansina 1985: 161, 199). Oral history served as the transmission system for information which was highly important for the identity of society (Barber and Barber 2004: 2). Rather than inventing stories to replace what had been before, each generation reshaped the tradition according to its own social agenda and cultural sensibilities (Finkelberg 2005: 11). Therefore, epic oral tradition cannot be approached using modern criteria of historicity (ibid.: 3). We tend to assume – wrongly – that events and details in a story are of equal 'value', and if we do not believe in specific elements, we reject the whole story as 'nonsense' or as a 'construct'. However, mythological narratives are neither all 'truth' nor untruth (Barber and Barber 2004: 27 f.).

From an archaeological point of view, historical and mythological narratives must be treated as hypotheses about the past, similar to a modern historian's own interpretation of the past (Hastrup and Meulengracht Sørensen 1987). Comparative anthropological studies from all over the world confirm that most myths developed out of actual events and real observations (Barber and Barber 2004). This does not, of course, mean that they can be accepted uncritically as historical truth, nor does it mean that all traditions automatically are unreliable (Vansina 1985: 195 ff.). The 'truth' must be understood in a selective cultural context that granted certain narratives and events greater value than others. This dialectic between present social agendas and their heritage in historical tradition implies that the same real event can be reported in widely different forms, a practice which is well illustrated in Germanic and Old Norse/Old English epics.

Among Germanic legends the great epic cycles of the Volsunga and the Nibelungen are probably the best known. They relate the story of the fall of the Burgundians after the Hunnic attack. The *Volsunga Saga*, which tells of Odin's grandchild Volsunga and his descendants, is known from a number of Old Norse sources, among others *The Poetic Edda*, written down in Iceland *c.* 1100, supposedly by Saemundur Frodhi. A short summary of the Sigurd cycle is found in Snorri's *Edda* from the thirteenth century. An unknown Icelandic author wrote *The Saga of the Volsungs* in the thirteenth century in prose narrative based on stories from older Norse poetry (Byock 1993). The same story is also known as *Sjurdar kvædi* in the Faeroe Islands, where it was recited in conjunction with the chain dance, a custom still practised as late as the nineteenth century. The German *Nibelungenlied* was written down around AD 1200 in the Bohemian-Austrian region by an unknown author, supposedly attached to the royal court,[1] and one of the more recent branches on the tree is Richard Wagner's interpretation in *The Ring of the Nibelungen*.

The historical basis of the story is the fate of the Burgundian kingdom, which had been founded on the left bank of the Rhine, around and to the south of Worms, in AD 413. In 437 King Gundicar/Gundaharius fell in battle, along with the majority of his people, in an attempt to halt the Huns. Attila is not recorded as having been personally involved in the attack, but he is linked in a natural and convincing way with the Burgundian kingdom's downfall. Attila, of course, was not solely responsible for its demise, and he himself would not long outlive it. According to fifth- and sixth-century sources, Attila died suddenly in AD 453, on the night of his wedding to Hildico, daughter of a Germanic king.[2] Although these sources attribute his death to an apoplectic stroke, rumour may have suggested that Hildico murdered Attila. In legends, with little respect for the chronological order of things, Hildico became a Burgundian princess, the sister of Gundicar; thus she gained a special status from her brother and the Burgundian people. The core of the legend is the story of the king's son Siegfried (Nordic: Sigurd the Fafnirsbane); his widow, the Burgundian princess Kriemhild (Nordic: Gudrun), the historic Hildico; her marriage to Etzel (Nordic: Atle), the historic Attila; and the final demise of King Gundicar (Nordic: Gunnar) and the other Burgundians (here called Gjukungs) (e.g. Gordon 1960: 111; Lukman 1943). The German tradition did not hold Etzel to be responsible for the death, and instead depicted him as a 'Heltenvater' (hero-father), the opposite to Atle in the Old Norse tradition, who is presented as cruel, and greedy for gold (Schulze 2007: 341).

Over the course of time other stories were incorporated, including that of the Gothic king Ermanaric (Nordic: Jörmunrek), attested in fourth-century AD historical sources as living on the northern shores of the Black Sea. He died, according to the Roman historian Ammianus Marcellinus, writing in AD 392–393, by committing suicide during the Hunnic attack of AD 375. A complete legend was composed around him, in which his wife Wunilda became Svanhild and was transformed, in the so-called *Svanhild Saga*, into Gudrun's daughter through a marriage to Sigurd (Lukman 1949). Later on, other historical characters appear; for instance, the Visigoth princess Brunhild and her sister Galswinth, wedded to two Merovingian brothers, King Sigibert of Austrasia and King Chilperic of Neustria, in the 560s. Legend thus transformed their dramatic and violent lives and deaths – described by Gregory of Tours – into a tale of conflict between Burgundians and Franks.

Another fragment of the drama of early medieval history is what might be called 'The Battle of the Huns'. The historical roots of this cycle are the fourth-century struggles of the Goths against the Huns and the destruction of Ermanaric's kingdom between the Vistula and the Black Sea in AD 376. These found an echo in the Anglo-Saxon legend of *Widsith*, in the Old Norse saga of *Hervarar* and *Heidrik's* crowning, and also in the *Gesta Danorum* of Saxo Grammaticus.[3] Of the three distinct versions, the one recorded in *Widsith* seems to be by far the oldest, although the date is the subject of lively debate. The Old English poem was transcribed into a single manuscript, the *Exeter Book*, between AD 970 and 1000. It is a collection of English religious verses, which was given to the cathedral by the first Bishop of Exeter who died in AD 1072. Two of the poems, named *Widsith* and *Deor*, differ remarkably from the others in scope, composition and language. The one relevant to us is *Widsith*. It is appraised by some as 'a relict of heathendom embedded in a Christian anthology', but drawing on much earlier traditions, without claiming to be an authentic record of a visit to the court of Ermanaric (Chambers 1912; Malone 1962; Rausing 1985; Davis 1992). To others it is a poem composed as a piece of 'pseudo-historical writing' in the tenth century AD and thus entirely invented (Niles 1999: 172), or a priori studied as a poem from the century in which it was written down (Hill 1984: 305–15).[4] One hundred and fifty years of commentary has not created any consensus. I propose that archaeology may hold the key to the historical authenticity of this and other epics. But first follows a brief presentation of the epic.

Widsith (Farway/Far journey) is the wandering singer/bard/skald who visits the court of Ermanaric and enumerates some seventy tribes and sixty-nine heroes/ kings. The poem is 'what a detractor could call the sort of things that result when a piece of language cannot make up its mind if it is a minimalist story or a shopping list' (Niles 1999: 171). Although the poem – or catalogue – is difficult to grasp, it obviously glorifies the ancient Goths and makes the Huns their enemy. Several times *Widsith* describes how the Goths of the Vistula had to defend their ancestral seats against Hunnic attacks. The historical basis of the story is the destruction of Ermaneric's kingdom and the subsequent migration of many Goths south across the Danube in and after AD 376 (Malone 1962: 103; Heather 1994: 13–14).[5] In the version in Saxo's *Gesta Danorum*, the war is turned into a struggle between Danes and Huns, but the Ostrogoths do appear under another name (Malone 1962: 103). The Icelandic version, in prose and verse alike, keeps the Goths but replaces the king (Malone 1962: 103). In the *Hervarar Saga*, the historical basis for the account of battles against the Huns is believed to be older than that of the other episodes, and the verses include a number of place names that point in the direction of central and eastern Europe, exactly where the Huns and the Goths met in the decades around AD 400 (Lönnroth 1995: 219). The three versions – those of the *Hervarar Saga*, Saxo's *Gesta Danorum*, and *Widsith* respectively – agree on some fundamentals: first, they tell a tale of warfare between the Huns and a Baltic 'nation'; second, they make the Huns the aggressor; third, they put the struggle in the Vistula valley and its environs; fourth, they tell the tale from the point of view of the Huns' foes – the defeated party (Malone 1962: 104).

The saga of *Dietrich of Bern*, written in Scandinavia in the thirteenth century, is a version of one of the great Germanic legends (Lukman 1941). Its historical core is centred round King Theodoric of the Ostrogoths, one of whose *sedes* (seats of power) was Verona ('Bern'), and another Ravenna, where he died in AD 526.[6] Although in the Scandinavian version Theodoric is only a minor character, while in German heroic poetry he is a central figure, his story was known in early medieval Sweden as he is named in an early ninth-century AD runic inscription from Rök – as inscribed memory (Connerton 1989: 4; Lönnroth 1977; Ralph 2005; Arwill-Nordbladh 2007). This long and unique inscription is difficult to understand. As a historical person, the king who 'nine generations ago ruled over the kingdom of Reid-mar' is identified as Theodoric and his seat as Ravenna. The rune-master further mentions that in his own time Theodoric sat fully armed on his horse, referring to Theodoric's equestrian statue erected in Ravenna, supposedly during his lifetime, but removed by Charlemagne to Aachen in AD 801.[7] The runic stone was raised by Varin to commemorate his dead son Vamod, and the allusion to the statue in Aachen indicates that learned men in Scandinavia, such as Varin, had opportunities to come in contact with the cultural world of Charlemagne and contemporary British and continental manuscripts (Arwill-Nordbladh 2007: 59). Whether or not Varin knew the *Dietrich Saga* or other stories about the Ostrogothic king Theodoric, it illustrates the persistence of great historical events and personalities in social memory.[8] It is commonly accepted that the Rök-stone was raised in the ninth century. The text specifies that Theodoric lived nine 'ages' ago. Obviously the past was measured in generations, and a generation approximates to thirty years. This places Theodoric in the early sixth century AD and thus corresponds with the historical dating of the Ostrogothic king (*c.* AD 455–526) (Arwill-Nordbladh 2007: 59).

Not much more than the names are left of what was once dramatic historical events, that is, the battles between the Huns, the Burgundians, the Goths, the

Gepids and the Lombards. The stories that survived are the closest we are likely to come to the actual events that gave rise to the Germanic legends. However, the similarities between the names of the kings of the Huns and those in the Nordic royal genealogies of the *Skjoldunge* and *Skilfinger* are quite remarkable. In the Nordic tradition the kings of the Huns become Danish and Swedish kings (Lukman 1943: 108). It confirms how loosely the legends were connected to their sources and how difficult it is to deduce any exact historical knowledge from them. What is important, however, is that the characters and events actually took place in Europe during the period AD 375 to 568, that is, the period between the Huns' first attack and the last Germanic migration, the Lombards' Italian migration, which is also the duration of the common animal styles (see Chapter 3 this volume). These shared Germanic legends go back to the formative centuries in which the Germanic kingdoms built themselves up from the foundations of the Roman Empire, even if only to collapse at a later stage. Strangely enough, though, there are practically no traces of the Late Antique Period to be found in them. They create a new beginning.

Germanic origin myths and legends arose out of the turbulent military encounters and social changes that led to the fall of the Western Roman Empire. When these transformative events were turned into myths and legends, order was brought to chaos. The Migration Period was a period of rapid changes and it led to the creation of a new socio-cosmological order. New gods and heroes merged with old ones, and a new tradition was invented that still retained an anchor to the past. But we should be open to the possibility that radical historical changes create radically new myths and new gods.

The enigma of *Widsith*

The only thing certain about *Widsith* is the date of its transcription; it is part of the *Exeter Book* from the late tenth century AD. Despite generations of learned exposition, it remains uncertain whether the poem records lost heroic songs going back to the Migration Period or must be regarded as an invention of the late tenth century, helping to shape the historical consciousness of those who read or heard it. For the primary reading of *Widsith* as 'authentic', we turn to the works of the two chief editors of modern times, R.W. Chambers' *Widsith: A Study in Old English Heroic Legend* (1912), and K. Malone's *Widsith* (1962), both philologists whose commentaries are learned to a degree that provide a benchmark for modern scholars. The strongest advocacy of the 'invented' reading is in John Niles' article 'Widsith and the anthropology of the past' (1999), where he deconstructs the poem in order to prove that it is entirely an early medieval text, composed in Britain in the aftermath of King Alfred's era, with the purpose of inventing a common glorious past.

Against this background of scholarly work we can either read the poem as fictitious, and therefore reject it, or we can accept it as a tenth century compilation of much older texts, originally composed in the sixth and early seventh centuries. Remarkably, it records tribes, kings and heroes of the Germanic migrations from the third to the middle of the sixth century, and it is without biblical lore. I shall

now critically re-evaluate the authenticity of *Widsith* before I test it against archaeological sources.

The poem consists of a catalogue of some seventy tribes and sixty-nine kings/
heroes, many of whom are historical persons known from the third, fourth and
fifth centuries, with the latest belonging to the sixth century AD. It lists tribal names
scattered all over Europe; however, most of the names are located in the countries
bordering the Baltic and the North Sea. To a modern reader the 143-line poem
is close to unintelligible. Even to a contemporary audience of the tenth century it
would have demanded a substantial familiarity with past myths and stories – a pre-
understanding rooted in oral tradition. Furthermore, there is no similarity to the
Old English poem *Beowulf*, today regarded as an epic poem composed some time
between the middle of the seventh and the end of the tenth century. All objects
described in *Beowulf*, such as swords, rings and goblets, are typical of the Scandinavian Migration Period.[9] This indicates that this lay was originally composed in
Scandinavia shortly after the events took place. This heroic narrative of more than
three thousand lines describes the deeds of one single person: a Scandinavian prince
named Beowulf. It is the only other manuscript known to have been transcribed at
the same time as *Widsith, c.* AD 1000 (Alexander 1973; Niles 2006). Where *Beowulf* is
an epic drama that may serve to recreate a glorious past, *Widsith* is a litany of names
without any dramatic moments and a minimal story line; however, the poem refers
to several of the persons mentioned in *Beowulf* (Rausing 1985:164). *Widsith* belongs
to an old skaldic tradition already obsolete at the time of its writing.

Against this background it is inconceivable that *Widsith* was a literary construction of the tenth century. It becomes far more intelligible if *Widsith* was composed
out of old lays nearly lost, in many ways resembling the enigmatic runic text on the
Rök-stone, an ancient relict embedded in a Christian anthology. It was given to the
cathedral of Exeter by its first bishop, Leofric, not because of its content but because
of the general status given to ancient lays in Britain in the late tenth century.

More recently, Kemp Malone (1962) carried out a remarkable re-evaluation.
Based on the composition of the poem, Malone argued that the author of *Widsith*
was a cleric with a special interest in the Germanic heroic past (ibid.: 112), and from
the evidence of the language he concluded that the poem was composed and written down in the latter part of the seventh century AD (ibid.: 116). Most of the text is
written in the West Saxon dialect of Old English, although it includes many elements
of other dialects. Altogether the text gives many indications of having had a long life
before the different parts were brought together to create the coherent whole of the
poem *Widsith* (ibid.: 116). Its composition is original; at least no other text is particularly like it. The only parallel to be found is a fragment of a stanza quoted in *Hervarar
Saga* (ibid.: 118; Lönnroth 1995: 22) in the part that tells of the battle between the
Huns and the Goths. This particular part of *Hervarar Saga* is regarded as the oldest
layer of tradition in the text and the specific stanza belongs to the oldest *edda*-tradi-
tion with roots in the Migration Period (Lönnroth 1995: 130, note 29).

Etymologically *Widsith* means 'far journey' or 'one who has travelled widely'. It
is evident that the skald/bard/scop is portrayed as a person central to creating and

upholding social memory. He is also given an identity, that is, a name and a tribe, and a social setting, that is, he is a lord with ancestral land in addition to having a professional career. However, the only thing in the poem 'that strikes one as fiction pure and simple is the personal history of the scop himself (Widsith)', as Malone writes (1962: 79).

The skald/bard/scop with the name of Widsith is introduced as an eyewitness to historical events and the author makes him visit royal courts of the third, fourth, fifth and sixth centuries, clearly to bring legitimacy to the narrative. However, the structure of the poem indicates that it has been composed from several fragments and episodes and Malone identifies different divisions and subdivisions, with there being three main sections of the speech, the First, Second, and Third 'Thule' (ibid.: 75).

The First Thula names thirty-two rulers, thirty-one tribes and one specific region. Malone identifies striking similarities between those names and names known from the *Finnsburg Fragment*, from *Beowulf*, and from *Tacitus*, and it is regarded as the oldest poem in the English language. Three of the kings are well-known historical figures: Attila, Ermanaric and Theodoric. The poet who composed the First Thula drew on knowledge which is only sporadically reflected in the classical literary sources in which Germanic kings were only mentioned when they were in personal contact with the Roman Empire. His sources of the past stem from a tribal tradition where place and time were secondary organising principles compared to fame. Of the thirty-two notable kings listed in the thula, the poem begins with the two most famous: Attila and Ermanaric, the Huns and the Goths. The tribal areas of these thirty-two kings all lay in Scandinavia and northern Germany. Five lines (45–9) are devoted to the Danish royalty of the Skjoldunge family, among others King Hrothgar who is the builder of the magnificent hall in Hlridargard (Lejre on Zealand), alluded to in *Beowulf*, in the *Hrólf saga Kraka*, and in the *Skjoldunga Saga*. In the First Thula, the Lombards are a tribe on the lower Elbe, already legendary in the north (ibid.: 83), which indicates the time of this poem. According to classical authors, the Lombards left their ancient homeland to settle along the Danube around Vienna in the late half of the fifth century (Menghin 1985). In the later part of the fourth century, Ermanaric's Gothic federation covered eastern and central Europe from the Baltic to the Black Sea. It was certainly a loose union of tribes with their own kings or rulers, but with Ermanaric as a superior king. Via the Goths on the Vistula and the political alliances that kept the north and the south in contact, Constantinople was included in the sphere of the Baltic area and the north. When Ermanaric died *c.* AD 375, the Huns rapidly replaced the Goths as the dominant political force in barbarian Europe for the next century.

Although the First Thula is restricted to tribes and kings from the fourth century onwards, it can hardly be composed before AD 530 (Malone 1962: 93). The Second Thula is approximately from the same time, and the Third Thula is, according to Malone, composed no earlier than AD 565 and before the Lombards' conquest of Italy around 570 (ibid.: 102). It is strictly limited to the Germanic/Scandinavian heroic age, since Ælfwin (the Lombard king Alboin of history) who conquered

Italy in 568, and had nearly completed the conquest when his wife had him murdered in 573 (ibid.: 126), is the latest of the heroes celebrated in *Widsith*.

Without dividing the poem into three original parts, or Thulae, as Malone did, Chambers came to the same conclusion regarding the date of *Widsith*: it had to be later than AD 568; however, not by much. For him it was most likely composed in the last decades of the sixth century or the first of the seventh (1912: 10). He also stressed the way in which the Huns are described: first as enemies, then as allies, and then again as the enemies of the Goths. The poet's familiarity with the complicated political relationship between the Huns and the Goths in the late fourth and early fifth centuries is in full accordance with our knowledge from other historical texts (Chambers 1912: 11). I shall now turn to archaeology and place names to further substantiate the *Widsith* epic's antiquity and its authenticity.

The topography of *Widsith* and the archaeology of Gudme

The First Thula, which counts tribes and kings from the fourth and fifth centuries, many known to Tacitus and/or Ptolemy, could hardly have been composed before AD 530, according to Malone (1962: 93). The composer of the first Thula, or the first thula-man, as Malone names him, clearly had the knowledge of a seafarer around the Baltic coast, and he might have been a seafarer, gathering information from personal visits to the tribes he mentions. The text centres on the Danish Islands and Jutland, and the composer shows a special interest in the Danes and the Anglo-Saxons (ibid.: 105). Malone presents the many similarities and historical connections to almost everything we can test, so we can hardly avoid seeing the story-teller as a true historian of his time, a person who had achieved professional training in some sort of school where he learned the tribal tradition about the past (ibid.: 87). Historical events are related as sober facts, not yet transmuted into heroic stories. The main purpose of the First Thula was to give 'poetical expression to a body of traditional lore thought of (not without reason) as history' as Malone expresses it (ibid.: 90). As a poet and historian he was the keeper of social memory among his people.

From the structure of the First Thula Malone concludes (ibid.: 86) that the thula-man belonged to the tribe of the Wrosnan. This tribal name, otherwise unknown to us, has, however, survived in the word Wrysn,[10] known from the medieval Danish *King Valdemar's Jordebog* from 1231. This is identified with the modern-day *Vresen*, an insignificant uninhabited Danish island in the Great Belt, 4–5km from the shoreline of south-eastern Funen. To Malone this is something of a mystery; however, he concludes: 'It seems reasonable to presume that the *Wrosnan* was an old tribe of the Danish islands who eventually lost their identity through migration. *Their chief seats lay perhaps in southern and southeastern Fyn, though we have no way of defining their holdings with precision*' (ibid.: 87, my italics).

Bearing in mind the nature of the skaldic institution and its attachment to kingly milieux, it might be relevant to bring archaeological and toponymic evidence into the discussion. Indeed, not far from the island of Vresen, on the south-eastern coast of Funen, lies Gudme – the home of the gods and the richest concentration of gold treasures in northern Europe (see Chapter 6 this volume). South-eastern Funen had already from the third century BC occupied a special place, thanks to the outstanding burial place at Langå north of Gudme, with over one hundred cremation graves from the second and first centuries BC (Albrectsen 1954). Three of these contained big cauldrons of iron and bronze, in addition to a unique bronze cauldron, from Capua and Etruria, already antiquities when they were placed in the ground. A Celtic wagon (like the famous wagons from the Dejbjerg bog) and several Celtic long swords, together with other weapons, and a couple of solid gold rings were buried here, too (Jensen 2003: 166 ff.). These graves break with the tradition of poorly furnished Late Bronze Age and Early Iron Age graves in the Danish area and are outstanding even in a north European context. They introduce, so to speak, the tradition of 'Fürstengräber' (chiefly graves) better known from the Roman Period (Hedeager 1992a). The locality of Gudme is only 4–5km south of Langå, and Møllegårdsmarken is even closer (cf. Figure 6.1). Its 2300 graves cover the period between the first century BC and the early fifth century AD (Albrectsen 1971; Christoffersen 1987). Here, as in the eastern part of Funen, rich graves with Roman imports are found. The coast at Lundeborg was an important landing place for Roman goods (Lund Hansen 1987; Hedeager 1992a; Thomsen 1994), and in the Migration Period for Byzantine gold (Thrane 1999). Thus, it has been argued that this area is one of the main royal and sacred centres in southern Scandinavia for most of the Iron Age. Here we find the kingly milieu in which a skaldic tradition such as that in *Widsith* would have been performed and maintained. And the epic itself points to this area as the home of the poet.

This can be further sustained. The last king of the First Thula to be mentioned (line 33) is 'Holen', king of the Wrosnan. To Malone, the man, as well as the place, is somewhat of a mystery, since they are otherwise unknown from other texts and the names themselves do not seem to fit anything expected. As already stated, Wrosnan is an unimportant island close to Gudme. The word 'holen' is usually identified with Old English *holegn*, which means 'holy', but to Malone 'this etymology gives a highly unsuitable royal name' (Malone 1962: 173).[11]

The archaeological evidence from Gudme, however, resolves the 'mystery'. Both king and place fit extremely well with the archaeological and etymological evidence of the fifth and sixth centuries AD in south-eastern Funen. The king last mentioned is the king of the tribe where the First Thula was composed in the middle of the sixth century. The unique cosmological qualities of Gudme implied that this place could neither give nor take a name in the same way as other places and kings. It seems fully reasonable that a king with a 'no-name' meaning 'holy', and a tribe named after a 'no-place', an uninhabited and seemingly inferior small island of the coast of Gudme, were meant to protect the Home of the Gods in the sixth century.

All royal families of the Early Middle Ages came from somewhere else, at least according to their genealogies (see Chapter 3 this volume). They encapsulate the special cosmic quality of distance, horizontally and vertically, as Mary Helms has argued (Helms 1993). However, their material attributes had to do the same. Whether Roman tableware or Byzantine gold, they represented another world and embodied the special qualities of 'cosmological distance' and 'biography'. They had to be brought from the outside world into the inner world by way of transformation. Gudme was in all probability a unique kingly and cosmological centre for foreign acquisitions and contacts with other kingly milieux. Maybe this was the central place for south Scandinavian would-be kings to obtain the qualities necessary to become kings. Therefore, its tribe never gave its name to, nor took its name from, the site of Gudme, because this was the Home of the Gods. The protector of the place was therefore without a spoken name. This phenomenon might be comparable to Oðin's many kennings, which mean that he is always called something else simply to avoid saying his real name.

Malone dates the composition of the first Thula just before AD 530, which is in the late Migration Period and the decades of Gudme's decline. For reasons we do not know, the whole settlement disappears, as does the tradition of the deposition of gold treasures in the area. This abrupt termination of a major royal site resonates well with Malone's conclusion (1962: 87): 'It seems reasonable to presume that the Wrosnan were an old tribe of the Danish islands who eventually lost their identity through migration.'

Jordanes, Paul the Deacon, Saxo Grammaticus, Snorri Sturluson, etc., all composed the ancient history of their people in times of immense social changes (see Part II). Jordanes wrote his *Gothic History* close to the estimated date of the First Thula, around AD 550, in a historical situation in which the Ostrogoths and the Amal dynasty faded away. In much the same way, the first part of *Widsith* could have been composed and transmitted (in oral form) to commemorate a glorious historical *époque*, which was nearly gone. It happened at a time when kingly lines in all parts of south Scandinavia gradually took over the concept of Gudme, in new places such as Helgö in Mälaren, Tissø on Zealand and Uppåkra in Scania. They were organised in roughly the same manner, and craft production and precious metals were vital to the sites.

Gudme represented the first generation of superior focal points in south Scandinavia, and it came to an abrupt end. Perhaps therefore, had it not been for the archaeological evidence, it would only have left a weak shadow of its existence in the place names and in the scant textual evidence of *Widsith*. However, other places rooted in the Heroic Age of the late Migration Period now come into being. Two places of exceptional reputation according to the written records are: Old Uppsala, the seat of the Ynglinga kings (e.g. Lindqvist 1936, 1949; Åberg 1947, 1949; Duczko 1996), in *Beowulf* named Skilfinger (Lukman 1943), housing the famous temple and sacred grove mentioned in the Viking Age (see Part III); the other is Lejre on Zealand (Niles 2006), the seat for the kingly line of the Danish Skjoldunge (Lukman 1943), housing a sacred grove similar to the grove in Old Uppsala. Archaeological evidence has verified the literary sources that these were superior places where cult and kingship were amalgamated through several centuries of the Late Iron Age and Viking Age. *Widsith* and other epics provide a historical frame of reference, which the archaeology can further detail and specify.

Widsith: a political narrative of the Migration Period

As demonstrated in Part II, all kingly lines of the Middle Ages were furnished with genealogies of a certain length and ancestors of special honour and great deeds. Also, they all have a migration myth as part of their history. They all descended from gods and heroes and except for the Scandinavians they all came from somewhere else – they had migrated.

However, the oldest tribal list we know of from the north is the First Thula of *Widsith*. It lists at least thirty-one kings and tribes and it ends with Holen Wrosnum, indicating that the poem was composed in his time. The first (lines 18–20) to be mentioned are:

> Ætla weold Hunum, Eormanric Gotum,
> Becca Baningum, Burgendum Gifica.
> Casere weold Crecum and Cælic Finnum
> (Widsith *lines 18–20*)

The list is organised according to importance and fame. Attila (AD 433–453) and the Huns are first, and second comes Ermanaric (died *c.* 375) and the Goths. Next follows the rulers of the Banings and the Burgundians, and in the third line the Caesar who is said to rule the Greeks, indicating the eastern Roman emperor. As number five in the list he is clearly subordinated.

The Second Thula lists fifty-four tribal names, indicating that the poet knew the world, and had travelled among foreign and famous royal families. Nine belong to tribes of peoples who are not Germanic: Huns, Idumings, Picts, Rumwalas, Scots, Scridfinns, Sercings, Serings and Wineds. They were all part of the world known to the people of the Migration Period. The other tribes belonged in Scandinavia, the Baltic, north-western Europe and along the Elbe, the Rhine, and the British Isles. Although this 'thula-man' knew Scandinavia quite well, the way he organised the tribal names indicates that he knew best the tribal lore of Jutland. He knew the Ostrogothic Empire and – at least by name – many of the tribes and peoples with whom they were in contact (Malone 1962: 92). There is no indication at all that he knew of the Goths in Italy, and there is no trace of the Visigoths or the Vandals in the information he gives. He is, like the composer of the First Thula, familiar with the Ostrogoths of the early days of Ermanaric.

The Second Thula begins:

> Ic wæs mid Hunum & mid Hreðgotum,
> mid Sweom & mid Geatum & mid Suthdenum
> (Widsith *lines 57–8*)

Again, this list of tribes and peoples begins with the two most famous, the Huns and the Ostrogoths. The composer of the Second Thula might have thought of Attila and Ermanaric as the rulers of the Huns and the Hreðgoths (Malone 1962: 175), but he only lists the tribal names, not the personal names. In the next line he moves on to Scandinavia, beginning with the Swedes of Uppland, the Geats (who lived on the Scandinavian peninsula between the Sweoms of Uppland to the north and the Danes of Scania to the south), and the south Danes. This indicates that he orders things from north to south.

The Third Thula (lines 99–103) only lists personal names, in all twenty of them. It begins and ends with Gothic kings. The first place is given to Hehca, the father of Ermanaric. The names in the beginning (lines 112–13) seem to reflect a chronological order; in line 112 they belong to the fourth and maybe the fifth century, while in line 113 they belong to much earlier times. After the Goths the poet turns to the Franks, the Scandinavians, the Lombards, and the Burgundians. The latest king mentioned in the thula and known as a historical person is Eadwin who died AD 565. However, the poet does not mention Ælfwin who conquered Italy c. 570, indicating that the poem was composed before this. Like the First and the Second Thula, the Third displayed knowledge of tribes with Baltic and North Sea connections. Interestingly enough, the poet shows no knowledge of later Gothic heroes such as Theodoric, indicating that the Vistula Goths were cut off from the southern part of the Goths after the death of Ermanaric. A central episode in the Third Thula (lines 119–22) is dedicated to the wars between the Huns and the Ostrogoths, where *Ætland leodum* (line 122) means 'against the people of Attila'. This is a kenning and means 'against the Huns'.[12]

All three thulas mention Attila and the Huns in prominent places. The First and the Second rank them first, and the Third devotes four lines to the description of the wars between them and the Ostrogoths. The same fight is central to the Icelandic *Hervarar Saga*, ch. 5: the battle between the Goths and the Huns. This particular part of the saga is regarded as the oldest, and there are obvious similarities to the First Thula in *Widsith*. Also, the Hunnic king – here called Humle – is mentioned first. They all tell the tale of battles between these two peoples, as does Saxo in *Gesta Danorum* book V (although he turns the Ostrogoths into the Danes). The earth-shattering historical events of the late fourth and early fifth centuries were remembered and passed on as a focal point of historical memory in northern Europe. They all picture the Huns as the aggressors, which they certainly were in the early days of Ermanaric.

The historical information about the Ostrogothic king Ermanaric comes from a contemporary source, Ammianus Marcellinus, and from the sixth-century Ostrogothic historian Jordanes. The first tells us of the extensive empire he built up and how it was seriously threatened by the attacks of the Huns (and Alans) and that the king died in mysterious circumstances, eventually committing suicide when he could no longer resist the Hunnic forces. It might be that Ermanaric sacrificed himself to the gods in order to save his people (e.g. Heather 1996: 98). It is a historical fact that his federation stretched along the rivers Vistula and Dniester, linking the Baltic shore to the Black Sea area and embracing a number of Slavic and Baltic tribes as well. After the death of Ermanaric, the Huns replaced his Ostrogothic supremacy.

It is these feuds and fights between the Ostrogoths and the Huns that remained the central narrative of northern poetry. In *Widsith* the tale of Attila clearly did not come from the Germans but from native Nordic tradition, which acquired it from the Goths in the Vistula area (Malone 1962: 128). Both *Hervarar Saga* and *Widsith* reflect a period in which there were severe ongoing conflicts as the Huns threatened the Goths in their ancient homeland in the Vistula basin (e.g. Wolfram 1990: 85 ff.; Heather 1996: 100ff.). After the death of Ermanaric, the Huns established supremacy in the Black Sea area and from there moved on to the Hungarian plain where they settled.

Later on, in the times of Attila, the Goths and the Huns might quite naturally have been allied. In the period between AD 434 and 445, Attila and his brother Bleda established supremacy over all the Germanic and other peoples between the Alps and the Baltic, and between the Caspian and somewhere east of the Rhine (Thompson 1996: 85). Jordanes reports in *Getica* (IX: 58): 'Romans borrow (names) from the Macedonians, the Greeks from the Romans, the Sarmatians from the Germans, and the Goths frequently from the Huns.' Whether the Huns used Germanic names, or whether the Latin sources altered the names and made them into Germanised versions, is impossible to know (Thompson 1996: 279; Heather 2006: 148), although marriages between Huns and Germans certainly took place; for example, Attila's last wife had the Germanic name Hildico (Thompson 1996: 164).

In *Widsith*, *Hervara Saga* and *Gesta Danorum* the battles between the Huns and the Goths are told from the perspective of the Goths (in Saxo from that of the Danes). Half a century later, in the time of Attila, the Huns and the Goths had established a partnership in which the Goths on the Vistula were part of the Hunnic confederation. Therefore we would expect that these epics represent a genuine historical tradition created in the north. This was one of the main conclusions of the work of Niels Lukman, *Skjoldunge und Skilfinge* (1943).

In his comparative analysis of Norse sagas, Lukman (1943) proposed that the figures of Haldan, Roo, Ottar and Adils represent the Hunnic kings named by Jordanes as Huldin, Roas, Octar and Attila. In contrast to other well-known European traditions, in which Attila remains king of the Huns, he and his forefathers are portrayed as Swedish and Danish kings in the Norse sagas. Although such transmissions are not uncommon in Norse tradition, there is a significant difference between other examples and this one in that it describes a number of historically well-attested persons before and after Attila, who are unknown in the European tradition. It suggests that the Skjoldunge/Skilfinger sagas represent an independent Norse tradition, which originates in the same historical events as the continental tradition, but was experienced in a different historical context (Lukman 1943: 108 ff.).

Without going too deeply into the work of Lukman, I find the main conclusions worth outlining in order to place them in a broader historical and archaeological context. Lukman identifies numerous such correspondences, among them many which are historically very specific, which lead him to detect an Adils/Beowulf tradition that goes back to a Hunnic rulership in Scandinavia in the late fourth and fifth centuries. However, Lukman contends that no proof can be provided by the written sources alone; archaeology must supplement them in order to reach a safer conclusion concerning the Hunnic presence in Scandinavia (ibid.: ch. 5); this will be considered in the following chapter.

9

HYPOTHESIS I: THE HUNS IN SCANDINAVIA

Historical framework: the impact of the Huns

The chief of the Huns, king Attila, born of his father Mundiuch, lord of the bravest tribes, sole possessor of the Scythian and German realms, something unheard of before, captured cities and terrified both empires of the Roman world, and, appeased by their prayers, took an annual tribute to save their remnants from plunder. And when he had accomplished all this by favour of fortune, he fell not by wound of the foe, nor by treachery of friends, but in the midst of his nation at peace, happy in his joy and without sense of pain. Who can rate this as death, when none believes it calls for vengeance?

(Getica *XLIX, 257*)

This was the song that was sung over the dead body of Attila when he died in AD 453 (Thompson 1996: 164). This short curriculum vitae is, so to speak, a compressed presentation of his position as the paramount ruler of Barbarian Europe and a superior to the Roman emperors, who paid him tribute. He kept his power through a sophisticated balance of terror and reward, well known as the strategy employed by later steppe empires, too. He never took, nor held land; he controlled space by movement and kept it by means of mobility and speed (Pohl 2001). Throughout the first millennium AD the nomadic system developed and expanded continuously. Its frontiers moved forward, neighbouring peoples were conquered and the 'ethnic' map and geopolitical configurations of western Eurasia were redrawn (Barfield 1989; Martynov 1991: ch. 5; Howard-Johnston forthcoming: ch.1). However, nomadic empires rose and fell with astonishing swiftness but the pastoral societies of the Eurasian steppes remained unchanged for ages; Herodotus' description of the Scythians from the fifth century BC is valid to the Mongols of the thirteenth century

AD. Therefore, the Mongol history is a pertinent analogy for studying the Huns and their strategy when meeting with the western world, and also their military techniques are comparable.[1] When the Mongols in 1237–42 invaded Europe (Chingis Khan died 1227), they held supremacy of the globe from Germany to Korea. During the thirteenth century the Mongols destroyed kingdoms and empires and left greater parts the Old World traumatised and transformed (Saunders 1971: 12). They practised genocide in a magnitude never witnessed since the ancient Assyrians who killed or deported whole nations. The Mongol conquests forever transformed the ethnic character of many regions where whole peoples were uprooted and dispersed. During their campaigns they encountered the world religions Buddhism, Islam and Christianity and they permanently changed their history (ibid.: ch.10).

Half a millennium earlier, in fifth-century Europe, the meeting with the Huns was likewise a historically well-attested intersection between structurally different societies with different religious systems and divergent perceptions of time and space – the Roman Empire, the agrarian Germanic warrior tribes, and the hypermobile Eurasian (pastoral steppe) warrior society – inexplicable without an effective central authority and relatively well-developed political institutions (Howard-Johnston forthcoming: ch. I).

These 'edges of time and space' might have opened up new ways of thinking and alternative perceptions of the world among the Germanic tribes. Those episodic transitions, as Anthony Giddens designates them, are defined as uneasy relations of symbiosis and conflict with, and partial domination over, surrounding societies (Giddens 1986: 245). The effect might be subversion or undermining of the ideological 'glue' that formerly held the society together (Giddens 1981: 23). The new glue that kept the world of Attila together was gold. 'Their greed for gold is prodigious' as the last of the great Roman historians, Ammianus Marcellinus, describes the Huns (Book 31, Ch. 2). It motivated the barbarian allies to seek out imperial gold in a never-ending spiral of consumption and violence. And it brought with it new social and religious institutions. This was the specific historical condition that characterised the pan-European 'world-system' during the first generations of the fifth century. But how far did this new 'world-system' of Attila extend? And what was its impact?

> Romulus (who had come from Italy to Attila as ambassador), an ambassador experienced in many affairs, took up the discourse and said that his (Attila's) very great fortune and the power derived from good luck exalted him so that he could not endure just proposals unless he thought they came from himself. By no one who had ever yet ruled over Scythia, or indeed any other land, had such great things been achieved in such a short time, since he ruled even the islands of the Ocean and, in addition to Scythia, held the Romans also to the payment of tribute. He is aiming, he said, at greater achievements beyond his present ones and desires to go against the Persians to expand his territory to even greater size.
>
> (Priscus *fr. 8*)[2]

From the conversation that followed between Romulus and Priscus, a Byzantine historian who travelled to the Hun court in AD 449 on a diplomatic mission and recorded his impressions (Gordon 1960), we understand that the former had a competent geographical knowledge of the Roman world and beyond. When he explicitly mentions 'the islands of the Ocean' to stress the power of Attila, this indicates that he in fact *knew* what he was talking about and may have presupposed that Priscus did the same. Clearly, to the north of continental Europe there is an ocean with islands, and scholars agree that it is the islands of the Baltic Sea to which he refers (Gibbon 2005: 370; Thompson 1996: 84 with references). It follows logically from the fact that the Huns gained supremacy over the Gothic tribes living in the north along the Vistula basin. According to this historical interpretation, the Huns' supremacy included part of Scandinavia.

From our knowledge of the military and political strategy of the Huns, it is most likely that they and their allied troops went to the north for a brief expedition during which they established local strongholds – by force and by diplomacy, during the first half of the fifth century AD. It would explain why Romulus is so precise about this particular item of information. It also explains the large number of ancient place names in Scandinavia with affiliation to the Huns; for example, *Húnar, Húnaherred, Hunna by, Hunneberg* (i.e. Liestøl 1924). If the Huns exercised a brief but significant political role in Scandinavia as 'cultural others', then it becomes easier to understand the cultural change and structural transformation of Scandinavian societies during this particular historical period (i.e. Hedeager 1992a, b, 2005b; Fabech 1994b; Näsman 1998; Kristoffersen 2000b; Myhre 2003a; Herschend 1998, 2009; Wiker 2001; Fredriksen 2006). This transformation materialised distinctly in the Nordic or Germanic animal style, which represents a new artistic expression and a new communicative strategy (Hedeager 2005a, b). Who inspired this new style?

Although the Huns for several reasons are the obvious candidates, they were not the only source of influence during this transformative period. Classical elements, figural compositions, carving-techniques, etc., from Roman, Gallo-Roman and Byzantine art have long been identified as decorative elements in the animal style (e.g. Roth 1979; Haseloff 1981). However, the whole *concept* of animals being the main organising principle in the new artistic expression[3] and – as argued above – in the cosmology can hardly be ascribed to the Roman world. It requires a different explanation.

All societies are influenced from the outside, traditionally labelled as innovation or diffusion. It is usually assumed to be an ongoing process that gradually adds new elements to an existing pattern, or material traits are transferred from one culture to another (Kristiansen 2005: 75, 151). However, the specific historical conditions that characterised the post-Roman era show a different pattern of rapid change, and the most likely candidates to trigger such large-scale changes were the Huns. For a rather brief period they held sway over large parts of Europe in various alliances. Based on contemporary Roman sources, the Huns have traditionally been viewed as an archaic, predatory people only held together by military activity and a continuous inflow of booty. However, it is hard to explain their military capacity and diplomatic vision without presupposing a sophisticated and effective central authority with an extensive reach. In the words of James Howard-Johnston, they 'plainly operated on an imperial scale, both in terms of territory and the diversity of subject peoples' (Howard-Johnston forthcoming: ch. I). From this new perspective we are right in asking what impact it had on Germanic societies and their institutions.

The impact of the Huns is most clearly seen in the epic poetry of central and northern Europe from this period. Attila and the Huns constitute a fixed point of social remembrance, so to speak, of an oral tradition of a *longue durée* thus codified in written form (see Chapter 8 this volume). In line with this I propose that these few decades of European history became decisive for reshaping the long-term cosmological history of northern Europe. It was a rapid episode of significant individual experiences that were later transformed into collective memory and thus became the foundation for a new historical and cosmological understanding of the world – a new beginning. Only archaeology can, however, provide the evidence to support or reject this hypothesis. And only archaeology can provide a first-hand dating of Old Norse mythology and its origin. We shall therefore begin with an analysis of material aspects of Hunnic influence and its acculturation.

Archaeological framework: transferable cosmologies

If the appearance of the Huns and the intersection between the Huns and the Germanic tribes generated a social and cultural transformation, we should expect the adoption of a new set of values and institutions, materialised in iconography, ruling regalia, monuments, buildings, etc. (Kristiansen and Larsson 2005: 10 ff.). As I shall argue, this is what characterises the archaeological record after AD 400 when Roman culture is replaced by Germanic culture. But first I shall discuss the nature of ritual exchange.

Like oral tradition, symbolic objects have the capacity to cross generations because they convey mythical information well known to people. Symbolic memory encapsulates in condensed form mythological knowledge and master narratives. When imbued with those qualities in the form of artwork and iconography, artefacts operate as social agents in networks of ritualised gift exchange (Gell 1992; Meskell 2004). They have their own curriculum vitae and may be perceived as acting independently. In Old Norse literature this is well attested regarding famous swords, helmets, necklaces, buckles and other personal adornments, named and thus personified (Hedeager 2001, 2004; Gansum 2004).

The importance of ritual exchange among Germanic and Nordic peoples is well attested. Social and political supremacy was formed through the circulation of specific objects of supreme quality. They were brought into being through a particular process of manufacturing or initiation. As already discussed in Chapter 6, they acquired an 'origin' through a process of transformation, what Mary Helms (1993) calls 'skilled crafting' and Alfred Gell (1992) terms 'a technology of enchantment'. Like people they had to go through a process of socialisation over time to gain a particular cultural identity.

During the first four centuries AD, Roman tablewares, weapons, jewellery, etc. served this function as the medium of gift exchange, due to their social and ideological supremacy (e.g. Hedeager 1992a). Manufactured within a supreme foreign culture, whether Roman or provincial, they were considered powerful and valuable (Hedeager 2001). They reached Germanic peoples as war booty and through ceremonial gift exchange in political alliances. In funerary rites they were buried with the dead because they encapsulated political alliances and the power of the person while alive. Such alliances were forged through the ritualised exchange of Roman tableware, emulating Roman lifestyle among Germanic elites.

However, from the late fourth century AD Roman goods stopped being consumed in social and ritual transactions. This fundamental change is accompanied by a significant change in material culture too, which reflected ideological disorder and loss of knowledge of Roman culture. At the same time, the new animal style was introduced (Salin 1904; Roth 1979; Haseloff 1981).

The importance of animals in religion and belief in shape changing are basic concepts in shamanistic systems of belief (i.e. Eliade 1964; Holmberg 1964; Chang 1983) with no relation to the Roman World (Salin 1903, 1904). However, the animal style incorporated elements of Roman techniques that were forged into a new language of signs, which resemble the highly complex and varied ancient Chinese and south Russian animal art (Salin 1903, 1904; Rostovtzeff 1929; Chang 1983). It developed first in south Scandinavia with the Nydam Style/Style I (Roth 1979; Haseloff 1981). However, Roth argues that the earliest figural compositions from the third and fourth centuries are attested from three areas with similar landscapes – south Scandinavia, south Slovakia and Hungary (Roth 1979: 45, 59) – indicating an already existing connection between selected areas of north and south-eastern Europe in the Late Roman Period. How are we to understand the dramatic ideological and cosmological changes that followed?

Archaeological framework: Hunnic material culture

The material evidence of the Huns is restricted to metal objects, where polychrome gold fittings with eagle heads – often in pairs – dominate (e.g. Werner 1956; Bona 1991; Koch 2007). The eagle or the falcon is a recurrent animal on gold fittings. It is known that Attila had two falcons as his heraldic weapon symbol,[4] and hunting with falcons and eagles has a long tradition among the steppe peoples of Central Asia (Kock 2007: 6). It is also well attested that predatory birds are the most valued helping spirits for shamans. Although the eagle – or eagles in pairs – motif is recurrent and important in the animal styles of the north, this does not provide a sufficient explanation for the development of the much richer animal style in Scandinavia. Animal art is, as Chang has demonstrated explicitly in his work on ancient China, closely interwoven with power:

> Clearly, if animals in Shang and Chou art were the principal medium
> employed by shamans to communicate with heaven, the possession of ani-
> mal-style ritual bronzes meant possession of the means of communication.
> Possessors of such means of communication were invested with wisdom and
> thus with power.
>
> (*Chang 1983: 80*)

Hunnic religious specialists were undoubtedly seers and shamans as are their Mongolian successors with their spirited representations of eagles and falcons, horses,
lions, etc. (Saunders 1971: 13; Morgan 2007: 37 ff.).[5] The Huns trusted haruspices
at a time when the Romans and the imperial Germans were Christianised, and
at a time when Roman edicts threatened with capital punishment those 'insane'
enough to consult them (Ammianus Marcellinus Book 28, Ch. 1). The specific
Hunnic method of foretelling the future, scapulimancy (divination from the
scorched shoulder-blade of a sheep), has Asiatic origins (Maenchen-Helfen 1973:
270; Morgan 2007: 37 ff.), and inscribed oracle shoulder-blades from sheep are
known from ancient China too (Chang 1983: fig. 3). The ritual is still conducted
among shamans/shamanesses of the Buriads who live in Mongolia today (Balogh
2007: 88 and pl.16a). In societies with a shamanistic world view, animals are essential, because they serve as helping spirits for the shaman's contact with the Other
World (e.g. Eliade 1964: 88–9). A common way to demand the help of animal spirits is by sacrificing an animal (Chang 1983: 69). Asiatic steppe peoples including the
Mongols, the ancient Chinese, the Siberians and the peoples of the Altai belong to
this animistic–shamanistic tradition (e.g. Rostovtzeff 1929; Chang 1983; Martynov
1991; Eliade 1964; Heissig 1996), as did the Huns.

Thus, the Huns brought with them a traditional Asiatic/Eurasian animistic–shamanistic belief system and it is accepted that such a belief system merged with
a Saami and a Nordic/Germanic belief system (Strömbäck 1935; Glosecki 1989;
Price 2001, 2002). It also resonated well with Gothic religious tradition. Already in
the third century the Goths came across a shamanistic culture when they reached
the Black Sea area. The intoxicating 'cannabis sauna' among the Scythians, which is
mentioned by Herodotus and was certainly also known among the Thracians, was
probably also used to send Gothic shamans on the desired 'trip' (Wolfram 1990:
107).

Within these religious systems, political supremacy went hand in hand with
the consolidation of religious power; when combined with wealth, art, myth and
ritual, it became a pathway to power (Chang 1983). Those who could provide
all these elements were considered superior. Now the Huns took over that role
from the Romans. In addition, this new belief system may have represented a most
welcome alternative to the adoption of the Christian faith among the north
European tribes.

The Huns also introduced a new medium of power: gold. During the same
decades of European history as the animal style came into being, gold constituted
the supreme institutional medium for Attila's policy (Thompson 1996: 94). Thus,

the immense number of gold hoards in the Nordic area, some of which contain significant Byzantine jewellery (Arrhenius 1990) can be ascribed to the policy of the Huns and the political situation in the Migration Period in general. The vast amounts of wealth reflected in these hoards situate Scandinavia within the realm of Hunnic policy and interaction. They point to the emergence of a new and more aggressive political system.

As a steppe empire, the Huns' sovereignty over vast territories was upheld through speed, mobility, violence and reward. Like other nomad peoples they never conquered land in order to control it (Thompson 1996: 60; Pohl 2001). Put another way, they controlled kings and their vassals and made them their allies, and kingdoms were reduced to vassals. As mounted warriors they were, theoretically at least, able to cross from one end of Europe to the other in a few weeks because of their outstanding capacity as horsemen who carried everything with them on horseback (Howarth 1994: 19). Ammianus Marcellinus describes them in the following way:

> their way of life is rough that they have no use for fire or seasoned food, but live on the roots of wild plants and the half-raw flesh of any sort of animal, which they warm a little by placing it between their thighs and the backs of their horses. They have no buildings to shelter them, but avoid anything of the kind as carefully as we avoid living in the neighbourhood of tombs; not so much as a hut thatched with reeds is to be found among them. They roam at large over mountains and forests, and are inured from the cradle to cold, hunger, and thirst. On foreign soil only extreme necessity can persuade them to come under roof, since they believe that it is not safe for them to do so.
>
> (*Ammianus Marcellinus, Book 31, Ch. 2*)

The Mongol conquests of the thirteenth century in general and the invasion of Europe in 1237–42 in particular represent a comparable historical sequence. The Mongols ruled the world from the German border to Korea, although they left only few traces behind (except for the *Secret History of the Mongols*). The culture of nomads is understandably poor. They had no permanent home, their institutions were movable, too, and social power was exercised in the hall or the felt-covered tent, *yurt* (Kennedy 2002: 45). Although Attila had a headquarters with impressive timber buildings to deal with foreign diplomats, all social, cultural, military, economic and religious institutions were transferable in space. Priscus reports on these institutions (Priscus fragm. 8). No doubt, Hun society incorporated a wide variety of specialists who performed and codified institutionalised behaviour, whether the young women in the welcome procession, the performers during the banquet, the women who embroidered the beautiful textiles, or the artisan smiths who transformed the Roman gold into elaborated diadems, earrings, and buckles, some inlaid with precious stone (Priscus fragm. 8; Chardaev 1991: 255–6), or into elaborate horse gear (see also Gabuev 2007: 293 ff.). Gift-giving was an essential part of diplomatic contact, although the distinction between gift and tribute is in reality often blurred (Pohl 2001: 453). No doubt the Huns, as did the Scythians and other steppe people, possessed sophisticated institutions that enabled them to incorporate tribute-paying vassal kings, who were also rewarded generously. The acquisition of gold and portable wealth constituted the purpose of diplomatic missions and the goal of Hunnic 'foreign policy' and warfare (e.g. Gibbon 2005: chs XXXIV–XXXV; Thompson 1996; Pohl 2001; Geary 2002; Heather 2006).

Thus the introduction of a new symbolic system in the late fourth and early fifth centuries can at best be ascribed to the imposition of Hunnic institutions and rule in which gold and animals were the media for social, religious and political power. It represents an 'episodic transition' that opened up a new type of social complexity and the adoption of a whole new set of social and cosmological values in Barbarian Europe. To evaluate the Hunnic impact, I put forward a hypothesis of the Hunnic presence in Scandinavia.

The Huns in Scandinavia: diagnostic features

Southern Scandinavia constituted part of Attila's sphere of dominion. The question is of what nature it was, and how it was materialised. Let us dwell a moment on the fact that without written evidence we should hardly have known of the Hunnic presence in Europe. Michel Kazanski is right in pointing out that 'the diversity of sources from which the material culture of the aristocracy of the empire of the Huns was drawn is indicative of the cosmopolitan character of Attila's court' (Kazanski 1993: 213). Therefore the scattered material evidence that has been identified as possessing diagnostic Hunnic features (Werner 1956; Bóna 1991; Koch 2007) becomes a yardstick for evaluating their presence also in the north.

Among the artefacts to which Joachim Werner called attention are the characteristic open-ended earrings of solid gold or silver, pot-bellied and with pointed ends (Figure 9.1). They are known from graves north and east of the Black Sea and from the Danube plain in Hungary (Werner 1956: 24–6, karte 10). However, Werner was not aware of nine similar earrings that have been found in Denmark, and one in southern Norway (Figure 9.2). They have never been identified as Hunnic, because nobody expected Hunnic items to appear there, despite the fact that Werner emphasised the type as one of the most significant and unambiguous Hunnic artefacts.[6] It is, however, striking that they are not found in any of the numerous Scandinavian gold hoards. Nearly all of them are single finds without clear context, and none of them come from bogs or wetlands, as do many of the gold hoards. It indicates that they were different from other gold artefacts, highly personal, and not a source of wealth. One find from a Migration Period burial in south-western Norway seems to confirm this and several of the finds in Denmark could therefore be from ploughed out burials.

Small bronze mirrors, frequently with the sun symbol on one side, are also characteristic Hunnic artefacts (Werner 1956: 19–24; Bóna 1991) (Figure 9.3). According to Werner (ibid.: fig. 4), they are present in graves from the Hunnic core area between the Danube and the Theiss, as well as north and east of the Black Sea and far into central Asia. They are closely linked to shamanistic practices (Heissig

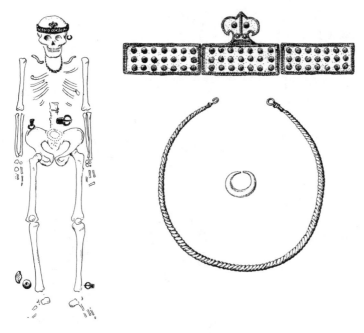

FIGURE 9.1   Hunnish woman's grave with an open-ended earring from Schipowo, Kurgan 2, Kazakhstan. Drawing by János Balatoni after Bóna (1991: 59, fig. 19).

1996: 253), even today among the Buriads in Mongolia (Balogh 2007: 96). Laboratory analysis testifies to the existence of one such mirror among the grave goods from the oldest inaugural burial in one of the three 'royal mounds' of Old Uppsala, the east mound, called 'Odin's Mound' (Arrhenius 1982, 1990; Bemmann 2007: 179). It has been argued that the bronze plate may rather be ascribed to a fibula (Duczko 1996: 78). However, the plate is exactly the size of the nomadic mirrors. A stone cairn covered the funerary fire, and at the centre a cremation urn was set into the ground. The cremated bones of a 10–14-year-old boy were found along with fragments of glass, gaming pieces, belt fittings, a bone comb and a spoon, together with fragments of gold filigree and *cloisonné*-work, etc. (Lindqvist 1936; for the latest discussion see Duczko 1996). There were fragments of bronze plates from a miniature leather helmet similar to the helmet in the 'princely grave' in Cologne Cathedral (Arrhenius and Sjøvold 1995) and from Avarian graves at Kerch (Arrhenius and Freij 1992:109). Also worth mentioning is a unique find of a solid tuft of human hair close to the urn. The burial is dated to the late Migration/early Vendel Period, probably the sixth century AD, although the exact date is under discussion (Åberg 1947; Lindqvist 1949; Duczko 1996; Ljungkvist 2008). However, the bronze mirror together with a solid tuft of hair is rather reminiscent of ceremonial burial practices among the Huns (they cut off their hair when in mourning, as in the case of Attila's funeral) although the burial took place after their disappearance from Europe.

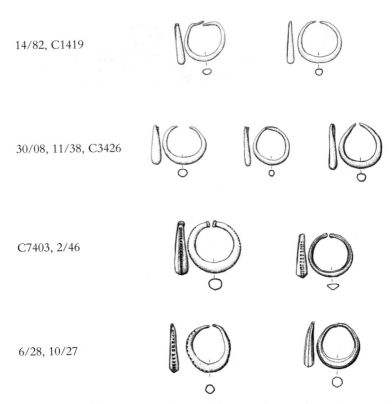

14/82, C1419

30/08, 11/38, C3426

C7403, 2/46

6/28, 10/27

FIGURE 9.2 Open-ended earrings of solid gold, pot-bellied and with pointed ends from Denmark. 14/82: Hammerslev, Randers county; C1419: Tjørn-elunde Mølle, Holbæk county; 30/08: Glumsø, Præstø county; 11/38: Denmark, unknown; C3426: Vejlstrup, Ringkøbing county; C7403: Vils, Thisted county; 2/46: Svendsmark, Præstø county; 6/28: Vindblæs, Ål-borg county; 10/27: Klipen, Åbenrå county. Registration numbers from the National Museum, Copenhagen. In addition, a gold ring similar to 6/28 is found in a weapon grave from Vesterbø grave 16, Rogaland, Nor-way (S 1428). Drawing: Bjørn Skaarup. © Lotte Hedeager.

Thus, one or two diagnostic artefact types ascribed to the Huns, pot-bellied, open-ended earrings and bronze mirrors, are attested in the north (Figure 9.4). The importance of animals, reflected in the development of Scandinavian and Germanic animal styles, the skilled crafting, 'the technology of enchantment', and the large number of gold hoards belong to the same cultural complex. However, the Hunnic presence took also more direct forms.

The confrontation with the Huns, although they might have included a mix-ture of ethnic groups, most certainly caused similar reactions in Scandinavia, as we know from Late Antique sources. At least some of the Huns clearly were of a dis-tinct ethnic Asiatic stock (Gibbon 2005: 367–8; Thompson 1996: 56; Maenchen-

FIGURE 9.3 Levice-Léva (Slovakia): grave with open-ended earring and mirror. Drawing by János Balatoni after Bóna (1991: 86, fig. 33).

Helfen 1973: 361 ff.; Heather 2006: 148; Geary 2002: 97). Ammianus Marcellinus describes them this way:

> They have squat bodies, strong limbs, and thick necks, and are so prodigiously ugly and bent that they might to be two-legged animals, or the figures crudely carved from stumps which are seen on the parapets of bridges. Still, their shape, however disagreeable, is human.
>
> (*Ammianus Marcellinus, Book 31, Ch. 2*)

They looked 'foreign', and their presence encapsulated fury, greed and power, but also reward, admiration and superiority. This may explain why faces with distinct Asiatic attributes are placed in central positions on the first generation of Danish and Norwegian square-headed brooches with elaborate animal ornamentation (Haseloff 1981) (Figures 9.5 and 9.6). It indicates that the Huns were present in the imagination of Scandinavian elites.[7] However, it may also indicate that such

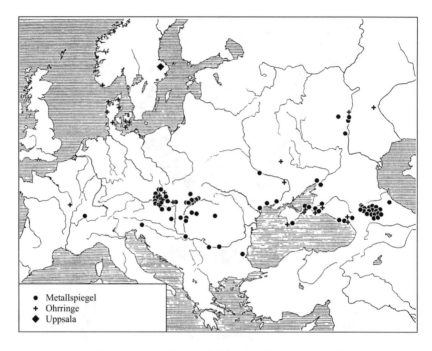

FIGURE 9.4 Distribution map of two of the most diagnostic artefacts related to the Huns: the pot-bellied, open-ended earrings of gold and silver and the bronze mirror. Redrawn by Per Persson after map from Werner (1956: map 10).

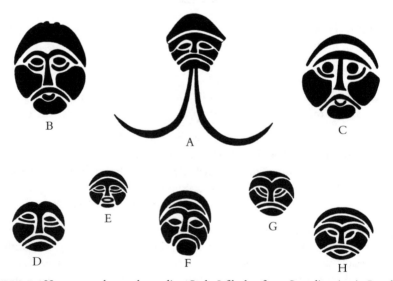

FIGURE 9.5 Human masks on the earliest Style I fibulae from Scandinavia: A: Lunde, Norway. B–C: Galsted, southern Jutland. D: Høstentorp, Zealand. E: Anda, Norway. F–H: Tveitane: Norway. After Haseloff (1981: Abb. 53).

FIGURE 9.6   Human masks as part of the ornamentation on brooches. A: Galsted, Southern Jutland. After Haseloff (1981: Abb. 9). B: Lunde, Lista, Norway. After Haseloff (1981: Abb. 3).

brooches were specially made on demand from the Hunnic elites and aimed as gifts to the Scandinavians.

A special find group, termed Hunnic funeral sacrifices ('Hunnische Totenopfer'), contains mounts from highly decorated harnesses, garments with applied gold decoration, saddle trappings and occasional lances or javelins with signs of intentional destruction found in small groups on dry land (Tomka 1987: 156 ff., 2007: 257, 2008). They are known from eastern and central Europe in the late fourth and early fifth centuries AD, and analogous ritual customs are ascribed to the mounted nomads of central Asia in later periods (Tomka 1987: 159; Bemmann 2007: 177 ff.). There are striking similarities between these funeral sacrifices and a group of finds from Scania in Sweden, from the sites of Sösdala, Fulltofta and Vennebo, that can be dated to the first half of the fifth century (Fabech 1991b: 94 ff.; Bemmann 2007).

In addition, the ceremonial dress carefully reproduced on the gold-foil figures from the late Migration Period onwards, and on the figures from the sixth- and seventh-century AD helmet plates (Watt 1999, 2004), is similar to the Caucasian caftans known from seventh-century burials (Holmqvist 1977: 214 Abb.12; Vierck 1978: 264–5, Abb.15; Watt 2004: 203; Mannering 2006) (cf. Figure 5.10) (Figures 9.7 and 9.8; cf. Figure 5.12). The short belted tunic, the traditional garment for Asiatic steppe nomads (whether short or long), was introduced into Scandinavia in the fifth

FIGURE 9.7 Helmet from Vendel grave 1, Sweden with figural plates. Drawing by O. Sörling (Stolpe and Arne 1927: pl. V).

FIGURE 9.8 Detail from the helmet from Vendel grave 1 (Figure 9.7). The small person wears a caftan. Drawing by O. Sörling (Stolpe and Arne 1927: pl. V).

and early sixth centuries AD and has been explained as a result of a 'Gothic cultural stream' ('gotischen Kulturstrom') or as an influence from the Avars (Vierck 1978: 264–6; Bender Jørgensen 2003, 2005; Näsman 2008: 116). However, the introduction of the *caftan* as the distinct male-warrior dress in Scandinavia from the late fifth century has recently been ascribed to direct Asiatic influence on Scandinavia (Mannering 2006: 197 f.). The change in military organisation towards an emphasis on mounted warriors is likewise explained as a result of direct connection with the eastern steppe cultures. It has been argued that the Huns (or later the Avars) brought the Hunnic saddle-type into Europe (Bóna 1991: 68; Scukin et al. 2006: figs 104–5; Popa 2007), as known from the chiefly burials at Vendel and Högom in Sweden (Engström 1997: 248 f.). Moreover, a dramatic change in Nordic arrowheads took place during the fifth century AD when the pointed awl-shaped type was introduced among elite warriors in western Scandinavia. Nomadic archers such as the Sagittarii in the Roman army and the Hunnic troops used this specific type of arrow with their characteristic composite bow. More than fifty such 'nomadic' arrowheads have been identified in Norway (Lindbom 2006: ch. 7).

To summarise: the mounted nomadic archer with an efficient composite bow, with caftan and saddle, is archaeologically attested in Scandinavia, as are Hunnic funeral sacrifices. This new warrior institution belonged in an elite environment, as reflected in burials and halls with gold-foil figures. Its introduction may be ascribed to the influence of returning warriors from the continent who encountered the mounted nomadic warriors and copied them when back home. However, I consider it more likely, when other archaeological indices are taken into consideration, that it reflects a more direct Nordic affiliation with the Huns and their allied troops during the fourth and fifth centuries.

Closely connected to the Germanic warrior-milieu is the 'Kolben' type arm-ring of solid gold known from chiefly and kingly graves, and from hoards of the late Roman and the Migration Period (Werner 1980; Arrhenius 1990; Lund Hansen 2001). It consists of a plain, massive, gold ring with thickened ends and was worn on the right arm (cf. Figure 6.6). Their size and form prevented them from being removed when in place. These rings are explained as *trustis dominica* symbolising an oath given to the king to confirm a lifelong military devotion (Arrhenius 1990: 132). Some of the early 'Kolben' rings were probably made in the Roman Empire during the fourth century AD. However, during the Migration Period their distribution indicates a more easterly production (ibid.: 130 and fig. 6.13). Their spatial distribution covers the entire area from the Black Sea to the Baltic islands, Sweden, Denmark, and from Norway. On the continent they mainly stay north of the Roman border, except for a few in Gaul/France, with Childeric's grave (he died in AD 481/82) at Tournai as the most prominent example.[8] Metal analysis has demonstrated that the content of silver in the alloy differs, which indicates different production centres. Some show a metal composition that corresponds to items from Hunnic graves, and Arrhenius has proposed that some 'Kolben' rings were of Hunnic origin. It seems likely that this *signum* of military rank, affiliation and loyalty was transmitted from late Roman to a Germanic/Barbarian context in the fifth century.[9] Here it was taken over by the Huns, as the spatial distribution of the 'Kolben' rings in the Migration Period reflects the Hunnic sphere of dominion.

Taken together, there is mounting archaeological evidence for a distinct Hunnic influence in selected areas of social, military and religious life in Scandinavia during the Migration Period. This influence also included new myths and their representation.

Evidence of a new cosmology

One of the most characteristic artefacts of the Migration Period is the gold bracteates (Mackeprang 1952; Axboe 2004, 2007). Their origin is traditionally ascribed to the Byzantine gold medallions with a portrait of the Roman emperor (Andrén 1991; Axboe 1991, 2007; Bursche 2000) (cf. Figures 3.8 and 3.9).[10] However, the bracteates were quickly transformed into a genuine Nordic medium of symbolic communication (e.g. Hauck 1985–89, 1991) (see Figure 4.20). The composition on some of the early bracteates illustrates the Old Norse myths of Baldur's death (Figure 9.9) and Tyr losing his hand in the mouth of the Fenris wolf (Figure 9.10) (Hauck 1978: 210, 1986; Roth 1986c: 10; Hedeager 2005a: 236–8) as well as Gunnar in the snake-pit as described in the *Lay of Atli*, part of the epic cycle of the *Volsungs* (Figure 9.11). The clear and unambiguous compositions suggest that these

| A | B | C |

FIGURE 9.9 Gold bracteates. 'Balder's death'. A: Bornholm. Drawing by Poul Wöhliche. B: Fakse, Denmark. C: Jutland, Denmark. Drawings by H. Lange. All after Hauck (1985–89; A: IK 595, B: IK 51, C: IK 165).

FIGURE 9.10 Gold bracteate. Trollhättan, Sweden. 'Tyr who loses his hand'. Drawing by H. Lange after Hauck (1985–89: IK 190).

FIGURE 9.11   Gold bracteate. Sigurd the Dragon Slayer (*Sigurd Fafnirsbani*). Söderby, Sweden. After Lamm et al. (2000: Tafel V).

myths were newly invented and held a central position in Old Norse belief system from the first half of the fifth century.

The largest group of bracteates, the so-called C-bracteates (Figures 9.12, 9.13, 9.14 and 9.15), illustrate a shamanistic representation of the soul journey: the head of a man in the disguise of a bird, travelling on a creature which looks like a horse but has a horn and beard (Hedeager 1997b, 2005a). Some of the figures on the early bracteates are very detailed and they show the head with pearls like the emperor or with what might be a diadem. The long hair is in a plait (Figures 9.12 and 9.13) and on a variation of the same motif the plait has turned into a bird (Figure 9.15).[11] The large number of bracteates with this motif underlines the importance of the soul journey, and it suggests that it was a new element in Old Norse religion that had to be propagated. Therefore the Roman emperor was replaced by the new 'king of the gods', Odin. With him was a new shamanistic practice introduced.

From Antique sources we hear of the Huns as exceptional horsemen. They looked, as Ammianus Marcellinus describes, as if man and horse were almost glued together as one creature, half-man and half-horse; in fact, what we see on some bracteates:

> they are ill-fitted to fight on foot, and remain glued to their horses, hardy but ugly beasts, on which they sometimes sit like women to perform their everyday business. Buying or selling, eating or drinking, are all done by day or night on horseback, and they even bow forward over their beasts' narrow necks to enjoy a deep and dreamy sleep. When they need to debate some important matter they conduct their conference in the same posture.
>
> (*Ammianus Marcellinus, Book 31, Ch. 2*)

FIGURE 9.12   Gold bracteate. Funen, Denmark. Drawing by H. Lange after Hauck (1985–89: IK 58).

FIGURE 9.13   Gold bracteate. Bjæverskov, Denmark. Drawing by H. Lange after Hauck (1985–89, IK 300).

That the Huns had long hair is certain; they might as well have worn it in a plate like other Asiatic steppe peoples. The elaborated diadems depicted on some of the bracteates heads can be ascribed to the specific Hunnic diadems of gold and inlaid stones (cf. Bóna 1991:147–9, pl. xiv, xv; Werner 1956: 61–8) (Figure 9.1).[12] The black shamanic costume among the Mongolian Buriads of today includes a metal crown-shaped helmet (Balogh 2007: 98 and pl. 18). The bearded and horned

FIGURE 9.14   Gold bracteate. Bjørnsholm, Denmark. Drawing by H. Lange after Hauck (1985–89: IK 25).

FIGURE 9.15   Gold bracteate. Hjørlunde, Denmark. Drawing by H. Lange after Hauck (1985–89: IK 79).

creature on the bracteates is a hybrid creature reminiscent of the Scythian ceremonial horse with artificial horns known from the frozen tomb at Pazyryk from the fifth century BC (Altheim 1959–62: 440 Abb. 8).

The Scandinavian warrior elites of the fifth century emulated the strongest symbol of the Roman emperor – the gold medallion – and transformed it into a symbol of barbarian power and supremacy by replacing its central motif with their new king of the Old Norse pantheon: Odin. It was also a powerful way to propagate the most important of the new myths that were introduced in the fifth century in Scandinavia. Some of these were turned into written-form *c*. 1200 and are thus recognisable in the iconography of the Migration Period, while others were lost and are incomprehensible to us.

Summarising the evidence

During the fifth and early sixth centuries AD, a structured transmission of symbols and material culture with affiliation to the Huns took place in Scandinavia. It triggered a process of cosmological and institutional invention. This 'episodic transition' represents a decisive and conscious religious change that sustained the rise of a new Germanic identity in opposition to the declining Roman west and its new Christian faith.

Prior scholars as Japetus Steenstrup (1893), Bernhard Salin (1903, 1904), Knut Liestøl (1924), Michael Rostovtzeff (1929), Guttorm Gjessing (1934), Ivar Lundahl (1934) and Niels Lukman (1943) have discussed Asiatic influences and Hunnic elements in the north during the Migration Period. However, since the Second World War most Scandinavian historians and archaeologists downplayed or even rejected such elements.[13] The most recent among them is Ulf Näsman (2008) who explicitly rejects the importance of the Huns altogether, especially their capacity to transform the political system of Barbarian Europe: 'it [the change in social and political structure] would have happened anyway, and not very much later. Had the Huns not succeeded, the Avars would plausibly have done so 193 years later [in Central Europe]' (Näsman 2008: 116). In this he accepts the structural interaction between east and west. However, the plausibility of his hypothesis can never be tested; it remains a counterfactual answer (see Hedeager 2009).

The hypothesis is supported by a new understanding of the nature of Hunnic rule, giving it the status of a steppe empire (Howard-Johnston 2007, forthcoming). It goes a long way to explain the immense political and ideological power the Huns exerted in restructuring barbarian Europe politically, ideologically and ethnically, and it provides a stronger historical and explanatory framework for their influence over Scandinavia. What Howard-Johnston makes clear is that the Huns were politically experienced in dealing with empires from their Chinese encounter, and thus entered western Europe not as barbarian hordes but as a well-organised and experienced nomadic empire. Walter Pohl (2001) demonstrates striking similarities between early medieval and thirteenth-century central Asian courts regarding their highly sophisticated political culture and thus supports this new view of the Huns.[14] And J.J. Saunders, dealing with the Mongols of the thirteenth century, points to the fact the modern historians still are struck with wonder at the Mongols extraordinary capacity in planning and co-ordinating their military campaigns. No doubt, he writes, the Mongol leaders were masters of the art of war such as the world scarcely saw before or has seen since. (Saunders 1971: 88). In a comparable historical context, eight hundred years earlier it seems plausible that the Huns also possessed all the necessary institutions and strategies to deal not only with the Roman Empire but also with less politically organised societies, such as the Germanic, whom they mobilised in their strategy against Rome and Byzantium. And it is likely that the Huns had the same effect on Europe as the Mongols eight centuries later where 'they were treated as something more than human, a dreadful visitation from hell; the frantic reports of refugees intensified instead of diminishing the fear and paralysis which gripped every land they approached' (Saunders 1971: 87). Contrary to the Mongols, the Huns did succeed in conquering western Europe and thus gained a more profound impact on the history of Europe.

10
HYPOTHESIS II: ATTILA AND THE RECASTING OF SCANDINAVIAN MYTHOLOGY

Ornamentation – Innovation – Migration: A hypothesis

Like myths and epic poetry, animal ornamentation was transformed and transmitted down through the centuries lasting up until the consolidation of Christianity *c.* AD 1200 to *c.* 1250. Quite clearly, the animals and the belief systems they encapsulated were incompatible with the Christian faith and world view and therefore they disappeared when Christianity was fully established *c.* AD 1200. It is no coincidence that the Old Norse heritage was written down at this moment on Iceland, where it has been upheld by a more traditional society. The fact that the Old Norse texts share central mythological motifs with the early bracteates of the fifth and early sixth centuries is a testimony to the *longue durée* of oral tradition and Norse religion (Axboe 2007: 121). This conclusion has implications for our understanding of the historicity of Old Norse religion.

In 1903 Bernhard Salin took up an already existing hypothesis[1] – that the cult of Odin arrived in Scandinavia during the late Roman and/or Migration Period (Salin 1903; see also Kaliff and Sundqvist 2004). Here, as in his pioneering work, *Die altgermanische Thierornamentik*, he put forward a hypothesis that has ever since been discussed among historians of religion and archaeologists in particular (Salin 1904). According to Salin, the introduction of animal ornamentation in Scandinavia was the result of influences from the Black Sea area. He argued for a migration from southern Russia into Scandinavia in the fourth century. The core of this historical event was reflected in the description of Odin and the Asir who came from Asia, Troy, or Byzantium to settle in Scandinavia. The story is told by Saxo Grammaticus in *The History of the Danes* (Book I: 25), and in its most detailed form by Snorri Sturluson in *Ynglinga Saga* (4), and in the Prologue to his *Edda*. Odin is portrayed as a powerful warrior chief or magician who settled in Scandinavia together with his warrior chiefs and let himself be worshipped as a god. To Salin the core of the story reflects a historical reality of migrating groups from the Crimean/Black Sea area: 'Dass aber in der Tradition ein Kern von Wahrheit steckte, dass sie nicht lediglich eine gelehrte und unkritische Mittelalterkonstruction ist, dürfte unbestreitbar sein' (However, it would seem indisputable that this tradition was not just a learned and uncritical medieval construction, but contained a core of truth) (ibid.: 148).

Central to the story are the wars between the Asir gods and the Vanir gods and later on the reconciliation and exchange of hostages. This part of the story is known from *The Prose Edda* (*Vǫluspá* 21–6) as well as from Snorri's *Edda: Gylfaginning* 22 and *Skáldskaparmál* 1. For older scholars the myth of the Vanir wars has mostly been seen as a reflection of a historical war between two opposing ethnic groups: a Scandinavian one with an old tradition of commemorating the Vanir gods of fertility, and a south-eastern warrior group with a belief in the Asir gods. This 'war of religion' among those who worshipped the Vanir gods and those who worshipped the Asir gods was the explanatory framework for most historians of Old Norse religion and many archaeologists. Since the Vanir are fertility deities and the Asir more warlike deities, the conflict has often been understood as a local fertility cult being overrun by a more warlike cult of invaders. To some, as Salin, this reflected historical events of the fourth century AD; to others the Asir–Vanir fight took place in the third millennium BC with the establishment of the Indo-Germanic Battle Axe culture. At that time the west European/south Scandinavian megalithic culture was replaced by the more 'advanced' battle-axe people. This historical event then stayed in the memory as the myth of the Vanir war and the pact of peace between the two groups (the Megalithic and the Battle-Axe groups).

However, from the early 1960s onwards scholars such as George Dumézil, Otto Höffler, Jan de Vries and W. Berts among others argued against any historical 'translation' of this narrative. Instead they claimed to offer a more scientific approach founded on structural comparison, particularly the work of Dumézil (1969). Based on comparative studies between Scandinavia, Europe and India, he claimed a shared origin of the main social divisions of all Indo-European societies, reflected in the nature of their most prominent gods. Although he had major difficulties in applying this structural tripartite division to the system of Old Norse (Davidson 1993: 154), he introduced new meaning into strange myths such as that of the early battle between the Vanir and the Asir. Like Claude Lévi-Strauss (e.g. 1963/1973), Dumézil employed a structural approach to the interpretation of myth, stressing the importance of polarity and contrast, but in doing that he omitted space and time from his system – in short 'history'. Instead, a timeless, unchanged Indo-European society took precedence.

The battle between the Asir and the Vanir was interpreted as the social conflict within a society in which the hierarchical followers of the king in control of magic-religious power (the Asir) stood against the rural population in control of fertility and wealth (the Vanir). Only through the pact between these two social classes was cosmic order and purpose recovered from apparent chaos. This scheme was applied both to the ancient Indian Vedic religion and to other Indo-Germanic societies (Lincoln 1999: ch. 7). To Dumézil the concordance between the Ancient Indian system of belief and the Old Norse was indisputable. The many similar elements, strikingly complex and strange, permitted Dumézil 'to be sure of what he was claiming' (Dumézil 1969: 33).

What is considered a scientific explanation within a timeless comparative structural approach of the history of religion can only be falsified or verified on archaeological grounds because archaeology represents independent contemporary sources. Therefore their historical value for dating is stronger than the historical sources, which are mostly much later than the actual events. At the bottom line the question remains whether the Asir–Vanir battle and reconciliation reflects historical events in the prehistoric Scandinavia/Germanic area or is an archetypical myth of cosmic social order within the Indo-European system of belief. Since the myth is referred to in *Voluspá* in *The Poetic Edda*, the core of the story – the battle, the reconciliation and the exchange of hostages – is no invention of Scandinavian narrators of the thirteenth century AD. However, the migration story of the Asir might of course be just that.

The migration story and myth of descent among the Scandinavians

Origin myths and migration stories are central to a majority of the early medieval ethnic histories, in particular those Germanic groups who claimed their origin in Scandinavia, such as the Ostrogoths, the Lombards, the Burgundians, the Anglo-Saxons and the Heruli. Although Christianised, in creating their royal genealogy they have Odin/Wotan/Gautr as the first king and progenitor of the royal stock and the royal family of the Ostrogoths, the Amals (Chapter 3 this volume). Jordanes called this first king 'Anses', who might either be identical with the Aeneas who wandered from Troy to the new city of Rome, according to Livy's national epic *History of Rome* (Sundqvist 2002: 149), or with the Asir, which Jordanes translates as *semideos* (demi-gods) (Simek 1996: 225). What interests us here is the fact that their identity and self-perception was tied up with the north and the pagan god of fury and magic (see Part III). Why is that?

The only peoples of Europe who apparently have no migration story recorded as part of their early Christian identity are the Scandinavians. It is evident that neither Christianity nor the new political/geographical realities of the early thirteenth century AD made Snorri or Saxo create one, although they do refer to royal genealogies of substantial length and divine origin. The ancestors of the Danish royal dynasty from Lejre on Zealand, the Skjoldungs, are identical to the Anglo-Saxon royal house of the Scyldings, well known from the Old English epic poem *Beowulf*, as well as *Widsith*. Scyld Scefing ('shield') is Odin's son and the progenitor of both royal lines (Simek 1996: 277). In Saxo's account in Book I, the father of the royal Danish line, the Skjoldung dynasty, is Humli/Humbli. From the Gothic Amal genealogy, Humli is known as the son of Gaut/Gapt/Gauts/Odin and older than Amal, the father of the Amali (the Ostrogothic royal line). This might reflect Gothic–Scandinavian relations of the third, fourth and fifth centuries AD (Wolfram

1990: 37). Thus, the royal dynasty of the Danes was descended from Odin and the Asir gods.

The Ynglings, on the other hand, are the Swedish royal dynasty from whom the first Norwegian king, Harald Fairhair (died *c.* AD 933) and the Norwegian royal line of the Ynglings are descended, as far down as the fourteenth century (Simek 1996: 378). The names of the early Swedish kings are retained in the poem *Ynglingatal*, composed in the ninth century AD, and adopted from there by Snorri's *Ynglinga Saga* and Ari's *Islendingabók*, as well as the Latin *Historia Norvegiae* (p. 26 this volume). In *Ynglingatal* the first king is Fjolnir; however, the prose texts name three gods before him – Snorri tells of Odin, Njorðr, and Yngvi-Freyr, and the two others of Yngvi, Njorðr, and Freyr. Angvi-Freyr (also known in the form Ingunar-Freyr) was considered to be the ancestor of the Ynglings, and Yngvi is frequently referred to as the ancestor of the Ynglings in skaldic poetry. Thus the royal dynasty of the Ynglings descended from the Vanir gods (ibid.: 378–9).

In *Germania* (2: 3–4), dating to the end of the first century AD, Tacitus tells of the Germanic tribe of the Ingaevones who, according to old traditions, descended from a son of Mannus ('man'). He was the one who gave them the name. The belief in a godly ancestor of the Nordic Germanic group named Inguaz or Inguan thus strengthens the information given by the skald Tjorðólf ór Hvíní in *Ynglingatal* and later on by Snorri and Ari about the sacred descent of the Ynglings, and the Vanir gods as their progenitors (Simek 1996: 378). Myths about the Germanic peoples' sacred descent are recorded from the time of Tacitus to the High Middle Ages as a mixture of myths, legends and historical facts. This is confirmed by the origin myths of the Germanic tribes as recorded in later times by Gregory of Tours, Jordanes, Bede, Paul the Deacon, etc. The Scandinavian migration story, however, differs significantly from the Germanic and Anglo-Saxon ones. It is not the tale of people on the move from north to south in Europe; on the contrary, it is a narrative about migration from the south-east of Europe to the north by Odin and his followers, the Asir. Snorri describes this move across Europe and the process of settling in south Scandinavia in detail in the Prologue to *The Prose Edda* (4, 5) and in the *Ynglinga Saga* (I, 1–5).

In the Prologue (translated by Jesse Byock 2005):

(3: He had a son named Voden, the one we call Odin)

4. Odin's journey Northward
Odin had a great gift of prophecy, as his wife also did, and through this learning he became aware that his name would become renowned in the northern part of the world and honoured more than kings. For this reason he was eager to set off from Turkey, and he took with him on his journey a large following of people, young and old, men and women. So, too, they took with them many precious things. Wherever they went on their travels, tales of their splendour were told, making them seem more like gods than men. They journeyed without stopping until they reached the north, where

they entered the region now called Saxland. There Odin settled down for a long time, taking possession of much of the land.

Odin had three of his sons guarding the country. One of them, Veggdegg, was a powerful king who ruled over East Saxland. His son was Vitrgils, whose sons were Vitta, the father of Heingest, and Sigar, the father of Svebdegg, whom we call Svipdag. Odin's second son, named Beldegg, we call Baldr; he held the land that is now called Westphalia. His son was Brand, and his son was Frjodigar, whom we call Frodi; his son was Freovin, his son was Wigg, whose son Gevis was called Gavir. Odin's third son was named Siggi, whose son was Rerir. The men of this family ruled in what is now called France, and from them come the family called the Volsungs.

From all of them, numerous and great families descend.

5. Odin's journey continues and the Æsir settle in the North
Then Odin set out, travelling north, and arrived in the country called Rheidgotaland. He took possession of all that he wanted in the land and made his son Skjold ruler. Skjold's son was named Fridleif and from him are descended the kindred known as the Skjoldungs, the family of the kings of Denmark. What is now called Jutland was then called Reidgotaland.

He then went northward to what is now called Sweden, where a king named Gylfi lived. When the king learned of the journey of these Asians, who were called Æsir, he went to meet them, offering to grant Odin as much authority in his kingdom as he wanted. Wherever they stayed in these lands a time of peace and prosperity accompanied their journey, so that all believed the newcomers were the cause. This was because the local inhabitants saw that they were unlike any others they had known in beauty and intelligence. Recognising the land's rich possibilities, Odin chose a place for a town, the one that is now called Sigtun. He appointed leaders and, in accordance with the customs of Troy, he selected twelve men to administer the law of the land. In this way he organised the laws as they had been in Troy, in the manner to which the Turks were accustomed.

Then he went north, continuing until he reached the ocean, which people believed surrounded all land. There, in what is now called Norway, he placed his son in power. This son was named Saeming, and Norway's kings, as well as its jarls and other important men of the kingdom, trace their descent to him, as it is told in Haleygjatal. Odin also had with him his son named Yngvi, who after him became a king in Sweden, and from whom those kinsmen called the Ynglings are descended.

The Æsir and some of their sons married women from the land where they settled, and their families increased. They spread throughout Saxland and from there throughout all the northern regions so that their language – that of the men of Asia – became the native tongue in all these lands. People think, because the names of their ancestors are recorded in genealogies, they can show that these names were part of the language that the Æsir brought here to the northern world – to Norway, Sweden, Denmark, and Saxland. In England, however, some names of ancient regions and places lead one to believe that the names originally came from another language.

(Prologue to The Prose Edda *4, 5)*

In *Ynglinga Saga* (translated by A. H. Smith):

(1) … To the south of the fells which lie outside all the inhabited land there runs through Sweden the Great the river which in proper speech is called the Tanais [river Don in Russia]; it was formerly called the Tanakvisl or Vanakvisl; it flows out into the Black Sea. In the older days the land between the Vanaforks was called Vanaland or Vanaheim [the home of the Vanes). This river divides the world into parts; that to the east is known as Asia, and that to the west as Europe.

(2) The land in Asia to the east of the Tanakvisl was called Asaland or Asaheim and the chief town in the land was called Asagarth (or Asagard). In the town there was the chief who was known as Odin and it was a great place for sacrificing. It was the custom for twelve chief priests of the temple to direct the sacrifices and to judge between men; they were called diar or drottnar; and them should all people serve and obey. Odin was the mighty warrior who had wandered far and won for himself many kingdoms; he was so victorious that he won every battle, and through that it came about that his men believed he must needs be winner in every fight. It was his wont when he sent his men to battle or on any other journey to lay his hands on their heads and give them this blessing; they then believed that all would go well with them. And so it was with his men; when they were hard beset on sea or land, they called on his name and always thought they got help from it; in him had they all their trust. He often went so far away that he was many years on the journey.

(3) Odin had two brothers; one was called Ve, the other Vili. These two ruled the kingdom when he was away. It once happened when Odin was gone far away and had been a long time from home that his people thought he would not come back. Then his brothers took it upon themselves to divide his goods in succession to him, but they both took to wife his spouse Frigga. But a little later Odin came home and once more took his wife to himself.

(4) Odin went with his army against the Vanes, but they withstood him well and defended their land. Each of them was in turn winner; both sides harried one another's land, and did each other great scathe. And when they both became weary of it, they arranged a meeting to make peace and gave each other hostages. The Vanes gave them their highest men, Niord the Wealthy and his son Frey, and the people of Asaland in return gave the man called Hæmir, whom they thought well fitted to be a leader, being a big and

218 The making of Norse mythology

handsome man. With him they sent Mimer, the wisest of men, and the Vanes in return gave the wisest of their men called Kvasir ...

(5) A great ridge of mountains goes from northeast to southwest dividing Sweden the Great from other kingdoms. To the south of the fells it is not far to the land of the Turks where Odin had great possessions. At that time the Roman Emperors were going far and wide over the world and in battle beat down all people; because of the unrest many lords fled from their lands. When Odin looked into the future and worked magic, he knew that his offspring would dwell and till in the northern parts of the earth. He, there-fore, set his brothers Ve and Vili over Asgarth and he himself went away and with him went all the priests and many of his folk. First he went to Gardarik [Russia] and from there he went south to Saxland [Germany]. He had many sons; he won kingdoms far over Saxland and set his sons as rulers over them. From there he went north to the sea and found himself a dwelling on an island, which is now called Odensö in Fyn. Then he sent Gefion north-east over the sound to look for land; she then came to Gylfi [king of Sweden], who gave her ploughland. Next she went to a giant's home and there begot four sons with a giant. She shaped them in the likeness of oxen, yoked them to plough and broke up the land unto the sea westwards opposite Odensö; it was called Selund [the old name for Zealand in Denmark], and there she dwelt afterwards. Skiold [according to various chronicles, was the founder of the old Danish Skjoldung line of kings and is identified with Scyld Sceafing of the Old English poem *Beowulf*], Odin's son, took her to wife and they lived in Leidra [Leidra was called Leire near Roskilde in Zealand, where all the Danish kings are buried even in our time]. There where she ploughed is now a lake or a sea called Löginn; the fjords in Löginn answer to the nesses in Selund.

... And then when Odin got to hear that there was good land to the east in Gylfi's country he went there and Gylfi came to terms with him because he deemed he had no power to withstand the Asaland people. Many dealings had Odin and Gylfi between themselves in cunning and charms, but the Asa people always won. Odin set his dwelling near Lögrinn [lake Mälar in Swe-den] where it is now called Gamla-Sigtuna [situated on the east side of the Uppsala fjord, near the present Sigtuna], and where he built a large temple for blood offerings according to the customs of his people. He conquered all the land round it, and called his place Sigtun. He gave the temple priests dwelling-places; Niord lived in Noatun, Frey near Uppsala, Heimdal by the Himenfjell, Thor in Trudvang, Balder in Breidablik; to all of them he gave good lands.

(9) Odin died in his bed in Sweden.

(Ynglinga Saga *I*, *1–5*)

This narrative is comparable to other Germanic myths of origin by being a mixture of historical facts and mythical transformations and with Odin as the progenitor of the royal stocks. What differs, however, is the direction of the migration, and the sacred nature of it. First, it is not the people themselves who are on the move, but their deity. Second, the movement is in the opposite direction to the Germanic migrations, from the Black Sea/East Roman area to the north. Third, the migration into Scandinavia is described in detail, as are the geographical strongholds for Odin's power in Denmark and Sweden, Odensø in Fyn and Sigtuna/Uppsala in the Mälar area, the stronghold of the Ynglinga kings. Also, Lejre on Zealand is mentioned as the home of the Skjoldunge royal family.

By stating Troy as the place of origin of the Asir, Snorri builds on one of the three *topoi* of origin stories in early medieval Europe: Troy, Palestine and Scandza. This Graeco-Roman tradition was invented under Augustus when Livy wrote his national epic *History of Rome* in which the Romans descended from the Trojan hero Aeneas who migrated from Asia Minor. This story became a prototype for genealogies and 'national histories' among the Germanic peoples who settled within the area of the Roman Empire as the first generation of 'barbarian' Christians (Sundqvist 2002: 149 ff.; Kaliff and Sundqvist 2004: 15 ff.). However, a majority of them state in addition their origin in Scandza. Those who lacked a migration myth of origin, such as the Franks, later on took ideas from Livy, Virgil and the Bible and they made Troy and Palestine their ancient homelands.

Although Aeneas and Asir have etymological similarities, like the Ostrogothic royal family the Amals, the Asir are not, however, an invention of thirteenth-century AD Scandinavian narrators. The Asir are well attested in *The Poetic Edda* as the biggest family of gods in Old Norse mythology and therefore significantly older than Snorri and his contemporary historians such as Saxo and Ari. The term *Asir* is also recorded in Gothic as *Ansis* (Latinised thus by Jordanes in *Getica* XIII, 78), and in Anglo-Saxon as *esa*. In German the name is only retained in some personal names, such as Ansila, Ansgeir, or Anshram (Simek 1996: 3). Therefore it might be that the Scandinavian narrators of the thirteenth century simply used the similarity of the names to connect the old Nordic genealogies with the classical tradition of origin since it is only they who give the account of the migration of the Asir from Asia and they place Asgard in Asia, too (Simek 1996: 3).

What is left over of the ancient Old Norse mythology in the Asir migration story is first of all the fact that their most important gods, Odin and his sons, belong to the Asir family, and, second, that the Asir are predominantly the gods of war and rulership, whereas the Vanir are the gods of fertility. Also deeply embedded in Norse cosmology is the fight between the Asir and the Vanir, the reconciliation and the exchange of hostages, reflecting the social practice of peacemaking in Scandinavian/Germanic societies in the Late Iron Age. The migration from Asia, Troy and the Byzantine Empire etc. might therefore be imbued with rhetoric and literary *topoi* with roots in Greek and Roman sources (Sundqvist 2002: 149; Kaliff andf Sundqvist 2004: ch. 3). It may equally well be argued, however, that the migration story, despite the Troy-*topos*, has a core of historical reality. Since the nineteenth century, scholarly arguments have swung between these opposite poles of interpretation.

Embedded knowledge – Greco-Roman tradition

I propose that the Scandinavian myths of origin and migration represent a similar narrative structure to other Germanic origin stories of the Migration Period. In Chapter 3 it has been argued that the origin myths of the Goths, the Langobards, etc. were so firmly rooted in the legitimacy of their identity and kingly authority that they could not be abandoned despite Christianisation. Stories of origin and royal genealogies transmitted fundamental cultural knowledge for the identity of the whole people. Therefore the authors had to strike a balance between new and old, and they did this by transforming oral histories into written form and imbuing them with rhetoric and literary *topoi* from Greek and Latin literature.

This deliberate attempt to maintain cultural (pagan) knowledge in a Romanised setting by transforming it from oral to written form during the fifth, sixth and seventh centuries AD is comparable to the political situation in Scandinavia in the twelfth and thirteenth centuries when Snorri and Saxo in particular legitimised the early Christian kings in a pagan past by writing *Heimskringla* (the History of the Kings of Norway) and *Gesta Danorum* (History of the Danes), among others. Saxo did it by writing in Latin, the language of the Church, and he too was strongly influenced by his classical learning. Snorri, writing in Old Icelandic, in addition to the royal genealogies, compiled or co-wrote *The Prose Edda*, a handbook for those aspiring Icelandic skalds who wanted to master the traditional forms of verse and the old tales essential to the imagery of Old Norse poetry. 'Edda' means great-grandmother, and it was regarded in Iceland as the authoritative handbook for training poets in traditional verse forms throughout the Middle Ages. *The Prose Edda*, written two centuries after the coming of Christianity, concentrates on what was still known of myths, legends and the use of traditional poetic diction. It is evident that the compilation of the *Edda* served to preserve old knowledge of the pre-Christian past, although it also shows an awareness of Latin literary genres of the Middle Ages (Byock 2005: xi–xii). *The Prologue*, however, differs significantly from the rest of the text in structure, the kind of genealogical information it contains, and in subject matter. It is composed in accordance with the Graeco-Roman tradition and thereby attempts to elevate the status of the *Edda* in the medieval Christian world by equating the traditional stories with the classical *topoi*, as Jordanes and Cassiodorus did in the sixth century AD. *The Prologue* may have been part of the original text, or it may have been added later (ibid.: xvi). The same narrative, however, is also presented in the opening section of *Heimskringla*, indicating that it is of a similar age to the main text. Was the migration story of Odin and the Asir an invention by Snorri or Saxo inspired by their classical learning, or did it reflect a core of historical reality, as the European origin myths of the Migration Period certainly did?

Attila's cosmological blueprint

For two generations of the fifth century AD, the inhabitants of most of Europe shared a common experience: the Huns. The importance of this painful historical event that accompanied the end of the Roman Period and recast the European political landscape needs to be emphasised, because the contemporary sources tend to favour the 'imperial' Germanic peoples in the former west Roman Empire who survived to write their history. The Huns themselves disappeared as suddenly as they had appeared, in the mid-fifth century AD, leaving only sparse physical traces behind. Those Germanic tribes who remained in northern Europe recounted their history entirely in oral form, with traditions about events kept and transmitted for so long as they were regarded as important or culturally significant. They were only written down in the early Medieval Period. I propose, however, that an essential core of the Migration Period's dramatic history was preserved in early medieval epic poetry and the Nordic sagas. Further, that these same themes are reflected in the material culture, too. The next passage will address the 'historical core' of the cultural transformations that took place during these few generations and their afterlife in Nordic cosmology/mythology.

In Snorri's migration story Odin and the Asir act in a strikingly similar way to the military and political strategy we know of from the Huns' brief expeditions during which they established strongholds – by force and by diplomacy. Snorri relates how Odin travelled north from the Black Sea to Scandinavia at great speed ('they journeyed without stopping'), how he set out on brief expeditions and sometimes stayed away for several years, and how he gave land to his sons and established political strongholds all over northern Europe and his sons became progenitors of the leading royal families in Scandinavia.

Snorri's comprehensive description of Odin as a paramount warrior chief and king of the Asir includes the following information. The correspondence with the historical Attila as the paramount chief and ruler is systematic and framed on a similar historical core (Table 1):

	Odin	Attila
1	Odin lived at the time when the Roman emperors were going far and wide over the world and in battle beat down all people	Attila lived at the time when Roman Emperors were going far and wide over the world and in battle beat down all people
2	Odin and the Asir came from Asia to Scandinavia (from the area east of the Tanais river (the River Don)	Attila and the Huns went from Asia to Scandinavia
3	Odin had wandered far and won many kingdoms	Attila had wandered far and won many kingdoms
4	Odin won every battle	Attila won every battle
5	Odin fought the war between the Asir and the Vanir – which he in fact did not win	Attila – and the Huns – fought the war between the Huns and the Ostrogoths – which he in fact did not win; they were allied
6	The unrest made people take flight from their land	The unrest made people take flight from their land – which they certainly did in the Migration Period

7	Odin's men called on his name when they needed aid, and they got help from it	We do not know whether the Huns did the same with the name of Attila
8	Odin often went so far that he was many years on a journey	Attila often went so far that he was many years on a journey – especially in the years AD 435–438, where he might have been in Scandinavia (with his brother Bleda)
9	Odin had great possessions in the land of the Turks (east of the Tanais river – this is to the east of the River Don in Russia)	Attila went on an expedition to the land north of the Caucasus and east of the River Don – in AD 451 (however, his headquarters was in the eastern part of the Hungarian plain)
10	Odin had three sons	Attila had three sons
11	Odin's favourite son was killed by his brother – his name was Beldegg – called Balder	Attila killed his brother Bleda (in 445)
12	Odin is a seer and shaman	The Huns had seers and shamans
13	Odin had two ravens[2]	Attila had two falcons as his heraldic weapon symbol[3]
14	Odin stilled the sea and turned winds in what way he would	Attila (and the Huns) could excite storms of wind and rain[4]
15	The Asir gods were unlike any other (in beauty and intelligence)	The Huns looked different (they were Asiatic)
16	Odin died in his bed	Attila died in his bed (in AD 453)

TABLE 1   The correspondence between Odin and Attila

To conclude, Snorri's migration story of Odin and the Asir displays so many and such striking similarities between the historical and archaeological facts of Attila and the Huns in the fifth century and their conquest of Scandinavia that they refer to one and the same sequence of historical events. The transformation of the story from a political historical to a mythological cosmological narrative is a prime example of the sacralisation of a new powerful ruling dynasty from outside. It accords well with a more universal phenomenon in which new ruling ancestors are elevated into *demi*-gods, and later founder-gods. The historical conquest is consequently transferred into a cosmological conquest where the new gods take precedence over the old. In this the political and religious–cosmological order is brought into balance. It further demonstrates the historical dynamics of religion, which derives from its ideological role of legitimising the social and political order. Attila and the Huns in fourth and fifth century AD Barbarian Europe amalgamated with Wodan/Wotan/Woden/Woutan, the old pan-Germanic god whose name meant 'possessed, frantic' (Glosecki 1989: 72) and thus became the paramount god of the Old Norse pantheon in the shape of Odin and his Asir,[5] a historical sequence that might be illustrated iconographically (Figure 10.1).

A

B

FIGURE 10.1 'Wotan/Attila' image on a bracteate from Jutland from the fifth/sixth century (A) and 'Odin' image on a helmet plate from Vendel grave 1 from the seventh century (B). The images illustrate the gradual transmission from magician to warrior; however, the animal followers are still present. A: Drawing by H. Lange after Hauck (1985–89: IK 25). B: Drawing by O. Sörling (Stolpe and Arne 1927: pl. VI).

11
STRANGER KINGS: INTRUDERS FROM THE OUTSIDE WORLD

I shall now reconsider the textual evidence for a Hunnic presence in Scandinavia. In 1943 Niels Lukman concluded in his doctoral thesis 'Skjoldunge und Skilfinger' that the Huns had impacted deeply on Scandinavian royal lineages and their history. But like the works of Malone and Chambers, the chief editors of *Widsith* (see Chapter 8 this volume), Lukman's thesis was academically ignored for decades. However, his masterly interpretation of Scandinavian history prior to AD 800 deserves attention.

Based on a wide variety of sources, Lukman reconstructed the histories of two prominent noble lineages of the north. He did so by mobilising many sources – Nordic, Old English and European – in which he identified recurring correspondences that testified to their historical authenticity. His results further indicated that the Skjoldunge–Skilfinger traditions must have been common knowledge for centuries before they left their mark in writing (see Lukman 1943: ch. I). Thus, Lukman identified an independent Norse tradition of the Huns, embedded in the royal sagas of the Skjoldunge–Skilfinger-tradition,[1] that is, the noble stocks attached to *Hlridargard* (Lejre) on Zealand and Old Uppsala in the Mälar area. This tradition originates in the same historical events as the continental tradition experienced from the north. It thus includes several well-attested historical persons before and after Attila, never mentioned in the European tradition. Although the two traditions refer to similar historical events, they are experienced from different historical perspectives (ibid.: 108 f.). The Norse figures in the Skjoldunge–Skilfinger tradition – Haldan, Roo, Ottar and Adils – correspond to the group of Hunnic kings mentioned by Jordanes in *Getica*: Huldin/Uldin (399–410), Ruga (422–34), Octar (?–430) and Attila (434–53). These correspondences, down to minute details, forced Lukman to conclude that the Huns most likely not only went to the north but in fact had established themselves as a ruling elite even before the time of Attila (during the time of Huldin), and that they remained in the region until the defeat of Attila's son and successor Ellac by the Ostrogoths in AD 455 (ibid.: ch. III, 154 ff.). Thus, according to Lukman, the Nordic saga-kings Haldan, Roo, Ottar and Adils were ethnic Huns, and some of the kings they installed in Denmark and Norway were explicitly named 'hund' (in Scandinavian 'hund' means 'dog', and ruling dogs are mentioned), a subordinate king is named 'Rakke' (yapping whelp in old Danish) and his courtiers are 'hunde' (ibid.: 49). It is telling, as Lukman points out, that all Scandinavian sources (*Widsith* included) accept the supremacy of Adils; *Gesta Danorum* and *Chronicon Lethrenses* (The Lejre Chronicle) only makes him less sympathetic than Snorri does in his *Ynglinga Saga*. In all sources Adils is a superior warlord. Interestingly, he is not described in the tradition of Viking heroes of the twelfth and thirteenth centuries when the sagas were composed, but as an equestrian warlord with two outstanding horses, 'Hravn' and 'Slöngver' as his *signum*. Like Attila's son Ellac, who shared the regency with his brothers and fell in battle against the Gothic people, Haldan's son Helge also shared the regency with his brother Roo and fell in battle in the east (historical-chronologically they belonged to different generations) (ibid.: 124). After this, the Hunnic dynasty came to an end. In Scandinavia, as in continental Europe, there followed a period without a king until the most famous of all the Skjoldunge kings, Hrolf Kraki, took over.

In the same way, Lukman (ibid.: ch. IV) demonstrates a series of correspondences between the *Hrólf saga Kraka*[2] and the Herulian history which cannot be derived from other continental histories, and which stand separately in the Norse tradition, including the final history of the decline of the Hunnic 'Empire'. Again, the correspondences are so many and so direct that the only satisfying explanation is that they go back to the Herulian relationship with the north and the historical return to Sweden of a group of Herulian chiefs and their followers in AD 512. Lukman makes a plausible case that the militarily experienced Herulian chiefs/ kings and their warriors came to play an important role after their return, among other things displayed in the *Hrólf saga Kraka* and its survival into the Viking Age and Early Middle Ages. Last, but not least, the title/name *erilar* (earl/jarl), well known from texts on Norwegian and Swedish rune-stones, derives from 'Herul', a reference to their position as a military elite on their return.

The historical evidence for the introduction of new royal lineages is supported by the reinvention of a monumental burial tradition. The Skjoldungs, the Skilfinger and the Ynglings are the three most prominent royal lineages of Norse saga-kings. The noble line of Skjoldungs was based in Lejre on Zealand. The Ynglings originated from Old Uppsala; however, a branch became kings in eastern Norway while the part remaining in Sweden were named the Skilfinger, and according to Lukman they included the early Hunnic kings. It is telling that these mytho-historical fixed-points are backed up archaeologically by groups of outstanding tumuli:[3] Old Uppsala (Duczko 1996; Bratt 2008), Borre (Myhre 2003a, b) and Lejre[4] (Niles 2006). In recent years monumental halls have been located in close vicinity to the mounds and in Lejre extensive excavations have unearthed a succession of huge ceremonial halls extending back to the fifth and sixth centuries (latest: Christensen 2008).

John Niles ascribes this introduction of the practice of building high-status monumental tumuli in the Nordic area to the influence of 'semi-nomadic peoples' from the steppe regions north of the Black Sea, although its origin lies further towards central Asia. The incursion into Europe of the Huns in the fourth and fifth centuries AD and the persistent contact between Scandinavia and the Black Sea region during these centuries constitute a historical explanation for the transmission of this elite burial practice that was to continue during the following centuries (Niles 2006: 192). The spectacular funeral of Attila on the Hungarian plain in AD 453, described in detail by Jordanes in *Getica*[5] a few generations later, was long remembered by singers and skalds as well as among learned people throughout the Middle Ages. The closest parallel to appear in the Norse sources is the description of Beowulf's funeral,[6] which may be influenced by this account (Niles 2006: 192 f.).[7] To conclude, the archaeological evidence of an invented tradition of monumental tumuli in Scandinavia (as well as in the Anglo-Saxon area),[8] the ritual display of war gear[9] and values, as well as the biased focus on the male warrior-hero in elite burials testify to a steppe tradition of monumental *kurgans* that became constitutive for the new royal lineages of the post-Hunnic era.

According to the historical tradition identified by Lukman, the Huns established themselves as a ruling elite of ethnic foreigners who remained in the area for several generations. This historical explanation concords well with the hypothesis put forward in Chapter 9, where it is argued on archaeological grounds that the Huns were present in Scandinavia, if only for a brief period during the reign of Attila. As numerous ethnographic studies have documented, stranger kings are a common phenomenon, whether constructed or real. Often their ancestor is a god or a king in the land of their origin and they themselves are descended from gods or semi-gods. Frequently they are of distinct ethnic stock, and their power is typically based on conquest (Sahlins 1985: 78 f.). If the Huns (and their multi-ethnic army) intruded into the Nordic realm using their familiar strategies as known from the continent, they installed themselves as rulers or their allies as vassal kings. However, their political dominance had to be institutionalised through a negotiation between violence and peace. In earthly terms it took place through a new ritualised system of gift-giving, feast and hoarding, institutionalising asymmetrical social relations and rooted a political hierarchy. Gold was *the* vehicle of both wealth and cosmological superiority through skilled crafting. Items of gold constituted ruling regalia for upholding cosmic and worldly order as exemplified by Odin's gold-ring Draupnir (see Chapter 1), the outcome of Volund's magic craftsmanship (see Chapter 6), and the gold-ring 'Svíagrís' ('Pig of the Swedes'), the regalia par excellence of King Adils (Attila) in Old Uppsala.[10] In the divine realm similar negotiations took place between the old Vanir gods and the intruding Asir gods who took their place as rulers in the Old Norse pantheon, as did the new earthly rulers in Uppsala and Lejre, surrounded by monumental barrows, new royal halls, temples and sacred groves (Lund 2009: 232–44).

Attila's sovereign power was grounded in a sophisticated political system of mutual violence and reward where imperial gold (from the outside world) was institutionalised as the medium for social, religious and political strategies (see Chapter 9). However, the king of the Huns was dreaded not only as a warrior but as a magician, too (Gibbon 2005: 372). It is reported that the Khan of the Geougen, who had been vanquished by Attila, believed that the Huns could make storms of wind and rain.[11] Also, King Adils in Old Uppsala explicitly grounded his supremacy on a potent combination of magic, gold and violence.

During the Migration Period, ruling kings were transformed into divine strangers by way of genealogy as the Germanic origin myths clearly attest (see Chapters 3 and 10). Their kings were descended from a god (Wotan, Odin), they came from somewhere else (e.g. Scandza), they were warriors and as semi-gods they were strangers from an outside realm. Distinct ruling families emerged as a political class in the 'Golden Age' of the fourth and fifth centuries AD: the lineages of the Skjoldungs, the Skilfingers, the Ynglings and the mythical Volsunga to name the most prominent in the north, the Ostrogothic Amal family being a prominent continental example. As semi-deities they constituted a superior social category, neither god nor man, by encapsulating foreign identity and sacred power.

Organising principles were those between chiefs, heroes and gods as one group, commoners as another. The cultural schemes of the Old Norse world allowed for this transgression. In the Christian world, however, God installed medieval kings; they were not descended from him. This explains why Snorri had to describe Odin as a human being who paradoxically was nonetheless worshipped as a god. It corresponds to the 'excuse' made by Paul the Deacon, who in *Historia Langobardorum* had to apologise for what he had to write about the way the Lombards received their name from Odin[12] (see Chapter 3). In the mythical scheme, however, it is well attested that Odin was a transgressor; he was the only god of the Norse pantheon who exceeded the boundary between realms and mixed with ordinary people; he was actually *seen*.

The Germanic peoples on the continent shared the structural schemes of their migration stories originating in Scandinavia. The archaeological evidence confirms such a relationship and suggests that particular types of myths originate in actual events. In a similar way, the Old Norse migration story of Odin and the Asir is the transformed mythological narrative of the Huns' conquest of Scandinavia. The military experience related to the Ostrogothic calamity might also be associated with the cosmic catastrophe and disorder reflected in the mythological war between the Asir and the Vanir (see Chapter 10).

Since all cultural systems function as a synthesis of stability and change, of past and present, diachrony and synchrony, each practical change is also a cultural reproduction, as Marshall Sahlins has argued (1985: ch. 5). A fateful event will always be inserted in a pre-existing category that is redefined, and therefore history is present in current action and mythology (cf. Beck et al. 2007). From this it becomes intelligible that in Norse mythology Attila was amalgamated with the already existing pan-Germanic god Wotan/Odin and the Huns with his Asir as his *comitatus* (retinue of warriors loyal to the king). The eruption of the Huns from the world 'out there' was a truly unprecedented earth-shattering event, of a kind not seen before. Attila[13] was therefore transformed and incorporated into an already existing mythology and system of belief as a stranger king, intruding from the outside realm. If events are defined as 'happenings that transform structures by disarticulating and rearticulating the schemas and resources of which structures are composed' (Sewell in Beck et al. 2007: 852),[14] thus the meeting with the Huns became such an event of universal dimensions to the Scandinavians. It institutionalised the *comitatus* system and a new hierarchical social order, it recast Norse mythology and kingship for centuries to come, and it came to represent a powerful northern counterforce to the victorious Christian regimes to the south.

NOTES

2 Written sources on the pre-Christian past

1 In general, modern scholars represent the 'positive' opinion, among others Vries 1956; Holtsmark 1964; Turville-Petré 1964.
2 For further discussion, see Andersson 1964; Callow 2006; and Nordal 2008.
3 For a critical view, see Niles (1999).

3 Origin myths and political/ethnical affiliations

1 Cf. H.M. Chadwick, *The Heroic Age*, Cambridge 1912, who first used the expression 'core of tradition' (Pohl 1994: 11, n.8). This process is clearly described by Liebeschuetz among others (Liebeschuetz 1992b). *Origo gentis* and *lex* are clearly connected – but, on the other hand, law was neither a defining trait nor a characteristic of ethnic identity (Amory 1993: 26).
2 Cf. a discussion in Wolfram 1990: 4; Goffart 1988: 36. My view differs from that of Goffart, who understands early medieval 'barbarian history' as that of fictitious literary texts, and their authors not only as reporters of the past but as inventors of the past they transmit (Goffart 1988: 15; see also Heather 1989: 114).
3 Vries 1956: § 372. North, on the other hand, argues that the Amal 'Gaut' and the Lombard 'Gausus' were names derived from Gothic *gáut*, and that *gáut* was an epithet denoting a ritual aspect of Enguz, a god whose name identifies him not only with Ingvi-Freyr but also with Ingui or Ing (North 1997). Although discussion about Gautr's identification is ongoing, his connection to the pagan Scandinavian pantheon seems clear. Discussion of the direction of influence through Europe from the etymological and literary evidence has to deal with the fundamental problem that written evidence does not appear in Scandinavia until the thirteenth century, by which time contacts seem to go from south to north. Therefore, the archaeological evidence is needed as an important – and independent – source of information.
4 According to Jordanes, several different Gothic origin myths existed, relating to regions named as Scandza, Thule or Britannia (*Getica* IV.25, V. 38). The common factor here was some mystical island, which according to Heather is only identifiable through Graeco-Roman geography (see Heather 1994: 66 which includes a discussion on the views of Goffart 1988: 84–96).

5 James argues that this myth was concocted by some erudite Frank, or Gallo-Roman, *c.* AD 600, to give the Franks a dignified ancestry by making them the equals of the Romans. The Frankish origin myth continued to develop and was well established by the tenth and eleventh centuries. As late as the eighteenth century, genealogies of the French kings began with Priam (James 1991: 235 ff.).

6 The main question is of course whether these myths really were told among the elite in the various groups – Goths, Lombards, Heruli or whatever. Heather is convinced that what we have in Cassiodorus and Jordanes are echoes of tales transmitted via a court literature, which also loved things classical, and can be shown to have worked classical elements into other material (pers. comm.). My point of departure is more anthropological, and I therefore hesitate to see the core of the Gothic origin myth as fundamentally different from the Heruli, for instance, which had no classical court literature.

7 As pointed out by Finnegan 1992: 277, interest in 'oral tradition', particularly 'myths' collected from overseas peoples or European 'folklore', also led historians to shift their focus away from current forms or meanings towards the search for the 'pure', 'original' or 'traditional' stages.

8 Vansina (1965, 1985) argues in his pioneering work on African material that oral history could be used as a historical source in a way parallel to written history. He claims that there is a kind of historical testimony, an 'original tradition' undergoing distortion through time until it is finally recorded by the historian as a historical testimony. For a discussion see e.g. Tonkin 1995: 83 ff.; Goody 1968; Dumville 1977; Willis 1981; Miller 1980; Byock 1993.

9 Discussions of this passage can be found in Heather 1989, 1993; Heather and Matthews 1991. Heather argues that the Amals' genealogy is more or less the fictitious work of Cassiodorus himself (1993: 344). On the role of rhetorical hyperbole in delineating the past and in staking claims to its heritage, see Lowenthal 1985.

10 The Amals themselves could equally well be a late construction of the fifth century: see the ongoing debate on whether the Amal tradition was 'real', in the sense that such a dynasty had provided kings in the fourth century for the Gothic Greuthungi (Wolfram 1990, 1994) or was a late invention (e.g. Heather 1995b).

11 If we accept this statement, it means that Humli, who is mentioned by Saxo Grammaticus, *Gesta Danorum*, Book I (*c.* AD 1200) as the founding father of the Danes, was already part of Scandinavian mythology in the sixth century. Heather, on the other hand, suggests Humli was a figure common to Germanic folklore (Heather 1994: 21).

12 For the ongoing discussion about the factual basis of the origin myth see Weibull 1958; Svennung 1967, 1972; Wagner 1967; Hachmann 1970; Goffart 1980: 22 ff., 1988: 85; Wolfram 1990: 324 ff.; Heather 1989, 1993, 1994; Pohl 1994; Bierbrauer 1994; Kaliff 2001.

13 Heather sees striking parallels between the rise of the Amals over at least two generations between *c.* 450 and *c.* 485, and the emergence of the Merovingians as the dominant Frankish dynasty at roughly the same time. Representatives of both families managed to defeat a series of rivals to incorporate ever-larger numbers of followers under their control (1995b: 149). There are clear differences, however, between the Amal and Merovingian genealogies.

14 Cited and translated in Heather 1995a. See Heather 1995b: 155.

15 Salin 1904 made the first typological and chronological distinction between the animal styles in Style I and II.

16 Lund Hansen 1992, however, dates the transitional period to 520/30.

17 Guy Hallsall 2007: 122–3 has criticised the proposed sixth- and seventh-century Iron Age origin of Old Norse religion of the Eddas. However, his parallel with Christianity is irrelevant, as one cannot compare textual and oral traditions. My book further falsifies his argument by anchoring the central myths of the Edda archaeologically in the fifth and sixth centuries.

4 Embodied in animals

1 In Denmark the Urnes Style is found on a major piece of church furniture, the twelfth-century altar from Liseberg church. In the Scandinavian settlements in Ireland, the style survived in a modified form at least until the 1130s and probably later (Wilson 2008: 337).
2 M.G.H., Epistolae III: 355. Cited by Speake 1980: 91.
3 M.G.H., Epistolae III: 301. Cited by Speake 1980: 92.
4 However, the impression of Style I as a 'lost language' with a deliberately 'hidden meaning' underlies the work of several scholars within the cultural historical paradigm as pointed out by Magnus 2001: 280 f.
5 For a critical discussion of Hauck's interpretation, see Starkey 1999.
6 Strömbäck 1935 was the first to identify the seið-complex in Old Norse religion and compare it to European and Siberian shamanism. The ongoing debate on the archaeology of shamanism is summarised by Whitley and Keyser 2003. See also Dillmann 1992; Price 2002, and Jóhanna Katrín Friðriksdóttir 2009: 418.
7 Enright 2006 explains how the Sutton Hoo whetstone sceptre, and thus the grave, as reflecting Celtic kingship theory. For a review see Hedeager 2007c.
8 Examples from the sagas of hamingja and fylgjur can be found in Orchard 2002.
9 See Strömbäck 1935: 164 f. for the different species.
10 For other examples, see Strömbäck 1935: 165 note 1; Mundal 1974; Jóhanna Katrín Friðriksdóttir 2009: 421.
11 Annales Lundenses in Danmarks Middelalderlige Annaler, published by E. Kroman 1980: 41–2. Translated from Latin by Tim A. Bolton. I am grateful to Tim Bolton for bringing this text to my attention.
12 Norse cosmology, it should be noted, was fundamentally different from the kind of 'sorcery' introduced to Scandinavia in the sixteenth and seventeenth centuries (Hastrup 1990; Raudvere 2001: 107).
13 Mentioned in Skáldskaparmál in Snorri Sturluson's Edda.
14 The following description of the eagle, the wolf, the wild boar and the bear is mainly based on Speake 1980 and Glosecki 1989.
15 For a comprehensive study of the changing human responses to wolves and their environment in medieval Britain and southern Scandinavia, see Pluskowski 2002.
16 There is a remarkable find from below the altar in Frösjö church in the Middle of Sweden (Jämtland), where parts of several bear skeletons dating from c. AD 1000 were found. Presumably they were sacrificed by hanging in a tree, together with a variety of other animal species. Unquestionably the bears at Frösjö represent a pre-Christian bear cult (Iregren 1989; Iregren and Alxandersen 1997).

5 Other ways of 'being in the world'

1 Dog graves might reflect personal and emotional relations, horses prestige and status, while the Sámi bears are a ritualising of nature (Jennbert 2003: 149). This explanation, however, does not question the basic concept of 'animal' in contrast to the human race.
2 The bog bodies cannot, however, be used as evidence for the Late Iron Age. They are mentioned here only to emphasise the customary nature of sacrificing humans.
3 For example, on the stone from Bote (Göransson 1999: 231).
4 From a reading of the Scandinavian written sources, Bolton (2006) concludes that criminals (as well as slaves) were commonly sacrificed.
5 Snorri Sturluson: Ynglinga Saga – including Ynglingatal, Historia Norwegiae et al. (see discussion in Sundqvist 2002: 253 ff. with references).
6 In Ynglings saga ch. 25, and in Ynglinga tal.
7 Flateyjarbók I, 191; translated O. Sundqvist 2002: 256.
8 Adam's account is crucial to the discussion of the Uppsala cult. It is widely regarded that there are details that cannot be accepted as authentic (Bolton 2006), but this does not

mean that all of Adam's text should be repudiated as pure fantasy (Sundqvist 2004). For a critical analysis see Hultgård (1997). The most radical criticism of the text (Janson 1998) rejects the information given concerning the cult in Uppsala and states that Adam's text only reflects polemics with the Church in the eleventh century. This theory has been convincingly refuted (Solli 2002: 157 f.; Sundqvist 2002: 117 ff.).

9 Based on astronomical calculations, Sundqvist (2002: 133) has pointed out that it is more likely that the sacrifice was performed every eight years.

10 This has been pointed out by Eldar Heide, University of Bergen. He also points to the tapestry from Överhogdal, Jämtland in Sweden found in a medieval Church in 1910, carbon dated to AD 900–1000 (Franzén and Nockert 1992). Here the antlers on a reindeer or a deer make up the tree. The top of the tree is a bird.

11 However, it is still unclear whether these remains belong to the pre-Christian period.

12 Lars Larsson, University of Lund, personal comments.

13 For a discussion and critique of oversimplification of the Middle Ages, see Cadden 1995.

14 For a definition, see for example Simek 1996: 82.

15 *Volsa tháttr* str.2. English translation from: Turville-Petré 1964: 256 f. (cited by Price 2002: 217).

16 Some have seen this tale and the names Volsi and Mornir as an unhistorical invention of the thirteenth/fourteenth century AD and thus plainly created in the High Middle Ages (Düwell 1971; Simek 1996: 365) while others regard it as a far more reliable source reflecting a genuine phallus cult (Näsström 2001: 150; Ström 1954, 1999: 87; Steinsland and Vogt 1979) directed towards the fertility god of the Old Norse, Freyr (Turville-Petré 1964; Steinsland 1997, 2005).

17 For a discussion and counterarguments, see Solli 2002: 74 ff. and Price 2002: 218. Recently the Eddic poem *Fjǫsvinnsmál* has been brought into the discussion. The central motif here, as in the *Volsa tháttr*, is interpreted as a 'split' *hieros gamos*. This might indicate a common ancient cult (Heide 1997).

18 *Volsa tháttr* ıstr.6, following Price 2002: 218.

19 *Volsa tháttr* str. 9. English translation in Price 2002: 218.

20 As known from the Volsunga saga, one of the legendary sagas, as well as the Volsunga-circle in the Eddic Poems.

21 Gro Steinsland has focused on the *hieros-gamos* element in the kingship ideology of Scandinavia (1991a) and the connection between eros and death (1997). Both Brit Solli 2002 and Neil Price 2002 have related sex, phallus and masturbation to *seiðr*-practice.

22 Cited in Sørensen 1973: 68 ff. and Foote and Wilson 1980.

23 Price 2002: 218 ff. has most recently convincingly argued for its relevance as a source for Swedish Viking Age. In several works Gro Steinsland discusses the erotic element in Nordic death rituals (i.e. 1991b, 1997).

24 Among the 177 names given to Odin ten are gallows names (Price 2002: 104).

25 For these two references I am indebted to Martin Carver, University of York. He also drew my attention to James Joyce's *Ulysses* and Joe Brady, who was hanged in Kilmainham prison in Dublin. When they cut him down 'his tool' was 'standing up in their faces like a poke'. Joyce offers a scientific explanation to this phenomenon: 'fracture of the cervical vertebrae and scission of the spinal chord would produce a violent ganglion stimulus of the nerve centres causing the pores of the *corpora cavernosa* to rapidly dilate so as to facilitate the flow of the blood to the penis' (1935: 315). Although not a medical expert, Joyce offers a current scientific explanation of the same phenomenon.

26 For the reference I am indebted to doctor Jens Lange, Stenlille, Denmark. He also drew my attention to the description by the novelist Albert Dam in *Syv Skilderier* (1962: 66–7).

27 Ran is the ruler of the realm of the dead at the bottom of the sea and that is where drowned people are expected to go (Simek 1996: 260).

28 For the most up-to-date research history, see Lamm 2004. For a discussion see Sundqvist 2002: 288; Zachrisson 2004a, b. Also, Clunies Ross 1994 has to some degree questioned

the *hieros gamos* – explanation. Alternatively, the gold-foil figures have been explained as shamans in different stages of action (Back Danielsson 1999)

29 Brink 1996: 260.

30 In addition to the pairs of figures, standing males and females with a staff or other attributes are found, as well as 'dancing' figures (Lamm 2004: 119).

31 In all sixty-three are known from Norway. Twenty one of these are found in barrows, three close to barrows. However, the find circumstances are often uncertain (Solberg 1999; Myhre 2006 Fig.2)

32 For a review of this debate, see Solli 2002: 122 ff.

33 Translation following Bandlien 2005: 99.

34 According to Norwegian trial records from the early fourteenth to mid-sixteenth century, verbal insults were the main reason for killing (Nøttveit 2006: 147).

35 *Gulathings law* 138.

36 In recent years, however, it has been argued that too close identification of an sei∂r with shamanism may weaken the focus on the specifically Norse type of divination (Bandien 2005: 57 with references; Mundal 2006).

37 *Grágás* 90.

38 The so-called Kidney daggers from the Middle Ages before AD 1500 are obviously phallic shaped. In Scandinavia they became more popular than any other type of dagger and they were worn hanging in front of the crotch in a clearly symbolic way. Using a phallus-shaped dagger against a person would be penetrative on a physical as well as a symbolic level. The daggers referred to a gender and norm system going back to the Viking Age and beyond, but still alive in the Middle Ages (Nøttveit 2006).

39 Snorri's *Edda* (2003: 94).

40 For a critical comment, see Jóhanna Katrín Fri∂riksdóttir 2009: 422–3.

41 Found in Sweden (e.g. Göransson 1999: fig. 13), and in Denmark (e.g. Jørgensen 2002).

42 Snorri's *Edda* 2003: 94.

43 From the *Dictionary of Old Norse Prose*, Orchard 2002.

44 *Grágás* 2; after Norrman 2000: 377.

45 The same pattern is found in the *Volsa thátthr* with the penis Volsi as synonymous with the phallic deity (Price 2002: 217). Heide 2006 includes the distaff in this discussion.

46 I fully agree with Price in his criticism of descriptions of Old Norse cross-dressing as 'drag' as being the use of a modern socio-sexual concept (Price 2002: 213).

47 Lärbro Tängelgårda I, IV, Sanda Sandegårda II, and Ihre (Göransson 1999: fig. 30).

48 One example is from Klinta on Öland (Price 2002: 142 f.). Another example is known from the Sámi area in Sweden (Zachrisson 1997). However, without osteological analysis of skeletal remains it is impossible to reveal 'cross-dressing'.

49 Hands were of great significance in healing: a healer, like a king or a hero, had to have healing hands. This may refer back to an old belief that humanity's supernatural powers were concentrated in the hands (Back Danielsson 1999, 2002, 2007).

50 These are defined as 'rites which accompany every change of place, state, social position and age' (Turner 1967: 94). All rites of transition comprise three phases: separation, margin (*limen*) and aggregation. During the liminal period, the state of the ritual subject – the 'passenger' – is ambiguous because 'he' passes through a realm that has only a few, if any, of the attributes either of the stage he has left or the stage he is going to reach (ibid.: 94).

51 For example, the bracteates from Allesø (Hauck 1985–89, IK 13), Nebenstedt (IK 308), and Darum (IK129).

52 For example, three bracteates from Trollhättan (Hauck 1985–89, IK 190).

53 For example, the bracteate from Fakse (Hauck 1985–89, IK 51).

54 In monastic communities of the Middle Ages, people who entered a monastery went through a process of restructuring personal identity through two stages: denial of one's previous identity, and constructing of an alternative new self. The process involved

negation of personal sexuality and rejection of personality and social status (Gilchrist 1994: ch.1.5, 2000).

55 Translated by Hollander 1994.
56 Translated by Hollander 1994.
57 Wiker 2001 argues that dress becomes more important during the Iron Age; influenced by Christianity the naked body disappears from artistic representations.

6 Commemorative places

1 The classic debate on gift-giving has in recent times been re-opened by the works of Marilyn Strathern 1988, Annette Weiner 1992, and Maurice Godelier 1999 among others.
2 This has generated a vast debate on 'agency' in archaeology; see Dobres and Robb 2000 and Meskell 2004 for a discussion.
3 Helms 1993 broadens the range of relevant craft activities beyond the production of material things. 'Skilled crafting' also includes the production of oratory, song, dance, instrumental musicianship, and navigation (ibid.: 14). This view is the one taken by Maurice Bloch 1974 too.
4 In this particular case I refrain from discussing iron technology and the extraction of iron ore as such, although this must have been of major importance in an Iron Age society.
5 This is true not only in Africa but also in most Indo-European-speaking societies of the past (i.e. Rowlands 1971: 216).
6 *Gylfaginning* ch. 5 (8); *Skáldskaparmál* ch. 32 (23).
7 *Vǫluspá* st. 11: 1–3, 12: 5; *Vafþrúðnismál* st. 25: 4–6.
8 *Alvíssmál*.
9 *Ynglingatal* st. 2.
10 Various forms of cultural transformation from a pagan to a Christian universe are suggested in the *Nibelungenlied*. The story told is not exactly the same, even though various elements, including the main characters, were kept. Changes are found, however, in the story's social context; for example, in terms such as honour, guilt and generosity, and in the depiction of certain relationships. The main difference between the *Volsunga Saga* and the *Nibelungenlied* is that the former represents a pagan universe, the latter a Christian one (Vestergaard 1992).
11 It is worth noting that an element of shamanistic practice was still present on Iceland in the late Middle Ages (Hastrup 1990: 388–9).
12 *Vǫlundarkviða* 24.
13 The name Gullveig, however, is known exclusively from *Vǫluspá* (21 and 22) in the *Poetic Edda*.
14 A similar depositional pattern characterised the Viking Age, although the hoards mainly consist of silver objects (Hedeager 1999b: 229–52).
15 The following is mainly based on Helms 1988 and 1993.
16 A possible ranking of these places can be found in Näsman 1999.
17 In several articles Fabech has developed this model in archaeological case studies, most recently 1998 and 1999. However, the model of ritual depositions in the cultural landscape, which plays an important part in Fabech's general model, has been the subject of debate; see Hedeager 1999b. In his thesis, *Gudarnas Platser* (The Places of the Gods – Sacral place-names and the sacral landscape) (2001), Per Vikstrand discusses the toponymic dimension of the sacral landscape in the Iron Age. The place names clearly indicate the sacred dimension of the landscape and the continuation of a cult in the landscape.
18 Eliade's phenomenologist approach has been criticised for being oversimplified and lacking historical and cultural context (e.g. Rennie 2007). However, I still find his work useful because of its comparative approach.
19 The descriptions in the *Poetic Edda* and in Snorri's *Edda* are not completely identical; for comparison of the sources see for example Simek 1996 and Orchard 2002.

20 *Gylfaginning* 2, 8, 9, 41; *Ynglinga Saga* 2, 5, 9.
21 *Grímnismal* 18.
22 According to the introduction to *Grímnismál, Skírnismál* and *Gylfaginning* 16, 49.
23 *Grímnismál* 8–10, 18–26; *Gylfaginning* 37–40.
24 This model has been applied to central places such as Old Uppsala (Sundqvist 2004), Helgö (Zachrisson 2004a, b), and Kaupang (Skre 2007b, c). It also fits well the spatial organisation of Uppåkra.
25 Gudme is suggested as the dominant centre in south Scandinavia during the Migration Period (Ringtved 1999). At the same time it is regarded as one of several rich archaeological settlements in south Scandinavia dating from the third to the sixth/seventh centuries AD (e.g. Fabech 1999; Näsmann 1999). For at discussion of a political model of Denmark based on Gudme and other 'central places', see Wickham 2005: 368 ff.
26 Neither Gudme nor Lundeborg have been fully published. The edited publication Nielsen et al. 1994 contains the most recent substantial articles about the investigations of 1984–91 and the finds. Several articles are published in *Frühmittelalterliche Studien* Bd. 21. Later the big hall and other houses were excavated. These are published by Sørensen 1994a, b and commented on by a variety of other authors. The Gudme/Lundeborg area occupied a prominent place in the importing of Late Roman objects into Scandinavia (Hansen 1987). Møllegårdsmarken is published *in extenso* by Albrectsen 1971; however, this was before the most recent excavations.
27 The foundation of the hall is dated to AD 300–400, that is, in the early stage of the settlement (Thrane 1999: 145, with references).
28 This is my suggestion. The excavator has reconstructed the building following the traditional ground plan of a farmhouse (Sørensen 1994b).
29 With the two golden horns from Gallehus in southern Jutland (stolen and melted down early in the nineteenth century) as the only exceptions.
30 The latest updated map of the excavated areas is shown in Sørensen 1994b: fig. 2.
31 Although the time difference between the written text and the iconography is several hundred years, it does not seem too daring to regard the gold bracteates as confirmation of the central religious complex and the central myths of the fifth and sixth centuries traced in the Old Norse literature from the Early Middle Ages, as argued by Hedeager 1999a; Solli 2002.
32 A twelfth-century visitor to Jerusalem, the Icelandic pilgrim Nicolas of Thverva, wrote of the *Holy Sepulchre*: 'The centre of the world is there; there, on the day of the summer solstice, the light of the sun falls perpendicularly from Heaven' (Ringbom 1951: 255, cited by Eliade 1961: 40). The *Apocalypse*, widely read and commented upon in medieval Europe, gives a detailed and enticing description of the heavenly city of Jerusalem: 'So in the Spirit he carried me away to a great high mountain, and showed me the holy city of Jerusalem, coming down out of heaven from God ... it had the radiance of some priceless jewel, like a jasper, clear as crystal. It had a great, high wall, with twelve gates ... The wall was built of jasper, while the city itself was of pure gold, brought as clear glass ... The twelve gates were twelve pearls, each gate being made from a single pearl. The streets of the city were of pure gold, like translucent glass' (part of the *Apocalypse* 21, 10–21, quoted by Andrén 1999: 351).
33 This is widely accepted among Scandinavian archaeologists and historians of religion. It was first developed by Steinsland (in the history of religion) and Herschend (in archaeology), based on textual and archaeological evidence. See Steinsland 1991, 1994a, 2005; Herschend 1997a: 49–59, 1998: 25–62.
34 Steinsland (i.e. 2005: 155) has argued that the gold-foil figures with an 'erotic couple' illustrates the holy wedding – *hieros gamos* – connected to the rulership in *Skírnismál*.
35 That is, *Gylfaginning* 48; in some early texts, however, Valhall was thought of as part of Hel (Simek 1996: 54).
36 *Gylfaginning* 48.
37 *Gylfaginning* 33.

7 The cosmic order of landscapes

1 My analysis of the hoards from the Migration Period and the Viking Age is based on Danish material and published as Hedeager 1999.
2 Relief brooches (gilded bronze or silver) belong to the elite female graves from the Migration Period, as do the bracteates, although only to a limited extent (Kristoffersen 2000b; Wiker 2000, 2001).
3 Concerning the gold-foil figures from Gudme/Lundeborg, two pieces have been found in the plough soil at the settlement area of Gudme, while a hoard of 102 pieces has, as already mentioned, been found in situ at Lundeborg (Thomsen et al. 1993: 89). The extensive trading and production activities connected to Lundeborg make the explanation that this particular hoard belonged to a craftsman's treasure the most obvious one. However, this hoard might just as well be understood as part of the same depositional pattern as the hoards from the Migration Period in that it is located just on the coast precisely at the strategic point where Tange Å, the stream inland from Lundeborg to Gudme, flows into the sea (see Thrane 1987: fig. 20).
4 Skovmand 1942, II: 39 and fig. 21; II: 40).
5 Skovmand 1942, II: 41.
6 Skovmand 1942, II: 8.
7 Skovmand 1942, II: 17–19.
8 Skovmand 1942, I: 4.
9 Skovmand 1942, III: 29 and 30.
10 101 of 291 hoards: 35 per cent.
11 58 of 291 hoards: 20 per cent.
12 98 of 291 hoards: 34 per cent.
13 34 of 291 hoards: 12 per cent.
14 This is based on the definition of these areas by Hyenstrand 1974: 153.

8 Knowledge production reconsidered

1 Various forms of cultural transformation from a pagan to a Christian universe are suggested in early Christian artwork, and in written form through examples such as the *Nibelungenlied*. The story is not exactly the same, even though various components including the main characters were kept. Changes are found, however, in the story's social context, that is, in terms such as honour, guilt, generosity and in the depiction of certain relationships (Vestergaard 1992). The myth has been reproduced throughout the centuries in many different parts of Europe.
2 Priscus *Fragm.* 23; Jordanes *Getica* XLIX.
3 The two oldest Danish chronicles, Svend Aggesen (c. AD 1180) and *Lejrekrøniken* (c. 1170) tell their own versions of Adils (=Attila) and his battle. Both in the Nordic countries and in England a great battle is described, in which Adils played a major role, always involved in crucial conflicts (Lukman 1943: 41).
4 For a thorough overview of the discussion, see Niles 1999.
5 Precisely how *Widsith* combines literary and oral traditions must of course remain a matter of debate. I have discussed a similar question in reference to Cassiodorus and the *Getica*. It must be stressed that I have never argued that any of these texts represent simply a written form of an oral tradition. They were written at the historical crossroads between a fading oral tradition and a new textual historical tradition.
6 J. Moorhead, *Theodoric* (Oxford, 1994). For the memory of Theodoric in the Early Middle Ages, see Löwe, 'Von Theodorich dem Grossen zu Karl dem Grossen', *Deutsches Archiv* 9 (1952), pp. 367 ff.
7 See F. Thürlemann 1977, 'Die Bedeutung der Aachener Theodorich-Statue für Karl den Grossen (801) und bei Walahfrid Strabo (829)', *Archiv für Kulturgeschichte* 59: 25–65.

8 Arwill-Nordbladh 2007 proposes that the text was affected by the 'Carolingian renaissance' with its copying of manuscript texts.
9 Niles 2008 goes through the images of 'the world of Beowulf'.
10 Chambers did not realise the connection between Wrosnan and Wrysn and placed Wrosnan as a coastal tribe somewhere between the Weser and the Elbe; however, he conceded that the identification is uncertain (1912: 202).
11 In Chambers' search for the meaning of *holen*, he concludes that neither of the explanations discussed are satisfactory (1912: 202).
12 Malone (1962: 103) argues that there is no reason to believe that Attila himself was ever involved in the battles. The historical wars between the Huns and the Ostrogoths took place in the late fourth century after the Huns' conquest of the southern part of Ermanaric's empire.

9 Hypothesis I: the Huns in Scandinavia

1 There is no evidence that the Mongols ever used gunpowder, guns or cannons (Saunders 1971: App. 2).
2 Gordon 1960: 91.
3 Salin 1903 argues for a south-eastern origin for Scandinavian animal ornamentation.
4 Lukman 1943:122; sources referred to in note 2.
5 Before conversion, shamans were religious specialists among the Goths (Wolfram 1990: 107).
6 For a discussion of the earrings, see Näsman 2008 and Hedeager 2009.
7 The heads are different from the Sarmatian-Alan human masks from the area around the Black Sea (Bóna 1991: fig.9; Carnap-Bornheim and Anke 2007). This difference is only to be expected. What is being portrayed in Scandinavia is a visual impression of people who looked different.
8 For a catalogue: see Kyhlberg 1986 and Lund Hansen 2001. The one in Childeric's grave is the heaviest known; its weight is more than 300g (Lund Hansen 2001: 178).
9 However, a few women of the most superior social stratum – such as the female grave in the Cologne cathedral – had this ring type. They might have been *reigning* queens (on behalf of an infant son, for example).
10 For a discussion of the influence from the Mithraic cult that reached Rome during the first century AD, see Kaliff and Sundström 2004. The central motif in the Mithras cult is the scene where the god kills the bull; this motif was known to all initiated into the Mithraic mysteries and is directed transferred to the C-bracteates, however, mixed with native Germanic ideas, mythology and style (Kaliff and Sundström 2004: 107 f.)
11 The motif of one of the Vendel helmets from the subsequent century has a close similarity to the motif on the bracteates. The depiction is normally explained as Odin with Hugin and Munin (on this occasion they are obviously different species: one is an eagle, the other is not a predatory bird). As a warrior he is in 'bird disguise' as he is wearing an eagle-helmet. A serpent joins him or is attached to the horse (Figure 10.1b).
12 The same image, however, has also been ascribed to silver coins struck for Constantine the Great (AD 306–337) (Axboe 2007: 67). This explanation is less convincing taken the time span of more than a century in consideration.
13 Recently, however, the American scholar John Niles has pointed to the possible impact of the Huns on the north: 'In part as a result of sustained contacts between the inhabitants of Scandinavia and the peoples of the steppes, in part because of the rapid, traumatic third- and fourth-century incursions of the Huns into Europe, the tribes inhabiting the land north of the Roman Empire adopted a number of customs whose origins lie farther to the south, in the direction of central Asia. Mound-building appears to have been one of them' (Niles 2006: 192).
14 It is also stated that Hunnic heritage has been preserved in the Hunnic name of sacred

'White City' (in the sources known by its Hun name *Ba cheng*), which together with building sacrifices is known from China to northern Europe (Obrusánzky 2008, fig. 4).

10 Hypothesis II: Attila and the recasting of Scandinavian mythology

1 In his work on the bracteates, Japetus Steenstrup presented the hypothesis that the bracteates were produced in Mongolia or Tibet, and brought with Odin and the Asir to Scandinavia (1893: 46 ff.).
2 This is found for example in Snorri's *Edda*, *Gylfaginning* 38–9.
3 Lukman 1943: 122; sources referred in note 2.
4 Gibbon 2005: 370 with references.
5 Among archaeologists the dissemination of the Odin cult across Scandinavia during the Late Iron Age is regarded as a significant aspect of an emerging dynastic ideology closely linked to the warrior elite and the *comitatus*, the body of armed men a king or chieftain could muster. Place names with Oden, which are scattered all over Scandinavia, are, however, absent on Iceland where Thor names are frequent.

11 Stranger kings: Intruders from the outside world

1 Lukman's research is based on an analysis and comparison of the entire text material in which members of noble stocks of the Skjoldunge–Skilfinger are mentioned. These include *Beowulf* and *Widsith*, the oldest Nordic saga, *Lejrekrøniken* from *c.* 1170, *Sven Aggesen's Chronicle* from the late twelfth century, Saxo's *Gesta Danorum* from *c.* 1200, *Historia Norvegiae* from *c.* 1170, Ari's list of Swedish and Norwegian kings from 1148, *Ynglingatal* and Snorri's *Ynglingasaga*, and the later *Skjoldungesaga* (Lukman 1943: 10 ff.). For European history and the history of the Huns, Lukman draws on the early medieval sources such as Jordanes, Priscus, etc. in addition to a wide variety of other sources not normally included in the study of the Huns, such as the Hungarian sagas and some Chinese sources.
2 Lukman's primary sources, in addition those mentioned for the Skjoldunge–Skilfingers, are the *Hrólf saga Kraka* from *c.* 1400 and the contemporary *Bjarkamál* as well as a Swedish Chronicle and *Historia Norvegiae*. Lukman's sources for the Herulian history are the continental ones (Lukman 1943: 12 ff., 125 ff.)
3 The mounds in Old Uppsala are the oldest; the oldest one is dated to the sixth century AD (for a discussion, see Ljungkqvist 2008).
4 Grydehøj has been dramatically diminished as a result of erosion and treasure-hunting. When it was built, it measured 40m in diameter and has an estimated height of 4–5m and is thus one of the most impressive burial mounds in southern Scandinavia from this period. In 1986 Grydehøj was carbon dated to AD 540–690; 630–50 has been suggested as a plausible date; however, the date remains uncertain (Andersen 2006: 154).
5 *Getica* ch. 49.
6 *Beowulf* lines 3137–83.
7 Tomka (2007: 253 f.) rejects the historical relevance of Jordanes' description. He sees it as a common historical *topos*.
8 Like Taplow from *c.* AD 630 and Sutton Hoo, Mound I, of a similar date.
9 'The Gelman's Tale' in Beowulf part XVIII, line 1143, mentions Hengest being killed by a sword named 'Hunlafing'. In Old English 'lafing' is a common way of describing swords as leavings, remains, or an heirloom, thus a heirloom left by the Huns (Dr Barbara West, UK – from an email correspondence, autumn 2009).
10 For example, *Hrólf saga Kraka* (chs 29 and 30). The biography of the gold-ring is known from *Skjoldunga saga* (Byock 1998: note 70).
11 The reference is given by Gibbon (2005: ch. XXXIV, note 14).
12 *Historia Langobardorum* I, 8.

13 I am open to the possibility that it was Attila's predecessor who constituted the first 'meeting with the Huns', and only later did Attila/Bleda become the dominant stranger king.
14 Beck et al. (2007) apply William Sewell's theory of the event from *The Logics of History: Social Theory and Social Transformation*. Chicago: University of Chicago Press (2005).

PRIMARY SOURCES, INCLUDING TRANSLATIONS

Adam of Bremen: *Beskrivelse af øerne i Norden*, translated and commented by A.A. Lund. Wormianum, Højbjerg. 1978.

Aeneid. See Virgil.

Alvíssmál. See *The Poetic Edda*.

Ammianus Marcellinus: *The Later Roman Empire (AD 354–378)*, selected and translated by W. Hamilton. With an introduction and notes by A. Wallace-Hadrill. Penguin Books Ltd, London. 1986.

Annales Lundenses. *Danmarks Middelalderlige Annaler*, published by E. Kroman, Copenhagen. 1980.

Ari Þorgilsson hinn Fróði: *Íslendingabók*. The Book of the Icelanders, translated by Siân Grønlie. Viking Society for Northern Research, vol. 18. University College London, London. 2006.

Bede: *Ecclesiastical History of the English People*, edited and translated by B. Colgrave and R.A.B. Mynors. Oxford. 1969.

Beowulf, text and translation, translated by John Porter. Anglo-Saxon Books, London. 1993.

Bjarkamál. I *Den norsk-islandske skjaldedigtning*, by Finnur Jónsson. B1 and B2, 800–1200. Rosenkilde & Bagger, Copenhagen. 1973.

Cassiodorus: *Variae*, translated with notes and introduction by S.J.B. Barnish. Liverpool University Press, Liverpool. 1992.

Codex Gothanum. In Paul the Deacon: *The History of the Lombards*, translated by W.D. Foulke. University of Pensylvania Press, Philadelphia. 1974 [1907].

The Cronicle of Fredegar. Die Chronik Fredegars und der Frankenkönige, Die Lebensbeschreibungen des Abtes Columban, der Bischöfe Arnulf und Leodegar, der Königin Balthilde, translated by Abel von Otto. Die Geschichtsschreiber der deutschen Vorzeit, vol. 2. Berlin. 1876.

De bello Gothico. See Procopius.

De origine actibusque Getarum. The Gothic history of Jordanes in English version, with an introduction and a commentary by Charles Christopher Mierow. Speculum Historiale, Cambridge. 1915.

Deor. In *The Exeter Book*. Early English Text Society, nos. 104,194. Poems I–VIII; including translations edited by Israel Gollancz, Poems IX–XXXII edited by W.S. Mackie. Oxford, Oxford University Press and Millwood, New York, Kraus Reprint. 1958–87.

Dietrich Saga. The saga of Thidrek of Bern, translated by E.R. Haymes. Garland library of medieval literature Series B, no. 56. Garland, New York. 1988.

Eddan, translated from Icelandic by Erik Brate. Klassikerförlaget, Stockholm. 1994.

Edictus Rothari. Die Gesetze der Langobarden, translated by Franz Beyerle. 1–3. Germanen-rechte, vol. 3. Witzenhausen. 1962–63.

Egils saga Skallagrímssonar. Egil Skallagrimssons saga, translated and introduced by Karl G. Johansson. Atlantis, Stockholm. 1992.

Eiríks saga rauða. *Eiríks saga rauða og Flatøbogens Grænlendingaþáttr samt uddrag fra Óláfssaga Tryggvasonar*, edited by G. Storm. STUAGNL 21. Copenhagen. 1891.

Eyrbyggja saga. *Eyrbyggja saga og Laxdæla saga*, after the Icelandic original texts by N.M. Petersen. Fr. Wøldikes forlagsboghandel, Copenhagen. 1863.

The Fight at Finnsburg: Finnsburg Fragment. In *Beowulf*, edited by F. Klaeber. Heath, Lexington. pp. 231–53.

Flateyjarbók, edited by G. Vigfusson and C.R. Unger. Malling, Copenhagen. 1860–68.

Fjǫlsvinnsmál. See *The Poetic Edda*.

Geographiké Hyphégesis. See Ptolemy.

Germania. See Tacitus.

Gesta Danorum. See Saxo Grammaticus.

Getica. See Jordanes: The Gothic History.

Gísla saga Súrssonar. Soga om Gisle Sursson: lang og kort versjon. Translated by Dagfinn Aasen, with an introduction by Else Mundal. Samlaget, Oslo. 1993.

Grágás. Stadarholsbok, reprinted after Vilhjalmur Finsen's edition. Odense Universitetsforlag, Odense. 1974.

Gregory of Tours, *Liber Historiae Francorum*. The History of the Franks, translated by L. Thorpe. Penguin Classics, London. 1974.

Grettirs saga. Grettes saga, translated by Ludvig Holm-Olsen. Norrøn saga, vol. 5. Aschehoug, Oslo. 1989.

Grímnismál. See *The Poetic Edda*.

Gulathings law. The Earliest Norwegian laws, being the Gulathing law and the Frostathing law, translated from Old Norwegian by L.M. Larson. Records of civilization, vol. 20. Columbia University Press, New York. 1935.

Gunnlaug Ormstungas Saga, translated by Hjalmar Alving. Fabel, Stockholm. 1989.

Guta Lagh med Gutasagan, compiled by T. Gannholm. Ganne Burs, Stånga. 1994.

Gutasaga. *Guta Lagh med Gutasagan*, compiled by T. Gannholm. Ganne Burs, Stånga. 1994.

Gylfaginning. See Snorri Sturluson: *Edda*.

Haraldskvæði. See Tórbjorn Hornklofi.

Háttatal. See Snorri Sturluson: Edda.

Hávamál. See *The Poetic Edda*.

Heimskringla. See Snorri Sturluson.

Helgakviða Hundingsbana I. See *The Poetic Edda*.

Hervarar Saga. *Isländska mytsagor*, translated and commented by L. Lönnroth. Atlantis, Stockholm. 1995.

Historia Ecclesiastica. See Bede.

Historia de gentibus septentrionalibus. See Olaus Magnus.

Historia Gothorum, Vandalorum et Suevorum. See Isidore of Seville.

Historia Langobardorum. See Paul the Deacon.

Historia Norvegiae, translated by P. Fisher, edited by I. Ekrem and L. Boje Mortensen, Museum Tusculanum, Copenhagen. 2003.

Historiae. See Gregory of Tours.

The History of the Danes. See Saxo Grammaticus: *Gesta Danorum.*

Hranfkels saga. Hrafnkel's saga and other Icelandic stories, translated with an introduction by H. Pálsson. Penguin, Harmondsworth. 1971.

Hrólf saga Kraka. *The Saga of King Hrolf Kraki,* translated with an introduction by J.L. Byock. Penguin Books, London. 1998.

Ibn Fadlon, Ahmad: *Risala.* Ibn Fadlan's journey to Russia: a tenth-century traveller from Baghad to the Volga River, translated with commentary by R.N. Frye. Markus Wiener Publishers, Princeton. 2005.

Ibn Rustah. *Studies on al-Ya'qūbī (d. after 905), Ibn Rustah (d.after 905) and al-Maqdisī (al-Muqaddasī) (d.about 1000).* Collected and reprinted, edited by Fuat Sezgin. Institut für Geschichte der Arabisch-Islamischen Wissenschaften, Frankfurt am Main. 1992.

Isidore of Seville: Historia Gothorum, Vandalorum et Suevorum. In *Isidore of Seville's History of the Goths, Vandals, and Suevi,* translated from Latin by G.B. Ford with an introduction by G. Doniniand. E.J. Brill, Leiden. 1970.

Íslendinga saga, by Sturla Þorðarson. Edited by T. Høskuldsdottir and E. Smith. Reykjavik. 1974.

Íslendingasǫgur. The Complete sagas of Icelanders, including forty-nine tales, edited by Viðar Hreinsson, introduction by Robert Kellogg. Leifur Eiríksson Publishing, Reykjavík. 1997.

Íslendingabók. See Ari Þorgilsson hinn Fróði.

Jordanes: *The Gothic History,* translated by C.C. Mierow. Princeton University Press, Princeton. 1915.

Kalevala. The Kalevala: an epic poem after oral tradition, by Elias Lönnroth. Translated from Finnish with an introduction and notes by Keith Bosley and a foreword by Albert B. Lord. Oxford University Press, Oxford. 1989.

King Valdemar's Jordebog. Kong Valdemars jordebog, published by Samfund til udgivelse af gammel nordisk litteratur by Svend Aakjær. Akademisk forlag, Copenhagen. 1989 [1926].

Landnámabók, efter Hauksbók, translated by J.R. Hagland. Erling Skjalgssonselskapet, Stavanger. 2002.

Laxdæla saga. Soga om laksdølane, translated by B. Fidjestøl. Norrøne bokverk. Oslo, Samlaget. 1994.

Lejrekrøniken. The Lejre Chronicle (Chronicon Lethrenses) chs 1–9 translated by Carole E. Newlands. Introduced and annotated by J.D. Niles. In J.D. Niles: Beowulf and Lejre. Arizona Center for Medieval and Renaissance Studies, Temple, AZ. 2006. pp. 311–27.

Liber Historiae Francorum, see Gregory of Tours.

Livy: *History of Rome.* The early history of Rome. Books I–V of The history of Rome from its foundation, by Titus Livius, translated by A. de Sélincourt with an introduction by R.M. Ogilvie. Penguin, Harmondsworth. 1971.

Lokasenna. See *The Poetic Edda.*

Monumentum Ancyramum. Res gestae divi Augusti, by Augustus Caesar. Text, translation and commentary by A.E. Cooley. Cambridge University Press, Cambridge. 2009.

Nibelungenlied. Das Niebelungenlied. Teubner, Leipzig. 1921.

Njal's saga, translated by M. Magnusson and H. Pálsson. Penguin, Harmondsworth. 1960.

Ólafs saga helga. See Snorri Sturluson.

Olaus Magnus: *Historia de gentibus septentrionalibus.* Historia om de nordiska folken, translated by J. Granlund. Gidlund, Stockholm. 1976.

Origo Gentis Langobardorum. *Leges Langobardorum*, edited by F. Beyerle. Germanenrechte, vol. 9. Witzenhausen. 1962.

Paul the Deacon: *Historia Langobardorum.* The History of the Lombards, translated by W.D. Foulke. University of Pennsylvania Press, Philadelphia, 1917/1974.

Pliny the Elder, *Natural History*, edited and translated by H. Rackham. Harvard University Press, Cambridge, MA. 1938.

The Poetic Edda, translated by L.M. Hollander. University of Texas Press, Austin. 1994.

Priscus, fragm. In C.D. Gordon: *The Age of Attila*. University of Michigan Press, Ann Arbour. 1960.

Procopius of Caesarea: *De bello Gothico (V–VIII); Wars*, translated by H.B. Dewing. William Heinemann, London. 1914–28.

The Prologue. See Snorri Sturluson: *Edda.*

Prose Edda. See Snorri Sturluson: *Edda.*

Ptolemy, Claudius: *Geographiké Hyphé. Geographica.* Edited by C.F.A. Nobbe. Tauchnitz, Lipsiae. 1966 [1843–45].

Reginsmál. See *The Poetic Edda.*

Risala. See Ibn Fadlan.

The saga of Gisli, translated by G. Johnston. Dent: London, 1963.

The Saga of Hardar. Harðar saga ok Hólmverja. I *Íslenzk fornrit*, vol. 13. Edited by Þórhallur Vilmundarson and Bjarni Vilhjálmsson. Reykjavík, Hið Íslenzka fornritafélag. 1991.

Saga of Hervarar and Heidrik's crowning. Hervarar saga ok Heiðreks, with notes and glossary by G. Turville-Petre. Introduction by Christopher Tolkien. Viking Society for Northern Research, text series vol. 2. Viking Society for Northern Research, University College, London. 1976.

The Saga of King Heidrek the Wise, translated by C. Tolkien. Icelandic texts. Thomas Nelson, London. 1960.

The Saga of the Volsungs, translated by J. Byock. University of California Press, Berkeley, CA. 1993.

Samtíðarsögur. Níunda alþjóðlega fornsagnaþingið, Akureyri 31.7.–6.8. 1994. International Saga Conference Akureyri 1994. Reykjavik. 1994.

Saxo Grammaticus: *Gesta Danorum*, translated by P. Fisher, edited by H.E. Davidson. D.S. Brewer, Cambridge. 1998.

Sjurdar kvæði. Die faröischen Lieder der Nibelungensage. Text, Lesarten und Übersetzung, vol. 1, Regin Smiður/Regin der Schmied, by K. Fuss. Göppinger Arbeiten zur Germanistik, vol. 427, edited by U. Müller, F. Hundsnurscher and S. Sommer. Kümmerle-Verlag, Göppingen. 1985.

Skáldskaparmál. See Snorri Sturluson.

Skírnismál. See *The Poetic Edda.*

Skjoldunga saga. Kong Skjold og hans slægt, Rolf Kraka, Harald Hildetand, Ragnar Lodbrog, translated by K. Friis-Jensen and C. Lund. Gad, Copenhagen. 1984.

Snorri Sturluson: *Edda*, translated and edited by Anthony Faulkes. Everyman, London. 1987.

Snorri Sturluson: *Heimskringla, or the lives of the Norse kings*, edited with notes by E. Monsen and translated into English with the assistance of A.H. Smith. Dover Publications, New York. 1990.

Snorri Sturluson: *Nordiska Kungasagor*, vol. 1. Från Ynglingasagan till Olav Tryggvasons saga, translated from Icelandic by K.G. Johansson. Fabel Bokförlag, Stockholm. 1991.

Snorri Sturluson: *Ólafs saga Helga*. Saga Óláfs konungs hins helga, by Snorri Sturluson. After handwritten pergament in Kungliga biblioteket in Stockholm no. 2 4to, with variants from other handwritten sources. Published for Kjeldeskriftfondet by Oscar Albert Johnsen and Jón Helgason. Commissioned by Jacob Dybwad; Norsk historisk kjeldeskrift-institutt, Oslo. 1941.

Snorri Sturluson: *The Prose Edda*, translated with an introduction and notes by Jesse L. Byock. Penguin Books, London. 2005.

Snorri Sturluson: *Ynglinga Saga*. In *Kongesagaer*, by Snorri Sturluson. Translated by Anne Holtsmark and Didrik Arup Seip. Norges kongesagaer. Oslo, Gyldendal. 1979.

Sonatorrek. In *Den norsk-islandske skjaldedigtning*, by Finnur Jónsson. B1 and B2, 800–1200. Rosenkilde & Bagger, Copenhagen. 1973.

Stjǫrnu-Oddadraumr, by Stjǫrn-Oddi Helgason. In *The Complete Sagas of Icelanders*, edited by Vidar Hreinsson et al. Leifur Eiríksson Publishing, Reykjavík. 1997.

Sturlungasaga, translated by K. Kålund and O. Hansen. Det Kongelige Nordiske Oldskrift-selskab. Gyldendal, Copenhagen. 1904.

Sven Aggesen's Chronicle. Sven Aggesøns historiske skrifter, translation based on Codex Arnæ-magnæanus 33, 4 by M.C. Gertz. Selskabet til Historiske Kildeskrifters Oversættelse. Rosenkilde & Bagger, Copenhagen. 1967.

Tacitus, P.C. *The Agricola and the Germania*, translated by H. Mattingly. Revised translation by S.A. Handford. Penguin Classics, London. 1982.

Thietmar of Merseburg: *Chronicon*, translated by Werner Trillmich. Ausgewählte Quellen zur deutschen Geschichte des Mittelalters, vol. 9. Wissenschaftliche Buchgesellschaft, Darmstadt. 1970.

Tórbjorn Hornklofi: Haraldskvæði. In *Den norsk-islandske skjaldedigtning*, by Finnur Jónsson. B1 and B2, 800–1200. Rosenkilde & Bagger, Copenhagen. 1973.

Vafþrúðnismál. See *The Poetic Edda*.

Variae. See Cassiodorus.

Virgil: *Aeneid*, translated by F. Ahl with an introduction by E. Fantham. Oxford University Press, Oxford. 2007.

Volsa tháttr. In *Den norsk-islandske skjaldedigtning*, by Finnur Jónsson. B1 and B2, 800–1200. Rosenkilde & Bagger, Copenhagen. 1973.

Volsunga saga. See *The Saga of the Volsunga*.

Vǫlundarkviða. See *The Poetic Edda*.

Vǫluspá. *Voluspå*, recomposed in Norwegian by Gro Steinsland and Preben Meulengracht Sørensen. Pax Forlag, Oslo. 1999.

Wars. See Procopius.

Widsith, edited by R.W. Chambers. Cambridge University Press, Cambridge. 1912.

Widsith, edited by K. Malone. Rosenkilde & Bagger, Copenhagen. 1962.

Ynglinga saga. See Snorri Sturluson: *Heimskringla*.

Ynglingatal, text, translation and comments by A. Noreen. Kungliga Vitterhets Historie och Antikvitets Akademiens Handlingar, Stockholm. 1925.

BIBLIOGRAPHY

Åberg, N. (1947) 'Uppsala högars datering', *Fornvännen*, 42: 257–89.

—— (1949) 'Vendelgravarna och Uppsala högar i deres historiska miljö', *Fornvännen*, 44: 193–204.

Albrectsen, E. (1954) *Fynske Jernaldergrave i Førromersk Jernalder*, Copenhagen: Ejnar Munksgaard.

—— (1971) *Fynske Jernaldergrave IV*, vol. 1–2, Odense: Odense Bys Museer.

Alexander, M. (1973) 'Introduction', in *Beowulf*, pp. 9–49, Harmondsworth: Penguin Classics.

Altheim, F. (1959–62) *Geschichte der Hunnen*, vols 1–5, Berlin: Walter de Gruyte.

Amory, P. (1993) 'The meaning and purpose of ethnic terminology in the Burgundian laws', *Early Medieval Europe*, 2(1): 1–28.

Andersen, H. (1998) 'Vier og lunde', *Skalk*, 1: 15–27.

Andersen, S. (2006) 'Lejre: Ship settings, Viking graves, Grydehøj', in J.D. Niles (ed.) *Beowulf and Lejre*, pp. 143–57, Medieval and Renaissance Texts and Studies 323, Temple, AZ: Arizona Center for Medieval and Renaissance Studies.

Andersson, T.M. (1964) *The Problem of Icelandic Saga Origins: A Historical Survey*, New Haven: Yale University Press.

Andrén, A. (1991) 'Guld og makt – en tolkning av de skandinaviska guldbrakteaternas funktion', in C. Fabech and J. Ringtved (eds) *Samfundsorganisation og Regional Variation*, pp. 245–55, Jysk Arkæologisk Selskabs Skrifter XXVII, Aarhus: Aarhus Universitetsforlag.

—— (1993) 'Doors to the Other World: Scandinavian death rituals in Gotlandic perspectives', *Journal of European Archaeology*, 1: 33–56.

—— (1998a) 'Världen från Lunds horisont', in C. Wahlöö (ed.) *Metropolis Daniae. Ett stycke Europa*, pp. 117–30, Årsbok till Medlemmarna av Kulturhistoriska Föreningen för Södra Sverige, Lund: Kulturhistoriska Föreningen.

—— (1998b) 'Från antiken till antiken', in S. Thorman and M. Hagdahl (eds) *Staden, Himmel eller Helvete*, pp. 142–93, Stockholm: Informationsförlaget.

—— (1998c) *Between Artifacts and Texts: Historical Archaeology in Global Perspective*, New York: Plenum Press.

—— (1999) 'Landscape and settlements as utopian space', in C. Fabech and J. Ringtved (eds) *Settlement and Landscape*, pp. 351–61, Aarhus: Aarhus Universitetsforlag.

—— (2000) 'Re-reading embodied texts – an interpretation of rune stones', *Current Swedish Archaeology*, 8: 7–32.

—— (2002) 'Platsernas betydelse. Norrön ritual och kultplatskontinuitet', in K. Jennbert, A. Andrén and C. Raudvere (eds) *Plats och Praxis*, pp. 299–342, Vägar till Midgård 2, Lund: Nordic Academic Press.

—— (2004) 'I skuggan av Yggdrasil', in A. Andrén, K. Jennbert and C. Raudvere (eds) *Ordning mot Kaos – studier av nordisk förkristen kosmologi*, pp. 389–430, Vägar till Midgård 4, Lund: Nordic Academic Press.

—— (2008) 'Lies about Gotland', in K. Chilidis, J. Lund and C. Prescott (eds) *Facets of Archaeology. Essays in honour of Lotte Hedeager on her 60th Birthday*, pp. 47–55, Oslo Archaeological series 10, Oslo: UniPub.

Andrén, A., Jennbert, K. and Raudvere, C. (eds) (2004) *Ordning mot Kaos – studier av nordisk förkristen kosmologi*, Vägar till Midgård vol. 4, Lund: Nordic Academic Press.

—— (eds) (2006) *Old Norse Religion in Long-term Perspectives*, Lund: Nordic Academic Press.

Anker, P. (1997) *Stavkirkene, deres egenart og historie*, Oslo: J.W.Cappelens Forlag.

Appadurai, A. (1986) 'Introduction: commodities and the politics of value', in A. Appadurai (ed.) *The Social Life of Things: Commodities in Cultural Perspective*, pp. 3–63, Cambridge: Cambridge University Press.

Arbman, H. (1943) *Birka. Untersuchungen und Studien*, vol. I, *Die Gräber*, Stockholm: Kgl. Vitterhets Historie och Antikvitets Akademien.

—— (1980) 'Båtgravarna i Vendel', i *Vendeltid*, pp. 19–30, Stockholm: Statens Historiska Museum.

Arrhenius, B. (1979) 'Ein Goldschmeidgrab von Hovgårdsberg Vendel, Uppland, Sweden', *Frühmittelalterliche Studien*, 13: 393–414.

—— (1982) 'Snorris Asa-Etymologie und das Gräberfeld von Altuppsala', in N. Kamp and J. Wollasch (eds) *Tradition als historische Kraft. Festschrift für Karl Hauck*, pp. 13–53, Berlin: de Gruyter.

—— (1990) 'Connections between Scandinavia and the east Roman Empire in the Migration period', in D. Austin and L. Alcock (eds) *From the Baltic to the Black Sea*, pp. 118–137, Studies in Medieval Archaeology, One World Archaeology 18, London: Unwin Hyman.

Arrhenius, B. and Freij, H. (1992) '"Pressbleck" fragments from the East Mound in Old Uppsala analyzed with a laser scanner', *Laborativ Arkeologi* 6, pp. 75–110, Stockholm: Stockholm University.

Arrhenius, B. and Sjøvold, T. (1995) 'The infant prince from the East Mound at Old Uppsala', *Laborativ Arkeologi* 8, pp. 29–37, Stockholm: Stockholm University.

Arwidsson, G. (1942) *Vendelstile, Email und Glas*. (Valgärdestrudien I). Uppsala: Uppsala Universitet.

—— (1977) *Valsgärde 7*, Die Grabfunde von Valsgärde III, Uppsala: Uppsala Universitets Museum.

Arwill-Nordbladh, E. (1991) 'The Swedish image of Viking Age women: Stereotype, generalization, and beyond', in R. Samson (ed.) *Social Approaches to Viking Studies*, pp. 53–64, Glasgow: Cruithne Press.

—— (1998) *Genuskonstruktioner i Nordisk Vikingatid. För och Nu*, GOTARC Series B, no. 9, Gothenburg: University of Gothenburg.

—— (2003) 'A reigning queen or the wife of a king – only? Gender politics in the Scandinavian Viking Age', in S.M. Nelson (ed.) *Ancient Queens*, pp. 19–40, Walnut Creek, CA: Altamira Press.

—— (2007) 'Memory and material culture – the rune-stone at Rök', in U. Fransson, M. Svedin, S. Bergenbrandt and F. Androshchuk (eds) *Cultural Interaction between East and West*, pp. 56–60, Stockholm: Stockholm University.

Ausenda, G. (1995) 'The segmentary lineage in contemporary anthropology and among the Langobards', in G. Ausenda (ed.) *After Empire. Towards an Ethnology of Europe's Barbarians*, pp. 15–45, Suffolk: The Boydell Press.

Axboe, M. (1991) 'Guld og guder i folkevandringstiden', in C. Fabech and J. Ringtved (eds) *Samfundsorganisation og Regional Variation*, pp. 187–200, Jysk Arkæologisk Selskabs Skrifter XXVII, Aarhus: Aarhus Universitetsforlag.

—— (1994) 'Gudme and the gold bracteates', in P.O. Nielsen, K. Randsborg and H. Thrane (eds) *The Archaeology of Gudme and Lundeborg*, pp. 68–77, Copenhagen: Akademisk Forlag.

—— (2004) 'Die Goldbrakteaten der Völkerwanderungszeit. Herstellungsprobleme und Chronologie', in *Ergänzungsbände zum Reallexikon der Germanischen Altertumskunde*, vol. 38, Berlin and New York: Walter de Gruyter.

—— (2005) 'Guld og guder', in T. Capelle and C. Fischer (eds) *Ragnarok. Odins verden*, pp. 41–56, Silkeborg: Silkeborg Museum.

—— (2007) *Brakteatstudier*, Nordiske Fortidsminder Series B, vol. 25, Copenhagen: Det kongelige nordiske Oldskriftselskab.

Axboe, M. and Kromann, A. (1992) 'DN ODINN PF AUC? Germanic, Imperial Portraits on Scandinavian Gold Bracteates', *Acta Hyperborea. Danish Studies in Classical Archaeology 4, Ancient Portraiture Image and Message*, pp. 271–305.

Back Danielsson, I-M. (1999) 'Engendering performance in the Late Iron Age', *Current Swedish Archaeology*, 7: 7–20.

—— (2002) '(Un)masking gender – gold foil (dis)embodiment in Late Iron Age Scandinavia', in Y. Hamilakis, M. Pluciennik and S. Tarlow (eds) *Thinking Through the Body. Archaeologies of Corporality*, New York and London: Kluwer Academic and Plenum Publisher.

—— (2007) *Masking Moments. The Transition of Bodies and Beings in the Late Iron Age Scandinavia*. Stockholm: Stockholm Universitet, Stockholm Studies in Archaeology 40.

Bæksted, A. (2001) *Nordiske Guder og Helte*, revised by J.P. Schjødt, 3rd edn, Copenhagen: Politikens Forlag.

Balogh, M. (2007) 'Shamanic traditions, rites and songs among the Mongolian Buriads: Meeting a shamaness and her assistant', *Shaman*, 15: 87–116.

Bandlien, B. (2005) 'Man or Monster. Negotiations of Masculinity in Old Norse Society', unpublished thesis, University of Oslo.

—— (2006) 'Maskulinitet, marginalitet og liminalitet i tidlig norrøn middelalder', in L. Skogstrand and I. Fuglestvedt (eds) *Det Arkeologiske Kjønn*, pp. 11–26, Oslo Archaeological Series 7, Oslo: Unipub.

Barber, E. Wayland and Barber, T.B. (2004) *When They Severed Earth From Sky. How the human mind shapes myth*, Princeton and Oxford: Princeton University Press.

Barfield, T.J. (1989) *The Perilous Frontier. Nomadic Empires and China, 221 BC to AD 1757*, Oxford and Cambridge, MA: Blackwell.

Barndon, R. (2004) 'A discussion of magic and medicines in East African iron working: actors and artefacts in technology', *Norwegian Archaeological Review*, 37(1): 21–40.

Barrett, J.C., Bradley, R. and Green, M. (eds) (1991) *Landscape, Monuments and Society. The prehistory of Cranborne Case*, Cambridge: Cambridge University Press.

Barth, F. (1969) 'Introduction', in F. Barth (ed.) *Ethnic Groups and Boundaries*, pp. 9–38, Oslo: Universitetsforlaget.

Bazelmans, J. (1992) 'The gift in the Old English epic Beowulf', paper presented at the conference Theory and Method in the Study of Material Culture, Leiden, August–September.

—— (1999) *By Weapons Made Worthy*, Amsterdam: Amsterdam University Press.

—— (2000) 'Beyond power. Ceremonial exchanges in Beowulf', in F. Theuws and J.L. Nelson (eds) *Rituals of Power from Late Antiquity to the Early Middle Ages*, pp. 311–76, Leiden: Brill.

—— (2002) 'Moralities of dress and the dress of the dead in Early Medieval Europe', in Y. Hamilakis, M. Pluciennik and S. Tarlow (eds) *Thinking Through the Body. Archaeologies of Corporality*, pp. 71–84, New York and London: Kluwer Academic and Plenum Publisher.

Beck, R.A., Bolender, D.J, Brown, J.A. and Earle, T.K. (2007) 'Eventful archaeology: The place of space in structural transformation', *Current Anthropology*, 48(6): 833–60.

Bemmann, J. (2007) 'Hinweise auf Kontakte zwischen dem hunnischen Herrschaftsbereich in Südosteuropa und dem Norden', in A. Koch and Historischen Museum der Pfalz Speyer (eds) *Attila und die Hunnen*, pp. 176–81, Stuttgart: Konrad Theiss Verlag.

Bender Jørgensen, L. (2003) 'Krigerdragten i Folkevandringstiden', in P. Rolfsen and F-A. Stylegar (eds) *Snartemofunnene i nytt lys*, pp. 53–79, Skrifter 2, Oslo: Universitetets Kulturhistoriske Museer.

—— (2005) 'Draktskikk', in E. Østmo and L. Hedeager (eds) *Norsk Arkeologisk Leksikon*, Oslo: Pax.

Bierbrauer, V. (1994) 'Archäologie und Geschichte der Goten vom 1.-7. Jahrhundert', *Frühmittelalterliche Studien*, 28: 51–171.

Bintliff, J.L. (ed.) (1991) *The Annales School and Archaeology*, Leicester and London: Leicester University Press.

—— (2004) 'Time, structure, and agency: The Annales, emergent complexity, and archaeology', in J.L. Bintliff (ed.) *A Companion to Archaeology*, pp. 174–94, Oxford: Basil Blackwell.

Bloch, Marc (1992 [1954]) *The Historian's Craft. With a preface by Peter Burke*, 7th edn, Manchester: Manchester University Press.

Bloch, Maurice (1974) 'Symbols, songs, dance, and features of articulation: Is religion an extreme form of traditional authority?' *Archives Européennes de Sociologie*, 15(1): 55–81.

Böhner, K. (1991) 'Die frühmittelalterlichen Silberphaleren von Eschwege (Hessen) und die nordischen Pressblechbilder', *Jahrbuch des Römisch-Germanischen Zentralmuseums Mainz*, 38: 681–743.

Boje Mortensen, L. (1991) *Civiliserede Barbarer. Historikeren Paulus Diaconus og hans forgængere*, Studier fra Sprog og Oldtidsforskning, Copenhagen: Museum Tusculanum.

Bolton, T. (2006) 'A textual historical response to Adam of Bremen's witness to the activities of the Uppsala-cult', in G. Steinsland (ed.) *Transformasjoner i vikingtid og norrøn middelalder*, pp. 61–91, Oslo: UniPub.

Bóna, I. (1991) *Das Hunnenreich*, Stuttgart: Konrad Theiss Verlag.

Bradley, R. (1998) *The Significance of Monuments*, London: Routledge.

Bratt, P. (2008) *Makt uttryckt i jord och sten. Store högar och maktstrukturer i Mälardalen under järnåldern*, Stockholm: Stockholm University.

Braudel, F. (1949) *La Méditerranée et le monde méditerranéen à l'époque de Philippe II*, Paris: Libraire A. Colin.

Brink, S. (1996) 'Political and social structures in Early Scandinavia', *TOR*, 28: 235–81.

Brink, S. (ed.) in collaboration with Price, N. (2008) *The Viking World*, London: Routledge.

Brøgger, A.W., Falk, H. and Shetelig, H. (1917) *Osebergfundet*, Kristiania.

Brøndsted, J. (1954) *Guldhornene*, Copenhagen: The National Museum.

—— (1960 [1940]) *Danmarks Oldtid. III. Jernalderen*, 2nd edn, Copenhagen: Gyldendal.

Brown, P. (1988) *The Body and Society. Men, women, and sexual renunciation in Early Christianity*, New York: Columbia University Press.

Bruce-Mitford, R. (1979) *The Sutton Hoo Ship Burial*, London: British Museum Publications.

Brück, J. (2004) 'Material metaphors. The relational construction of identity in Early Bronze Age burials in Ireland and Britain', *Journal of Social Archaeology*, 4: 307–33.

—— (2006) 'Fragmentation, Personhood and the Social Construction of Technology in Middle and Late Bronze Age Britain', *Cambridge Archaeological Journal*, 16: 297–315.

Brulet et al. (1990) 'Das merowingische Gräberfeld von Saint-Brice', in R.Pirling (ed.) *Tournai, die Stadt des Frankerkönigs Childeric. Ergebnisse neu Ausgrabungen, Katalog*, pp. 17–34. Krefeld.

Brumfield, E.M. (2000) 'On the archaeology of choice', in M-A. Dobres and J. Robb (eds) *Agency in Archaeology*, pp. 249–55, London: Routledge.

Budd, P. and Taylor, T. (1995) 'The faerie smith meets the bronze industry: magic versus science in the interpretation of prehistoric metal-making', *World Archaeology*, 27(1): 133–43.

Bursche, A. (2000) 'Roman gold medallions in Barbaricum. Symbols of power and prestige of Germanic élite in late Antiquity', in B. Kluge and B. Weisser (eds) *Akten – Proceedings – Actes, XII. Internationaler Numismatischer Kongress Berlin 1997*, pp. 758–71, Berlin: Staatliche Museen zu Berlin.

Bynum, C.W. (2001) *Metamorphosis and Identity*, New York: Zone Books.

Byock, J.L. (1982) *Feud in the Icelandic Saga*, Berkeley: University of California Press.

—— (1990) *Medieval Iceland. Society, Sagas and Power*, Berkeley: University of California Press.

—— (1993) 'Introduction', in *The Saga of the Volsungs*, trans. J.L. Byock, pp. 1–29, Middlesex: Hisarlik Press.

—— (1998) 'Introduction', in *The Saga of King Hrolf Kraki*, trans. J.L. Byock, pp. vii–xxxii, Harmondsworth: Penguin.

—— (2001) *Viking Age Iceland*, London: Penguin Books.

—— (2005) 'Introduction', in *Snorri Sturluson: The Prose Edda*, trans. J.L. Byock, pp. ix–xxxv, London: Penguin Classics.

Cadden, J. (1995) *The Meaning of Sex Difference in the Middle Ages*, Cambridge: Cambridge University Press.

Callmer, J. (1991) 'Territory and dominion in the Late Iron Age in southern Scandinavia', in K. Jennbert, L. Larsson, B. Petré and B. Wyszomirska-Werbart (eds), *Regions and Reflections: In Honour of Märta Strömberg*, pp. 257–73, Stockholm: Almqvist and Wiksell International.

Callow, C. (2006) 'Reconstructing the past in medieval Iceland', *Early Medieval Europe*, 14(3): 297–324.

Carmichael, D. (1994) 'Places of power: Mescalero Apache sacred sites and sensitive areas', in D.L. Carmichael, J. Hubert, B. Reeves and A. Schanche (eds) *Sacred Sites, Sacred Places*, pp. 89–98, One World Archaeology, London: Routledge.

Carnap-Bornheim, C. and Anke, B. (2007) 'Geschichtsdarstellungen im reiternomadischen Milieu', in A. Koch and Historischen Museum der Pfalz Speyer (eds) *Attila und die Hunnen*, pp. 263–7, Stuttgart: Konrad Theiss Verlag.

Carruthers, M. (1990) *The Book of Memory: A Study of Memory in Medieval Culture*, Cambridge: Cambridge University Press.

Chambers, R.W. (ed.) (1912) *Widsith: A Study in Old English Heroic Legend*, Cambridge: Cambridge University Press.

Chang, K.C. (1983) *Art, Myth, and Ritual. The path to political authority in ancient China*, Cambridge, MA: Harvard University Press.

Chapman, J. and Gaydarska, B. (2007) *Parts and Wholes. Fragmentation in prehistoric context*, Oxford: Oxbow Books.

Chardaev, V.M. (1991) 'Gold und geschmeide bei den Nomaden des 4.-14. Jahrhunderts n.Chr.', in R. Rolle, M. Müller-Wille and K. Schietzel (eds) *Gold der Steppe. Archäologie der Ukraine*, pp. 255–8, Schleswig: Archäologisches Landesmuseum, Christian-Albrechts-Universität.

Christensen, A.E., Ingstad, A.S. and Myhre, B. (1992) *Oseberg-dronningens grav*, Oslo: Schibsted.

Christensen, T. (2008) 'Ældste Lejre', *Skalk*, 6: 18–24.

Christie, N. (1995) *The Lombards*, The Peoples of Europe, Oxford: Blackwell.

Christoffersen, J. (1987) 'Møllegårdsmarken – Struktur und Belegung eines Gräberfeldes', *Frühmittelalterliche Studien*, 21: 85–100.

Clanchy, M.T. (2001) *From Memory to Written Record. England 1066–1307*, Oxford: Blackwell.

Clover, C.J. (1986) 'The long prose form', *Arkiv för Nordisk Filologi*, 101: 10–39.

—— (1993) 'Regardless of sex: Men, women, and power in Early Northern Europe', *Speculum. A Journal of Medieval Studies*, 68(2): 363–88.

Clunies Ross, M. (1994) *Prolonged Echoes. Old Norse myths in medieval Northern society, vol. 1: the Myths*, Odense: Odense University Press.

—— (1998) *Prolonged Echoes. Old Norse myths in medieval Northern society, vol. 2: The reception of Norse myths in medieval Iceland*, Odense: Odense University Press.

—— (2000) 'Women skalds and Norse poetics', in S. Hansson and M. Malm (eds) *Gudar på Jorden. Festskrift till Lars Lönnroth*, pp. 85–96, Stockholm: Symposium.

—— (2008) 'The creation of Old Norse mythology', in S. Brink (ed.) in collaboration with N. Price *The Viking World*, pp. 231–4, London: Routledge.

Cohan, S. and Shires, L.S. (1988) *Telling Stories: Theoretical Analysis of Narrative Fiction*, London: Routledge.

Collinder, B. (1972) 'Inledning', in *Snorres Edda*, pp. 7–29, Stockholm: Forum.

Collingwood, R.G. (1946) *The Idea of History*, Oxford: Oxford University Press.

Conkey, M. and Hastorf, C. (1990) 'Introduction', in M. Conkey and C. Hastorf (eds) *The Use of Style in Archaeology*, pp. 1–4, New Directions in Archaeology, Cambridge: Cambridge University Press.

Connerton, P. (1989) *How Societies Remember*, Cambridge: Cambridge University Press.

—— (2006) 'Cultural memory', in C. Tilley, W. Keane, S. Küchler, M. Rowlands and P. Spyer (eds) *Handbook of Material Culture*, pp. 315–24, London: Sage Publications.

Croke, B. (1987) 'Cassiodorus and the Getica of Jordanes', *Classical Philology*, 82: 117–34.

Curta, F. (2007) 'Some remarks on ethnicity in medieval archaeology', *Early Medieval Europe*, 15(2): 159–85.

Daim, F. (1982) 'Gedanken zum Ethnosbegriff', *Mitteilungen der anthropologischen Gesellschaft in Wien*, 112: 58–71.

—— (ed.) (1992) *Awarenforschungen I–II*, Wien: Institut für Ur- und Frühgeschichte der Universität Wien.

Dam, A. (1962) *Syv Skilderier*, København: Gyldendal.

Davidson, H. Ellis (1978) 'Shape-changing in the Old Norse sagas', in J.R. Porter and W.M.S. Russel (eds) *Animals in Folklore*, pp. 126–42, Cambridge: D.S. Brewer.

—— (1982 [1969]) *Scandinavian Mythology*, revised edn, London: Hamlyn.

—— (1988) *Myths and Symbols in Pagan Europe*, Manchester: Manchester University Press.

—— (1990 [1964]) *Gods and Myths of Northern Europe*, Harmondsworth: Penguin.

—— (1993) *The Lost Beliefs of Northern Europe*, Routledge: London.

Davis, C.R. (1992) 'Cultural assimilation in the Anglo-Saxon royal genealogies', *Anglo-Saxon England*, 21: 23–36.

Dedekam, H. (1925) 'To tekstilfragmenter fra folkevandringstiden. Evebø og Snartemo', in *Bergens Museums Aarbok 1924–25*, pp. 1–57, Hist.-Antik. Række 3, Bergen: Bergen Museum.

Díaz-Andreu, M., Lucy, S., Babic, S. and Edwards, D. (eds) (2005) *The Archaeology of Identity*, London: Routledge.

Dillmann, F.-X. (1992) 'Seiður og shamanismi i Íslendingasögunum', *Skálskaparmál* 2: 20–33.

Dobres, M.-A. and Robb, J. (eds) (2000) *Agency in Archaeology*, London: Routledge.

Dover, K.J. (1989 [1978]) *Greek Homosexuality*, 2nd edn, Cambridge, MA: Harvard University Press

Dowson, T.A. (ed.) (2000a) 'Queer Archaeologies', *World Archaeology*, 32(2).

—— (2000b) 'Why queer archaeology? An introduction', *World Archaeology*, 32(2): 161–5.

—— (2000c) 'Homosexuality, queer theory and archaeology', in J. Thomas (ed.) *Interpretive Archaeology*, pp. 283–9, London: Leicester University Press.

du Bois, T.A. (1999) *Nordic Religions in the Viking Age*, University of Pennsylvania Press: Philadelphia.

Duby, G. (2000) *Art and Society in the Middle Ages*, Cambridge: Polity Press.

Duczko, W. (1996) 'Uppsalahögarna som symbol och arkeologiska källor', in W. Duczko (ed.) *Arkeologi och Miljöarkeologi i Gamla Uppsala*, Occasional papers in Archaeology 11, pp. 59–96, Uppsala: Uppsala University.

Dumézil, G. (1969) *De Nordiske Guder*, Copenhagen: Fremad.

Dumville, D.N. (1977) 'Kingship, Genealogies and Regnal Lists', in P.H. Sawyer and I.N. Wood (eds) *Early Medieval Kingship*, pp. 72–104, Leeds: University of Leeds.

Düwell, K. (1971) *Das Opferfest von Lade und die Geschichte vom Völsi*, Göttingen: K.M. Halosar.

—— (1978) 'Runeninschriften', in Ahrens, C. (Herausgeg) *Sachsen und Angelsachsen*, pp. 219–29, Ausstellung des Helms-Museums. Hamburgisches Museum für Vor- und Frühgeschichte.

Earle, T. (1990) 'Style and iconography as legitimation in complex chiefdoms', in M. Conkey and C. Hastorf (eds) *The Use of Style in Archaeology*, pp. 61–72, New Directions in Archaeology, Cambridge: Cambridge University Press.

—— (2004) 'Culture Matters in the Neolithic transition and emergence of hierarchy in Thy, Denmark: Distinguished Lecture', *American Anthropologist*, 106(1): 111–25.

Eliade, M. (1961) *The Sacred and the Profane. The Nature of Religion*, New York: Harper & Row.

—— (1964) *Shamanism. Archaic techniques of ecstacy*, London: Penguin Books.

—— (1978 [1962]) *The Forge and the Crucible*, 2nd edn, Chicago: The University of Chicago Press.

—— (1984) *A History of Religious Ideas*, vol. 2, Chicago: The University of Chicago Press.

—— (1997) *Patterns in Comparative Religion*, London: Sheed and Ward.

Elias, N. (2004 [1939]) *The Civilizing Process*, revised edn, Oxford: Basil Blackwell.

Ellis, H.R. (1943) *The Road to Hel: a study on the conception of the dead in Old Norse literature*, Cambridge: Cambridge University Press.

Ellmers, D. (1970) 'Zur Ikonographie nordischer Goldbrakteaten', *Jahrbuch des Römisch-Germanischen Zentralmuseums Mainz*, 17: 201–84.

Engelstad, E. (1991) 'Images of power and contradiction: feminist theory and post-processual archaeology', *Antiquity*, 65(248): 502–14.

Engström, J. (1997) 'The Vendel chieftains – a study in military tactics', in A. Nørgård Jørgensen and B.L. Clausen (eds) *Military Aspects of Scandinavian Society in a European Perspective, AD 1–1300*, pp. 248–55, PNM Studies in Archaeology & History 2, Copenhagen: The National Museum.

Enright, M.J. (1996) *Lady with a Mead Cup*, Dublin: Four Courts Press.

—— (2006) *The Sutton Hoo Sceptre and the Roots of Celtic Kingship Theory*, Dublin: Four Courts Press.

Fabech, C. (1991a) 'Samfundsorganisation, religiøse ceremonier og regional variation', in C. Fabech and J. Ringtved (eds) *Samfundsorganisation og Regional Variation. Norden i Romersk Jernalder og Folkevandringstid*, pp. 283–303, Jysk Arkæologisk Selskabs Skrifter XXVII, Aarhus: Aarhus Universitetsforlag.

—— (1991b) 'Booty sacrifices in Southern Scandinavia: A reassessment', in P. Garwooet, D. Jennings, R. Skeates and J. Toms (eds) *Sacred and Profane*, pp. 88–99, Oxford University Committee for Archaeology Monograph 32, Oxford: Oxbow Books.

—— (1994a) 'Reading society from the cultural landscape. South Scandinavia between sacral and political power', in P.O. Nielsen, K. Randsborg and H. Thrane (eds) *The Archaeology of Gudme and Lundeborg*, Copenhagen: Akademisk Forlag.

—— (1994b) 'Society and landscape. From collective manifestations to ceremonies of a new ruling class', in H. Keller and N. Staubach (eds) *Iconologia Sacra. Festschrift für Karl Hauck*, pp. 132–43, Berlin and New York: Walter de Gruyter.

—— (1998) 'Kult og samfund i yngre jernalder – Ravlunda som eksempel', in L. Larsson and B. Hårdh (eds) *Centrala Platser, Centrala Frågor*, pp. 137–64, Stockholm: Almqvist & Wiksell International.

—— (1999) 'Organising the Landscape. A matter of production, power, and religion', in T. Dickinson and D. Griffiths (eds) *The Making of Kingdoms*, pp. 37–47, Anglo-Saxon Studies in Archaeology and History 10, Oxford: Oxford University Committee for Archaeology.

Ferguson, G. (1961) *Signs & Symbols in Christian Art*, Oxford: Oxford University Press.

Finkelberg, M. (2005) *Greeks and Pre-Greeks. Aegean Prehistory and Greek Heroic Tradition*, Cambridge: Cambridge University Press.

Finnegan, R. (1992) *Oral Traditions and the Verbal Arts*, London: Routledge.

Fischer, S. (2005) *Roman Imperialism and Runic Literacy*, Uppsala: Uppsala University.

Fischer Drew, K. (1993) *The Laws of the Salian Franks*, Philadelphia: University of Pennsylvania Press.

Fisher, P. (1980) 'Introduction', in H. Ellis Davidson (ed.) *Saxo Grammaticus. The History of the Danes. Book I–IX*, trans. P. Fisher, pp. 1–14, Cambridge: Brewer.

Flores, N.C. (1996) 'Introduction', in C. Flores (ed.) *Animals in the Middle Ages. IX–VXI*, New York and London: Garland.

Fokkens, H. (1996) 'The Maaskant project', *Archaeological Dialogues*, 3(2): 196–215.

Foley, J.M. (1995) *The Singer of Tales in Performance*, Bloomington and Indianapolis: Indiana University Press.

Fonnesbech-Sandberg, E. (1985) 'Hoard finds from the Early Germanic Iron Age', in K. Kristiansen (ed.) *Archaeological Formation Processes*, pp. 175–90, Copenhagen: The National Museum.

Foote, P. and Wilson, D.M. (1980) *The Viking Achievement*, London: Sidgwick & Jackson.

Foucault, M. (1985) *The History of Sexuality: the Use of Pleasure*, London: Penguin.

Fowler, C. (2004) *The Archaeology of Personhood*, London: Routledge.

Franklin, A. (1999) *Animals & Modern Cultures*, London, Thousand Oaks: Sage Publications.

Franzén, A-M. and Nockert, M. (1992) *Bonaderne från Skog och Överhogdal och andra medeltida väggbeklädnader*, Stockholm: Kgl. Vitterhets Historie och Antikvitets Akademien.

Fredriksen, P.D. (2006) 'Two graves – three metaphors', in R. Barndon, S.M. Innselset, K.K. Kristoffersen and T.K. Lødøen (eds) *Samfunn, Symboler og Identitet – Festskrift til Gro Mandt på 70-årsdagen*, pp. 271–82, UBAS Nordisk, Bergen: University of Bergen.

Friðriksdóttir, Jóhanna Katrín (2009) 'Women's Weapon. A re-evaluation of magic in the Íslendingasögur', *Scandinavian Studies* 81(4): 409–36.

Fuglesang, S.H. (1982) 'Early Viking Art', *Acta ad Archaeologiam et Artium Historiam Pertinentia*, II: 125–73.

Gabuev, T. (2007) 'Ein hunnerzeitliches Fürstengrab aug dem Kaukasusgebiet', in A. Koch and Historischen Museum der Pfalz Speyer (eds) *Attila und die Hunnen*, pp. 293–7, Stuttgart: Konrad Theiss Verlag.

Gaimster, M. (1998) *Vendel Period Bracteates on Gotland. On the significance of Germanic art*, Acta Archaeologica Lundensia Series in 8, no. 27, Stockholm: Almqvist & Wiksell International.

Gansum, T. (1999) 'Mythos, Logos, Ritus. Symbolisme og gravskikk i lys av gudediktene i den eldre Edda', in I. Fuglestvedt, T. Gansum and A. Opedal (eds) *Et Hus med Mange Rom. Vennebok til Bjørn Myhre på 60-årsdagen*, pp. 439–504, AmS-Rapport 11B, Stavanger: Arkeologisk Museum.

—— (2003) 'Hår og stil og stiligt hår: Om langhåret maktsymbolik', in P. Rolfsen and F.-A. Stylegar (eds) *Snartemofunnene i nytt lys*, pp. 191–221, Universitetets Kulturhistoriske Museums Skrifter 2, Oslo: University of Oslo.

—— (2004) 'Role the bones – from iron to steel', *Norwegian Archaeological Review*, 37(2): 41–57.

—— (2008) 'Hallene og stavkirkene – kultbygninger i en overgangstid', in K. Chilidis, J. Lund and C. Prescott (eds) *Facets of Archaeology. Essays in honour of Lotte Hedeager on her 60th Birthday*, pp. 199–213, Oslo Archaeological Series 10, Oslo: UniPub.

Garber, M. (1997) *Vested Interests*, London: Routledge.

Gasparri, S. (1983) *La Cultura Tradizionale Dei Longobardi*, Spoleto: Centro Italiano di Studi Sull'alto Medioevo.

—— (2000) 'Kingship rituals and ideology in Lombard Italy', in F. Theuws and J.L. Nelson (eds) *Rituals of Power, From Late Antiquity to the Early Middle Ages*, pp. 95–114, Leiden: Brill.

Geary, P. (1978) *Furta Sacra. Thefts of relics in the Central Middle Ages*, Princeton: Princeton University Press.

—— (1983) 'Ethnic identity as a situational construct in the Early Middle Ages', *Mitteilungen der Anthropologischen Gesellschaft in Wien*, 113: 15–26.

—— (1988) *Before France and Germany. The creation and transformation of the Merovingian world*, Oxford: Oxford University Press.

—— (2002) *The Myth of Nations. The Medieval Origins of Europe*, Princeton: Princeton University Press.

Geisslinger, H. (1967) *Horte als Geschichtsquelle*, Offa-Bücher Neue Folge 19, Neumünster: Wachholtz.

Gell, A. (1992) 'The technology of enchantment and enchantment of technology', in J. Cooter and A. Shelton (eds) *Anthropology, Art and Aesthetics*, pp. 40–63, Oxford: Clarendon Press.

—— (1998) *Art and Agency. An Anthropological Theory*, Oxford: Clarendon Press.

Gerberding, R.A. (1987) *The Rise of the Carolingians and the Liber Historiae Francorum*, Oxford: Clarendon Press.

Gibbon, E. (2005 [1776–88]) *The History of the Decline and Fall of the Roman Empire*, abridged edn, ed. and trans. D. Womersley, London: Penguin Classics.

Giddens, A. (1981) *A Contemporary Critique of Historical Materialism*, London: Macmillan.

—— (1986) *The Constitution of Societies*, Cambridge: Polity Press.

Gilchrist, R. (1994) *Gender and Material Culture*, London: Routledge.

—— (2000) 'Unsexing the body: The interior sexuality of medieval religious women', in R.A. Smidt and B.L. Voss (eds) *Archaeologies of Sexuality*, pp. 89–103, London: Routledge.

—— (2008) 'Magic for the dead? The archaeology of magic in Later Medieval burials', *Medieval Archaeology*, 52: 119–59.

Ginzburg, C. (1983) *The Night-Battles: Witchcraft and Agrarian Cults in the Sixteenth and Seventeenth Centuries*, London: Routledge.

Gjessing, H. (1915) 'Et gammelt kultsted i Sandeid. Frugtbarhetsgudeparets dyrkelse i Ryfylke og paa Jæderen', *Maal og Minne*, 65–79.

—— (1979 [1934]) 'Attila og det enegga sverdet', in *Universitetets Oldsaksamling 150 år. Jubileumsbok 1979*, pp. 127–35, Oslo: University of Oslo.

Glosecki, S.O. (1989) *Shamanism and Old English Poetry*, New York and London: Garland Publishing.

—— (2000) 'Movable beasts', in N.C. Flores (ed.) *Animals in the Middle Ages*, pp. 3–23, New York and London: Garland.

Godelier, M. (1999) *The Enigma of the Gift*, Chicago: The University Press of Chicago.

Goffart, W. (1980) *Barbarians and Romans*, Princeton: Princeton University Press.

—— (1988) *The Narrators of Barbarian History*, Princeton: Princeton University Press.

Goody, J. (ed.) (1968) *Literacy in Traditional Societies*, Cambridge: Cambridge University Press.

Göransson, E.-M. (1999) *Bilder av Kvinnor och Kvinnlighet. Genus och kroppsspråk under övergången till kristendom*, Stockholm Studies in Archaeology 18, Stockholm: Stockholm University.

Gordon, C.D. (1960) *The Age of Attila*, Ann Arbour: The University of Michigan Press.

Gormsen, H. (1967) *Retsmedicin. Rets- og Socialmedicin samt Medicinallovgivning*, 2nd edn, Copenhagen: F.A.D.L.s Forlag.

Gosden, C. (2006) 'Material culture and long-term change', in C. Tilley, W. Keane,

S. Küchler, M. Rowlands and P. Spyer (eds) *Handbook of Material Culture*, pp. 425–42, London: Sage Publications.

Gosden, C. and Hill, J.D. (2008) 'Introduction: re-integrating "Celtic" art', in D. Garrow, C. Gosden and J.D. Hill (eds) *Rethinking Celtic Art*, pp. 1–14, Oxford: Oxbow Books.

Gosden, C. and Marshall, Y. (1999) 'The cultural biography of objects', *World Archaeology*, 31(2): 169–78.

Gosden, C., Marrais, E. de and Renfrew, C. (eds) (2004) *Rethinking Materiality*, Cambridge: The McDonald Institute.

Graham, W.A. (1987) *Beyond the Written Word. Oral aspects of scripture in the history of religion*, Cambridge: Cambridge University Press.

Graham-Campbell, J.A. (1980a) *Viking Artefacts: a selected catalogue*, London: British Museum Press.

—— (1980b) *The Viking World*, London: Frances Lincoln.

Graves, R. (1961) *The White Goddess*. London: Faber.

Grieg, S. (1922) 'Smedverktøy i Norske Gravfunn', *Oldtiden: tidsskrift for norsk forhistorie*, 9: 21–95.

Grønbech, W. (1954) *Kultur und Religion der Germanen*, vol. 2, Stuttgart: W. Kohlhammer Verlag.

Gunnell, T. (1995) *The Origins of Drama in Scandinavia*, Cambridge: D.S. Brewer.

—— (2006) '"Til holts ek gekk": The performance demands of *Skírnismal*, *Fáfnismál* and *Sigrdrífumál* in liminal time and sacred place', in A. Andrén, K. Jennbert and C. Raudvere (eds) *Old Norse religion in long-term perspectives*, pp. 238–42, Lund: Nordic Academic Press.

—— (2008) 'The performance of the Poetic Edda', in S. Brink (ed.) in collaboration with N. Price *The Viking World*, pp. 299–303, London: Routledge.

Gustafsson, G. (1900) 'Et fund af figurerede guldplader', *Foreningen til norsk Fortidsmindesmerkers Bevarings Aarsberetning*, 1886–99: 87–95.

—— (1906) *Norges Oldtid. Mindesmærker og Oldsager*, Kristiania: Norsk Folkemuseum.

Haaland, G. and Haaland, R. (2007) 'God of war, worldly ruler, and craft specialists in the Meroitic Kingdom of Sudan', *Journal of Social Archaeology*, 7(3): 372–92.

Haaland, R. (2004) 'Technology, transformation and symbolism: Ethnographic perspectives on European Iron Working', *Norwegian Archaeological Review*, 37(1): 1–19.

—— (2006) 'Ritual and political aspects of iron working; iron in war and conflict', in K. Kroeper, M. Chłodnicki and M. Kobusiewicz (eds) *Archaeology of Early Northeastern Africa*, pp. 135–52, Studies in African Archaeology 9, Poznań: Poznań Archaeological Museum.

Haaland, R. and Haaland, G. (2008) 'Craft specialization, caste identities and political centralization. On the use of Anthropological perspectives in reconstructuring archaic forms of economic organization', in K. Chilidis, J. Lund and C. Prescott (eds) *Facets of Archaeology. Essays in honour of Lotte Hedeager on her 60th birthday*, pp. 155–67, Oslo Archaeological Series 10, Oslo: UniPub.

Haardh, B. (1996) *Silver in the Viking Age. A Regional-Economic Study*, Acta Archaeologica Lundensia Series in 8, no. 25, Stockholm: Almqvist & Wiksell International.

Hachmann, R. (1970) *Die Goten und Skandinavien*, Berlin: Walter de Gruyter.

Hägg, I. (1985) *Die Textilfunde aus dem Hafen von Haithabu*, Bericht über dis Ausgrabungen in Haithabu 20, Neumünster: Karl Waccholtz Verlag.

Halperin, D.M. (1995) *Saint Foucault: Towards a Gay Hagiography*, Oxford: Oxford University Press.

Halsall, G. (1992) 'The origins of the "Rheiengräberzivilisation": forty years on', in

J. Drinkwater and H. Elton (eds) *Fifth-Century Gaul: A Crisis of Identity?*, pp. 196–207, Cambridge: Cambridge University Press.

—— (2005a) 'The Barbarian invasions', in P. Fouracre (ed.) *The New Cambridge Medieval History I, c.500–c.700*, pp. 35–55, Cambridge: Cambridge University Press.

—— (2005b) 'Their sources and their interpretation', in P. Fouracre (ed.) *The New Cambridge Medieval History I, c.500-c.700*, pp. 56–90, Cambridge: Cambridge University Press.

—— (2007) *Barbarian Migrations and the Roman West*, Cambridge: Cambridge University Press.

Halvorsen, E.F. 1960 'Galder', *Kulturhistorisk Leksikon for Nordisk Middelalder* 5. København.

Hamerow, H. (2005) 'The earliest Anglo-Saxon kingdoms', in P. Fouracre (ed.) *The New Cambridge Medieval History I, c.500-c.700*, pp. 263–90, Cambridge: Cambridge University Press.

Hansen, J. (2006) 'Offertradition og religion i ældre jernalder i Sydskandinavien – med særlig henblik på bebyggelsesofringer', *Kuml*, 2006: 117–67.

Hansen, U. Lund (1987) *Römischer Import im Norden*, Nordiske Fortidsminder ser. B, vol. 10, Copenhagen: Det kongelige nordiske Oldskriftsselskab.

Harding, J. (2005) 'Rethinking the greater divide: Long-term structural history and the temporality of event', *Norwegian Archaeological Review*, 38(2): 88–101.

Hardt, M. (1998) 'Royal treasures and representation in the Early Middle Ages', in W. Pohl and H. Reimitz (eds) *Strategies of Distinction. The Construction of Ethnic Communities, 300–800*, pp. 255–80, Leiden: Brill.

Härke, H. (1992a) 'Changing symbols in a changing society: the Anglo-Saxon weapon burial rite in the seventh century', in M. Carver (ed.) *The Age of Sutton Hoo*, pp. 149–66, Suffolk: The Boydell Press.

—— (1992b) *Early Anglo-Saxon Shields*, London: The Society of Antiquaries of London.

—— (ed.) (2000a) *Archaeology, Ideology and Society. The German Experience*, Frankfurt am Main: Peter Lange.

—— (2000b) 'The circulation of weapons in Anglo-Saxon societies', in F. Theuws and J.L. Nelson (eds) *Rituals of Power. From Late Antiquity to the Early Middle Ages*, pp. 377–99, Leiden: Brill.

Harrison, D. (1991) 'Dark Age migrations and subjective ethnicity: the example of the Lombards', *Scandia*, 57(1): 19–36.

Haseloff, G. (1956) 'Die langobardischen Goldblattkreuze. Ein Beitrag zur Frage nach dem Ursprung von Stil II', *Jahrbuch des Römisch-germanischen Zentralmuseums Mainz*, 3: 143–63.

—— (1970) 'Goldbrakteaten-Goldblattkreuze', *Neue Ausgrabungen und Forschungen in Niedersachsen*, 5: 24–39.

—— (1981) *Die germanische Tierornamentik der Völkerwanderungszeit*, vols I–III, Berlin and New York: Walter de Gruyter.

—— (1984) 'Stand der Forschung: Stilgeschichte Völkervanderungs- und Merowingerzeit', in M. Høgestøl, J.H. Larsen, E. Straume and B. Weber (eds) *Festskrift til Thorleif Sjøvold på 70-årsdagen*, Universitetets Oldsaksamlings Skrifter 5, Oslo: University of Oslo.

Hastrup, K. (1990) 'Iceland: Sorcerers and paganism', in B. Ankarloo and G. Henningsen (eds) *Early Modern Witchcraft. Centres and Peripheries*, pp. 383–401, Oxford: Clarendon Press.

Hastrup, K. and P. Meulengracht Sørensen (1987) 'Indledning', in K. Hastrup and P. Meulengracht Sørensen (eds) *Tradition og Historieskrivning*, pp. 7–14, Acta Jutlandica LXIII: 2, Aarhus: Aarhus Universitetsforlag.

Hauck, K. (1970) *Goldbrakteaten aus Sievern: spätantike Amulett-Bilder der 'Dania Saxonica' und die Sachsen-'Origo' bei Widukund von Corvey*, Münstersche Mittelalter-Schriften 1, Munich: W. Fink.

—— (1972) 'Zur Ikonologie der Goldbrakteaten IV: Metamorphosen Odin's nach dem Wissen von Snorri und von Amulettmeistern der Völkerwanderingszeit', in O. Bandle, H. Klingenberg and F. Maurer (eds) *Festschrift für S. Gutenbrunner*, pp. 47–70, Heidelberg: Winter.

—— (1978) 'Götterglaube im Spiegel der goldenen Brakteaten', in C. Ahrens (ed.) *Sachsen und Angelsachsen*, pp. 185–218, Veröffentlichungen des Helms-Museums 32, Hamburg: Helms-Museum.

—— (1983) 'Text und Bild in einer oralen Kultur. Antworten auf die zeugniskritische Frage nacn der Erreichbarkeit mündlicher Überlieferung im frühen Mittelalter', *Frühmittelalterliche Studien*, 17: 510–645.

—— (1985–89) (ed.) *Die Goldbrakteaten der Völkerwanderungszeit*, vols 1–5, with contributions from M. Axboe, C. Düwel, L. von Padberg, U. Smyra and C. Wypior, Münster Mittealterschriften 24, Munich: Wilhelm Fink Verlag.

—— (1986) 'Methodenfragen der Brakteatendeutung', in H. Roth (ed.) *Zum Problem der Deutung frühmittelalterlicher Bildinhalte*, pp. 273–96, Akten des 1. Internationalen Kolloquiums in Marburg a.d. Lahn, 15. bis 19. Februar 1983, Sigmaringen: Jan Thorbecke Verlag.

—— (1987) 'Gudme in der Sicht der Brakteatenforschung', *Frühmittelalterliche Studien*, 21: 147–81.

—— (ed.) (1991) 'Der historische Horizont der Götterbild-amulette aus der übergangsepoche von der Spätantike zum Mittelalter', Bericht über das Colloqium vom 28.-11.- 1.12.1988 in Bad Homburg, Göttingen: Abhandlungen der Akademie der Wissenschaften in Göttingen, Philol.-Hist. Klasse.

—— (1994) 'Gudme as Kultort und seine Rolle beim Austausch von Bildformularen der Goldbrakteaten', in P.O. Nielsen, K. Randsborg and H. Thrane (eds) *The Archaeology of Gudme and Lundeborg*, pp. 78–88, Copenhagen: Akademisk Forlag.

Heaney, S. (2008) 'Introduction', in *Beowulf*, translated by S.Heaney. New York, London: W. W. Norton & Compagny, pp. vii–xxiv.

Heather, P. (1989) 'Cassiodorus and the rise of the Amals: Genealogy and the Goths under Hun domination', *Journal of Roman Studies*, LXXIX: 103–28.

—— (1993) 'The historical culture of Ostrogothic Italy', in *Teoderico il Grande e i Goti d'Italia. Atti del XIII Congresso internazionale di studi sull'Alto Medioevo*, pp. 317–53, Spoleto: Centro italiano di studi sull'alto Medioevo.

—— (1994) *Goths and Romans 332–489*, 2nd edn, Oxford: Clarendon Press.

—— (1995a) 'The Huns and the end of the Roman Empire in the Western Europe', *English Historical Review*, 110: 4–41.

—— (1995b) 'Theoderic, king of the Goths', *Early Medieval Europe*, 4(2): 145–73.

—— (1996) *The Goths*, Oxford: Blackwell.

—— (1998) 'Disappearing and reappearing of tribes', in W. Pohl and H. Reimitz (eds), *Strategies of Distinction: The Construction of Ethnic Communities, 300–800*, pp. 92–111, Leiden: Brill.

—— (2006) *The Fall of the Roman Empire. A new History of Rome and the Barbarians*, Oxford: Oxford University Press.

Heather, P. and Matthews, J. (1991) *The Goths in the Fourth Century*, Liverpool: Liverpool University Press.

Hedeager, L. (1988) *Danernes Land, Danmarkshistorie 2, 200 f.Kr.-700*, Copenhagen: Gyldendal og Politiken.
—— (1991) 'Die dänischen Golddepots der Völkerwanderungszeit', *Frühmittelalterliche Studien*, 25: 73–88.
—— (1992a) *Iron-Age Societies*, Oxford: Basil Blackwell.
—— (1992b) 'Kingdoms, ethnicity and material culture: Denmark in a European perspective', in M. Carver (ed.) *The Age of Sutton Hoo*, pp. 279–300, Suffolk: The Boydell Press.
—— (1993) 'The creation of Germanic identity: *A European origin myth*', in P. Brun, S. van der Leeuw and C. Whittaker (eds) *Frontiéres d'empire. Nature et signification des frontiéres romaines*, pp. 121–32, Collection Mémoires 5, Nemours: Musée de Préhistoire d'Ile-de-France.
—— (1997a) *Skygger af en Anden Virkelighed*, Copenhagen: Samlerens Forlag.
—— (1997b) 'Odins offer. Skygger af en shamanistisk tradition i nordisk folkevandringstid', *TOR*, 29: 265–78.
—— (1998) 'Cosmological endurance: pagan identities in early Christian Europe', *European Journal of Archaeology*, 1(3): 382–96.
—— (1999a) 'Skandinavisk dyreornamentik. Symbolsk repræsentation af en før-kristen kosmologi', in I. Fuglestvedt, T. Gansum and A. Opedal (eds) *Et hus med mange rom. Vennebok til Bjørn Myhre på 60-årsdagen*, pp. 219–38, AmS-Rapport 11A, Stavanger: Arkeologisk Museum.
—— (1999b) 'Sacred topography. Depositions of wealth in the cultural landscape', in A. Gustafsson and H. Karlsson (eds) *Glyfer och Arkeologiska Rum. In honorem Jarl Nordbladh*, pp. 229–52, Gothenburg: University of Gothenburg.
—— (1999c) 'Myth and art: a passport to political authority in Scandinavia during the Migration Period', in T. Dickinson and D. Griffiths (eds) *The Making of Kingdoms*, pp. 151–6, Anglo-Saxon Studies in Archaeology and History 10, Oxford: Oxford University Committee for Archaeology.
—— (2000) 'Europe in the Migration Period, The formation of a political mentality', in F. Theuws and J.L. Nelson (eds) *Rituals of Power. From Late Antiquity to the Early Middle Ages*, pp.15–57, Leiden: Brill.
—— (2001) 'Asgard reconstructed? Gudme – a "central place" in the North', in M. de Jong and F. Theuws (eds) *Topographies of Power in the Early Middle Ages*, pp. 467–507, Leiden: Brill.
—— (2003) 'Beyond mortality – Scandinavian animal style AD 400–1200', in J. Downes and A. Ritchie (eds) *Sea Change: Orkney and the Northern Europe in the later Iron Age AD 300–800*, pp. 127–38, Balgavies: The Pinkfoot Press.
—— (2004) 'Dyr og andre mennesker – mennesker og andre dyr. Dyreornamentikkens transcendentale realitet', in A. Andrén, K. Jennbert and C. Raudvere (eds) *Ordning mot Kaos*, pp. 219–52, Vägar till Midgård 4, Lund: Nordic Academic Press.
—— (2005a) 'Animal representations and animal iconography', *Studien zur Sachsenforschung*, 15: 231–45.
—— (2005b) 'Scandinavia', in P. Fouracre (ed.) *The New Cambridge Medieval History I, c.500-c.700*, pp. 496–523, Cambridge: Cambridge University Press.
—— (2007a) 'Scandinavia and the Huns: An interdisciplinary approach to the Migration Era', *Norwegian Archaeological Review*, 40(1): 42–58.
—— (2007b) 'Comments by James Howard – Johnston and Frands Herschend, and reply by Lotte Hedeager', *Norwegian Archaeological Review*, 40(2): 199–207.

—— (2007c) 'Review: Michael J. Enright: The Sutton Hoo Sceptre and the Roots of Celtic Kingship Theory', *Norwegian Archaeological Review*, 40(1): 110–12.

—— (2009) 'Paradigm exposed: Reply to Ulf Näsman', *Fornvännen*, 103(4): 279–83.

—— (2010) 'Split bodies in the late Iron Age/Viking Age of Scandinavia', in K. Rebay-Salisbury, M.L.S. Sørensen and J. Hughes (eds) *Body Parts and Bodies Whole. Changing relations and meanings*, pp. 111–18, Oxford: Oxbow.

Hedeager, L. and Tvarnø, H. (2001) *Tusen års Europahistorie*, trans. K.A. Lie, Oslo: Pax.

Heide, E. (1997) 'Fjølsvinnsmål. Ei oversett nøkkelkjelde til nordisk mytologi', unpublished thesis, University of Oslo.

—— (2006) 'Spinning seiðr', in A. Andrén, K. Jennbert and C. Raudevere (eds), *Old Norse Religion in Long-term Perspectives*, Lund: Nordic Academic Press, pp. 164–70.

Heissig, W. (1996) 'Recent East Mongolian shamanistic traditions', in J. Pentikäinen (ed.) *Shamanism in Northern Ecology*, pp. 249–66, Berlin and New York: Mounton de Gruyter.

Hellmuth Andersen, H., Madsen, H.J. and Voss, O. (1976) *Danevirke*, Aarhus: Jysk Arkæologisk Selskab.

Helms, M. (1988) *Ulysses' Sail: An Ethnographic Odyssey of Power, Knowledge and Geographical Distance*, Princeton: Princeton University Press.

—— (1993) *Craft and the Kingly Ideal. Art, Trade and Power*, Austin: University of Texas Press.

—— (1998) *Access to Origins. Affines ancestors and aristocrats*, Austin: University of Texas Press.

Herbert, E. (1984) *Red Gold of Africa*, Madison: University of Wisconsin Press.

—— (1993) *Iron, Gender and Power*, Bloomington: Indiana University Press.

Hermann, P. (2009) 'Concepts of memory and approaches to the past in Medieval Icelandic literature', Scandinavian Studies 81(3): 287–308.

Herschend, F. (1978–79) 'Två studier i ölandska guldfynd. I: Det myntade guldet, II: Det omyntade guldet', *TOR*, XVIII: 33–294.

—— (1995) 'Hus på Helgö', *Fornvännen* 90: 221–8.

—— (1997a) *Livet i Hallen*, Opia 14, Uppsala: Uppsala University.

—— (1997b) 'Striden i Finnsborg', *TOR*, 29: 295–333.

—— (1998) *The Idea of the Good in Late Iron Age Society*, Opia 15, Uppsala: Uppsala University.

—— (1999) 'Halle', in *Reallexikon der Germanischen Altertumskunde*, vol. 13, pp. 414–25, Berlin: Walter de Gruyter.

—— (2001) *'Journey of Civilisation'*, Opia 24, Uppsala: Uppsala University.

—— (2009) *The Early Iron Age in Scandinavia. Social Order in Settlement and Landscape*, OPIA 46, Uppsala: Uppsala University.

Hill, J. (1984) 'Widsið and the tenth century', *Neuphilologische Mittelilungen*, 85: 305–15.

Hills, C. (2003) *Origins of the English*, London: Duckworth.

Hines, J. (1984) *The Scandinavian Character of Anglian England in the pre-Viking Period*, BAR British series 124, Oxford: British Archaeological Reports.

—— (1989) 'Ritual hoarding in Migration-Period Scandinavia: A review of recent interpretations', *Proceedings of the Prehistoric Society*, 55: 193–205.

—— (1993) *Clasps, Hektespenner, Agraffen. Anglo-Scandinavian clasps of classes A–C of the 3rd to the 6th centuries AD. Typology, diffusion and function*. Stockholm: Kungl. Vitterhets Historie och Antikvitets Akademien.

—— (1994) 'The becoming of English identity, material culture and language in Early Anglo-Saxon England', *Anglo-Saxon Studies in Archaeology and History* 7: 49–59.

—— (1995) 'Cultural change and social organization in Early Anglo-Saxon England', in G.Ausenda (ed.), *After Empire. Towards an Ethnology of Europe's Barbarians*, pp. 75–87. Woodbridge: Boydell.

—— (2003) 'Myth and reality. The contribution of archaeology', in M. Clunies Ross (ed.) *Old Norse Myths and Society*, pp. 19–39, Odense: University Press of Southern Denmark.

Hjørungdal, T. (1991) *Det Skjulte Kjønn. Patriarkal tradisjon og feministisk visjon i arkeologien belyst med fokus på en jernalderkontekst*, Acta archaeologica lundensia Series in 8, no. 19, Stockholm: Almqvist & Wicksell International.

Hobsbawm, E.J. and Ranger, T. (eds) (1983) *The Invention of Tradition*, Cambridge: Cambridge University Press.

Hodder, I. (1982) *Symbols in Action*, Cambridge: Cambridge University Press.

—— (1986) *Reading the Past*, 1st edn, Cambridge: Cambridge University Press.

—— (1987) *Archaeology as Long-Term History*, Cambridge: Cambridge University Press.

Hodder, I. and Hutson, S. (2003 [1986]) *Reading the Past*, 3rd edn, Cambridge University Press: Cambridge.

Hohler, E.B. (1999) *Norwegian Stave Church Sculpture*, vols I–II, Oslo: Scandinavian University Press.

Høilund Nielsen, K. (1997) 'Retainers of the Scandinavian king: An alternative interpretation of Salin's Style II (sixth – seventh centuries AD)', *Journal of European Archaeology*, 5(1): 151–69.

—— (1998) 'Animal style – a symbol of might and myth. Salin's Style II in a European context', *Acta Archaeologica*, 69: 1–52.

—— (1999) 'Ulvekrigeren. Dyresymbolik på våbenudstyret fra 6.-7. århundrede', in O. Højris, H.J. Madsen and T. Madsen (eds) *Menneskelivets Mangfoldighed*, pp. 327–34, Aarhus: Aarhus Universitetsforlag.

—— (2002) 'Fra antikristne symboler til "ophitisk kunstsmag"', in K. Høilund Nielsen and S. Kristoffersen (eds) *Germansk dyrestil (Salins Stil I-III). Et historisk perspektiv*, Hikuin, 29: 7–14.

—— (2005) '… *the sun was darkened by day and the moon by night … there was distress among men …* – on social and political development in 5th- to 7th-century southern Scandinavia', *Studien zur Sachsenforschung*, 15: 247–86.

Høilund Nielsen, K. and Kristoffersen, S. (eds) (2002) *Germansk dyrestil (Salins Stil I-III). Et historisk perspektiv*, Hikuin, 29: 15–74.

Holmberg, U. (1964) *The Mythology of All Races. Volume IV. Finno-Urgric, Siberian*, New York: Cooper Square Publishers.

Holmqvist, W. (1951) 'Dryckeshornen från Söderby Karl', *Fornvännen*, 1951: 33–65.

—— (1977) 'Figürliche Darstellungen aus frühgeschichtlicher Zeit', *Studien zur Sachsenforschung*, 1: 197–214.

Holtsmark, A. (1964) *Studier i Snorres Mytologi*, Oslo: Universitetsforlaget.

—— (1992) *Fornnordisk Mytologi*, Lund: Studentlitteratur.

Hougen, B. (1935) *Snartemofunnene*, Norske Oldfunn VII, Oslo: Universitetets Oldsaksamling.

Howard-Johnston, J. (2007) 'Comments by James Howard-Johnston and Frands Herschend, and reply by Lotte Hedeager', *Norwegian Archaeological Review*, 40(2): 199–207.

—— (forthcoming) *The Struggle for Mastery in Western Eurasia, 200–800 A.D.*, Oxford.

Howarth, P. (1994) *Attila, King of the Huns*, London: Constable.

Howe, N. (1989) *Migration and Mythmaking in Anglo-Saxon England*, Yale: Yale University Press.

Hultgård, A. (1997) 'Från ögonvittnesskildring till retorik. Adam av Bremens notiser om Uppsalakulten i religionshistorisk belysning', in A. Hultgård (ed.) *Uppsalakulten och Adam av Bremen*, pp. 9–50, Uppsala: Nora.

—— (1999) 'Fornskandinavisk hinsidestro i Snorre Sturlusons spegling', in U. Drobin (ed.) *Religion och Samhälle i det Förkristna Norden. Et symposium*, pp. 109–24, Odense: Odense Universitetsforlag.

Hyenstrand, Å. (1974) *Centralbygd-Randbygd. Strukturella, ekonomiska och administrativa huvudlinjer i mellansvensk yngre jernålder*, Acta Universitas Stockholmiensis, Studies in North-European Archaeology 5, Stockholm: Almquist & Wiksell.

Imer, L.M. (2004) 'Gotlandske billedsten – dateringen af Lindqvists gruppe C og D', in *AArbøger for nordisk oldkyndighed og historie*, 2001: 47–111, Copenhagen: Det Kgl. Nordiske Oldskriftselskab.

Ingold, T. (1994) 'Introduction', in T. Ingold (ed.) *What is an Animal?*, pp. 1–16, One World Archaeology 1, London: Routledge.

—— (2000) *The Perception of the Environment*, London and New York: Routledge.

Iregren, E. (1989) 'Under Frösö kyrka – ben från en vikingatida offerlund?', in L. Larsson and B. Wyszomirska (eds) *Arkeologi och Religion*, pp. 119–33, Lund: Lund University.

Iregren, E. and Alexandersen, V. (1997) 'De döda berätter', in I. Zachrisson (ed.) *Möten i Gränsland. Samer och Germaner i Mellanskandinavien*, pp. 81–116, Stockholm: Statens Historiska Museum.

Jakobsson, A. Hed (1999) 'Towns, plots, crafts and fertility', *Current Swedish Archaeology*, 7: 37–53.

—— (2003) *Smältdeglars Härskare och Jerusalems Tillskyndare*, Stockholm Studies in Archaeology 25, Stockholm: Stockholm University.

Jakobsson, M. (1997) 'Burial layout, society and sacred geography', *Current Swedish Archaeology*, 5: 79–98.

James, E. (1991) *The Franks*, Oxford: Basil Blackwell.

Janson, H. (1998) *Templum Nobilissimum. Adam av Bremen, Uppsalatemplet och konfliktlinjerna i Europa kring år 1075*, Gothenburg: Historiska Institutionen, University of Gothenburg.

Jansson, K. (2003) 'Tolv graver och en guldgubbe från Visingsö', *Fornvännen* 98: 127–30.

Jansson, S.B.F. (1987 [1963]) *Runes in Sweden*, Stockholm: Gidlunds.

Janzén, A. (1947) 'De fornsvenska personnamnen', in A. Janzén (ed.) *Nordisk Kultur. Personnamn*, pp. 236–68, Stockholm: Albert Bonniers förlag.

Jennbert, K. (2003) 'Animal graves', *Current Swedish Archaeology*, 11: 139–52.

—— (2004) 'Människor och djur', in A. Andrén, K. Jennbert and C. Raudvere (eds) *Ordning mot Kaos*, pp. 183–217, Vägar till Midgård 4, Lund: Nordic Academic Press.

—— (2006) 'The heroized dead', in A. Andrén, K. Jennbert and C. Raudvere (eds) *Old Norse Religion in Long-term Perspectives*, pp. 135–40, Lund: Nordic Academic Press.

Jensen, J. (2003) *Danmarks Oldtid. Ældre Jernalder 500f.Kr.- 400 e.Kr.*, Copenhagen: Gyldendal.

—— (2004) *Danmarks Oldtid. Yngre Jernalder og Vikingetid 400 – 1050 e.Kr.*, Copenhagen: Gyldendal.

Jensen, J.S., Bendixen, K., Liebgott, N-K. and Lindahl, F., with contributions from Grinder-Hansen, K. and Posselt, G. (1992) *Danmarks Middelalderlige Skattefund c.1050–c.1550*, vols I–II, Nordiske Fortidsminder Series B, vols 12/1–2, Copenhagen: Det Kongelige Nordiske Oldskriftselskab.

Jesch, J. (1991) *Women in the Viking Age*, Woodbridge: The Boydell Press.

Jochens, J. (1996) *Old Norse Images of Women*, Philadelphia: University of Pennsylvania Press.

—— (1998) *Women in Old Norse Society*, Ithaca and London: Cornell University Press.

Johansen, B. (1996) 'The transformative dragon. The construction of social identity and the use of metaphors during the Nordic Iron Age', *Current Swedish Archaeology*, 4: 83–102.

Jones, A. (1998) 'Where eagles dare. Landscape, animals and the Neolithic of Orkney', *Journal of Material Culture*, 3: 301–24.

—— (2007) *Memory and Material Culture*, Cambridge: Cambridge University Press.

Jones, S. (1997) *The Archaeology of Ethnicity*, London: Routledge.

Jong, M. de (2001) 'Religion', in R. McKitterick (ed.) *The Early Middle Ages*, pp. 131–64, Oxford: Oxford University Press.

Jong, M. de and Theuws, F. (eds) (2001) *Topographies of Power in the Early Middle Ages*, Leiden: Brill.

Jørgensen, L. (1994) 'The find material from the settlement of Gudme II – composition and interpretation', in P.O. Nielsen, K. Randsborg and H. Thrane (eds) *The Archaeology of Gudme and Lundeborg*, pp. 53–63, Copenhagen: Akademisk Forlag.

—— (1995a) 'The warrior aristocracy of Gudme: The emergence of landed aristocracy in Late Iron Age Denmark?', in H.G. Resi (ed.) *Produksjon og Samfund*, pp. 205–20, Varia 30, Oslo: Universitetets Oldsaksamling.

—— (1995b) 'Stormandssæder og skattefund i 3.-12. århundrede', *Fortid og Nutid*, 2: 83–110.

—— (2002) 'Kongsgård – kultsted – marked. Overvejelser omkring Tissøkompleksets struktur og function', in K. Jennbert, A. Andrén and C. Raudvere (eds) *Plats och Praxis. Studier av nordisk förkristen ritual*, pp. 215–48, Lund: Nordic Academic Press.

Jørgensen, L. and Vang Petersen, P. (1998) *Guld, magt og tro*, Copenhagen: The National Museum.

Joyce, J. (1935) *Ulysses*. Hamburg: Odyssey Press.

Kaliff, A. (1997) *Grav och Kultplats*, AUN 24, Uppsala: Uppsala University.

—— (2001) *Gothic Connections*, OPIA 26, Uppsala: Uppsala University.

Kaliff, A. and Oestigaard, T. (2004) 'Cultivating Corpses – A comparative approach to disembodied mortuary remains', *Current Swedish Archaeology*, 12: 83–104.

Kaliff, A. and Sundqvist, O. (2004) *Oden och Mithraskulten. Religiös acculturation under romersk järnålder och folkvandringstid*, OPIA 35, Uppsala: Uppsala University.

Karlsson, L. (1983) *Nordisk Form. Om djurornamentik*, Stockholm: Statens Historiska Museum.

Kazanski, M. (1993) 'The sedentary elite in the "Empire" of the Huns and its impact on material civilisation in Southern Russia during the Early Middle Ages (5th–7th Centuries AD)', in J. Chapman and P. Dolukhanov (eds) *Cultural Transformations and Interactions in Eastern Europe*, pp. 211–35, Aldershot, Brookfield, USA, Hong Kong, Singapore and Sidney: Avebury.

Kendrick, T.D. (1938) *Anglo-Saxon Art*, London: Methuen.

Kennedy, H. (2002) *Mongols, Huns and Vikings*, London: Cassell.

Kilger, C. (2008) 'Kombinationer av föremål – de vikingatida mittspännedepåerna', in K. Childis, J. Lund and C. Prescott (eds) *Facets of Archaeology. Essays in honour of Lotte Hedeager on her 60th Birthday*, pp. 323–38, Oslo Archaeological Series vol. 10, Oslo: UniPub.

Klindt-Jensen, O. and Wilson, D. (1965) *Vikingetidens Kunst*, Copenhagen: The National Museum.

Knapp, A.B. (ed.) (1992) *Archaeology, Annales and Ethnohistory*, Cambridge: Cambridge University Press.

Knapp, A.B. and Meskell, L.M. (1997) 'Bodies of evidence in prehistoric Cyprus', *Cambridge Archaeological Journal*, 7(2): 183–204.

Knüsel, C. and Ripley, K. (2000) 'The Berdache or man-woman in Anglo-Saxon England and early medieval Europe', in W.O. Frazer and A. Tyrell (eds) *Social Identity in Early Medieval Britain*, pp. 157–91, Leicester: Leicester University Press.

Koch, A. and Historischen Museum der Pfalz Speyer (eds) (2007) *Attila und die Hunnen*, Stuttgart: Konrad Theiss Verlag.

Koch, R. (1969) *Katalog Esslingen. Die vor- und frühgeschichtlichen Funde in Heimatmuseum*, vol. II, *Die merowingischen Funde*, Veröffentlichungen des Staatlichen Amtes für Denkmalpflege Stuttgart A14/II, Stuttgart: Müller & Graff.

Kopytoff, I. (1986) 'The cultural biography of things: commoditization as process', in A. Appadurai (ed.) *The Social Life of Things: Commodities in Cultural Perspective*, pp. 64–91, Cambridge: Cambridge University Press.

Kousgård Sørensen, J. (1985) 'Gudhem', *Frühmittelalterliche Studien*, 19: 131–38.

Krag, C. (1991) *Ynglingatal og Ynglingesaga. En studie i historiske kilder*, Oslo: Universitetsforlaget.

Kristiansen, K. (1996) 'Die Hortfunde der jüngeren Bronzezeit Dänemarks. Fundumstände, Funktion und historische Entwicklung', in *Archäologische Forschungen zum Kultgeschehen in der jüngeren Bronzezeit und frühen Eisenzeit Alteuropas*, pp. 255–70, Ergebnisse eines Kolloquiums in Regensburg 4.-7. Oktober 1993, Bonn: Universitätsverlag Regensburg GMBH.

—— (2004) 'An essay on material culture', in F. Fahlander and T. Oestigaard (eds) *Material Culture and Other Things*, pp. 259–78, Gotarc Series C. no. 61, Gothenburg: University of Gothenburg.

—— (2005) 'Theorising diffusion and population movement', in C. Renfrew and P. Bahn (eds) *Archaeology. The Key Concepts*, pp. 75–9, London: Routledge.

Kristiansen, K. and Larsson, T.B. (2005) *The Rise of Bronze Age Society. Travels, Transmissions and Transformations*, Cambridge: Cambridge University Press.

Kristoffersen, S. (1995) 'Transformation in Migration Period animal art', *Norwegian Archaeological Review* 28(1): 1–17.

—— (2000a) 'Expressive objects', in D. Olausson and H. Vandkilde (eds) *Form – Function – Context*, pp. 265–74, Acta Archaeologica Lundensia, Stockholm: Almqvist & Wiksell.

—— (2000b) *Sverd og Spenne. Dyreornamentik og Social Kontekst*, Studia Humanitas Bergensis 13, Kristiansand: Høyskoleforlaget.

—— (2004) 'Bridal jewels – In life and death', in T. Oestigaard, N. Anfinset and T. Saetersdal (eds) *Combining the Past and the Present*, pp. 31–7, BAR International Series 1210, Oxford: British Archaeological Reports.

Kromann, A. (1994) 'Gudme and Lundeborg – The coins', in P.O. Nielsen, K. Randsborg and H. Thrane (eds) *The Archaeology of Gudme and Lundeborg*, pp. 64–7, Copenhagen: Akademisk Forlag.

Krüger, S.H. (1988) 'Bjørneklør fra vestlandske graver', in S. Indrelid, S. Kaland and B. Solberg (eds) *Festskrift til Anders Hagen*, pp. 357–66, Arkeologiske Skrifter 4, Bergen: University of Bergen.

Kyhlberg, O. (1986) 'Late Roman and Byzantine solidi', in A. Lundström and H. Clarke (eds) *Excavations at Helgö*, vol. X, pp. 13–126, Stockholm: Almqvist & Wiksell International.

Lamm, J.P. (2004) 'Figural gold foils found in Sweden', in H. Clarke and K. Lamm (eds) *Excavations at Helgö*, vol. XVI, pp. 41–142, Stockholm: Kungl Vitterhets Historie och Antikvitets Akademien (KVHAA).

Lamm, J.P., Hydman, H., Axboe, M., Hauck, K., Beck, H., Behr, C. and Pesch, A. (2000) 'Der Brakteat des Jahrhunderts', *Frühmittelalterliche Studien*, 34: 1–93.

Laqueur, T. (2003 [1990]) *Making Sex: Body and Gender from the Greeks to Freud*, Cambridge, MA: Harvard University Press.

Larsson, L. (ed.) (2004) *Continuity for Centuries. A ceremonial building and its context at Uppåkra, southern Sweden*, Uppåkrastudier 10, Stockholm: Almqvist & Wiksell International.

—— (2007) 'The Iron Age ritual building at Uppåkra, southern Sweden', *Antiquity* 81: 11–25.

Larsson, L. and Hårdh, B. (eds) (1998) *Centrala Platser, Centrala Frågor*, Acta Archaeologica Lundensia Series in 8, no. 28, Lund: Lund University.

Layton, R. (1991) *The Anthropology of Art*, Cambridge: Cambridge University Press.

Le Jan, R. (2000) 'Frankish giving of arms and rituals of power: Continuity and change in the Carolingian Period', in F. Theuwe and J.L. Nelson (eds) *Rituals of Power*, pp. 281–309, Leiden: Brill.

Lee, M.M. (2000) 'Deciphering gender in Minoan dress', in A.E. Rautman (ed.) *Reading the Body*, pp. 111–23, Philadelphia: University of Pennsylvania Press.

Lévi-Strauss, C. (1963/1973) *Structural Anthropology*, vols 1–2, Middlesex: Penguin Books.

Lie, H. (1952) 'Skaldestudier', *Maal og Minne*, 1952: 1–92.

Liebeschuetz, J.H.W.G. (1992a) *Barbarians and Bishops*. Oxford: Clarendon Press.

—— (1992b) 'Alaric's Goths: nation or army?', in J. Drinkwater and H. Elton (eds) *Fifth-Century Gaul: A Crisis of Identity*, pp. 75–83, Cambridge: Cambridge University Press.

Liestøl, K. (1924) 'Hune-heren', *[Norsk] Historisk Tidsskrift*, 5(5): 453–67.

Lincoln, B. (1999) *Theorizing Myth. Narrative, Ideology, and Scholarship*, Chicago and London: The University of Chicago Press.

Lindblad, G. (1954) *Studier i Codex Regius af Äldre Eddan*, Lund: Gleerup.

Lindbom, P. (2006) *Vapen under Wreccornas Tid, 150 – 500 e.Kr*, AUN 36, Uppsala: Uppsala University.

Lindow, J. (2001) *Norse Mythology. A guide to the gods, heroes, rituals, and beliefs*, Oxford: Oxford University Press.

—— (2003) 'Cultures in contact', in M. Clunies Ross (ed.) *Old Norse Myths, Literature and Society*, pp. 89–109, Odense: University Press of Southern Denmark.

Lindqvist, S. (1936) *Uppsala Högar och Ottarshögen*, Monografiserie 13, Stockholm: Kgl. Vitterhets Historie och Antikvitets Akademien.

—— (1941–42) *Gotlands Bildsteine*, vols I-II, Stockholm: Kgl. Vitterhets Historie och Antikvitets Akademien.

—— (1949) 'Uppsala högars datering', *Fornvännen*, 44: 33–48.

Lindstrøm, T.C. and Kristoffersen, S. (2001) 'Figure it out! Psychological perspectives on perception of Migration Period animal art', *Norwegian Archaeological Review*, 34(2): 65–84.

Ljungkvist, J. (2008) 'Dating two royal mounds of Old Uppsala', *Archäologisches Korrespondenzblatt*, 38(2): 263–82.

—— (2006) *En hira atti rikR. Om elit, struktur och ekonomi kring Uppsala och Mälaren under yngre järnålder*, AUN 34, Uppsala: Uppsala University.

Lönnroth, L. (1977) 'The riddles of the Rök-stone: A structural approach', *Arkiv för Nordisk Filologi*, 92: 1–57.

—— (1986) 'Dómaldi's death and the myth of the sacral kingship', in J. Lindow, L. Lönnroth and G.W. Weber (eds) *Structure and Meaning in Old Norse Literature*, pp. 73–93, Odense: Odense University Press.

—— (1995) *Isländska Mytsagor*, commented and trans. L. Lönnroth, Stockholm: Atlantis.

Lowenthal, D. (1985) *The Past is a Foreign Country*, Cambridge: Cambridge University Press.

Lucy, S. (2005) 'Ethnic and cultural identities', in M. Díaz-Andreu, S. Lucy (eds) *The Archaeology of Identity*, pp. 86–109, London: Routledge.

Lukman, N. (1941) *Didreks Saga og Theoderics Historie*, Studier fra Sprog- og Oldtidsforskning, Copenhagen: Povl Branner.

—— (1943) *Skjoldunge und Skilfinger. Hunnen- und Herulerkönige in Ostnordischer Überlieferung*, Copenhagen: Gyldendal.

—— (1949) *Ermanaric hos Jordanes og Saxo*, Studier fra Sprog- og Oldtidsforskning, Copenhagen: Povl Branners Forlag.

Lund, J. (2006) 'Vikingetidens værktøjskister i landskab og mytologi', *Fornvännen* 101: 323–41.

—— (2008) 'Banks, Borders and Bodies of Water in a Viking Age Mentality', *Journal of Wetland Archaeology*, 8: 53–72.

—— (2009) 'Åsted og Vadested. Et studie af vikingetidens deponeringer som indfaldsvinkel til det cognitive landskab', unpublished thesis, Oslo: University of Oslo.

Lund Hansen, U. (1987) *Römischer Import im Norden. Warenaustausch zwishen dem Römischen Reich und dem freien Germanien*, København: Det kongelige nordiske Oldskriftselskab.

—— (1992) 'Die Hortproblematik im Licht der neuen Diskussion zur Chronologie und zur Deutung der Goldschätze in der Völkerwanderungszeit', in K. Hauck (ed.) *Der historische Horizont der Götterbild-Amulette aus der Übergangsepoche von der Spätantike zum Frühmittelalter*, pp. 183–94, Göttingen: Vandeenhoeck & Ruprecht.

—— (2001) 'Gold rings – symbols of sex and rank', in B. Magnus (ed.) *Roman Gold and the Development of the Early Germanic Kingdoms*, pp. 157–88, Stockholm: Almqvist & Wiksell International.

Lundahl, I. (1934) *'Hunner' som benämning på invånare i Medelpad*, Stockholm: Kunglig Ortnamskommissionen.

Lundborg, M.D. (2006) 'Bound animal bodies', in A. Andrén, K. Jennbert and C. Raudvere (eds) *Old Norse Religion in Long-term Perspectives*, pp. 39–44, Lund: Nordic Academic Press.

Lundström, A. (1968) 'Helgö as frühmittelalterlicher Handelsplatz in Mittelschweden', *Frühmittelalterliche Studien*, 2: 278–90.

Mackeprang, M. (1952) *De nordiske Guldbrakteater*, Århus: Jysk Arkeelogisk Selskab.

Madsen, C. and Thrane, H. (1995) 'Møllegårdsmarkens veje og huse', *Fynske Minder*, 1995: 77–91.

Maenchen-Helfen, O.J. (1973) *The World of the Huns. Studies in their history and culture*, M. Knight (ed.), Berkeley: University of California Press.

Magnus, B. (2001) 'The enigmatic brooches', in B. Magnus (ed.) *Roman Gold and the Development of the Early Germanic Kingdoms*, pp. 279–95, Konferenser 51, Stockholm: Kgl. Vitterhets Historie och Antikvitets Akademien.

—— (2002) 'Ørnen flyr – om Stil I i Norden', *Hikuin*, 29: 105–18.

Magnúsdottir, A. (2008) 'Women and sexual politics', in S. Brink (ed.) in collaboration with N. Price *The Viking World*, pp. 40–8, London: Routledge.

Malone, K. (ed.) (1962) *Widsith*, Copenhagen: Rosenkilde & Bagger.

Mann, M. (1986) *The Sources of Social Power*, vol. I, *A history of power from the beginning to A.D. 1760*, Cambridge: Cambridge University Press.

Mannering, U. (1998) 'Guldgubber. Et billede af yngre jernalders dragt', unpublished thesis, University of Copenhagen.

—— (1999) 'Sidste skrig', *Skalk*, (4): 20–7.

—— (2006) 'Billeder af Dragt. En analyse af påklædte figurer fra yngre jernalder i Skandinavien', unpublished thesis, University of Copenhagen.

—— (2008) 'Iconography and costume from the Late Iron Age in Scandinavia', in M. Gleba, C. Munkholt and M.L. Nosh (eds) *Dressing the Past*, pp. 59–67, Oxford: Oxbow Books.

Mansrud, A. (2004) 'Dyrebein i graver – en kilde til jernalderens kult og forestillingsverden', in A- L. Melheim, L. Hedeager and K. Oma (eds) *Mellom Himmel og Jord*, pp. 82–111, Oslo Archaeological Series 2, Oslo: University of Oslo.

—— (2006) 'Flytende identiteter? – dyrebein i graver og førkristne personoppfatninger', in T. Østigård (ed.) *Lik og ulik. Tilnærmninger til variasjon i gravskikk*, pp. 133–57, University of Bergen Archaeological Series 2, Bergen: University of Bergen.

—— (2008) '"Stykkevis og delt" – noen refleksjoner omkring forholdet mellom kropp, identitet og personoppfatning I det førkristne samfunnet', in K. Chilidis, J. Lund and C. Prescott (eds.) *Facets of Archaeology. Essays in honour of Lotte Hedeager on her 60th Birthday*, pp. 385–96, Oslo Archaeological series vol. 10. Oslo: UniPub.

Maret, P. de (1985) 'The smith's myth and the origin of leadership in Central Africa', in R. Haaland and P. Shinnie (eds) *African Iron Working*, pp. 73–87, Oslo: Norwegian University Press.

Markus, R.A. (1990) *The End of Ancient Christianity*, Cambridge: Cambridge University Press.

Marrais, E. de, Castillo, L.J. and Earle, T. (1996) 'Ideology, Materialization, and power strategies', *Current Anthropology*, 37(1): 15–31.

Marrais, E. de, Gosden, C. and Renfrew, C. (eds) (2004) *Rethinking Materiality – the engagement of mind with the material world*, Cambridge: McDonald Institute for Archaeological Research.

Martel, S. (2007) 'Gender ambiguity and gold bracteates in the Scandinavian Iron Age', *Nicolay Arkeologisk Tidsskrift*, 101: 67–75.

Martynov, A.I. (1991) *The Ancient Art of Northern Asia*, ed. and trans. by D.B. Shimkin and A.M. Shimkin, Urbana and Chicago: University of Illinois Press.

Mauss, M. (1990 [1959]) *The Gift*, trans. W.D. Halls, London: Routledge.

Melheim, A.-L., Hedeager, L. and Oma, K. (eds) (2004) *Mellom himmel og jord*, Oslo Archaeological Series 2, Oslo: University of Oslo.

Menghin, W. (1985) *Die Langobarden. Archäologie und Geschichte*, Stuttgart: Konrad Theiss Verlag.

Meskell, L. (1996) 'The somatization of archaeology: Institutions, discourses, corporeality', *Norwegian Archaeological Review*, 29(1): 1–16.

—— (1999) *Archaeologies of Social Life. Age, Sex, Class et cetera in Ancient Egypt*, Oxford: Blackwell.

—— (2000a) 'Re-em(bed)ding sex: domesticity, sexuality, and ritual in New Kingdom Egypt', in R.A. Schmidt and B.L. Voss (eds) *Archaeologies of Sexuality*, pp. 253–62, London: Routledge.

—— (2000b) 'Writing the body in archaeology', in A.E. Rautman (ed.) *Reading the Body*, pp. 13–21, Philadelphia: University of Pennsylvania Press.

—— (2004) *Object Worlds in Ancient Egypt. Material biographies past and present*, Oxford and New York: Berg.

Meskell, L.M. and Joyce, R.A. (2003) *Embodied Lives. Figuring Ancient Maya and Egyptian Experience*, London: Routledge.

Meulengracht Sørensen, P. (1983) *The Unmanly Man. Concepts of sexual defamation in Early Northern society*, The Viking Society Studies in Northern Civilisation 1, Odense: Odense University Press.

—— (1989) 'Moderen forløst af datterens skød', in A. Andrén (ed.) *Medeltidens Födelse*, Lund: Gyllenstiernska Krapperupsstiftelsen.

—— (1991a) 'Om eddadigtenes alder', in G. Steinsland, U. Drobin, J. Pentikäinen and P. Meulengracht Sørensen (eds) *Nordisk Hedendom. Et symposie*, pp. 217–28, Odense: Odense Universitetsforlag.

—— (1991b) 'Håkon den Gode og guderne. Nogle bemærkninger om religion og central-magt i det tiende århundrede – og om religion og kildekritik', in P. Mortensen and B. Rasmussen (eds) *Høvdingesamfund og Kongemagt*, pp. 235–44, Jysk Arkæologisk Selskabs Skrifter 22(2), Højbjerg: Jysk Arkæologisk Selskab.

—— (1992) *Fortælling og Ære. Studier i islændigesagaerne*, Aarhus: Aarhus Universitetsforlag.

Milde, H. (1988) '"Going out into the day": Ancient Egyptian beliefs and practices concern-ing death', in J.M. Bremer, T.P.J. van den Hout and R. Peters (eds) *Hidden Futures: Death and Immortality in Ancient Egypt, Anatolia, the Classical, Biblical and Arabic-Islamic World*, pp. 15–35, Amsterdam: University of Amsterdam Press.

Miller, D. (1999) 'Artefacts and the meaning of things', in T. Ingold (ed.) *Companion Ency-clopedia of Anthropology*, pp. 396–419, London: Routledge.

Miller, J.C. (1980) 'Listening to the African past', in J.C. Miller (ed.) *The African Past Speaks: Essays on Oral Tradition and History*, pp. 1–59, Folkestone: Dawson.

Miller, W.I. (1990) *Bloodtaking and Peacemaking. Feud, law, and society in Saga Iceland*, Chicago and London: The University of Chicago Press.

Mitchell, J.P. (2006) 'Performance', in C. Tilley, W. Keane, S. Küchler, M. Rowlands and P. Spyer (eds) *Handbook of Material Culture*, London: Sage Publications.

Mitchell, S. (2008) 'The heroic and legendary sagas', in S. Brink (ed.) in collaboration with N. Price *The Viking World*, pp. 319–22, London: Routledge.

—— (2009) 'Odin, Magic, and a Swedish Trial from 1484', *Scandinavian Studies*, 81(3): 263–86.

Moore, H.L. (1999 [1994]) 'Understanding sex and gender', in T. Ingold (ed.) *Companion Encyclopedia of Anthropology*, pp. 813–30, London: Routledge.

—— ([1994] 2000) 'Bodies on the move: gender, power and material culture', in J. Thomas (ed.) *Interpretive Archaeology*, pp. 317–28, London: Leicester University Press.

Moreland, J. (2001) *Archaeology as Text*, London: Duckworth.

Morgan, D. (2007) *The Mongols*, Cambridge MA, Oxford UK: Blackwell.

Morphy, H. (1989) 'Introduction', in H. Morphy (ed.) *Animals into Art*, pp. 1–17, London: Unwin Hyman.

—— (1999) 'The anthropology of art', in T. Ingold (ed.) *Companion Encyclopedia of Anthropology*, pp. 648–85, London: Routledge.

Morris, I. (2000) *Archaeology as Cultural History*, Oxford: Blackwell.

Morris, K. (1991) *Sorceress or Witch? The image of gender in Medieval Iceland and Northern Europe*, Lanham: University Press of America, Lanham.

Motz, L. (1983) *The Wise One of the Mountain: Form, Function and Significance of the Subter-ranean Smith*, Göppinger Arbeiten zu Germaanistik 379, Göppingen: Kümmerle.

—— (1993) 'The host of Dvalinn', *Collegium Medievale*, 6(1): 82–96.

—— (1994) 'The magician and his craft', *Collegium Medievale*, 7(1): 5–29.

Müller, G. (1967) 'Zum Namen *Wolfhetan* und seinen Verwandten', *Frühmittelalterliche Stu-dien*, 1: 200–12.

—— (1968) 'Germanische Tiersymbolik und Namengebung', *Frühmittelalterliche Studien*, 2: 202–17.

Müller, S. (1880) 'Dyreornamentikken i Norden. Dens Oprindelse, Udvikling og Forhold til samtidige Stilarter. En arkæologisk Undersøgelse', *Aarbøger for nordisk Oldkyndighed og Historie*, 1880: 185–403.

Mundal, E. (1974) *Fylgjemotiva i Norrøn Litteratur*, Oslo: Universitetsforlaget.

—— (2006) 'Theories, explanatory models and terminology', in A. Andrén, K. Jennbert and C. Raudvere (eds) *Old Norse Religion in Long-term Perspectives*, pp. 285–8, Lund: Nordic Academic Press.

Myhre, B. (2003a) 'The Iron Age', in K. Helle (ed.) *The Cambridge History of Scandinavia*, pp. 60–93, Cambridge: Cambridge University Press.

—— (2003b) 'Borregravfeltet som historisk arena', *Viking*, LXVI: 49–73.

—— (2006) 'Fra fallos til kors- fra horg og hov til kirke?', *Viking*, LXIX: 215–50.

Napier, A.D. (1986) *Masks. Transformation and Paradox*, Berkeley: University of California Press.

Näsman, U. (1984) *Glas och Handel i Senromersk tid och Folkvandringstid*, Uppsala: Uppsala University.

—— (1991) 'Sea trade during the Scandinavian Iron Age: Its character, commodities and routes', in O. Crumlin-Pedersen (ed.) *Aspects of Maritime Scandinavia AD 200–1200*, pp. 23–40, Roskilde: Vikingeskibshallen.

—— (1998) 'The Scandinavians' view of Europe in the Migration Period', in L. Larsson and B. Stjernquist (eds) *The World-View of Prehistoric Man*, pp. 103–21, papers presented at a symposium in Lund, May 5–7 1997, Konferencer 40, Stockholm: Kgl. Vitterhets Historie och Antikvitets Akademien.

—— (1999) 'The Etnogenesis of the Danes and the making of a Danish kingdom', in T. Dickinson and D. Griffiths (eds) *The Making of Kingdoms*, pp. 49–64, Anglo-Saxon Studies in Archaeology and History 10, Oxford: Oxford University Committee for Archaeology.

—— (2008) 'Scandinavia and the Huns. A source-critical approach to an old question', *Fornvännen*, 103: 111–18.

Näsström, B-M. (1996) 'Offerlunden under Frösö kyrka', in S. Brink (ed.) *Jämtlands kristnande*, pp. 65–85, Uppsala: Lunne Böcher.

—— (2001) *Blot. Tro och offer i det förkristna Norden*, Stockholm: Norstedts.

—— (2006) *Bärsärkarna. Vikingetidens elitsoldater*, Stockholm: Norstedts.

Nielsen, K.M. (1985) 'Runen und Magie', *Frühmittelalterliche Studien*, 19: 75–97.

Nielsen, P.O. (1994) 'The Gudme-Lundeborg Project. Interdisciplinary research 1988', in P.O. Nielsen, K. Randsborg and H. Thrane (eds) *The Archaeology of Gudme and Lundeborg*, pp. 16–22, Copenhagen: Akademisk Forlag.

Nielsen, P.O., Randsborg, K. and Thrane, H. (eds) (1994) *The Archaeology of Gudme and Lundeborg*, Copenhagen: Akademisk Forlag.

Niles, J.D. (1999) 'Widsith and the anthropology of the past', *Philological Quarterly*, 78: 171–213.

—— (2006) *Beowulf and Lejre*, Medieval and Renaissance Texts and Studies 323, Temple, AZ: Arizona Center for Medieval and Renaissance Studies.

—— (2008) 'Afterword. Visualizing Beowulf', in *Beowulf. An illustrated edition*, trans. S. Heaney, pp. 213–48, New York and London: W.W. Norton & Co.

Nordal, G. (2008) 'The Sagas of the Icelanders', in Brink, S. (ed.) in collaboration with N. Price, *The Viking World*, London: Routledge, 315–18.

Nordberg, A. (2003) *Krigarna i Odins Sal*, Stockholm: Religionshistoriska institutionen, Stockholm University.

Norrman, L. (2000) 'Woman or warrior? The construction of gender in Old Norse myth', in G. Barnes and M. Clunies Ross (eds) *Old Norse Myths, Literature and Society*, pp. 375–85, Proceedings of the 11th International Saga Conference 2–7 July 2000 at the University of Sydney, Sydney: Centre for Medieval Studies, University of Sydney.

North, R. (1997) *Heathen Gods in Old English Literature*, Cambridge: Cambridge University Press.

Nøttveit, O-M. (2006) 'The kidney dagger as a symbol of masculine identity', *Norwegian Archaeological Review*, 39(2): 138–50.

Obrusánszky, B. (2008) 'Tongwancheng, the city of Southern Huns', in *Hunnen zwischen Asien und Europa. Aktuelle Forschungen zur Archäologie und Kultur der Hunne*, pp. 17–24, Herausgegeben vom Historischen Museum der Pfalz Spyrer, Langenweissbache: Beier und Beran.

Oestigaard, T. (1999) 'Cremations and transformations: When the dual cultural hypothesis was cremated and carried away in urns', *European Journal of Archaeology*, 2: 345–64.

—— (2000) 'Sacrifices of raw, cooked and burnt humans', *Norwegian Archaeological Review*, 33(1): 41–58.

—— (2007) *Transformatøren. Ildens mester i Jernalderen*, Gotarc Series C, Gothenburg: University of Gothenburg.

Olason, V. (2000) 'Topography and world view in Njáls saga', in S. Hansson and M. Malm (eds) *Gudar på jorden. Festskrift till Lars Lönnroth*, pp. 131–41, Stockholm: Symposion.

Olausson, L. Holmqvist (1990) '"Älgmannen" från Birka. Presentation av en nyligen undersökt krigargrav med människooffer', *Fornvännen*, 85: 175–82.

Olsén, P. (1945) *Die Saxe von Valsgärde*, Valsgärdestudien II, Uppsala: Almquist & Wiksell.

Oma, K. (2004) 'Hesten og det heilage. Materialiseringa av eit symbol', in L. Melheim, L. Hedeager and K. Oma (eds) *Mellom Himmel og Jord*, pp. 68–81, Oslo Archaeological Series 2, Oslo: Unipub.

—— (2007) *Human-Animal Relationships: Mutual becomings in Scandinavian and Sicilian households 900–500 BC*, Oslo Archaeological Series 9, Oslo: Unipub.

Orchard, A. (2002 [1997]) *Norse Myth and Legend*, London: Cassell.

Ørsnes, M. (1966) *Form og Stil i Sydskandinaviens yngre Germanske Jernalder*, Copenhagen: The National Museum.

Oxenstierna, E (1956) *Die Goldhörner von Gallehus*, Lidingö.

Parry, J. and Bloch, M. (1993) 'Introduction: Money and the morality of exchange', in J. Parry and M. Bloch (eds) *Money and the Morality of Exchange*, pp. 1–32, Cambridge: Cambridge University Press.

Petersen, P. Vang (1994) 'Excavations at sites of treasure trove finds at Gudme', in P.O. Nielsen, K. Randsborg and H. Thrane (eds) *The Archaeology of Gudme and Lundeborg*, pp. 30–40, Copenhagen: Akademisk Forlag.

—— (2005) 'Odins fugle, valkyrier og bersærker', in T. Capelle and C. Fischer (eds) *Ragnarok. Odins Verden*, pp. 57–86, Silkeborg: Silkeborg Museum.

Pluskowski, A.G. (2002) 'Beasts in the woods. medieval responses to the threatening wild', unpublished thesis, University of Cambridge.

Pohl, W. (1980) 'Die Gepiden und die gentes an der mittleren Donau nach dem Zerfall des Attilareiches', in H. Wolfram and F. Daim (eds) *Die Völker an der mittleren und unteren Donau im fünften und sechsten Jahrhundert*, pp. 240–305, Denkschriften der Österreichischen Akademie der Wissenschaften 145, Wien: Österreichische Akademie der Wissenschaften.

—— (1994) 'Tradition, Ethnogenese und leterarische Gestaltung: eine Zwischenbilanz', in K. Brunner and B. Merta (eds) *Ethnogenese und Überlieferung*, pp. 9–26, Wien: Oldenbourg Verlag.

—— (ed.) (1997) *Kingdoms of the Empire: the integration of Barbarians in Late Antiquity*, Leiden: Brill.

—— (2000a) *Die Germanen*, München: Oldenbourg Verlag.

—— (2000b) 'Identität und Widerspruch: Gedanken zu einer Sinnesschichte des Frühmittelalters', in W. Pohl (ed.) *Die Suche nach den Ursprüngen: Von der Bedeutung des frühen Mittelalters*, pp. 23–35, Wien: Verlag der Österreichischen Akademie der Wissenschaften.

—— (2001) 'The *regia* and the *hring* – barbarian places of power', in M. de Jong and F. Theuws (eds) *Topographies of Power in the Early Middle Ages*, pp. 439–66, Brill: Leiden.

—— (2004) 'Gender and ethnicity in the early Middle Ages', in L. Brubaker and J.M.H. Smith (eds) *Gender in the Early Medieval World. East and West, 300–900*, pp. 23–43, Cambridge: Cambridge University Press.

Pohl, W. and Reimitz, H. (eds) (1998) *Strategies of Distinction: The Construction of Ethnic Communities, 300–800*, Leiden: Brill.

Popa, A. (2007) 'Frühhunnenzeitliche Besiedlung zwishen Ostkarpaten and Dnjester,' in V.A. Koch and Historischen Museum der Pfalz Speyer (eds) *Attila und die Hunnen*, pp. 169–73, Stuttgart: Konrad Theiss Verlag.

Price, N. (ed.) (2001) *The Archaeology of Shamanism*, London: Routledge.

—— (2002) *The Viking Way. Religion and War in Late Iron Age Scandinavia*, AUN 31, Uppsala: Uppsala University.

—— (2005) 'Sexualität', in *Reallexikon der Germanischen Altertumskunde*, pp. 244–57, Berlin and New York: Walter de Gruyter.

—— (2006) 'What's in a name? An archaeological identity crisis for the Norse gods (and some of their friends)', in A. Andrén, K. Jennbert and C. Raudvere (eds) *Old Norse Religion in Long-time Perspectives*, pp. 179–83, Lund: Nordic Academic Press.

—— (2008) 'Dying and the dead: Viking Age mortuary behaviour', in S. Brink in collaboration with N. Price (eds) *The Viking World*, pp. 157–73, London: Routledge.

Puhvel, J. (1970) 'Aspects of equine functionality', in J. Puhvel (ed.) *Myth and Law among the Indo-Europeans*, pp. 159–72, Studies in Indo-European Comparative Mythology, Berkeley: University of California Press.

Ralph, B. (2005) 'Den gåtfulla Rökstenen', in E. Ahlstedt et al. (eds) *Under Ytan. Populärvetenskapliga föreläsningar hållna under Humanistdagarna den 12.-13. november 2005*, pp. 263–9, Humanistdagboken 18, Gothenburg: University of Gothenburg.

Rasmussen, K. (1929) *Intellectual Culture of the Iglulik Eskimos*, Copenhagen: The National Museum.

Ratke, S. and Simek, R. (2006) 'Guldgubber. Relics of Pre-Christian law ritual', in A. Andrén, K. Jennbert and C. Raudvere (eds) *Old Norse Religion in Long-term Perspectives*, pp. 259–64, Vägar till Midgård 8, Lund: Nordic Academic Press.

Raudvere, C. (1993) *Föreställningar om Maran i Nordisk Folktro*, Lund Studies in History of Religions 1, Lund: Lund University.

—— (2001) 'Trolldóm in Early Medieval Scandinavia', in K. Jolly, C. Raudvere and E. Peters (eds) *Witchcraft and Magic in Europe. The Middle Ages*, pp. 73–171, Philadelphia: University of Pennsylvania Press.

—— (2003) *Kunskap och Insikt i Norrön Tradition*, Vägar til Midgård 3, Lund: Nordic Academic Press.

—— (2004) 'Delen eller helheten. Kosmologi som empirisk och analytiskt begrepp', in A. Andrén, K. Jennbert and C. Raudvere (eds) *Ordning mot Kaos – studier av nordisk förkristen kosmologi*, pp. 59–98, Lund: Nordic Academic Press.

Rausing, G. (1985) 'Beowulf, Ynglingatal and the Ynglinga Saga', *Fornvännen*, 80(3): 163–77.

Rautman, A.E. and Talalay, L.E. (2000) 'Introduction. Diverse approaches to the study of gender in archaeology', in A.E. Rautman (ed.) *Reading the Body. Representations and remains in the archaeological record*, pp. 1–12, Philadelphia: University of Pennsylvania Press.

Rennie, B. (ed) (2007) *The International Eliade*, New York: State University of New York Press.

Ricoeur, P. (1989) *Time and Narrative*, vol. 3, trans. K. McLaughlin and D. Pellauer. Chicago: Chicago University Press.

Rimmon-Kenan, S. (1983) *Narrative Fictions: Contemporary Poetics*, London: Methuen.

Ringbom, L.I. (1951) *Graltempel und Paradies*, Stockholm: Wahlstrom & Widstrand.

Ringtved, J. (1999) 'The geography of power: South Scandinavia before the Danish kingdom', in T. Dickinson and D. Griffiths (eds) *The Making of Kingdoms*, pp. 49–64, Anglo-Saxon Studies in Archaeology and History 10, Oxford: Oxford University Committee for Archaeology.

Roe, P.G. (1995) 'Style, society, myth, and structure', in C. Carr and J.E. Neitzel (eds) *Style, Society, and Person*, pp. 27–76, New York and London: Plenum Press.

Rosenwein, B. (1989) *To Be the Neighbour of Saint Peter. The social meaning of Cluny's property, 909–1049*, Ithaca and London: Cornell University Press.

Rostovtzeff, M. (1929) *The Animal Style in South Russia and China*, Princeton: Princeton University Press.

Roth, H. (1979) *Kunst der Völkerwanderungszeit*, Frankfurt am Main: Propyläen Verlag.

—— (ed.) (1986a) *Zum Problem der Deutung frühmittelalterlicher Bildinhalte*, Akten des 1. Internationalen Kolloquiums in Marburg a.d. Lahn, 15. bis 19. februar 1983, Sigmaringen: Jan Thorbecke Verlag.

—— (1986b) 'Stil II – Deutungsprobleme. Skizzen zu Pferdmotiv und zur Motivkoppelund', in H. Roth (ed.) *Zum Problem der Deutung frühmittelalterlicher Bildinhalte*, pp. 111–28, Akten des 1. Internationalen Kolloquiums in Marburg a.d. Lahn, 15. bis 19. februar 1983, Sigmaringen: Jan Thorbecke Verlag.

—— (1986c) 'Einführung in die Problematik, Rückblick und Ausblick', in H. Roth (ed.) *Zum Problem der Deutung frühmittelalterlicher Bildinhalte*, pp. 9–24, Akten des 1. Internationalen Kolloquiums in Marburg a.d. Lahn, 15. bis 19. februar 1983, Sigmaringen: Jan Thorbecke Verlag.

—— (1986d) *Kunst und Kunsthandwerk im Frühen Mittelalter*, Stuttgart: Theiss Verlag.

Rowlands, M. (1971) 'The archaeological interpretation of prehistoric metal working', *World Archaeology*, 3(2): 210–24.

—— (1993) 'The role of memory in the transmission of culture', *World Archaeology*, 25(2): 141–51.

—— (1999) 'The cultural economy of sacred power', in P. Ruby (ed.) *Les Princes de la Protohistoire et l'Émergence de l'État*, pp. 165–72, Actes de la table ronde internationale organisée par le Centre Jean Bérard et l'École francaise de Rome, Naples, 27–29 octobre 1994, Naples and Rome: Centre Jean Bérard and École Française de Rome.

Rudenko, S.I. (1970) *Kul'tura naseleniya Tsentral'nogo Altaya v skifskoye vremya* (The Culture of the Population of the Central Altay in Scythic Times), Leningrad: Izd AN SSSR.

Russell, W.M.S. and Russell, C. (1978) 'The social biology of werewolves', in J.R. Porter and W.M.S. Russell (eds) *Animals in Folklore*, pp. 143–82, Cambridge: Brewer.

Sahlins, M. (1981) *Historical Metaphors and Mythical Realities*, Ann Arbor: University of Michigan Press.

—— (1985) *Islands of History*, London and New York: Tavistock Publications.

Salin, B. (1903) 'Heimskringlas tradition om asarnes invandring. Ett arkeologiskt-religions-historiskt udkast', in *Studier tillägnade Oskar Montelius 9/9 1903 af lärjungar*, Stockholm.

—— (1904) *Die altgermanische Thierornamentik*, Stockholm and Berlin: Asher.

—— (1922) 'Fyndet från Broa i Halland, Gotland', *Fornvännen*, 7: 89–206.

Saunders, J.J. (1971) *The History of Mongol Conquests*, Philadelphia: University of Pennsylvania Press.

Saunders, N.J. (1999) 'Biographies of brilliance: pearls, transformations of matter and being, c. AD 1492', *World Archaeology*, 31(2): 243–57.

Schier, K. (1981) 'Zur Mythologie der Snorra Edda: Einige Quellenprobleme', in U. Dronke, G.P. Helgadottir, G.W. Weber and H. Bekker-Nielsen (eds) *Speculum Norroenum: Norse Studies in memory of Gabriel Turville-Petré*, pp. 405–20, Odense: Odense Universitetsforlag.

Schjødt, J.P. (1990) 'Horizontale und vertikale Achsen in der vorchristlichen skandinavischen Kosmologie', in T. Ahlbäck (ed.) *Old Norse and Finnish Religions and Cultic Place-Names*, pp. 35–57, Stockholm: Almqvist & Wiksell International.

—— (2004) *Initiation, liminalitet og tilegnelse af numinøs viden. En undersøgelse af struktur og symbolik i førkristen nordisk religion*, Aarhus: Det teologiske Fakultet, Aarhus University.

—— (2008) *Initiation between Two Worlds. Structure and Symbolism in Pre-Christian Scandinavian Religion*, Odense: The University Press of Southern Denmark.

Schmidt, R.A. and Voss, B.L. (eds) (2000) *Archaeologies of Sexuality*, London: Routledge.

Schulze, U. (2007) 'Der weinende König und sein Verswinden im Dunkel des Vergessens', in A. Koch und Historischen Museum der Pfalz Speyer (eds) *Attila und die Hunnen*, pp. 337–45, Stuttgart: Konrad Theiss Verlag.

Scukin, M., Kazanski, M. and Sharov, O. (2006) *Des les goths aux huns: Le nord de la mer noire au Bas-empire et a l'epoque des grandes migrations*, BAR International Series 1535, Oxford: British Archaeological Reports.

Sedlmayr, H. (1950) *Die Entstehung der Kathedral*, Zurich: Atlantis Verlag.

Sehested, F. (1878) *Fortidsminder og Oldsager fra Egnen om Broholm*, Copenhagen.

Shanks, M. (1993) 'Style and the design of a perfume jar from an archaic Greek city state', *Journal of European Archaeology*, 1: 77–106.

Shanks, M. and Hodder, I. (1995) 'Processual, postprocessual and interpretive archaeologies', in I. Hodder, M. Shanks, A. Alexandri, V. Buchli, J. Carman, J. Last and G. Lucas (eds) *Interpreting Archaeology*, pp. 3–33, London and New York: Routledge.

Shennan, S.J. (ed.) *Archaeological Approaches to Cultural Identity*, One World Archaeology, London: Unwin Hyman.

Simek, R. (1996) *Dictionary of Northern Mythology*, Cambridge: Brewer.

Skinner, M.B. (2005) *Sexuality in Greek and Roman Culture*, Oxford: Blackwell.

Skovmand, R. (1942) 'De Danske Skattefund fra Vikingetiden og den Ældste Middelalder indtil omkring 1150', *Årbøger for Nordisk Oldkyndighed og Historie*, 1942: 1–275.

Skre, D. (1998) *Herredømmet – Bosetning og Besittelse på Romerike 200–1350 e.Kr.*, Oslo: Scandinavian University Press.

—— (2007a) 'The dating of *Ynglingatal*', in D. Skre (ed.) *Kaupang in Skiringssal*, pp. 407–29, Norske Oldfund 22, Aarhus: Aarhus University Press.

—— (2007b) 'The emergence of a central place: Skiringssal in the 8th Century', in D. Skre (ed.) *Kaupang in Skiringssal*, pp. 431–43, Norske Oldfund 22, Aarhus: Aarhus University Press.

—— (2007c) 'Towns and markets, kings and central places in South-western Scandinavia c. AD 800', in D. Skre (ed.) *Kaupang in Skiringssal*, pp. 445–69, Norske Oldfund 22, Aarhus: Aarhus University Press.

—— (2008a) 'Post-substantivist towns and trade AD 600–1000', in D. Skre (ed.) *Means of Exchange*, pp. 327–42, Norske Oldfund 23, Aarhus: Aarhus University Press.

—— (2008b) 'Dealing with silver: Economic agency in South-Western Scandinavia AD 600–1000', in D. Skre (ed.) *Means of Exchange*, pp. 343–55, Norske Oldfund 23, Aarhus: Aarhus University Press.

Smith, J.M.H. (2005) *Europe after Rome. A New Cultural History 500–1000*, Oxford: Oxford University Press.

Søby Christensen, A. (2002) *Cassiodorus Jordanes and the History of the Goths*, Copenhagen: Museum Tusculanum Press.

Sofaer, J.R. (2006) *The Body as Material Culture*, Cambridge: Cambridge University Press.

Solberg, B. (1999) '"Holy white stones", Remains of fertility cult in Norway', in U. von Freeden, U. Koch and A. Wieczorek (eds) *Völker an Nord- und Ostsee und die Franken*, pp. 99–106, Aktens des 48. Sachsensymposiums in Mannheim vom 7. bis 11. September 1997, Bonn: Rudolf Habelt GmbH.

Solli, B. (1998) 'Odin – the queer? Om det skeive i norrøn mytologi', in *Universitetets Oldsaksamlings Årbok*, 1997/1998, pp. 7–42, Oslo: University of Oslo.

—— (2002) *Seid-Myter, sjamanisme og kjønn i vikingenes tid*, Oslo: Pax.

—— (2004) 'Det norrøne verdensbildet og ethos', in A. Andrén, K. Jennbert and C. Raudvere (eds) *Ordning mot kaos*, pp. 253–87, Vägar till Midgård 4, Lund: Nordic Academic Press.

Sørensen, M.L.S. (1992) 'Gender archaeology and Scandinavian Bronze Age studies', *Norwegian Archaeological Review*, 25(1): 31–49.

—— (1997) 'Reading dress: the construction of social categories and identities in Bronze Age Europe', *Journal of European Archaeology*, 5(1): 93–114.

—— (2000) *Gender Archaeology*, Cambridge: Polity Press.

Sørensen, P. Østergaard (1994a) 'Houses, farmsteads and settlement pattern in the Gudme area', in P.O. Nielsen, K. Randsborg and H. Thrane (eds), *The Archaeology of Gudme and Lundeborg*, pp. 41–7, Copenhagen: Akademisk Forlag.

—— (1994b) 'Gudmehallen. Kongeligt byggeri fra jernalderen', *Nationalmuseets Arbejdsmark*, 1994: 25–39.

Sørensen, S. (1973) *De Russisk-Nordiske Forhold i Vikingetiden*, Copenhagen: Gyldendal.

Spangen, M. (2005) 'Edelmetalldepotene i Nord-Norge', unpublished thesis, University of Tromsø.

Speake, G. (1980) *Anglo-Saxon Animal Art and its Germanic Background*, Oxford: Clarendon Press.

Staecker, J. (2004) 'Hjältar, kungar och gudar', in Å. Berggren, S. Arvidsson and A-M. Hållas (eds) *Minne och Myt. Kunsten at Skapa det Förflutna*, pp. 39–78, Lund: Nordic Academic Press.

Starkey, K. (1999) 'Imagining an Early Odin. Gold bracteates as visual evidence?' *Scandinavian Studies*, 71(4): 373–92.

Steenstrup, J.J.S. (1893) *Yak-Lungta-Bracteaterne*, Copenhagen: Bianco Luno.

Steinsland, G. (1990) 'De nordiske gullblekk med parmotiv og norrøn fyrsteideologi', *Collegium Medievale*, 3(1): 73–94.

—— (1991a) *Det Hellige Bryllup og Norrøn Kongeideologi*, Oslo: Solum.

—— (1991b) 'Dødsbryllupet. Betraktninger omkring død og eros, 'hellige hvite sten', gotlanske billedstener og Oseberg-graven', in G. Alhaug, K. Kruken and H. Salvesen (eds) *Heidersskrift til Nils Hallan på 65-årsdagen*, pp. 421–35, Oslo: Novus.

—— (1994a) 'Eros og død i norrøn kongeideologi: kan mytisk herskerideologi kaste lys over forestillinger og riter knyttet til død, begravelse og gravkult?', in J.P. Schjødt (ed.) *Myte og Ritual i det Førkristne Norden*, pp. 141–57, Odense: Odense Universitetsforlag.

—— (1994b) 'Eros og Død – de to hovedkomponenter i norrøn kongeideologi', in *Studien zum Altgermanischen; Festschrift für Heiko Uecker*, pp. 626–47, Berlin: Walter de Gruyter.

—— (1997) *Eros og Død i Norrøne Myter*, Oslo: Universitetsforlaget.

—— (2005) *Norrøn Religion. Myter, riter, samfunn*, Oslo: Pax.

Steinsland, G. and Meulengracht Sørensen, P. (1994) *Menneske og Makter i Vikingenes Verden*, Oslo: Universitetsforlaget.

Steinsland, G. and Vogt, K. (1979) 'Den gamle tro', in I. Semmingsen, N.K. Monsen, S. Tschudi-Madsen and Y. Ustvedt (eds) *Vår Fjerne Fortid*, pp. 129–63, Norges Kulturhistorie 1, Oslo: Aschehoug.

Sten, S. and Vretemark, M. (1999) *Kungshögarna i Gamla Uppsala, gamla Uppsala socken i Uppland*, Rapportserie från Samlingsenheten, Statens Historiska Museum, Osteologisk Rapport 1999(1), Stockholm: Statens Historiska Museum.

Steuer, H. (1987) 'Helm und Ringschwert – Prunkbewaffnung und Rangabzeichen germanischer Krieger. Eine Übersicht', *Studien zur Sachsenforschung* 6: 189–236.

—— (1989) 'Archaeology and History: Proposals on the social structure of the Merovingian Empire', in K. Randsborg (ed.) *The Birth of Europe: Archaeology and Social Development in the First Millennium A.D.*, pp. 100–22, Analecta Romana Instituti Danici, Supplementum XVI, Roma: L'Erma di Bretschneider.

Stoklund, M., Nielsen, M.L., Holmberg, B. and Fellow-Jensen, G. (eds) (2006) *Runes and their Secrets. Studies in Runology*, Copenhagen: Museum Tusculanum Press.

Stolpe, H. and Arne, T.J. (1927) *La nécropole de Vendel*, Monografiserien 17, Stockholm: Kungl. Vitterhets Historie och Antikvitetsakademien.

Strathern, M. (1988) *The Gender of the Gift: problems with women and problem with society in Melanesia*, Berkeley: University of California Press.

Straume, E. (1986) 'Smeden i jernalderen, bofast – ikke bofast, høy eller lav status', in *Universitetets Oldsaksamling Årbok*, 1984/85, pp. 45–58, Oslo: University of Oslo.

Ström, F. (1954) *Diser, Nornor, Valkyrjor*, Stockholm: Almqvist & Wiksell.

—— (1999 [1961]) *Nordisk Hedendom*, Gothenburg: Akademiförlaget.

Strömbäck, D. (1935) *Sejd. Textstudier i nordisk religionshistoria*, Stockholm and Copenhagen: Hugo Geber and Levin & Munksgaard.

—— (1970) 'Att helga land. Studier i Landnáma och det äldsta rituella besittningstagandet', in *Folklore och Filologi. Valda uppsatser utgivna av Gustav Adolfs Akademien 13.8.1970*, pp. 135–65, Uppsala.

Sundqvist, O. (1995) 'Review of C. Krag Ynglingatal og Ynglingesaga, 1991', *Svensk Religionshistorisk Årsskrift*, 4: 158–62.

—— (1997) 'Myt, historia och härskare', in O. Sundqvist and A.L. Svalastog (eds) *Myter och Mytteorier*, pp. 93–120, Religionshistoriske forskningsrapporter från Uppsala 10, Uppsala: Uppsala University.

—— (2002) *Freyr's Offspring. Rulers and religion in ancient Svea society*, Uppsala: Uppsala University.

—— (2004) 'Uppsala och Asgård. Makt, offer og kosmos i forntida Skandinavien', in A. Andrén, K. Jennbert and C. Raudvere (eds) *Ordning mot Kaos – studier av nordisk förkristen kosmologi*, pp. 145–79, Vägar till Midgård 4, Lund: Nordic Academic Press.

Svennung, J. (1967) *Jordanes und Scandia*, Kritisch-exegetische Studien, Stockholm: Almquist & Wiksell.

—— (1972) 'Jordanes und die gotische Stammsage', in U.E. Hagberg (ed.) *Studia Gothica*, pp. 20–56, Antikvariske Serien 25, Stockholm: Kgl. Vitterhets Historie och Antikvitets Akademien.

Tapper, R. (1994 [1988]) 'Animality, humanity, morality, society', in T. Ingold (ed.) *What is an Animal*, pp. 47–62, One World Archaeology 1, London: Routledge.

Taylor, T. (1996) *The Prehistory of Sex: Four Million Years of Human Sexual Culture*, London: Fourth Estate.

Teillet, S. (1984) *Des Goths á la nation gothique. Les origines de l'idée de nation en Occident du Ve au VIIe siècle*, Paris: Société d'Edition 'Les Belles Lettres'.

Theuws, F. and Alkemade, M. (2000) 'A kind of mirror for men: Sword depositions in late Antique Northern Gaul', in F. Theuwe and J.L. Nelson (eds) *Rituals of Power*, pp. 401–76, Leiden: Brill.

Theuws, F. and Nelson, J.L. (eds) (2000) *Rituals of Power, from Late Antiquity to the Early Middle Ages*, Leiden, Boston and Köln: Brill.

Thomas, J. et al. (2006) Comments on Jan Harding (2005), *Norwegian Archaeological Review*, 39(1): 80–97.

Thompson, E.A. (1996 [1948]) *The Huns*, revised and with afterword by P. Heather, Oxford: Blackwell.

Thomsen, P.O. (1994) 'Lundeborg – an early port of trade in South-East Funen', in P.O. Nielsen, K. Randsborg and H. Thrane (eds) *The Archaeology of Gudme and Lundeborg*, pp. 23–9, Copenhagen: Akademisk Forlag.

Thomsen, P.O., Blæsild, B., Hardt, N. and Michaelsen, K.K. (1993) *Lundeborg – en handelsplads fra jernalderen*, Svendborg: Svendborg Museum.

Thrane, H. (1987) 'Das Gudme-Problem und die Gudme-Untersuchungen', *Frühmittelalterliche Studien*, 21: 1–48.

—— (1998) 'Materialien zur Topographie einer eisenzeitlichen Sakrallandschaft um Gudme auf Ostfünen in Dänemark', in A. Wesse (ed.) *Studien zur Archäologie des Ostseeraumes. Von der Eisenzeit zum Mittelalter. Festschrift für Michael Müller-Wille*, pp. 235–47, Neumünster: Wachholtz.

—— (1999) 'Gudme', in *Reallexikon der Germanischen Altertumskunde*, vol. 13, pp. 142–8, Berlin and New York: Walter de Gruyter.

Tinn, M. (2007) *De Første Formene. Folkekunstens abstrakte formspråk*, Oslo: Instituttet for sammenlignende kulturforskning/Novus.

—— (2009) 'Innsikt eller overblikk. Merleau-Pontys diskusjon av kroppen og den kartesianske erkjennelse', in J. Lund and L. Melheim (eds) *Håndverk og Produksjon. Et møte mellom ulike perspektiver*, pp. 61–82, Oslo Archaeological Series 12, Oslo: Unipub.

—— (unpublished) 'Worlds without words. Abstract meaning in textile folkart'.

Tomka, P. (1987) 'Der hunnische Fundkomplex von Pannonhlma', in G. Bott (ed.) *Germanen, Hunnen und Awaren. Schätze der Völkerwanderungszeit*, pp. 156–61, Nuremberg: Verlag des Germanisches Nationalmuseum.

—— (2007) 'Über die Bestattungssitten der Hunnen', in A. Koch und Historischen

Museum der Pfalz Speyer (eds) *Attila und die Hunnen*, pp. 253–57, Stuttgart: Konrad Theiss Verlag.

—— (2008) 'Zwischen Hsiung-nu und Hunnen aus archäologischer Sicht', in Historischen Museum der Pfalz Spyrer (eds) *Hunnen zwischen Asien und Europa*, pp. 91–100, Aktuelle Forschungen zur Archäologie und Kultur der Hunne, Langenweissbache: Beier und Beran.

Tonkin, E. (1995) *Narrating our Pasts. The social construction of oral history*, Cambridge: Cambridge University Press.

Treherne, P. (1995) 'The warrior's beauty: the masculine body and self-identity in Bronze Age Europe', *Journal of European Archaeology*, 3(1): 105–44.

Trigger, B.G. (1989) *A History of Archaeological Thought*, Cambridge: Cambridge University Press.

Turner, V. (1967) *The Forest of Symbols*, Ithaca and London: Cornell University Press.

Turville-Petré, E.O.G. (1964) *Myth and Religion of the North*, London: Weidenfeld & Nicolson.

Van Dyke, R. and Alcock, S. (eds) (2003) *Archaeologies of Memory*, Oxford: Blackwell.

Van Gennep, A. (1960) *The Rites of Passage*, London: Routledge & Kegan Paul.

Vansina, J. (1965) *Oral Tradition: A Study in Historical Methodology*, London: Routledge.

—— (1985) *Oral Tradition as History*, London: James Currey.

Veit, U. (1989) 'Ethnic concepts in German prehistory: a case study on the relationship between cultural identity and archaeological objectivity', in S.J. Shennan (ed.) *Archaeological Approaches to Cultural Identity*, pp. 35–56, One World Archaeology, London: Unwin Hyman.

—— (2000) 'Gustaf Kossinna and his concept of a national archaeology', in H. Härke (ed.) *Archaeology, Ideology and Society. The German Experience*, pp. 40–64, Frankfurt am Main: Peter Lang.

Vestergaard, E. (1992) 'Völsunge-Nibelungen Traditionen. Antropologiske studier i en episk traditions transformation i forhold til dens sociale sammenhæng', unpublished thesis, Aarhus University.

Veyne, P. (1988) *Did the Greeks believe in their Myths? An essay on the Constitutive Imagination*, Chicago and London: The University of Chicago Press.

Vierck, H. (1967) 'Ein Relieffibelpaar aus Nordendorf in bayerische Schwaben', *Bayerische Vorgeschichtsblätter*, 32: 104–43.

—— (1978) 'Zur seegermanischen Männertracht', in C. Ahrens (ed.) *Sachsen und Angelsachsen*, pp. 263–70, Ausstellung des Helms-Museums, Hamburg: Hamburgisches Museum für Vor- und Frühgeschichte.

Vikstrand, P. (2001) *Gudarnas Platser. Förkristna sakrala ortsmann i Mälarlandskapen*, Uppsala: Kungl. Gustaf Adolfs Akademien för svensk folkkultur, Uppsala University.

Voss, B.L. (2000) 'Feminisms, queer theories, and the archaeological study of past sexualities', *World Archaeology*, 32(2): 180–92.

Voss, B.L. and Schmidt, R.A. (2000) 'Introduction', in B.L. Voss and R.A. Schmidt (eds) *Archaeologies of Sexuality*, pp. 1–23, London and New York: Routledge.

Vries, J. de (1956) *Altgermanische Religionsgeschichte*, vol.1, Berlin: Walter de Gruyter.

Wagner, N. (1967) *Getica. Untersuchungen zum Leben des Jordanes und zur frühen Geschichte der Goten*, Quellen und Forschungen zur Sprach- und Kulturgeschichte der germanischen Völker, N.F. 22, Berlin: Walter de Gruyer.

Wallis, R.J. (2000) 'Queer shamans: autoarchaeology and neo-shamanism', *World Archaeology*, 32(2): 252–62.

Wamers, E. (1987) 'Die Völkerwanderungszeit im Spiegel der germanischen Heldensagen', *Germanen, Hunnen und Avaren*, pp. 69–94, Nuremberg: Germanisches Nationalmuseums.

—— (1993) 'Insular art in Carolingian Europe: The reception of old ideas in a new empire', in R.M. Spearman and J. Higgitt (eds) *The Age of Migrating Ideas*, pp. 35–44, Edinburgh: National Museum of Scotland.

Watt, M. (1991) 'Sorte Muld', in P. Mortensen and B. Rasmussen (eds) *Høvdingesamfund og Kongemagt*, pp. 89–108, Jysk Arkæologisk Selskabs Skrifter XXII: 2, Aarhus: Aarhus Universitetsforlag.

—— (1999) 'Gubber', in *Reallexikon der Germanischen Altertumskunde*, vol. 3, pp. 132–42, Berlin: Walter de Gruyter.

—— (2004) 'The gold-figure foils ("guldgubbar") from Uppåkra', in L. Larsson (ed.) *Continuity for Centuries. A ceremonial building and its context at Uppåkra, Southern Sweden*, pp. 167–221, Uppåkrastudier 10, Stockholm: Almqvist & Wiksell International.

Weibull, C. (1958) *Die Auswanderung der Goten aus Schweden*, Gothenburg: Elander.

Weiner, A.B. (1992) *Inalienable Possessions. The Paradox of Keeping-While-Giving*, Berkeley: University of California Press.

Weiner, J.F. (1999) 'Myth and metaphor', in T. Ingold (ed.) *Companion Encyclopedia of Anthropology*, pp. 591–612, London: Routledge.

Weir, A. and Jerman, J. (1986) *Images of Lust. Sexual Carvings on Medieval Churches*, London and New York: Routledge.

Wells, P.S. (2009) *Barbarians to the Angels. The Dark Age Reconsidered*, London, New York: Norton.

Wenskus, R. (1961) *Stammesbildung und Verfassung*, Köln: Böhlau.

Werner, J. (1935) *Münzdatierte austrasische Grabfunde* (Germanische Denkmäler der Völkevanderungszeit 3). Berlin, Leipzig.

—— (1956) *Beiträge zur Archäologie des Attila-Reiches*, Munich: Verlag der bayerischen Akademie der Wissenschaften.

—— (1963) 'Tiergestaltige Heilsbilder und germanischhe Personennamen', *Deutsche Vierteljahresschrift für Literaturwissenschaft und Geistesgeschichte*, 37: 377–83.

—— (1980) 'Der goldenen Armring des Frankenkönigs Childerich und die germanischen Handgelenkenringen der Jüngeren Kaiserzeit', *Frühmittelalterliche Studien*, 14: 1–49.

Whitley, D.S. and Keyser, J.D. (2003) 'Faith in the past: debating an archaeology of religion', *Antiquity*, 77(296): 385–93.

Wickham, C. (2005) *Framing the Early Middle Ages. Europe and the Mediterranean, 400–800*, Oxford: Oxford University Press.

Wiedgren, M. (1998) 'Kulturgeografernas bönder och arkeologernas guld – finns det någon väg til syntes?', in L. Larsson and B. Hårdh (eds) *Centrala Platser, Centrala Frågor*, pp. 281–96, Acta Archaeologica Lundensia Series in 8, no. 28, Stockholm: Almqvist & Wiksell International.

Wiker, G. (2000) 'Gullbrakteatene – i dialog med naturkreftene', unpublished thesis, University of Oslo.

—— (2001) 'Om konstruksjon av ny menneskelig identitet i jernalderen', *Primitive Tider*, 4: 51–72.

—— (2008) 'Balders død – en krigerinitiasjon? En ikonografisk tolkning av "Drei-Götter-brakteatene"', in K. Chilidis, J. Lund and C. Prescott (eds) *Facets of Archaeology. Essays in Honour of Lotte Hedeager on her 60th Birthday*, pp. 509–26, Oslo: Unipub.

Williams, C.A. (1999) *Roman Homosexuality: Ideologies of Masculinity in Classical Antiquity*, Oxford: Oxford University Press.

Willis, R.G. (1981) *A State in the Making: Myth, History and Social Transformation in Pre-Colonial Ufipa*, Bloomington: Indiana University Press.

Wilson, D. (1992) *Anglo-Saxon Paganism*, London: Routledge.

—— (2008) 'The development of Viking art', in S. Brink (ed.) in collaboration with N. Price, *The Viking World*, pp. 323–38, London: Routledge.

Wolfram, H. (1970) 'The shaping of the early Medieval Kingdom', *Viator*, 1: 1–20.

—— (1990) *History of the Goths*, Berkeley: University of California Press.

—— (1994) 'Origo et religio. Ethnic traditions and literature in early medieval texts', *Early Medieval Europe*, 3(1): 19–38.

—— (2004) 'Auf der Suche nach den Ursprüngen', in W. Pohl (ed.) *Die Suche nach den Ursprüngen: Von der Bedeutung des frühen Mittelalters*, pp. 11–22, Wien: Verlag der Österreichischen Akademie der Wissenschaften.

Wood, I. (1983) *The Merovingian North Sea*, Alingsås: Viktoria Bokförlag.

—— (1990) 'Ethnicity and the ethnogenesis of the Burgundians', in I.H. Wolfram and W. Pohl (eds) *Typen der Ethnogenese unter besonderer Berücksichtigung der Bayern*, pp. 53–69, Vienna: Verlag der Österreichischen Akademie der Wissenschaften.

—— (1994) *The Merovingian Kingdoms*, London: Longman.

Zachrisson, I. (1997) *Möten i Gränsland. Samer och Germaner i Mellanskandinavien*, Stockholm: Statens Historiska Museum.

Zachrisson, I. and Iregren, E. (1974) *Lappish Bear Graves in Northern Sweden. An Archaeological and Osteological Study*, Early Norrland 5, Stockholm: Kungl. Vitterhets Historie och Antikvitets Akademien.

Zachrisson, T. (1998) *Gård, Gräns, Gravfält. Sammanhang kring ädelmetalldepåer och runstenar från vikingetid och tidigmedeltid in Uppland och Gästrikland*, Stockholm Studies in Archaeology 15, Stockholm: Stockholm University.

—— (2004a) 'The holiness of Helgö', in H. Clarke and K. Lamm (eds) *Excavations at Helgö*, vol. XVI, pp. 143–76, Stockholm: Almqvist & Wiksell International.

—— (2004b) '"Det heliga på Helgö" och dess kosmiska referenser', in A. Andrén, K. Jennbert and C. Raudvere (eds) *Ordning mot Kaos – studier av nordisk förkristen kosmologi*, pp. 343–88, Vägar till Midgård 4, Lund: Nordic Academic Press.

INDEX